EXPOSITION

EXPOSITION

of

DANIEL

By

H. C. LEUPOLD

BAKER BOOK HOUSE
Grand Rapids, Michigan

Reprinted 1969 by
Baker Book House Company

EXPOSITION OF DANIEL

ISBN: 0-8010-5531-8

Twentieth printing, July 1989

Manufactured in the United States of America

To

MY BELOVED WIFE

INTRODUCTION

1. Daniel

The Hebrew proper name "Daniel" means either "God is judge" or "God is my judge," depending on whether the *i* within the word is regarded as the connective (*yodh compaginis*) or as the pronominal suffix for "my." In forms of this sort it is almost impossible to tell whether the one or the other of these two is meant.

There is a distinct reference to Daniel, the prophet, the author of the book current under his name, in the book of Ezekiel, the prophet, namely in the following three passages: Ezek. 14:14, 20; 28:3. In the first two of these passages Daniel is mentioned in connection with two other worthies of the Old Testament, Noah and Job, all three being considered outstanding examples of righteousness, who might deliver their own souls in a land visited by the just judgment of God even if all others should perish. In the third instance Daniel is held up to the king of Tyre as a paragon of wisdom with whom the king of Tyre could hardly hope to measure himself, proud though he might be of his own superiority.

The date for the passage Ezek. 14:14, 20 is determined by a comparison of the following passages: 8:1 compared with 1:2 yields the result that chapter 14 of Ezekiel should be assigned to the year 591 B. C. inasmuch as Jechoniah's captivity began in 597 B. C. However, Daniel was led into captivity in 604. Consequently this word was written fourteen years after Daniel was taken to Babylon and eleven years (cf. Dan. 1:5) after Daniel's elevation to the prominent position at the court of the king of Babylon. For the reference in Ezek. 28:3 the date-passage is 26:1. Con-

(5)

sequently this latter passage is to be dated about five
years later than the preceding one. We give the conclusion to be drawn in the words of *Keil*: "It will in no
way appear surprising to us to find that the fame of
his righteousness and his wonderful wisdom was so
spread abroad among the Jewish exiles that Ezekiel
was able to point to him as a bright example of these
virtues."

This had to be said to make it apparent that the
natural reference that Ezekiel makes to the chief character of the book of Daniel is entirely in order and
supports the historical evidence in favor of the prominence of Daniel in his day and age, for criticism has
tried to invalidate this testimony of Ezekiel's to Daniel
by several devices. The first of these is to claim that
Ezekiel must be referring to "a famous personality
from antiquity" (*Meinhold*). Archaeology knows of a
Daniel from the Ras Shamra tablets, who was the son
of the god El. But Ezekiel would hardly put such a
mythological personage by the side of Noah and Job.
But, as we have just pointed out in the quotation from
Keil, it is not necessarily the length of time that has
elapsed that determines whether a man has just claim
to fame. Because of unusually brilliant achievements
some men enjoy a high reputation while they are still
comparatively young. Why not, then, mention two
men from hoary antiquity and one whose fame has but
recently been established, and that by circumstances
that brought him emphatically to the attention of all
the faithful in Israel?

A second device that is calculated to invalidate
Ezekiel's support of the historicity is to make Daniel's
achievements appear as trifling as possible. *Cornill*
(*Einleitung*, p. 241) quotes *Reuss* with approval,
where the latter labels Daniel at the time of Ezekiel's
prophecy as *ein babylonischer Student*, "a Babylonian
student." Daniel could have been eighteen years old
when he began his studies of Babylonian lore and

would, eighteen years thereafter, have been thirty-six years old. Many a man has made his mark long before that time, even in the realm of politics. *Reuss's* statement of the case is hardly fair.

It is plainly an overstatement, even of the negative position, to say that there is "no reference to Daniel as a historic person in the Old Testament" (*Montgomery*). For by such a sweeping statement the whole book of Daniel with its more than seventy references to Daniel is branded as unhistorical and unreliable, and the three references of Ezekiel are ignored.

Kliefoth says very soberly in reference to this aspect of the matter: "This testimony (Ezek. 14 and 28) for the existence and for the authenticity of his (Daniel's) book is so utterly clear and simple that it has cost those who were unwilling to accept it much trouble to impair it (*es zu verdunkeln*)." He adds, by way of further explanation: "It is obvious that Ezekiel does not quote these three names in the interest of history but as an example for his thesis, and therefore he does not follow a strictly chronological order but a factual sequence, moving to a climax from Noah, who was able to save his family, through Daniel, who was at least able to save his friends, to Job, who did not even save such."

The entire issue is beclouded when attention is drawn to the fact that Daniel was in the list of those who returned from the Exile as also his friends, Hananiah, Mishael, and Azariah, are said to be. A comparison of the passages involved (see Ezra 8:2; Neh. 10:6 referring to men who came in 457 B. C.; Neh. 3:23, 24; 10:2; Ezra 10:28; Neh. 3:30, referring to the same date; Neh. 8:4, again of the same date) immediately yields the result that these could not have been the contemporaries of the men mentioned in the book of Daniel but were men who by accident bore the same names as the persons who are prominent in Daniel's book.

2. The Author

We regard Daniel to be the author of this book.
The internal evidence amply supports this claim.
Though nothing in the first six chapters of the book
indicates that the Daniel mentioned in it is the author,
yet from chapter 7 onward the following instances
occur where both the first person and the name Daniel
are combined: 7:2, 15, 28; 8:1, 15, 27; 9:2, 22; 10:1,
2, 7, 11, 12; 12:5. This fact, coupled with the obvious
unity of the book, indicates that Daniel wrote all of it.
If in the first half of the book he is pleased to refer to
himself objectively, that is a mode of procedure that
was common in antiquity. If, after he has acquainted
his reader with himself, he prefers to turn to the use
of the first person, that in itself is no insuperable difficulty in the way of unity of authorship. This claim
could be invalidated only by strong contrary evidence,
which, as we shall observe, is in no sense offered by
negative criticism.

Why should interpreters be so strongly opposed to
accepting such clear evidence? This is merely one
phase of the effort to impugn the credibility of the
book as a whole, which effort again rests on certain
strong presuppositions. Of what nature these presuppositions are is quite correctly stated by *Kliefoth*
who makes the following very sober evaluation: "If
a man accepts a notion of a God, who either is nothing
more than the natural laws, or is so completely bound
to his own natural laws that He is unable to break
through them by any free act of His own, such a man,
we say, cannot conceive of an actual miracle nor of a
true prophecy. But he who thus finds his path blocked
by his own peculiar conceptions, which eliminate both
miracles and prophecy, must of necessity dispose of
this book in some way, even if it be in the way followed by the old heathen Porphyry in his critical and sub-
versive comments, for in this book Daniel experiences
miracles and receives prophecies." This type of char-

acterization is resented by negative criticism and is described as bigoted and unjust but remains basically true and just after all, much as we may regret to say it.

We must take up in order some of the points that are said to conflict with the possibility of authorship by Daniel.

For one thing, it is asserted that, if the author had lived at the court of King Nebuchadnezzar and had known both the king and the Babylonian language, he could have used only one form of this proper name, and that the spelling "Nebuchadrezzar," a form appearing rather frequently in Jeremiah. However, the "secondary form," as *K. W.* calls it, appears so very commonly (II Chron., Jer., Dan., Ezra, Neh., Esther, and I Chron.) that it must be obvious that the spelling with *n* came very naturally to the Jews and could, therefore, be used most readily by Daniel even though he was writing at the Babylonian court.

More serious would seem to be the objection that Daniel could not be the author of a book that reports his own death. In proof of the fact that he does this the passage 1:21 is cited: "And Daniel continued even unto the first year of King Cyrus." However, it becomes immediately apparent that the statement concerning the death of Daniel first has to be inserted into this passage before it can be found there. The verse in question carries us up to a certain year without asserting that Daniel died in that year. It was important, however, to mention that year itself as being one that Daniel lived to see.

Here may be the place to discuss the assertion that the author of the book, who was not Daniel, it is said, gives indication of the fact that he knew his position to be inferior to that of the true and great prophets of *Yahweh* in that he never once ventures to use a statement such as "thus saith *Yahweh*." This argument is specious inasmuch as only a special form of words is considered without giving attention to the fact that their equivalent most obviously appears within the book, and that rather frequently. The exact form of words as such means little if, as is the case, the book records that it was the grace and the power of God that enabled the man Daniel to interpret visions and dreams (see 2:22, 23, 30, 45; 4:8, 9; 5:11, 12), and when it further records that an angel from God gave Daniel an interpretation of the particular visions that had been given to him to see (see 7:16; 8:16-19; 9:22, etc.). Arguments of this sort are calculated (we regret to say it) to throw sand into the eyes of the unwary.

In this connection we merely report another approach which in itself constitutes a mere claim, which is made, no doubt, in good faith but is very misleading in its unmodified form. We refer to the claim of some (e. g., *Farrar*) who assert that they who attempt to hold to the belief of authorship of this book by Daniel do so "in defiance of masses of opposing evidence." In all fairness it should be reported that in support of the idea of authorship by Daniel there is a mass of supporting evidence, which we have found not only as strong as, but much stronger than, the evidence that has been submitted by negative criticism. In fact, to record our sober conviction, we believe that before the very bar of reason the negative position has been utterly demolished and Daniel's authorship brilliantly vindicated.

The next negative contention is that Daniel is unlike the noted prophets of the Lord in that he avoids the use of the distinctive name for the true God, *Yahweh*. In doing that he is said to be more like those later writers, who, the nearer we get to New Testament times, studiously avoid this most holy name. Says one of the critics: "So we find in the Book of Daniel a similar avoidance of the awful Tetragrammaton." Let anyone look for himself. A hurried count tells me that this name actually appears no less than seven times. Do you call that "avoidance"? We know that these seven instances appear within one chapter, namely, the ninth, where Daniel makes his confession to the God of his fathers. But what about the avoidance of this name in the other chapters? The answer is simple: the divine names are used according to their meaning and thus with fine propriety. When a true Israelite speaks to the God of his fathers, what could be more in order than the ancient name of the covenant God? The other chapters deal very largely with Israel in its relation to the nations round about, the Gentiles. For them God is not *Yahweh* but the Creator God who made them, the God to be feared—*Elohim*. The critical mode of presenting the argument involved has hardly been fair and unbiased.

But what about the resemblance, even the "close resemblance between Daniel and other apocryphal books"? Aside from the fact that "other" in this quotation obviously begs the question, this in no sense argues for the fact that, since apocryphal books frequently follow the thought patterns of Daniel, therefore Daniel must be derived from them. There is another obvious possibility. This possibility agrees beautifully with the idea that Daniel was the author of the book. For when in the days during and after Antiochus Epiphanes the close correspondence between the events of those days and the prophecies of Daniel became obvious, the book of Daniel must have begun to enjoy great respect. We can readily understand why at such a time men should have begun to write in imitation of the book of Daniel even though what they wrote is now usually classed as belonging to the "Apocrypha." They that advance this critical argument fail to consider that of several possibilities they were choosing only the one that supported their side of the question.

At first glance the following counterargument from *Koenig's Einleitung* seems to have quite a bit more substance than most of the preceding objections. Pointing to the passage, Ezek. 28:3, where the king of Tyre is addressed—sarcastically, by the way: "Thou art wiser than Daniel." *Koenig* asks: Is there any likelihood "that the king of Tyre would be reminded of Daniel as of a notable wise man?" One objection along the same line comes to our mind: Even if Daniel's fame had spread quickly among his own people, would fifteen years suffice to have made him so famous that the king of Tyre could appropriately be reminded of him? However, this objection vanishes if we remember that, though the king of Tyre is addressed, this does not mean that the prophetic discourse was delivered before the king in his own palace. It is not even necessary that he should ever have had this word brought to him. Note a similar situation in Jer. 25:15ff. where the prophet Jeremiah gives the kings of the nations to drink of the cup of the wrath of God. This could not be carried out according to the letter. It was a rhetorical figure, a dramatic way of saying that God would visit their evil ways upon them. So the Ezekiel passage is a dramatic presentation of the idea that the proud king of Tyre is by no means as wise and as invincible as he thinks. This was a thought to be conveyed to Israel by the prophet. If Ezekiel then uses a comparison that Israel comprehends and the king of Tyre does not, that in no wise conflicts with the purpose of the passage.

The bulk of critical opinion of our day is unanimous in calling this book a pseudonymous production. To speak plainly, it is their critical contention that Daniel did not write it; furthermore, that Daniel could not have written it; in fact, it does not truthfully bear the name of Daniel.

If the authorship by Daniel is denied, the question must naturally be asked, "Why did the author, or some contemporary of his, put this book forth under the name of Daniel?" Many critical explanations have been offered, which we have always regarded to be of the most dubious sort. They certainly failed to make the ethics of the procedure acceptable. But now one of the most recent and scholarly critics—Charles—has come to the fore with a frank admission of the inadequacy of the explanations offered heretofore. He says: "It must be confessed that the grounds which scholars have in the past adduced for the use of pseudonymity by Jewish teachers have quite failed to justify themselves at the bar of the ordinary conscience" (p. xxi). We feel that this concession delivers us from the necessity of proving at length what we have always believed to be the case.

Yet Charles, too, regards the book of Daniel to be pseudonymous. What new and more satisying justification of pseudonymity does he offer? He says: "When once the prophetic Canon was closed, no book of prophetic character could gain canonization as such, nor could it gain a place among the sacred writings at all unless its date was believed to be as early as the time of Ezra. On this ground, the prophetic type of man was forced to resort to pseudonymity to obtain a hearing, and so to issue his work under the name of one of Israel's ancient worthies of a date earlier than Ezra or at all events contemporary with him."

This explanation of Charles's is, in our opinion, not one whit better than any that went before. It takes the position that "prophetic men," if they could not gain a hearing in the Canon and have their works listed among the canonical writings by fair means, would naturally resort to means that were dubious. For it is most reprehensible to let a book go forth as the work of an illustrious saint or prophet when it was obviously not written by him. Forgery, no matter how ambitious its purpose, is still forgery. "At the bar of the ordinary conscience" this verdict will still have to be rendered.

Had the "prophetic type of man" who was the author of the book been sure of its merits and its true inspiration he could well have permitted the book to be tried by the ordinary test of time. If his views of inspiration did not include faith in the providence of the God who inspired men, faith, I say, strong enough to hold that God would preserve what He had inspired, then such an author had neither a strong nor an adequate faith. We for our part doubt that God was wont to employ such instruments. If he must help the Almighty and His cause by questionable means he plays a part that is analogous to that played by Jacob and Rebecca in securing the blessing of the first-born. Somehow the issue involved in such cases is so clear that we have little difficulty in getting children to see what is at stake. How much more readily would the Jews, of whom we have clear proof that they watched zealously over the Canon, have rejected any books whose authenticity was bolstered up by spurious claims!

Besides, this contention of Charles's makes the age of Ezra appear as a purely arbitrary limit of the period of canonical writings. Several statements in the first book of the Maccabees make it obvious that the Jews were merely waiting for a competent prophet to appear, and that they would readily have submitted to the judgment of such a one. No true prophet would, therefore, have had difficulty in getting a hearing. Cf. I Macc. 4:46 and 9:27; also 14:41.

Other arguments against Daniel's authorship of the book will be considered under other headings in this Introduction or in the comments upon individual passages in connection with which the objections are treated.

3. Historical Background

At the time the prophet Daniel writes the kingdom of Judah has been overthrown. That fact was so grievous a shock to the people of God that even they who firmly believed in the providence of God had severe difficulties to overcome. For though the kingdom of Judah had always been more or less small, except in the days of David and Solomon, it had, nevertheless, on significant occasions enjoyed the providential care of God to such an extent that wavering faith again and again saw the sovereign power of God displayed in a most heartening way. Some, in a sense of superstition, and others, in a sense of belief in the providence of God, had held that such a calamity as the overthrow of God's city and God's Temple could never take place. Now the unexpected had happened.

Besides, the overthrow had been wrought with that distinctive thoroughness that had marked the efforts of the Assyrians—deportation, a violent up-rooting, and a complete transplanting—a process from which no nation had ever recovered in the past. And now, as we know, with this particular nation (Israel) were tied up all the gracious promises of God. Were these promises cancelled? Could God achieve the impossible, humanly speaking? At least those who were none too well established in the faith had very grievous difficulties in their thinking; and even the faithful needed enlightenment and reassurance.

Besides, as God foreknew, and as the next developments very clearly showed, the kingdom of God was not going to be re-established in the form of a visible entity like unto what Israel had known since the days of David. Israel's independence, except for the brief flare-up at the time of the Maccabees, was a thing of the past. Israel was destined to be a very inferior nation under foreign domination.

Parallel with this series of disappointments ran the very obvious fact that the world power was running on mightily and forging to the forefront. It might well be possible that Babylon would give way to Persia, and Persia in turn to the Greeks. But it was always world power, dominating the world and having grandeur and military resources and all things else that make for success at its disposal. How paltry God's ancient people always seemed by contrast! Besides, in the Greek empire, which was soon to come, there was to appear the added advantage of having one language dominate within the empire as a unifying force and as an expression of the great power resident in these empires.

True, somewhat strange phenomena were appearing in the world of religions. Idolatry was breaking down and losing its hold on the peoples generally, at least on the more advanced nations. Well might the Israelite wonder whether the time for the setting-up of the kingdom of the Messiah had not, perhaps, drawn near after all.

It must also be remembered that very grievous times were again about to descend upon the people of God. The trying events of the times of Antiochus Epiphanes were in the offing.

Did the times and the impending future not very clearly call for some revelation of God whereby the nations might be revealed in their weakness and their striving in its futility; and on the other hand, whereby the assurance of ultimate victory for the people of God and all His holy objectives might be set forth in a manner adequate for these new times and conditions? Even humanly speaking, it was almost imperative that a comprehensive revelation be given, setting forth the issues of the kingdom of God versus the world power and what truths might afford a safe anchorage in the strange and troublous times that were then trying men's souls.

In addition, it seemed to be such a suitable time for God to teach some substantial lessons to the Gentiles, who, because of the internal collapse of their own religions, might from this time forth be more susceptible to impressions emanating from the true God through His prophets. It can be conceived of as a wholesome thing that the representatives of the world power heard the truth about their power as well as about the true and living God whom they held in rather low esteem. His kingdom would last forever; theirs would be overthrown.

Even from the point of view of these elementary considerations we can see how eminently fitting it was that God should give the messages of the book of Daniel at this time.

4. Time of Composition

Our statements on the question of authorship give our answer to the question as to the time of composition of the book. If Daniel lived to see the fall of Babylon under Belshazzar and was then already an old man, and also labored under Darius the Mede for a time and in his own book recorded this activity of his, the most reasonable time to assign for the composition or the completion of his book would be the decennium following the fall of Babylon—538 B. C. to 528 B. C.

The majority of commentators of the present time are of quite a different opinion, an opinion that is built almost exclusively (though this is not always readily admitted) on the fact that the eleventh chapter tells of things with such minute detail that, as they think, only one who was living during or after the things recorded occurred could have done justice to them. But because after a given point the exact pattern of history is left behind, the conclusion is drawn that at that point the author was beginning to deal with things that lay in the future and could, therefore, no longer write accurately. This given point is definitely 166 B. C.- 165 B. C. by common consent of all who are critically inclined. *Cornill (Einleitung,* p. 242) aims to be very impressive when he tells us that we are able to determine the date of writing "almost to the very day." Lest we fail to give due credence to what he thus tells us, he assures us that the traditionalists are getting rarer and rarer. Of course, this particular year was the first year of the Maccabean uprising.

Others do not consider the case quite so simple. They have a far more elaborate scheme of composition that they believe can be detected. That of *Montgomery* is relatively simple in this respect. He feels that the two halves of the book are too different from one another to be derived from one source. Therefore the first half is classed as pre-Maccabean, dating from the third century; the second half only is ascribed to the time of the beginning of the uprising of the Maccabees.

A number of questions that could be discussed in this connection will more appropriately fit into the next category.

5.   Integrity—Historical Accuracy

Volumes have been written on this subject. The critics are wont to find the wildest sort of historical inaccuracies. *Meinhold* (*Einleitung*) uses the very derogatory language *die wunderbarsten historischen Schnitzer,* i. e. "the most remarkable historical blunders." But even *Montgomery,* who, on the whole, is very fair-minded, was compelled to concede that in these and in similar assertions the "critics overreached themselves."

Some are inclined to object to the miracles as such inasmuch as they feel that a certain mania for miracles pervades the book. Any reader must concede that the miracles are more common in Daniel than in many other portions of the Scriptures. But that is merely in harmony with the fact that, according to the Scriptures, miracles predominate in certain eras, are bunched together for a time and then for a time fail to put in their appearance. Only the wisdom of God can determine when such eras have arrived, and why just during such times miracles are in order, and why they are not allowed to come to the forefront at another time. Some of the ages marked by miracles are those of Moses and the Exodus, Elijah and Elisha, and the age of the blessed Savior and His holy apostles. The only other time comparable to these is the time of Daniel. But since it pleased God to stress both His omnipotence and His omniscience in an unusual way, it must be conceded that there is a propriety about having them appear in this age. Miracles speak a language that the duller ear of the heathen can comprehend.

When the question of the integrity of the book is raised, that often means: May it be ascribed to Daniel, to whom the statements in the book itself ascribe it? One objection that some feel stands in the way is the apocalyptical character of the book. Behind that objection lies the observation that apocalyptical books begin to flourish in the Maccabean age and not yet in the days of Daniel. We have indicated above where the solution of this seeming difficulty lies.

But if individual items under this head are stressed, then these have to be examined one by one. An item of this sort is the claim that a marked "characteristic of this later Apocalyptic" is "a theological determinism which regards all history as foreordained, a copy stamped from the drama already enacted above, involving the exact calculation of secular days and years . . ." That may all be true with regard to the "later Apocalyptic." But when the claim is added that "determinism is a far more definite factor in the theology of the book than elsewhere in the Old Testament," we must enter a protest. For that is a point of view foisted upon the book of Daniel. It is, like many other matters in the other prophets, pure prophecy. As such it foretells what things will come to pass without in any sense creating a pattern within which coming events must fall. To question the possibility of such prophecy and to call it some kind of determinism are in essence questioning the foreknowledge of God. Either God foreknows, or He does not. If He does He can communicate to man as much of this knowledge as it may be beneficial for man to know. By communicating such knowledge to man God has not

shaped the course of history. Else foreknowledge is
not foreknowledge.

In the effort to prove a late date for the book the
claim has been stressed that Daniel appears, not in the
list of the Hebrew prophets in the stricter sense, but
in the third division of the Hebrew canon, the "Writings," where our book occupies a somewhat late place.
But, as has been pointed out again and again, the sequence of books in the Hebrew canon is not chronological. Besides, there is no proof for the origin of any
book in this group or elsewhere in the canon later than
the time of Malachi, that is, about 400 B. C. Not to
class Daniel with the other prophets marks a very
correct observation on the part of the Jewish guardians
of the Old Testament canon. For, in fact, Daniel was
not sent to the people of God with a message to proclaim to them day by day as other prophets were. For
that matter, Daniel was a statesman, who never re-
linquished this position of his. True, his message had
an import also for his own people. But he was primarily
God's voice to heathen monarchs. To indicate this fact
the Jews grouped his book in a separate category.

The answer to the foregoing objection, which
answer is an entirely valid and satisfactory one, has
been given so often and has never been refuted that it
begins to strike the present writer as a strange kind
of unwillingness to learn when interpreters fail to
note pertinent facts.

Much along the same line as the preceding criticism is the one that points to the fact that in his
famous book "Ecclesiasticus," listed among the acknowledged Apocrypha, Jesus Sirach fails to list Daniel in his famous series of mighty heroes of the Biblical
record. But this list, as anyone can read, is not an
attempt to name exhaustively all men deserving to be
called "famous men" (Ecclesiasticus 44:1). None of
the Judges of Israel are mentioned except Samuel. In
the list of those who were active in the days of the

Restoration even Ezra is passed by although Nehemiah is mentioned. Who will account for this? The omission of Daniel's name in this uncanonical book therefore proves nothing more than that its author either forgot Daniel at the moment or, perhaps, was not even so much of an admirer of Daniel.

But what about the statement that neither Haggai nor Zechariah, neither Ezra nor Nehemiah offer a syllable in regard to the book of Daniel? If this silence is construed to mean that they do not contain the name of Daniel nor a quotation from him in a direct statement by him, then the presupposition must be that it is fair to expect books as short as all these are to take cognizance of all contemporary literature—which is certainly an absurd expectation. But viewing the evidence of the case rightly, we feel that this is a claim that ought to be inverted. As *Keil* puts it: "Not only was Zechariah acquainted with Daniel's prophecies, but Ezra also and the Levites of his time make use of (Ezra 9 and Neh. 9) the penitential prayer of Daniel (ch. 9)." The correspondence between these prayers of penitence ought to be especially obvious to any careful reader. Ezra and Nehemiah had learned the true and deep lesson of their predecessor.

Much has been made of the fact that more than two hundred years before the beginning of the Greek era the names of Greek musical instruments appear in Daniel (cf. 3:5 and all parallels). A *possible* explanation would, of course, be that the author wrote some time after the Greek era began. But just as possible is the explanation that contacts between Babylon and Greece are far more ancient than men had formerly surmised. It has been pointed out (*Keil*) that, upon the testimony of Strabo, a Greek was found in the army of Nebuchadnezzar, and, upon the testimony of Eusebius, that Greeks followed Esarhaddon (682 B. C.). But it is common knowledge how strongly the names of musical instruments retain the designation of the land from which they originally came. But the question involves so many difficulties that some modern commentators no longer feel free to use this against authorship by Daniel.

We have discussed at length the question whether there is a conflict between Dan. 1:1 and Jer. 25 on the question of dates and have there (1:1) shown that these two statements do not contradict one another.

Nor is it safe any longer to stress the claim that history knows of no Belshazzar inasmuch as up to very recent times the only record available in regard to him was the Biblical. *Montgomery* sums up the situation very aptly in the words: "The existence of Belshazzar at the end of the Chaldean dynasty was strikingly demonstrated by the discovery of the name on the Nabonidus Cylinder, in which he appears as Nabonidus' son." For a further discussion of the subject see chapter 5. *Cornill* had waxed so bold as to say in his day that, if the king under whom Babylon was destroyed be called Belshazzar, this is even "at variance with the assured testimonies of the Old Testament." Men have since become more cautious.

Then there is the somewhat difficult problem of identifying Darius the Mede (5:31). It will be observed that in our comments we take the position that this personage may have been the Gubaru spoken of in the Nabonidus-Cyrus Chronicle as being appointed over Babylon by Cyrus after the conquest of the city. Mark well that we claim nothing more than that this identification is possible. For the present we remind only of the fact that this identification has not been disproved.

Under the head of historical inaccuracies must come the critical claim that in the account of Daniel both Nebuchadnezzar and Darius are not presented with historical fidelity but are patterned after that wretched fiend of the eleventh chapter, Antiochus Epiphanes. For—so it is claimed—if the book was written in the second century then it must present these two kings merely as prototypes of this later and bitter enemy of the Jews. Critics must do something like that if they want to salvage the unity of the book. But this supposition is erroneous on a number of counts as we shall also show in part when we come to the chapters in which these kings are dealt with. Some of the critics have come to see this point. They admit that it is "erroneous . . . to argue that the portraiture of these two kings was modelled after the arch-tyrant Antiochus." In fact, the difference between these two kings on the one hand and Antiochus on the other is so pronounced that it would never occur to the ordinary reader of the book.

A rather impressive argument, on the other hand, is the one advanced by the critics on the score of the language in evaluating the amount of non-Hebrew elements found in the book. When, for example, an impressive list of seventeen Persian words is assembled, and it is pointed out that "his Persian vocabulary is more extensive than his Babylonian," one is apt to be puzzled, at least for a moment. For one is inclined to wonder how Daniel, who was rather an old man at the time the Persians overcame Babylon, should have absorbed so much of a coloring of Persian at so late a date. Yet we definitely feel that the case is grossly overstated when it is given this form: "But why should even a royal official, who was a Semite and had enjoyed most of his life and experiences under Babylonian monarchs, be so contaminated in the diction of his old age with vocabulary of the new empire" (*Montgomery,* p. 21)? For a careful examination of the list presented at once reveals the fact that at least twelve of the seventeen words listed are in the class of governmental terminology used at governmental headquarters— names of officials, technical terms, and the like. If Daniel moved in the circles of the new Persian government he must have become immediately aware of the new regime that the Persians set up, their new nomenclature to designate the new officials. Not only that, but he must have seen that to use the old terminology would have confused the new generation for which he was writing. Being familiar with the new terminology, he would have used it with facility and accuracy, especially if he wrote his book near the end of his days, and even if he merely revised certain parts near the end of his life in order to bring terms up to date. This very reasonable supposition leaves so trifling an amount of Persian words that it would be absurd to want to base any substantial claims on their presence in the book.

We must mention briefly a claim, met with rather frequently, that tries to prove a late date for the book by pointing to 9:1, 2, where it is said that Daniel "understood by the books the number of the years whereof the word of Jehovah came to Jeremiah the prophet . . . even seventy years." It is claimed that the plural "books" indicates the existence of an Old Testament canon which was all but complete, and since men of this school have already given late dates down to 350 or even 250 B. C. to certain books, it must needs follow, by this style of reasoning, that we have in this passage an indication of the comparatively late date of the book and of the fact that the traditional date is impossible. But it must be conceded that the term used—"the books"—has the utmost latitude. All the needs of the case would be met if what Daniel had in hand was any group of prophetical books, whether one of the rolls that later Judaism was familiar with or any other collection of prophetic writings that were extant about the year 540 B. C. This counterclaim of ours is so obvious that we feel that it is quite unnecessary to try to establish our point at any further length.

Nor need we go into a lengthy investigation of the claim that the developed angelology of the book is like that of the period of the Maccabees. For everyone can well see that, even on the basis of the conservative position, this observation can be explained very readily. For if the book of Daniel was written somewhere around 535 B. C., what does it matter if a book written after 150 B. C. has the same type of angelology? Are we so dull as not to be able to see that this allows for the very reasonable assumption that the later of the two books has an angelology like the first because the author of the second learned from the first? Must this similarity mean that the book of Daniel was written at the time of the composition of the books of the Maccabees? Again, criticism has chosen the one of two possibilities that suits its purposes and stressed it as though it were the only possible one. Such arguments have no compelling force.

We should have no difficulty with the claim that "hitherto neither has his (Daniel's) name been discovered nor the faintest trace of his existence" in historical or monumental records. Though it is emphasized that he had the prominent position that he did at the court of Nebuchadnezzar, it must be remembered that, according to the very statements of the book itself, this involved nothing more than that he was found to be "ten times better than all the magicians and enchanters that were in all his [the king's] realm" (1:20); or that the king "made him to rule over the whole province of Babylon and to be chief governor over all the wise men of Babylon" (2:48); or that Daniel was one of the three presidents that ruled over the domains of Darius (6:1), which realm, as we show in connection with this chapter, was only little Babylon, the district, not the Persian Empire. Looking at this aspect of the case only for the present, we shall have to admit that there were many governors of Babylon or men of inferior position, like that of being chief of the wise men, whose names have been lost. By accident some few names of the vast total have been discovered. Does that make all those whose names have not been

discovered characters of fiction? Nor dare we forget
that no trace of Moses, Joshua, David, Solomon, Isaiah,
or even of Christ and his twelve apostles has been
found in contemporary historical records. Some men
seem to forget that our faith is not based on history,
and that the Scriptures do not get their validity from
confirmation by extant historical documents.

To bring this matter of the treatment of the so-
called historical inaccuracies to a close, since we have
touched upon at least those issues which are most
frequently mentioned, we would remind the reader
that these are in no sense dead issues. One of the most
recent introductions to the Old Testament (*Pfeiffer's*,
pp. 753-758) within the space of five pages has the
following criticisms to make under the head of the
"Historical Background" alone. We merely list phrases
and sentences at random: "deliberately obscure language"; "some verses defy interpretation"; "historical recapitulations in obscure oracular language";
"information sketchy and erroneous"; "the first historical reference (1:1f) is incorrect"; "the writer has
confused the statement"; "contradiction with facts";
"another anachronism"; "to add to the confusion";
"in the author's muddled mind"; "the author concluded that the kings of Persia from Cyrus to Alexander were only four, where they were eleven"; "author's
misconceptions"; "this unhistorical tale seems to be
a confused reminiscence"; "the author's information
is extremely vague."

The matter boils down to this: the critical objections have been answered time and again in such a
manner as to satisfy those that still believe in the
veracity of God's Word, who also are fully convinced
that, on the basis of sound logic, not one valid objection
against the historical truth of the Bible can be pointed
out. They who raise the claim that "the historicity of
the Book of Daniel is an article of faith" are correct

only when they accept the equally valid claim: *The correctness of the critical position is an article of faith.*

We must confess to our utter inability to understand the position of those who spend page after page of argument in an endeavor to discredit and honeycomb the credibility of the book and its basic reliability and then give us the bland assurance: "Yet no words of mine can exaggerate the value which I attach to this part of our Canonical Scriptures." We do not question the writer's honesty. But we fail utterly to comprehend how such a position can be maintained. Surely, the effect of these extensive arguments, which are designed to stress the errors and the inaccuracies at great length, will be so strongly to confuse the lay reader as well as many of the clergy as to make it utterly impossible for them to read the book with anything other than confusion, if not a painful uneasiness that will make all constructive approaches to the book basically futile.

6. Purpose

In setting forth the historical background (above) we had occasion to dwell at length upon the purpose of the book from the positive point of view.

A few further considerations under that head may be appended.

The Book of Daniel was in an outstanding sense a book of comfort, designed for evil days as well as for good days. By the help of it Israel could discern that its oppressions were, indeed, going to be heavy, but, on the other hand, that they were foreknown by God and were therefore not to be dreaded too much. For if an all-knowing God had seen what would transpire He must at the same time be an omnipotent God who would be able to deliver His own, as well as a faithful God who would not suffer them to be tempted above what they were able.

But in making this claim we have no thought about history's being regarded as a kind of "drama already enacted above" after some sort of deterministic pattern. They that charge the book with such thoughts and doctrines do violence to its teachings and hasten to draw conclusions that are far from warranted by the contents of the book.

In claiming that this is a book of comfort we are at the same time defining our position over against those who, having deflated the book by their criticisms, arrive at the conclusion that it is "impossible to ascertain a deep moral tone" or, for that matter, any particular "doctrinal significance" in the things set forth in the book. The moral purpose is of the highest. This book is in no sense inferior to the books of the other great prophets in the divine truths that it sets forth and in the confident spirit in which it propounds them. As for the doctrines offered by the book, they do happen to be clothed in a form that is for the most part different from that which we are wont to observe in prophecy elsewhere. But despite all that we may well claim that what this book teaches is set forth nonetheless clearly.

This defines our position also over against all those who see in the Book of Daniel only things that are heavily veiled. This view they advance in connection with the term "apocalyptic," which covers a multitude of irregularities. In the sense in which the term is used, namely, as referring to certain types of religious literature that specialize in mystery and attempts to disclose the unknown future, in this sense we absolutely reject the claim that Daniel belongs to this kind of literature. It does not deal with these subjects in the manner of the traditional literature of this class of writings. It does not offer cryptic messages. But it is, indeed, the original after which many spurious and inferior copies have been patterned. It is in a class by itself. The apocalyptic literature is a feeble and an unreliable imitation, safe only in so far as it says exactly the same things that Daniel says. In other words, the Bible has two valid apocalypses— Revelation and Daniel. Every other apocalypse is spurious. The valid and the spurious should not be classed under the one head.

7. Language

The Book of Daniel is bilingual. From 2:4 to 7:28 it is written in Aramaic; the rest is Hebrew. After an introductory chapter in Hebrew the second chapter makes the transition to the Aramaic at the point where it is being stated that the Chaldeans spoke to the king in the Aramaic language, which language is still called "Syrian" in the American Standard Version and "Syriack" in the King James translation. In days of old it was frequently, if not generally, referred to as "Chaldee," due to a misunderstanding. The propriety of the transition into the Aramaic at the point where these Chaldeans speak in Aramaic must be conceded.

That does not as yet answer the much-debated question, "What led Daniel to use this language in a book which was designed for the use of the people of God?" As we indicate in connection with the comments on 2:4 we hold that, since this part of the book is primarily the portion which was designed to teach the world powers of those days a lesson, it is written in the language which was the world language in those days.

This seems to be the meaning of the following words, quoted from *Charles* (p. xxxiv) : "In a work in which the visions of the King of Babylon were interpreted, Aramaic, which was the *lingua franca* of the whole East at the time, was naturally considered suitable." Though *lingua franca* means a hybrid or mixed language it comes also to mean "an international language." Again he says (p. lxxx) : "Aramaic as the language of commerce and diplomacy was the *lingua franca* of the ancient world alike in the East and in the West."

Since we include chapter seven in the first half of the book and regard this half as a unit we have no particular problem under this head as they have who have the partition of the book come at the end of the sixth chapter. Being the world language, the Aramaic was, of course, also understood in this portion of the book by the Jews, for whom it was also designed as a part of their sacred Scriptures. In any case, the transition from the Hebrew to the Aramaic had already set in by this time as is also indicated by the fact that a later postexilic book—Ezra—was in part written in Aramaic as well.

Two difficulties call for discussion. The first is that of the so-called difference between the East and the West Aramaic. It used to be asserted rather confidently that the Aramaic of this book bears such a close resemblance to the Western Aramaic that is found in Jewish sources that originated in Palestine about this time or later that it must be classed as Western Aramaic. This claim was then naturally followed by the contention that Daniel, who had spent practically three-fourths or more of his life farther east, where the Eastern Aramaic was spoken, would naturally have written in the Eastern Aramaic had he written this book. So this claim was made to militate against authorship of the book by Daniel.

However, the course that the discussion took ran about as follows: *Driver* and those of his school pressed the claim rather strongly. *Wilson* proved rather exhaustively, also on the basis of the papyri, that such a claim cannot be substantiated. It is now conceded by writers like *Montgomery* that Wilson proved his point. *Charles* formulates his findings in a thesis which runs thus (p. lxxix) : "The differentiation of Aramaic into Eastern and Western cannot from existing documents and inscriptions be established before the first century B. C., if so early." He then adds that other recent authorities on Aramaic such as Baumgartner and Bauer-Leaner have come to the same conclusion. They who claim that the book was written in the Western Aramaic have not gone into the case with sufficient thoroughness.

The second difficulty lies in the claim that the Aramaic of the book is, of necessity, rather late and cannot have been written in the sixth century B. C., which is the date set for its composition by conservative scholarship. So *Farrar* quotes *Driver* in what seems a rather forceful statement of the case as saying : "The *Persian* words *presuppose* a period after the Persian empire had been established ; the *Greek* words *demand*, the *Hebrew supports*, and the *Aramaic permits* a date after the conquest of Palestine by Alexander the Great." But, to begin with, this rather aggressive claim hardly ventures to press the date of the writing of the book down past 300 B. C. In the second place, it originates with *Driver*, regarding whom *Wilson* has shown that he did not go into the question of language with sufficient thoroughness. In the third place, it is advanced by *Farrar*, who himself admits that this whole question "involves delicate problems on which an independent and a valuable opinion can only be offered by the merest handful of living scholars, and respecting which even these scholars sometimes disagree."

But since this phase of the discussion, apparently spurred on by *Wilson's* investigations, at least in part, a more thoroughgoing investigation has taken place, headed very largely by *Charles*.

One of the arguments which *Charles* advances in support of the late date of the Book of Daniel seems almost final in its thoroughness and convincing power.

It runs as follows: As far as the Aramaic language from 800 B. C. to 100 A. D. is concerned, five distinct periods of development are discernible, of which Ezra and Daniel plainly represent the third and the fourth, and so Daniel in particular must be assigned to the second century B. C. His five periods run as follows:

I. 800-500 B. C., represented by the Zinjirli Inscriptions and Aramaic letters of the time of Assurbanipal.

II. 500-400 B. C., represented by Assuan and Elephantine documents in the West and by a variety of documents in Asia Minor and Arabia in the East.

III. Toward the close of the Fourth Century, ca. 325 B. C., represented primarily by the Aramaic portions of the Book of Ezra.

IV. Second Century, involving the Aramaic sections of the Book of Daniel.

V. 100 B. C.-150 A. D., covered by Nabataean and Palmyrene Inscriptions.

That this development of the Aramaic language is not a fanciful notion but is amply supported by evidence appears from the various grammatical subdivisions offered by Charles under this head. He lists such data as the use of the emphatic state, personal pronoun endings, certain letters displaced by others, assimilation of *n*, personal and demonstrative pronouns, suffixes, causative verb forms, imperfect and participial forms, Hophals and derived infinitives.

To all this he adds more than a dozen examples of words and phrases used idiomatically and makes a clear-cut differentiation of usage in regard to the five periods in question.

We call this inductive proof at its best. We might be inclined to take issue with a number of the writer's findings or consider his evidence insufficient in quite a number of other cases, but by far the bulk of his proofs would still be unassailed and unassailable.

We still hold that the final conclusion drawn is erroneous. All Charles proves is that the Aramaic of the Book of Daniel, as we now have it, is of the type that would have been written in the second century B. C. But that claim *does not prove that the age to which the Aramaic portions of the book now belong is the same as the age in which the book was originally written.*

We are surprised that Charles did not note this obvious point, for he is far from claiming that the Book of Daniel was written in one piece, and that it remained unaltered thereafter. He tells the story of a rather hectic career that the book or portions of it are supposed to have had till it finally attained its present shape and form. We know little about such varied fortunes of Biblical books though the critical claims would construe a strange textual history for almost every one of them. We on our part, however, are meeting the critic on his own ground and are as· suming for the moment that the Aramaic portions of Daniel, since they were written in the world language, may, for that matter, have been brought up to date in spelling and endings and the like as late as the second century B. C. The particular reason for this revision may well have been the fact that the Book of Daniel was being appreciated anew in the troublous times under Antiochus Epiphanes.

From even the conservative point of view such an assumption is quite reasonable. It would not necessitate the loss of a single word or the alteration of the meaning of a single sentence. It would be entirely parallel, let us say, with the fortunes of Luther's translation of the Bible, when the original of Luther of the sixteenth century is compared with reprints of the nineteenth and the twentieth centuries. Certain consonants are dropped, others are added; some are doubled; some endings are changed; new spellings appear. The changes involved could be made the subject of a detailed study such as Charles has made of the Aramaic of Daniel. Yet who, knowing the issues that are involved, would hesitate for a moment to claim that the nineteenth-century edition is Luther's translation, true to the original to all intents and purposes, different only in spelling, which in this instance is a very secondary consideration? Or, to press the case home a little more pointedly, who, because of the nineteenth-century spelling, would venture the claim that Luther could not have been the author of the translation? Or furthermore, who would venture to claim that someone had taken unseemly liberties with the Bible or with a particular translation in bringing it up to date? Similar cases in large number could be cited from the study of comparative philology or from the history of the development of languages.

We cite Luther's translation as a parallel because the German orthography has undergone more extensive variations than has the English during the last four centuries.

So we reiterate, though Charles may have fixed the age to which the Aramaic of the present Book of Daniel belongs—and we honestly believe he did—he has not proved anything about the age in which the Aramaic of that book was written, nor can he on the basis of the critical position.

8. Style

A brief statement on the subject of the style of the book. Even the casual reader is impressed with the dignity of the typical Biblical style of this book, its naturalness, and the general absence of any particular rhetorical ornamentation. Certain portions repeat in public explanation what was given in the initial private explanation (cf. 4:10-17 with v. 20-26; also 7:1-14 with v. 17-27). The second statement of the case is at the same time so manifestly different from the original as to constitute a distinct commentary upon it.

Aside from this it must be obvious that historical narratives and visions plus their explanations do not lend themselves naturally to impassioned flights of oratory such as are found in the book of Isaiah, for example. Nor does this difference constitute a criticism of the style of the writer. It rather does credit to his discernment. He recognizes the limitations imposed by the situation. In expounding visions a man must hold closely to the original which appeared to him. The simpler his style, the more likely is he to furnish a clear explanation. Exposition as a type of discourse never possesses the flexibility found in hortatory paragraphs. But that is no criticism. Who would expect flights of eloquence in describing the beasts at the beginning of chapter 8? The author deserves the highest commendation for observing these proprieties.

Yet here again criticism has launched into attacks that are calculated to undermine the respect of men for this good book. Here is the manner after which one writer of this type finds fault with the book; he senses "a certain artificiality of diction, a sounding rhetorical stateliness, enhanced by dignified paraphrases and leisurely repetitions" and adds that "this is sometimes carried so far as to make the movement of the book heavy and pompous." Why this same author should take *Reuss* to task for having asserted in a similar vein: "*Der Styl ist unbeholfen, the Figuren grotesk, die Farben grell,*" is more than we can detect, for he himself later refers to the "grotesque and gigantic emblems of Daniel." Men speak thus about a book when they find themselves entirely out of sympathy with it. In this case the added motive must be noted of making this appear as a late and an inferior book, not such a one as the great and mighty prophets of the days of Israel's creative period would have produced. Therefore this same critic adds that in this book we may trace "none of that 'blasting with excess of light,' none of that shuddering sense of being uplifted out of self, which marks the higher and earlier forms of prophetic inspiration." Again he charges: "Yet surely it has but little of the sublime and mysterious beauty, little of the heart-shaking pathos, little of the tender sweetness of consolatory power, which fill the closing book of the New Testament." The critic may wax very eloquent in his faultfinding, but just what he misses other devout readers may have found in the book in ample measure. So we must point to the fact that he is offering personal reactions and subjective criticisms rather that scientific findings that have any practical value.

We have little sympathy with the claim that "this style of symbolism" as it is found in the book of Daniel "originated among the Jews from their contact with the graven mysteries and colossal images of Babylonian worship." This could apply to neither of the two dreams of Nebuchadnezzar, nor to the tale of the three men in the fiery furnace, nor to Daniel in the lions' den. This must refer only to chapters 7 and 8. But there again the thing described is a dream which was sent to Daniel by the Almighty. Daniel is, therefore, not the author of the dream, but God is. The critical claim practically amounts to this, that *God's* style and imagery were borrowed from these Babylonian sources, which, to say the least, is a precarious claim.

Under the head of style the question of metrical structure comes in for discussion. Are portions of the book poetic, or is it all prose? Some claim that sections or verses such as the following at least bear evidence of metrical structure: 3:31; 4:1, 2, 7b-9, 11-14 and the greater part if not all of vv. 31-34; 6:27, 28; 7:9, 10, 13, 14, 23-27; 9:24; 12:3. As long as nothing more is meant than that a kind of rhythmical prose is used when the strain of diction rises to a higher level, we can agree that something analogous to poetry and a kind of metrical structure are involved. But such claims may be stressed beyond what is reasonable and should be advanced with great care.

9. The Hebrew Portions of the Book, a Translation?

Charles presents a seemingly impressive array of arguments in support of his contention that the section 1—2:4 and the section 8—12 are from different translators, his basic assumption being that the Hebrew portions of the book are translated from an Aramaic original. As proof Charles advances seven arguments, which we shall refute briefly. Although much learning has been expended on some of these critical hypotheses which aim to discredit the authorship of this book by Daniel as well as the integrity of the book as a whole, it can be demonstrated that this learning is still but a futile assault upon the integrity of the book as such.

a) It is claimed that, since we find the so-called *waw apodosis* in 1:2, 18, 20 and not at all in chapters 8—12, this is a notable difference of Hebrew style, especially since these last five chapters contain as many as 133 verses. However, upon the frank admission of Charles, the *waw apodosis* is a "rare classical idiom." It would be easy, we are sure, to produce many sections of 133 verses in which no *waw apodosis* occurs even though the same author may have used this construction in a chapter preceding such a section. Its mere absence in the chapters in question therefore proves nothing.

b) It is said: "The translator of 1—2:4 uses twice the *oratio obliqua* instead of the *oratio directa*— a sign of late Hebrew: i. e., in 1:3 . . . and 2:2." We are not so sure that indirect discourse is late Hebrew. But assuming it to be for the sake of argument, the proof would apparently run thus, that he who has used a type of expression that appears late in a language must thereafter in the same document, having his choice of this or the alternate form of expression, always use the one he employed once or twice before. For no one will venture to claim that, if indirect discourse is a sign of late Hebrew, direct discourse has entirely vanished from late Hebrew. Why must it follow that, having shown one type of expression to have been used twice, a man has proved that this is a stylistic peculiarity that bars an author from the use of an alternate available form?

c)   "In 1:4 . . . 'the literature and language of the Chaldeans' " is said to be "bad Hebrew, being found only twice elsewhere in the Old Testament." We fail to see the force of this argument. Is it to run thus: because in the first of two sections "bad Hebrew" appears, some more "bad Hebrew" would have to appear in the second section, otherwise this section could not be ascribed to the same author? We admit the fact that the phrase in question is not the customary form of expression found in Hebrew. Only two similar instances of this construction can be cited. To designate it as "bad Hebrew" makes the construction appear in too unfavorable a light.

d)   The fourth instance cited has to do with two different meanings of the idiom *'amadh liphney* as it is used first in 1:5 and 19 and then in 8:4, 7; 11:16. Since the writer admits "this of course may be accidental," we feel exactly as he does and dismiss the case.

e)   We are told that the supposed translator uses the divine name *'adhonay* ("Lord") in 1:2 but never in chapters 8—12. This argument is based on the impossible and unreasonable assumption that, if an author uses one divine name of the four or five commonly known, he must within the next four or five chapters use that same name again, either a few times or regularly. Subjective preference on the part of critics plays into such matters so largely that to try to cover the issues by arbitrary rules of this sort borders on decrees invented to impress the uninformed.

f) The next argument is based on the fact that one and the same verb (*'asah*) is used with two different prepositions "to express mainly the same idea" (1:13 and 11:7). Surely, Charles would not venture to claim that this constitutes ground for postulating two different authors. In all languages we find ourselves confronted with a choice of prepositions with one and the same verb which involve very little if any difference in meaning. Sometimes we use the one; sometimes the other. Therefore the conclusion does not follow that two different translators have been shown to be at work.

g) Lastly it is claimed that the author has a "strange fondness for singular forms which have apparently plural suffixes." Charles cites 1:16 and compares 1:5, 8, 10, 15, and then points out that in chapters 8—12 none such are found. But most amazing is the fact that the first four passages listed offer the same noun. Consequently the seemingly long array of instances reduces itself to *two*. Then the reference— given later—to *Gesenius-Kautzsch* (93ss) reveals that the forms are not so unusual, and that they only seemingly have plural suffixes. We fail to see how any interpreter could list such a trivial thing as a mark of style that is prominently present in one instance and noticeably absent in another and so a clear indication of the work of two different writers.

Our impression of all these arguments is that they are about as inconsequential as they can be, and that they do not even begin to prove the original contention that two different translators worked at the Hebrew portions of Daniel.

10. Emending the Text according to the Translations

It seems necessary also to dispose of the difficulties arising from another prominent trend followed by the critics of the Masoretic text of Daniel as well as of all other Old Testament books. We refer to the

trend of giving a large measure of critical priority to
the Greek translations by way of evaluating what may
have been the original Hebrew or Aramaic text of the
book of Daniel. Critics are very strongly of the opinion
that the Masoretic text of Daniel cannot be that of the
original text of the book. In fact, the Masoretic text is
said to be secondary. The other versions that are used
for corrective purposes are Theodotion's Greek, the
Septuagint, the Syriac Peshitta, and the Vulgate.

It must be remembered, of course, that already in
the early Christian Church the Septuagint translation
of Daniel had been displaced by Theodotion's better
Greek version, and so the Septuagint version of Daniel
was lost till it reappeared in an old library about 1771.
Both it (usually referred to by the old symbol LXX)
and Theodotion's version (usually referred to as Th.)
are used generously to emend the Masoretic text (usually referred to as MT).

How strongly this critical approach is reinforced
appears from claims such as this: there are twelve
passages where LXX, Th., Pesh., and Vulgate fail to
support MT; LXX and Th. supply the missing date;
sometimes a single version preserves the original; MT
is frequently untrustworthy, the original being preserved only in LXX; the text contains dislocations,
interpolations, Hebrew words misused, Aramaic words
of a later period, and misused phrases. (These positions are largely those of Charles).

Such an array of charges might well disturb the
average reader and make him lose all confidence in the
text commonly found in Hebrew Bibles and drive him
to the conclusion that everything about the Book of
Daniel is uncertain. Or he might cast himself upon the
mercy of critical scholarship as the only agency capable of bringing order out of chaos.

However, there is so much to be said on the subject of the priority and, generally speaking, the integrity of the Masoretic text that, we believe, any man,

weighing the evidence carefully, must feel impelled to take quite a different view of the situation. Certain textual difficulties will be encountered, it is true, but not such as are of a serious nature.

We shall give a rather extended treatment of the case because the whole approach to the Book of Daniel is determined by an interpreter's attitude toward the text; and also because the critical claims to the contrary are rather positively advanced and rather extensively elaborated. For a more detailed statement of the positive side of the matter *Koenig's Einleitung*, p. 104ff, may be compared. We have derived quite a bit of the following presentation from this source.

To begin with, the grandson of Jesus Sirach, who wrote the famous introduction to his grandfather's book, which book is called Ecclesiasticus, and who wrote this introduction about a hundred years or more B. C., remarked in the course of it about the inadequacy of the available translation of the Hebrew Scriptures into Greek. He must have been referring to the Septuagint version. Such an opinion, coming from so early a date, dare not be disregarded. This version was available already then.

It should not be overlooked that there are numerous indications that the Septuagint version represented the theological viewpoint of Judaism that was current at the time and consistently made corresponding changes in the text. Most notable of all these changes is the translation of *Yahweh* by κύριος, which is really *'adhonay* ("Lord"), the form regularly substituted by Jewish readers for *Yahweh*.

It can be shown that the Septuagint version continually makes attempts to smooth out the difficulties of the Masoretic text by renderings that are interpretative rather than exact, or that remove minor inequalities of the text. Translations are apt to do that in any case. The Septuagint does it rather obviously.

When, lastly, several versions such as the Septuagint, the Targums, and the Vulgate, as well as the Samaritan Pentateuch can be cited in support of a textual reading that differs from MT, this should not impress us unduly even though for the moment it would seem to argue for a text that is different from the Masoretic text as being basic for all of these. For the point mentioned above, that the Septuagint reflects the general theological position of the postbiblical age, merely again comes to the fore here. The current Jewish tradition, long carried on orally in a practically fixed form, found expression in all these versions and is more or less uniformly expressed in them all.

On the basis of these arguments we may well maintain the claim of the priority of the current Masoretic text and use it as a text which stands in little need of correction by the versions. Yet, any true scholar will consistently compare the versions throughout for any possible help on occasional points.

11. Bibliography

A. *Commentaries*

Behrmann, Georg. *Das Buch Daniel,* in Nowack's *Handkommentar.* Goettingen: Vandenhoeck und Rupprecht, 1894.

Charles, R. N. *Book of Daniel.* Oxford: Clarendon Press, 1929.

Driver, S. R. *Daniel,* in the *Cambridge Bible for Schools and Colleges.* Cambridge University Press, 1900.

Farrar, F. W. *The Book of Daniel,* in *The Expositor's Bible.* Grand Rapids, Mich.: Wm. B. Eerdmans Publishing Company, 1943.

Fausset, A. R. *The Book of Daniel,* in *Jamieson, Fausset and Brown's Critical and Explanatory Commentary.* New York: George H. Doran Co., 1934.

Haevernick, H. A. C. *Das Buch Daniel.* Hamburg: Perthes, 1832.

Keil, C. F. *The Book of the Prophet Daniel*, in the *Keil and Delitzsch Commentary in Clark's Foreign Theological Library*. Edinburgh: T. and T. Clark, 1891.

Kliefoth, Th. *Das Buch Daniels*. Schwerin: Sandmeyer, 1868.

Luther, M. *Auslegung des Propheten Daniel*, 1530. (Chapters 11 and 12) *Luthers Saemmtliche Werke*, VI, 6. St. Louis: Concordia Publishing House, 1897.

Marti, Karl. *Das Buch Daniel*, in *Kurzer Handkommentar zum A. T.* Tuebingen and Leipzig: J. S. B. Mohr, (Paul Siebeck), 1901.

Meinhold, J. *Das Buch Daniel*, in *Strack und Zoecklers Kommentar*. Noerdlingen: C. N. Beck, 1889.

Montgomery, James A. *The Book of Daniel*, in the *International Critical Commentary*. New York: Charles Scribner's Sons, 1927.

Thomson, J. E. H. *Daniel*, in *the Pulpit Commentary*. New York: Funk and Wagnalls Co. (Introduction written 1896).

Wright, Charles H. H. *Daniel and His Prophecies*. London: Williams and Norgate, 1906.

Zoeckler, O. *Der Prophet Daniel*, in *Langes Bibelwerk*. Bielefeld and Leipzig: Velhagen and Klasing, 1870.

Kelly, William. *Notes on the Book of Daniel*. New York: Loizeaux Brothers, nd.

Ironside, H. A. *Lectures on Daniel the Prophet*. New York: Loizeaux Brothers, 1920.

Behrmann, Charles, Farrar, Marti, Meinhold, and Montgomery represent the critical position with varying degrees of intensity. The presupposition on the part of each of these writers is a very unreliable Hebrew text, which is first to be reconstructed. The reconstruction is usually determined very largely by the exegetical result that is desired. Charles represents the most learned and most extreme efforts in this direction. Montgomery is usually rather fair in his statement of positions other than his own. But on the whole, so much attention is given to the purely critical appraisal of the contents of the book that the message of the prophet, as it is finally allowed to stand, makes rather meager fare. Farrar displays the most heat in the disparagement of conservative views although he aims to set forth the message of the book as being of unusual value.

Among the conservative writers Haevernick is a bit out of date. Fausset is rather brief. Luther still deserves careful reading. Zoeckler has just a mild tinge of the critical at times. Keil is marked by sober and constructive exposition. He is superseded by the masterful discussion of Kliefoth, who displays rare thoroughness and a remarkable insight into the peculiar nature of Daniel's prophecies. A more delightful and reliable guide than Kliefoth could hardly be found.

Thomson, otherwise sound and good, uses too much space to determine the original Aramaic from which he believes portions of the Hebrew text as we now have it were derived. All such theories are simply not susceptible of proof. Among more recent writers Wright has boldly championed the authorship of the book by Daniel.

Kelly and Ironside accept the book as revelation from the pen of Daniel himself but force millennialistic constructions into passages that are utterly free of such thoughts.

B. *Dictionaries*

Buhl, Frants. *Gesenius' Handwoerterbuch ueber das alte Testament.* Leipzig: F. C. W. Vogel, 1905.

Brown, Driver, Briggs. *A Hebrew and English Lexicon of the Old Testament* (based on Gesenius). New York: Houghton, Mifflin Co., 1907.

Koenig, Eduard. *Woerterbuch zum alten Testament.* Leipzig: Dieterich, 1922. (2. and 3. edition).

C. Versions

Holy Bible, Revised Version, American Standard
Edition, 1901.

King James Version.

Luther's *German Bible.*

Smith, J. M. Powis. *The Old Testament, An
American Translation* (Daniel by Alex. R. Gordon).
Chicago: University of Chicago Press, 1927.

Hebrew Bible (Leteris) also *Biblia Hebraica,*
edited by Rud. Kittel. Leipzig: J. C. Hinrichs, 1906.
Daniel by M. Loehr.

Rahlfs, Alfred. *Septuaginta.* Stuttgart: Privi-
legierte Wuertembergische Bibelanstalt, 1935. This
offers both the old Septuagint text of the Greek as well
as the version of Theodotion.

D. Miscellaneous

Hengstenberg, E. W. *Christologie des Alten Testaments* (vol. 3). Berlin: Ludwig Oehmigke, 1856. This
work offers about 200 pages in support of the traditional interpretation of the "seventy weeks."

Koenig, Eduard. *Einleitung in das Alte Testament.*
Bonn: Eduard Weber, 1893.

Koenig, Eduard. *Die messianischen Weissagungen
des Alten Testaments.* Stuttgart: Chr. Belser, 1923.

Mauro, Philip. *The Seventy Weeks and the Great
Tribulation.* Boston: Hamilton Bros., 1923.

Moeller, Wilhelm. *Der Prophet Daniel* (40 pp.,
Extract from his *Einleitung*). Zwickau: Sachsen,
Johannes Herrmann, nd.

Wilson, Robert Dick. *Studies in the Book of Daniel.* New York: G. P. Putnam's Sons, 1917.

Boutflower, Charles. *In and Around the Book of
Daniel.* London: Society for Promoting Christian
Knowledge, 1923.

Fuerbringer, L., "Kleine Danielstudien," *Concordia
Monthly,* April—September, 1938.

Wilson, Robert Dick, "The Origin of the Ideas of Daniel," *Princeton Theological Review,* April, 1923, 161ff.

———. "The Influence of Daniel," *Princeton Theological Review,* July, 1923, 337ff; October, 1923, 541ff.

———. "The Background of Daniel," *Princeton Theological Review,* January, 1924, 1ff.

———. "The Prophecies of Daniel," *Princeton Theological Review,* July, 1924, 377ff.

———. "On the Hebrew of Daniel," *Princeton Theological Review,* April, 1927, 177ff.

CHAPTER I

Preface

In this first chapter we find such facts concerning Daniel and his companions as are essential to the proper understanding of the rest of the book. This chapter may, therefore, very properly be designated as the Preface to the book. Nothing is written in it that could not be presented by Daniel concerning himself. What seems to be praise of self (v. 17-20) is a record of achievements whose attainment is very specifically ascribed to God, as a gift that He bestowed upon Daniel for very special purposes. A man who enjoyed so rare a reputation for righteousness on the one hand (Ezek. 14:12-20) and for wisdom on the other during his lifetime (Ezek. 28:3) could, no doubt, have written much more about himself, had he been minded to sing his own praises. Yet the things that he does present concerning himself are indispensable for the proper understanding of the rest of the book.

1. **In the third year of the reign of Jehoiakim, king of Judah, came Nebuchadnezzar, king of Babylon, unto Jerusalem and besieged it.**

The very first phrase of this book comes in for its share of criticism—*bishnath shalosh*, "in the third year." The writer is charged with having confused the issues referred to in II Kings 24:1, where the three years of Jehoiakim's submission to Nebuchadnezzar are recorded, and with having used them in calculating what year of Jehoiakim's reign witnessed Daniel's deportation--surely a very clumsy bit of confusion if the author had really been guilty of it. Or it is simply asserted that for the historical event referred to in this verse "there is no historical corroboration" (*Mont-*

gomery)—a statement which cannot be denied, for no historian besides Daniel records this assault upon Jerusalem. Or again, the fact recorded is treated as though it were highly suspicious because no further proof for its genuineness can be adduced. *Driver* says (*Introduction to the Literature of the Old Testament,* p. 498) in reference to the fact that the "third" year is mentioned, "Though it cannot, strictly speaking, be disproved" yet it "is highly improbable."

This calls for a more detailed examination of the statements involved.

If no secular historian, strictly speaking, except Josephus, of whom we shall speak later, makes any reference to the event under consideration, we may well limit ourselves to demonstrating how the Biblical material under this head is to be coordinated. From II Chron. 36:4, 5 we learn that it was Pharaoh Necho who deposed Jehoahaz and made Eliakim, his brother, king over Judah, changing his name to Jehoiakim; also that Jehoiakim reigned eleven years. The years usually assigned to him run from 608—597 B. C. Upon this basis we should have to fix the date that Dan. 1:1 gives as 606 or 605 B. C.

The prophet Jeremiah (46:2) gives us the next fact that helps us to establish the sequence of events, for he informs us that while Pharaoh Necho was at the Euphrates River in Carchemish his army was smitten by Nebuchadnezzar, king of Babylon, "in the fourth year of Jehoiakim son of Josiah." This would fix the date of the battle at Carchemish at 604 B. C. It was while Pharaoh Necho was enroute to Carchemish that Josiah sought to encounter him and was slain (II Kings 23:29, 30).

However, this notable fourth year of Jehoiakim's, which was the first year of Nebuchadnezzar's actual reign as king, was important in Jeremiah's ministry from another point of view, for this was the year in which Jeremiah uttered the significant prophecy recorded in 25:1-9 of his book, the ninth verse of which assures Israel that this very Nebuchadnezzar, who had just ascended the throne, would come against Judah "and against all nations round about" and would "utterly destroy them." Because this was the most definite form that predictions against Jerusalem and Judah had taken up to this time, Jeremiah gives us the very year in which he received this word and carefully coordinates it with the corresponding year of Nebuchadnezzar's reign, saying that Jehoiakim's "fourth year" was Nebuchadnezzar's "first year."

Another statement made by Jeremiah in the same year is reported in chapter 36. The fulfillment of the command involved in v. 1—8, namely, to write all his messages, apparently could not, however, be brought about until the next year. For Jeremiah had been cast into prison (cf. v. 5) as a result of the message spoken in chapter 25. Such words were considered seditious and treasonable. Being unable to appear at the house of the Lord, Jeremiah took steps to have the summary of "all the evil" (v. 3) which the Lord purposed to do unto the people of Judah recorded; and so the prophet dictated his words to Baruch. This procedure consumed some time, and so the book could not be read before "the fifth year of Jehoiakim" (v. 9). Jeremiah therefore asks Baruch to wait with the public reading of these messages until a sufficiently large number of people could be found to hear them. The first occasion for a larger concourse of people was "the fast day" (v. 6 and 9) of the fifth year. We know that such voluntary fast days, according to the example of Zechariah 7:5, were observed as anniversary days of great national calamities. From this it would appear that the fifth-year fast day of Jehoiakim's time must have commemorated the capture of the city by Nebuchadnezzar in Jehoiakim's *fourth* year (604 B. C.). From this we conclude that, after Nebuchadnezzar had disposed of the Egyptians at Carchemish on the Euphrates, he also came down and conquered Jerusalem, though none of the other historical or prophetical books of the Bible mentions this conquest of the Holy City, no doubt because it was but one of several such conquests that occurred in these years, and in a sense a minor one. In any case, evidence points to a conquest of Jerusalem by Nebuchadnezzar in Jehoiakim's fourth year, which was Nebuchadnezzar's first year.

It was on the occasion of this public reading in the fifth year of Jehoiakim that Baruch's book was taken from him and read by Jehudi (36:21) before the king, who displayed his calloused disregard of the divine warning by burning the manuscript leaf by leaf after it had been read. Hereupon Jeremiah received a divine commission to prepare a new book and also foretold the disgraceful end to which Jehoiakim would come (v. 30).

We assemble the rest of the available material in order to get as complete a picture of the events of these years as possible. From II Kings 24:1 we learn that Jehoiakim's submission to Nebuchadnezzar lasted three years. If, as we just saw, the only occasion of Nebuchadnezzar's capture of the city that occurred at this time—disregarding what Dan. 1:1 offers under this head—would be this ominous fourth year of Jehoiakim, that is to say, 604 B. C., then it seems best to assume that the three years of submission referred to in II Kings 24:1 would have run from 604 to 601 B. C. In the same passage we are told that at the expiration of these three years Jehoiakim rebelled against Nebuchadnezzar. But the great Babylonian monarch apparently was not in a position to advance at once against Jerusalem in person. But he did dispatch "bands of the Chaldeans" (v. 2) "against Judah to destroy it." The prophetic writer of Kings knows that this was Jehovah's doing, and he ascribes the coming of these bands as well as those of the Syrians, Moabites, and Ammonites to His sovereign control. Though

Judah was thus harassed, Jerusalem was apparently not taken at once.

Yet we do know that in the seventh year of Nebuchadnezzar (see Jer. 52:38) this king carried away captives from Judah to the number of 3,023. This would have been the eleventh year of Jehoiakim, or 597 B. C. This must also have been the occasion referred to in II Chron. 36:6, when Jehoiakim was "bound in fetters" *to be carried to Babylon.* Yet Nebuchadnezzar apparently did not carry out this purpose, for in the providence of God the statement of Jeremiah (36:9) about Jehoiakim's unfortunate end had to be fulfilled. But II Chron. 36:7 does state positively that at this time also some "of the vessels of the house of Jehovah" were taken to Babylon and put into the temple of the mighty monarch.

All these things happened before the last two expeditions, when Jerusalem was finally taken and utterly destroyed, namely, the expeditions in the eighteenth and the nineteenth years of Nebuchadnezzar, 587 and 586 B. C.

If these are the only references to the capture of Jerusalem in the days of Jehoiakim, where does our verse (1:1 of Dan.) fit into the picture inasmuch as it does not coincide with any of the instances mentioned? Three solutions of the problem have been attempted. The first of these is the simplest and has much to commend it. It asserts that Dan. 1:1 refers to an event that is distinct from all the others mentioned in the Scriptures. In other words, Nebuchadnezzar came not only in 604 B. C., the first year of his reign, and in 597, the seventh year of his reign, but also in 605, the year before he became king in his own right. If the question is raised: "Why is there no other reference to this expedition of 605, especially in the historical books, Kings and Chronicles; or also by Jeremiah, who in 52:28-30 mentions the three different occasions on which Nebuchadnezzar carried away captives from Jerusalem and even tells how many the king took on each occasion?" we answer: "The raid in 605 was not a major capture like the three mentioned by Jeremiah; besides, only a handful of princes was carried away as v. 3 indicates." Daniel, however, has a very particular reason for referring to the event because it was the occasion of his own deportation to Babylon.

There is, however, one objection to the position that we are taking that must be met before we proceed. It is pointed out that, as we concede above, Nebuchadnezzar became king in 604; but Dan. 1:1 ascribes this capture of the Holy City to "Nebuchadnezzar, *king* of Babylon." However, the difficulty is by no means serious. We need merely to assume that the proleptic use of the title occurs here even as we Americans might tell how our first *president* acquitted himself very creditably in Braddock's campaign, yet we all know that many years were to pass before he became president. We see no difficulty in the way of using the title proleptically. *Wilson*[1] has devoted a whole chapter to this use of the word "king" and has fully established this proof.

One historical fact seems to stand in the way of our solution. It is pointed out that, if Nebuchadnezzar had advanced to Jerusalem in 605 B. C., before the battle of Carchemish in 604 B. C., he would have had the Egyptians in his rear, who had gone to the Euphrates already in 608 and, according to Josephus,[2] were at this time in possession of all of Syria. However, another passage in Josephus[3] indicates the course events were taking, and how this may be understood.

---

1. Wilson, Robert Dick, *Studies in the Book of Daniel*, New York: Putnam, 1917, pp. 83-95.

2. Josephus, Flavius, *Antiquities of the Jews*, Hartford: The S. S. Scranton Co., 1916, translated by Whiston, Book X, Chap. VI, 1, p. 311.

3. Josephus, Flavius, *Against Apion*, Hartford: The S. S. Scranton Co., 1916, translated by Whiston, p. 891.

Josephus is quoting from the Chaldean historian Berosus, who relates that Nabolasser (i. e., Nabopolassar), Nebuchadnezzar's father, had heard that a governor whom he had set over Egypt had revolted. Being himself old, Nabopolassar delegated his son to take the rebel in hand. This Nebuchadnezzar set out to do; but while he was engaged in the task, his father took sick and died. When the report of this reached the son, he committed his captives to his friends and, choosing a small but select retinue, hastened across the desert to Babylon to quell an incipient disorder. When we are told, however, that among the captives just mentioned there were "Jews, and Phoenicians and Syrians, and of the nations belonging to Egypt," we notice that Judah had apparently been involved in this conquest of Nebuchadnezzar's in 605 B. C., and that, apparently, there was no permanent garrison at Carchemish to reckon with. For, as our first citation from Josephus also shows, the Egyptian king, Necho, took his great army to Carchemish in 604 in order there to encounter Nebuchadnezzar. Consequently the statement about an Egyptian garrison at Carchemish is revealed as an ungrounded assumption, and we find incidental corroboration of the campaign Daniel describes in 1:1, which we may allow to stand as having occurred in 605 B. C.

We feel, therefore, that the simplest solution of the seeming difficulty is to assume that, though we have no other record of a campaign of Nebuchadnezzar's against Jehoiakim in 605 B. C., we are fully justified in letting this claim stand. If the result is: *three* such campaigns during Jehoiakim's reign, that need not at all surprise us in view of the frequency of campaigns against Syria and Egypt by Babylonian or Chaldean monarchs.

Thomson draws attention to the fact that this verse does not make the statement that the city of Jerusalem itself was captured. One corner of what belonged to the city, namely, the Temple area, perhaps fell into the hands of the Chaldeans, for they were able to take vessels of the Temple and carry them away to Babylon. In connection with the siege also certain youths fell into their hands. Viewing the case thus, as the statement of v. 1 actually gives it, would make our claim all the more reasonable that this was a minor expedition, and this latter fact would explain why there are no other references to it in the records that we have available.

Two other solutions of the problem have been offered because of unwillingness to concede the possibility of three such campaigns. One is the fact that the verb "came," *ba'*, may also be taken in the sense "he set out" rather than in the sense "he arrived." At least the following passages may be cited for this usage: Gen. 45:17; Num. 32:6; II Kings 5:5; Jonah 1:3, and perhaps I Sam. 22:5. *Keil* and *Zoeckler* defend this view; so does *Hengstenberg*. *Kliefoth* refuses to allow its use in connection with military expeditions, but he must have overlooked Num. 32:6. In any case, the contention built upon this fact is that, though Nebuchadnezzar started in the *third* year of Jehoiakim's reign, he did not arrive until the *fourth*. If it is asked, "Why mention his departure rather than his arrival?" *Keil* suggests very properly that this reflects the point of view of the aged writer, Daniel, who was himself living at Babylon as he wrote and would thus naturally use this point of departure, and adds: "For him, a Jew advanced in years, naturally the first movement of the expedition threatening and bringing destruction to his fatherland, whether it moved directly or by a circuitous route upon the capital, would be a significant fact . . . the fatal commencement of the march of the Chaldean host would have a mournful significance." *Montgomery* may call the contention based on the verb *ba'* "absurd," but we could regard the above reasoning well grounded and entirely admissible if we did not feel that the preceding explanation is simpler and more to the point. However, if an interpreter cannot believe that Nebuchadnezzar made three expeditions to Judah in eleven years he may accept this second view as being one that eliminates all difficulties.

For that matter, there is one more possible approach to this problem, an approach that also harmonizes the statements found in Scriptures but relieves the commentator of the necessity of accepting the possibility of three expeditions by Nebuchadnezzar in eleven years. In Babylonia, for example, it was not customary to designate the unexpired part of the last year of the reign of the deceased king as the first year of his successor but to call this remaining fraction of the year "the year of the beginning of his reign." The next year that began with the first of Nisan would then be reckoned as the "first year of his reign." The Egyptians did not make this distinction and would class the unexpired year as "the first" and the next as "the second year" of a king's reign. It is commonly agreed that the Hebrews followed the Egyptian manner of reckoning. Since *Wilson*[4] has given the fullest treatment of this point, we give his summary: "To harmonize perfectly the apparent anachronism of Dan. 1:1 and Jer. 25:1, we have only to suppose that Jeremiah writing in Palestine used the manner of reckoning common in that country, and that Daniel writing in Babylon used the method there employed." We still believe that the first solution offered above is the simplest of all. It goes on the assumption that one manner of reckoning the years of the reign of kings is used consistently by the Biblical writers of this period, and that two different expeditions are referred to.

From what was written above we can conclude very readily what it was that induced Nebuchadnezzar to besiege Jerusalem in the third year of Jehoiakim's

4. *op. cit.* pp. 60-82.

reign. All Syria, including Judah, had been under Egyptian control. Nebuchadnezzar sought to establish his claim to this contested territory. Jehoiakim, having been elevated to the throne by Pharaoh Necho (II Chron. 36:4), would naturally regard himself as a vassal of the Egyptian king and would refuse to hail Nebuchadnezzar as his sovereign lord.

The name "Nebuchadnezzar" should, according to its Babylonian form, be spelled "Nebuchadrezzar," with an "r," for the Babylonian has *Nabu-kudurri-usur*, which perhaps means, "Nebo protect the boundary" (*BDB*), or "Nebo protect the crown." In any case, *BDB* lists twenty-seven instances where the form is spelled "incorrectly." If about thirty-one instances of the correct spelling are available, that at least allows the conclusion that the incorrect form was very commonly used among the Jews. The incorrect form cannot, therefore, be used as an argument against authorship of the book by Daniel because Daniel was writing for Jews and using a form of the king's name that he apparently knew was commonly in use among them.

On the form *wayyatsar*, "he besieged," see *G. K.* 67x. *Shenath* is construct, a usual construction in such cases; frequently *shanah* is repeated. But cf. *G. K.* 134O.

2. And the Lord gave Jehoiakim, king of Judah, into his hand and some of the vessels of the house of God; and he brought them to the land of Shinar, to the house of his god; and the vessels he brought to the treasure house of his god.

We learn from II Chron. 36:5 why it was that the Lord's favor was not in evidence over against Jehoiakim: "he did that which was evil in the sight of *Yahweh*, his God." Consequently *'adhonay*, "the Lord of all," gave him, though he was "king of Judah," into his enemy's hand. The city was not well prepared for a siege, and so at least the Temple which was located on its northeast corner was taken. Since trophies of war, especially temple spoils, were always a welcome token of victory in the capital city of a king, Nebuchadnezzar took "some of the vessels of the house of God." *Qetsath,* an Aramaic form, means "end." "From the end of," *miqtsath,* naturally comes to mean "some of"— the *min* being partitive.

The question is raised, "Does *waybhi'em,* 'and he brought them,' refer to the deportation of the vessels only or to the deportation of the vessels and the captives?" We hold the solution to be very simple. Captives have not been mentioned, except the king, and he was not deported. Consequently the writer is disposing of the vessels first; the suffix "them" can refer grammatically only to the vessels. Of these it is said that they were taken "to the land of Shinar," the ancient name of the wicked land, which is first used in Gen. 10:10 and 11:2, and here comes into use again as the wicked spirit of olden times is revived in the oppression of God's people, cf. Zech. 5:11 for a similar use. Shinar is, of course, Babylon.

It is not "the choicest of the vessels" that are taken as *Gordon* erroneously translates; just "some." To dispose of this minor item first, Daniel records how the king first brought them "to the house of his god," thereby acknowledging the help of his god, who gave these trophies into his hands. They are then deposited "in the treasure house of his god"—no doubt, a building separate from the "house" or temple proper yet near by and in the same complex of buildings. It matters little whether one translates *'elohaw* as "his god" or "his gods." Both are permissible grammatically. The former seems the more feasible. So the vessels are disposed of briefly in order to come to the more important issue of the captives. The vessels will reappear in chapter five.

3, 4. And the king told Ashpenaz, the chief of his eunuchs, to bring some of the children of Israel,

namely of the royal stock and of the nobility, young men in whom there was no blemish whatever, but who were handsome in appearance, such as showed capacity in all forms of wisdom and possessed a wide range of knowledge and unusual understanding, and who were capable of standing in the palace of the king, and to teach them the writing and the speech of the Chaldeans.

The author now concerns himself with the story as to how certain captives came to Babylon—captives who are to figure very prominently in the chapters that follow. If the statements of *Josephus*, quoting *Berosus*, referred to above are considered in this connection, it may well seem that, as Nebuchadnezzar was about to make his hurried trip back across the desert to quell incipient difficulties, he gave orders to Ashpenaz to select certain promising youths. In later Hebrew the expression *'amar le* no longer means "he said to" but "he commanded," which we have rendered by the more colloquial "he told," which in the English also comes to mean "command."

The meaning of the word "Ashpenaz" is uncertain. *K. W.* builds on an Armenian parallel root which means "guest-friend or stranger." In any case, this Ashpenaz holds the very influential position of "chief of his eunuchs." He receives his orders, it appears, in the land of Judah because the verb "to bring," *lehabhi*, is the same as the one that is used in v. 2 with reference to the bringing of the vessels of the Temple to Babylon. The king desires to grace his court with eminent captives from subjugated nations. By this means he gathers a select body of talented young men about him, who might be an ornament to any court and be doubly attractive by being so very heterogeneous a group from many nations. It would at the same time gratify the king's vanity to have such representatives of many nations on display as trophies of war. This would hardly have been a very numerous body of the young men selected to represent Israel. Yet only the best stock was permissible. Therefore the king leaves orders that these lads are to be either "of the royal stock" (Hebrew: "of the seed of the kingdom"—the noun "of the kingdom" being used for the adjective "kingly") or "of the nobility." For this latter noun the Hebrew uses *partemum*, i. e., "nobles."

Referring to this word, *Meinhold* constructs an objection to authorship by Daniel by advancing the claim that "this Persian word in the mouth of an exilic author is passing strange" (*hoechst sonderbar*). Yet we need to feel no alarm, for the Persian origin of the word is not yet demonstrated. *Buhl* offers a choice of one of two derivations: the word is either a *Persian* loanword, *fratama*, πρῶτος, i. e., first, or, following *Haupt*, he suggests the *Assyrian parsumu*, "old man." Critics should use uncertain terms with proper caution. The double *waw, umin . . . umin*, is distributive: "as well . . . as also," *K. S.* 376 a.

4. We now have, as it were, a set of specifications laid down by the king with reference to the ones to be chosen. They must also be "young men," *yeladhim*, a term also meaning "child" but here apparently referring to youths—estimates of age run from ten to twenty years. In these there dared be "no blemish whatever"— Hebrew: "not any spot"—for these youths were to grace the royal court. In addition, they were to be men "who were handsome in appearance"—Hebrew: "good of appearance." Many of the ancients could hardly conceive of a good man's having a homely or unsightly appearance. Beauty was regarded almost as a virtue. The major emphasis, however, lay in the field of mental endowment because learning of a very particular sort was to be imparted to these young captives. Therefore three double expressions cover the requirements under this head.

We have rendered the first clause "such as showed capacity in all forms of wisdom." The Hebrew says: "having insight in all wisdom." Since "wisdom," *chokhmah,* usually means *constructive* wisdom, this requirement seems to involve the idea that the men in question be more than idle dreamers or theorists. We prefer to render the second expression "who possessed a wide range of knowledge," for the Hebrew participle with a cognate object emphasizes the wide range of knowledge: "knowing knowledge." The original of the third expression reads: "having insight of knowledge." That surely must mean that they are to possess insight that probes beneath the surface, for the root *bun* involves "having discernment." We have sought to capture this shade of thought by the idea of possessing "unusual understanding." We therefore believe that the three qualifications specified are quite distinct from one another.

Montgomery blurs the issue when he says, "The three phrases are simply accumulative and do not permit analysis into distinct mental functions." Nor do we feel that *Gordon d*oes very well to render *chokhmah* as "learning." All these requirements are expressed by participles which are plainly present and come to a climax in the practical purpose involved: "who were capable of standing in the palace of the king." Here *'amadh,* to "stand," has the technical meaning of standing in the capacity of servants or of doing service. Thus far the whole set of demands depends on the infinitive used in v. 3, "to bring."

A second infinitive, which, like "to bring," depends on "he told" (v. 3) rounds out the official's orders, namely, "to teach them," *lelammedham.* Two subjects were to be taught them: "the writing and the speech of the Chaldeans." *Sepher* originally means "script" or "writing." So *K. W.* But *BDB* uses "writing" also in the sense of "book learning." The "writing" no doubt came first, namely, the unusually difficult Babylonian as well as the Sumerian script. But, surely, it was taught so that, through it, the "learning" might be acquired as *A. V.* and *A. R. V.* quite properly render the word. A separate study, of course, was to learn to use the "speech," *lashon,* or language of the Chaldeans. The term "Chaldeans," *Kasdim,* here designates a special class of learned men, who were, perhaps, the "astrologers" (*K. W.*) among the people. Puzzling as it is to have a people and one select class of that people designated by one and the same name, this usage is too clearly established in Scripture to call for quibbling. *Meinhold* at once charges the writer with a blunder, claiming that such a double use of the name is "most unlikely" (*hoechst unwahrscheinlich*). He could have contented himself with saying that we do not now possess the facts that furnish us with an entirely adequate explanation.

The Chaldeans as a nation were long crowded into the background (cf. Isa. 23:13) although they appear as early as Abraham's time (Gen. 11:28) as dwelling near the mouth of the Euphrates. They then become the ruling class (Hab. 1:6), at least already when Nabopolassar, father of Nebuchadnezzar, comes to the throne. The term *Kasdim,* according to a Babylonian phonetic rule, "s" before a dental becoming "l," is rendered in Greek as Χαλδαιοι, i. e., Chaldeans. Some advance the idea that they were of Aryan extraction. Most scholars class them as Semitic, an idea with which Gen. 11:28 seems to agree.

What did this, which we may sum up as "the learning of the Chaldees," involve in detail? *Pinches,* writing in the *International Standard Bible Encyclopedia,* suggests the following: "The learning of the Chaldeans . . . comprised the old languages of Babylonia (the two dialects of Sumerian, with a certain knowledge of Kassite, which seems to have been allied to the Hittite; and other languages of the immediate neighborhood) ; some knowledge of astronomy and astrology; mathematics, which their sexagesimal system of numeration seems to have facilitated; and a certain amount of natural history. To this must be added a store of mythological learning, including legends of the Creation, the Flood. . . . They had likewise a good knowledge of agriculture, and were no mean architects, as the many celebrated buildings of Babylon show" (article: "Chaldea"). We feel that Pinches has given a good and correct summary of the type of things that were to be offered to these young captives as subjects to be learned.

5. **And the king assigned to them a regular daily portion of the king's delicacies and of the wine which he drank, and that they were to be trained for three years; and at the end of that period they were to stand before the king.**

The advantages that were to accrue to these young men are now mentioned. In the first place, they were to eat of the food prepared for the royal board. In days of old lavish display characterized royal courts in the matter of food and of drink. To have huge quantities of rare delicacies prepared and to have a large retinue at court consuming these dainties were reckoned a truly royal distinction. In this instance, after the lads were brought to Babylon, it was the king himself who apportioned or "assigned" to them a share in food and in drink of his table.

The Hebrew idiom describes their allotment as "a portion of the day in its day." We should say "a regular daily portion." The "delicacies" are *pathbagh* in Hebrew, which is always written *path-bagh*, with the hyphen, in the text, apparently because of a popular etymology, which was a misconception, for the Hebrew word *path* meant a "bit" or "morsel." Yet that root is not involved in this instance, for interpreters seem pretty much agreed that this is a Persian loan word from the *Sanskrit pratibagha*, which appears also in Greek and is transliterated ποτί-βαζις. The old-Persian form is nearest to the Hebrew *pati-baga*. To what extent the Babylonians may have been familiar with it in days of old we cannot say, nor how it ever came into the Hebrew. "The wine which he drank" is described as "the wine of his drinking." If we compare Solomon's luxury in matters of food and of drink (I Kings 4:21), all of which was, no doubt, on a far more modest scale, there can hardly be any doubt about it that these youths were really being allowed the utmost of indulgence by this assignment. Biblical parallels are found in Gen. 43:34; II Sam. 11:8; II Kings 25:30.

We regard also the next item as a distinct advantage the young men enjoyed: "they were to be trained (*gadhal* in the Piel, 'to bring up children') for three years." The course of training might not be an easy one, for Babylonian learning was a thoroughgoing and very substantial thing. Yet there was the desirable prospect "at the end of that period" to be among those that stood before the king. The phrase *'amadh liphney*, "stand before," is the equivalent of "becoming the servant of" and was commonly in use.

The construction of this verse is a bit loose: "assign" has as its object first "portion," *debhar*, then the infinitive *gaddelam*, "to be trained." See G. K. 114p and *K. S.* 413v. Again the infinitive construction goes over into the finite verb, "they were to stand," *ya 'amdhu*. See *K. S.* 413e. There is no need of rearranging the verse as Charles, following Marti, does.

6, 7. Now among these there were, of the children of Judah, Daniel, Hananiah, Mishael, and Azariah. The prince of the eunuchs appointed names for them. For Daniel he appointed the name of Belteshazzar; for Hananiah, that of Shadrach; and for Mishael, that of Meshach; and for Azariah, that of Abednego.

How many were selected for this very special course of training we cannot say. Four are mentioned as coming "from the children of Judah." So Daniel very modestly identifies himself as *Calvin* points out. The presupposition seems to be that the entire group was rather small if only four represent the tribe of Judah, for the Ten Tribes had already been removed by the Captivity of Samaria. Of these four Daniel alone is mentioned elsewhere in the Scriptures, namely in Ezek. 14:14, 20 and 24:17.

This being the first mention of Daniel, here must be the place to discuss one of the current objections to the historical credibility of our book. Ezekiel's reference to Daniel has aroused suspicion in the minds of some who cannot believe that a contemporary could have ventured to classify Daniel among the mighty patriarchal heroes such as Moses and Job, and do that after Daniel had been on the scene only ten or fifteen years at the most and could not have been older than about thirty-five years. However, it must be remembered that, when an oppressed and uprooted nation saw so consistent an exponent of courage, wisdom, and true faithfulness as Daniel was, distinguish himself in so very eminent a position in the Babylonian state, such a man would also, from a purely human point of view, be likely to be idolized. How much more if the mainspring of his life was true godliness! Cf. also Introduction, 1.

The Hebrew names of these men are characteristic of that people. "Daniel" meant "(my) judge is God." "Hananiah" meant "gracious is *Yahweh*." "Mishael" meant "who is He that is God?" "Azariah" means "*Yahweh* hath helped." All the names are of a kind that might in evil days be given to children by godly parents.

"The prince of the eunuchs," being a man of some consequence, has the duty of giving these lads new names. Parallel cases are found in the Scriptures in II Kings 23:34 and 24:17, where the Egyptians and the Babylonians follow the same course. The change of name involved the idea that the god of those who bestowed the new name was to be honored rather than the god of the vanquished. In days of old most names were theophoric, i. e., they had the name of the deity incorporated. The new names are not easily interpreted because of our imperfect knowledge of Babylonian or of the mode of transliteration of Babylonian names.

Belteshazzar is said to be a compound of *balat*, "life," and *sar-usur*, "protect." Others have conjectured that *balat* might be the name of the god Saturn (see *BDB*). By pointing the name *Bel*, the Hebrews apparently thought they had discovered the name of the Babylonian divinity *Bel* in this name, an idea that is incorporated also in 4:8 (*English*). Most scholars reject this idea on the basis of *their* knowledge of Babylonian, which they seem to think is far superior to Daniel's, to whom it was a living language, and who wrote 4:8 advisedly. I prefer to trust Daniel in this matter rather than the still fragmentary knowledge of Babylonian that our scholars have.

"Shadrach" means "command of Aku," being compounded of *Sudur* and *Aku*, "*Aku*" being the moon-god. These names, of course, bear a decidedly polytheistic flavor.

"Meshach" is contracted from *Mi-sha-aku*, which means "who is what Aku (the moon-god) is?" The Hebrew has similar compounds for proper names, "Mishael" itself being one of these. In this instance *Aku* is substituted for *'El*, a name of the true God, meaning literally the "Strong One."

"Abednego" means "servant of Nebo," the latter half of the word, *nego*, being a corruption, either intentional or unintentional, of the correct name of the god.

8. **Now Daniel solemnly resolved that he would not defile himself with the king's delicacies, nor with the wine of which he drank. Therefore he requested**

of the prince of the eunuchs that he might not defile himself.

It has been pointed out (*Kliefoth*) that there are really three things of a distinctly heathen character with which Daniel and his three companions had to reckon as daily issues: the acquisition of heathen wisdom, the bearing of heathen names, the eating of heathen food. The first two of these were things that could not involve conscientious scruples. For though it had fallen to the lot of these men to master heathen wisdom and sciences, that duty did not involve the acceptance of everything that was taught them in the sense that they were under necessity of believing those elements which were distinctly heathen lore. These men could guide themselves by the example of the man Moses, who passed through a similar experience without detriment to his faith. The second experience, that of having their names changed, was a thing to be suffered. Though these youths may not have used their new names, it was impossible to check heathen men if they were desirous of calling them by a new name. That was a thing to be borne, even if not approved of. But in the matter of the eating of food from the king's table more serious issues were involved.

All meals served at the king's table were feasts, and among the heathen feasts were feasts in honor of the gods. That involved that a portion of the meat to be served would first be dedicated to some god in sacrifice. The eating of the remainder meant sharing in the sacrificial meal, which was, of course, in honor of the god to whom a portion had been sacrificed. To share in such a feast was the equivalent of honoring such an idol, admitting his claims and existence, and so practically denying the one true God. For that reason Daniel refused such contamination. The companions of Daniel are not mentioned, it would seem, because Daniel at first acted alone in the matter, and only later did the others follow suit.

The Hebrew idiom describes what Daniel did as "laying upon his heart not to defile himself." There were no outward scruples. Daniel laid his resolve "upon his heart." We endeavor to catch the force of this idiom by rendering the verb he "solemnly resolved." The verb *ga'al* in the Hithpael means "to defile himself" and refers to more than ceremonial defilement because sinning in the matter of idol-meat would be more than an outward shortcoming. Daniel takes the requisite steps to escape such contamination: he politely makes his request to be excused from eating such food. He does not, by stubborn and tactless opposition, needlessly make a martyr of himself. He does not provoke others to persecute him. He simply states his case as objectively and as clearly as he can. There is always the added possibility that the meat of animals not slaughtered in the proper manner or of unclean animals might have been involved.

The construction *'asher lo'* equals the customary *pen,* for "that not," cf. *G. K.* 157.

Daniel's position is said to reflect very accurately the attitude common in the age of the Maccabees. In proof of this contention passages from the apocryphal books are cited, which are, indeed, a corroboration of this claim. Eleazar's example is touched upon (II Macc. 6:18-31); also Esther's in the additions to Esther in the *Septuagint,* (4:14 and 5:4); then Judith's example (Jth. 10:5); and lastly that of Judas and his followers (II Macc. 5:27). True as all this is, it in no wise proves that the book of Daniel was written at this late date. Why should a very godly man like Daniel not have insight and strength of character sufficient to enable him to discern these issues and to take a stand that is worthy of a consistent servant of the true God? It was, it is true, only in his day that situations such as these began to arise; but this touch in the book is to be expected at this point. Critics had better not draw illogical and ill-founded deductions from this simple historical fact.

9, 10. Now God granted Daniel favor and sympathy in the sight of the prince of the eunuchs. Yet the prince of the eunuchs said to Daniel: "I for my part am afraid of my lord, the king, who hath appointed your food and drink. For why should he observe your faces to look more strained than those of the lads that are of your age? So you would forfeit my head to the king."

We are first told what the immediate reaction of the prince of the eunuchs to Daniel's request was. It is not to be denied that so influential a personage might have dealt very inconsiderately with so unimportant a character as Daniel was. Daniel's request might have been construed as insubordination, meddlesomeness, queerness. He might have put himself permanently into the bad graces of this prince. Instead, God, who in manifold instances controls the hearts of men for the good of His own children, in this case so influenced this court official that he displayed toward Daniel both "favor and sympathy"—"favor," *chesedh,* just plain "good-will"; "sympathy," *rachamim,* plural of intensity in the sense of a deep-seated feeling for a man and for his objectives, which is really the root meaning of "sympathy."

Yet the prince of the eunuchs said—we take the *waw* of *wayyo'mer* to be adversative—in effect, "I dare not grant your request." To show that he is kindly disposed toward Daniel he gives the Hebrew lad a full explanation of his relation to the king in this matter. Behind that explanation there lurks the phantom of an absolute monarch. Him the prince fears, for it might well happen that, because of a change in diet, the lad Daniel might lose weight. At least, so it appears to the court official who apparently had never met a man who voluntarily chose humbler fare when the royal dainties were within his reach. If, then, the monarch should happen to notice that one of his Hebrew proteges looked pale and wan, an inquiry might follow, all the more so if the other lads of the same age had a healthy color. The inquiry might soon disclose that the king's precept in the matter of food and drink had been presumptuously altered by the prince. Absolute imperial power being what it was in those days, the prince would receive but short shrift and lose his head; and they who in the last analysis would have "forfeited" his head to the king would have been these very youths. Surely, that was not what they intended. So they must realize the difficulty of the prince's position.

We have translated *zo‘aphim* "more strained," *A. R. V.* reads "worse looking." *Za‘aph* really means "to be excited," "to look worried." Nothing more than a wanness or paleness is implied. In the *Piel chûbh* means "to inculpate my head with the king" (*BDB*), which is poor enough English and recommends the above rendering. It might have been better to translate the *'asher lammah,* (v. 10), which also *A. R. V.* renders "for why," "lest," ὅπως μή a late usage of this combination which both *BDB* (p. 554a) and *K. S.* (396q) support, for it actually amounts to the regular *pen* after a verb of fearing.

11-13. So Daniel said to the steward whom the prince of the eunuchs had appointed over Daniel, Hananiah, Mishael, and Azariah: "Put thy servants to the test for ten days and let us have vegetables to eat and water to drink. Then let our appearance be examined before thee as well as the appearance of the lads who are wont to eat the king's delicacies. Then deal with us according to what you see."

Though the Hebrew continues the narrative by a *wayyo 'mer,* "and he said," this indicates the next step that Daniel takes in an effort to keep from sinning against his conscience. So it is best to translate, "*Then he said.*" This change in tactics on Daniel's part is obscured by the *A. V.* which renders, "Then said Daniel to *Melzar.*" The Hebrew *hammeltsar* can hardly be a proper name because of the article that is prefixed. *Meltsar* may mean "steward" although we concede that the meaning is dubious. The Assyrian *matstsaru,* "keeper" or "guardian," does not seem to strike quite close enough. The suggestion of *Meinhold* to draw on the Persian word *mulsaru,* "cellarer," would be very helpful but for the fact that it is *modern* Persian. This "steward" happens to be the intermediary between the prince of the eunuchs and these young courtiers, who, by the way, have by this time aligned themselves with Daniel (plural used) and offer their own request together with his. This request is very modest. It involves no unseemly or unreasonable risk. Besides, the steward will hardly have had direct contact with the king and therefore does not need to observe such extreme caution as does the prince of the eunuchs.

12. The request limits itself to a test of ten days. *Nas* is *Piel* imperative, short form, from *nasah,* "to tempt." The Old English "prove" (*A. V.*) is covered by our "put to the test." "Ten days" constitute a reasonably short period, yet one that is long enough to test the merits of the case. Since the food defiled by idol sacrifices was meat and wine, a part of the former of which was laid on the altar, and a part of the latter poured out as a libation, "vegetables," *zero'im,* "things sowed," would be outside of the pale of the defiled things. So would "water." The privations involved were really not rigorous. For under the head of "things sowed" would come grains, and so bread was not stricken from the menu. Many a savory dish could be prepared despite these restrictions. These young men were not confined to "pulse" (*A. V.*), that is, peas and beans.

13. Daniel is certain that God is well pleased with the obedience of His servants and will not let them be put to shame. So the next step in his proposal is to have a comparison made at the expiration of the ten days, and to have it made in the steward's presence (*lephaneykha*). Daniel has also common sense on his side. Overrich fare such as the luxuriously appointed table of the king offered in unlimited amounts to all who had access to his board was not as conducive to good health as was plain, substantial food. Nothing could be fairer than that the steward should then deal with the lads according to what he sees. Daniel has no doubt that, if an improvement is noted in his own appearance and that of his companions, the steward will allow them to do according to their scruples of conscience. We believe that even in this simple and practical proposition Daniel displays the wisdom for which he later became justly famous.

Tir'eh has *tsere* rather than *seghol*, a form of writing designed to mark the jussive or voluntative rather than the imperfect, *G. K.* 75hh. It may be translated "see" or "think best."

14-16. So he gave heed to them in this matter and put them to the test for ten days. And at the end of the ten days their appearance was better, and they were fatter of flesh than all the youths that were eating the royal delicacies. So the steward took away their delicacies and the wine they were to drink and gave them vegetables.

It may seem that a disproportionate amount of emphasis is being given to a secondary matter. But the meticulous care exercised by these young men in doing the will of their God is perhaps the strongest indication that could be found of their complete allegiance to their God. Their determination shows also how clearly they discerned what issues were at stake, and how correctly they were getting their bearings in the matter of making an adjustment in reference to daily contact with heathen life. The issues involved were not trifles. In this matter they had to take a stand. *Farrar* has failed to comprehend the issues when he remarks, "It is difficult to conceive that there was less chance of pollution in being elaborately trained in heathen magic and dream interpretation than in eating Babylonian food." For, in the first place, "the learning of the Chaldeans" was not on the low and cheap level that the present-day meaning of the term "magic" involves. In the second place, there was not merely the *possibility* of pollution in eating the king's food. Such pollution was inescapable: such eating meant a denial of the true God.

The *le* before *dabhar* means "in reference to," *K. S.* 33or. The *min* before *getsath* is temporal, *K. S.* 401g. *Beri'ey* is *constructio ad sensum*, it no longer applies to their *"appearance"* but to *them.* In v. 16 *hayah* with the participle *nose'* is better adapted to express the permanence of the new arrangement.

17. And as for these four youths, God gave them knowledge and understanding of all literature [writings] and wisdom; and to Daniel he gave insight into every sort of vision and dreams.

This is practically a summary of the achievements of these youths during their three years of training. We are not told how hard they studied, or how difficult their subjects were. Yet there can be no doubt that the ground to be covered was considerable, and that they applied themselves diligently to their tasks, imbued with a sense of responsibility and desirous of being found fully equipped in case God should desire to use them in more responsible positions. But what can man achieve by his own strength or endeavor? Consequently nothing is said about their own achievements. But what God gave them as a blessing and a free gift and, in a limited sense, as a reward for their faithful endeavors, that merits to be recorded.

One set of gifts was bestowed on all four alike—something their heathen companions could not achieve as is indicated by the independent nominative "as for these four youths"—and these gifts comprised "knowledge and understanding of all literature and wisdom." Considering this gift of God as a whole, we take it to imply a type of insight that was superior to what Babylonian lore could afford an individual. By that we mean an enlightenment that comes from on high and discerns clearly between heathen blandishments and godly truth. We mean a discernment that enabled these four to sit in judgment on all secular learning that was offered them and to evaluate it according to the estimate of the all-wise God. Such discernment is, of course, never a product of the unaided human mind.

The individual gifts involved in this greater gift from God were, first of all, "knowledge," *madda'*, the ability to penetrate through the mists of heathen uncertainty and to detect what was actually true; secondly, "understanding of all literature or writings," a mastery of the entire body of the extant writings, based on penetrating insight (*haskel*, "to have insight"); and lastly "wisdom," *chokhmah*, constructive ability rightly to apply the knowledge acquired, and to do so in the fear of God. It must be granted that these were no trivial gifts, and that they fitted these youths for responsible positions. *Thomson* very aptly quotes *Jerome* in this connection, who assumes that "they learned not that they might follow, but that they might judge and correct." *Thomson*, however, discards this suggestion in the course of his exposition.

To Daniel was given a very special talent in addition to the above: "insight into every sort of vision and dreams." All men are familiar with dreams; they come during sleep. "Visions" are beheld also in a waking state; they are seen either as a still picture or as a scene of action. Where such dreams or visions were divinely inspired or were to serve a special purpose Daniel had ability for seeing what they meant.

The sentence structure of this verse needs to be inspected. The nominative absolute ("these four youths") is regularly resumed by a summarizing word, usually in the nominative. In this case the structure breaks, and a *dative* (*lahem*) picks up the thread. Again, the objects of "gave" are first a noun, then an absolute infinitive (*haskel*), then again a noun, *K. S.* 223b; 233a.

Very appropriately, as *Thomson* suggests, the facts recorded here may be regarded as rather strong evidence against the theory of late authorship of the book. For it is well known with what abhorrence the Jews of Maccabean times regarded the acquirement of Greek learning. In fact, everything Greek was assiduously avoided (cf. II Macc. 4:14). How, then, could an author, writing in that particular period, suggest that his hero freely absorbed heathen lore and so practically encouraged his contemporaries to do the same?

18-20. Now at the end of the days which the king had appointed to bring them in the prince of the eunuchs brought them in before Nebuchadnezzar. And the king interviewed them; and out of the entire number there were none found to be compared with Daniel, Hananiah, Mishael, and Azariah. So they entered the king's service. And in all matters of discriminating wisdom, about which the king inquired of them, he found them ten times better than all scholars and enchanters throughout his kingdom.

By the skillfully arranged narrative suspense has been created as to how these lads fared at the end of their period of preparation. We are told briefly what the test revealed. The three years are summarized by the very general term *yamin*, "days." The king had left a standing order to have them brought before him

at that time. The prince of the eunuchs arranged to
have his charges presented. They are actually con-
ducted into the king's presence, apparently by the
prince himself. The king personally conducts the inter-
view. "The king spoke with them" must mean he "interviewed" them. These four stood out from the entire
number as clearly as God-given wisdom excels humanly
acquired knowledge. At once the result is appended, in
characteristic Hebrew fashion, "they entered the
king's service." The Hebrew idiom merely says, "They
stood before the king" (*A. V.*), but this regularly
means to fill the position of some sort of servitor.

The examination has been disposed of too briefly.
Consequently the writer reverts to it: in every matter
the king inquired from them they were "ten times
(Hebrew: *yadhôth*, 'ten *hands*') better," not only than
their contemporaries, that is, the lads who were
trained simultaneously with them, but even "ten times
better than all scholars and enchanters throughout his
(the king's) kingdom." That is most superlative praise.
Yet, if God had equipped these youths, the praise that
this account bestows is to be accorded to God rather
than to these diligent young men. The words written
do not give the impression of being the self-commenda-
tion of one who happened to be one of the four who
excelled.

The wise men of Babylon are lumped together
under the two terms "scholars and enchanters." Previously, in v. 4, a different term was used, apparently to
describe the entire body—"Chaldeans." In 2:2, where
the classification is more detailed, *four* names are used,
the first two being identical with the two occurring
in this verse. "Scholars," *chartummim*, a word akin to
the root *cheret* meaning "stylus" or pen. This deriva-
tion induces *K. W.* to deduce that the *chartummim* were
wielders of the stylus, *Griffelfuehrer*, and so "scholars." The word is used as a designation for the wise
men who were summoned to interpret Pharaoh's dream

(Gen. 41:8) and there is parallel with *chakhamim,* "wise." However, the "enchanters" or "conjurers" (*BDB*) are called *'ashshaphîm,* from the Assyrian root *asipu,* meaning "to conjure." Apparently here, too, the point of view was that a man who was skilled enough to conjure or call up the dead (necromancy) was a man of unusual knowledge. Apparently, then, the two words as such imply a high type of learning, whether it be Egyptian or Babylonian.

In v. 18 *waybhi'em* is a consecutive clause which attaches itself to a preceding adverbial phrase, which again is the equivalent of an adverbial clause, *K. S.* 366 l. In v. 20 "discriminating wisdom" is *chokhmath bînah,* i. e., "wisdom of insight." Also the nominative absolute *debhar,* etc., which is taken up again by the verb *yimtsa'em,* agrees only indirectly with this verb— a break in the construction, *K. S.* 341 i. In fact, the consecutive imperfect follows after a noun and not after a clause, *K. S.* 366 r.

21. And Daniel continued even unto the first year of King Cyrus.

Comparing superficially with 10:1, it has pleased many commentators to charge the author with error on the basis of his own later statement. However, though this verse is naturally a kind of summary it does .not aim to tell when Daniel died but how long he lived, and that reckoned in terms of reigns of kings. Before his mind's eye the author, reviewing, of course, his own life, sees a succession of notable figures rise to power and fall again: Nebuchadnezzar II (602—), Amel Marduk (562—), Nergal-shar-usur (560—), Labashi-Marduk (556—), Nabunaid (555—), and lastly Cyrus, who came and conquered Babylon in 538 to top off all his other conquests. From 602-538 in terms of monarchs—what a span of useful and prominent activity! The few years of the reign of Cyrus in which Daniel figured need not be mentioned.

Much as critics have remonstrated about having
wayhi, "he was," translated "continued" (*A. V.*), one
of their number freely admits the correctness of the
translation. *Montgomery* says: "Despite the objection
of commentators, the use of *hayah,* 'remained, continued,' is found elsewhere. The present phrase is exactly duplicated in Jer. 1:3, cf. Ruth 1:2." He also
concedes that *'adh,* "unto," need not mark the utmost
limit or "exclude the remoter future" and cites Ps.
110:1 and 112:8 as parallel cases. Ps. 110:1 is especially
clear: the expression "until I make thine enemies thy
footstool" (in Hebrew "until," *'adh* with the infinitive) surely does not imply that the Lord's dominion
ends when His enemies are subdued; it may properly
be said to *begin* then.

Interpreters love to refer to *Pusey's* fine comment
on this verse. He says: "Simple words, but what a
volume of tried faithfulness is unrolled by them! Amid
all the intrigues indigenous at all times in dynasties
of Oriental despotism, amid all the envy toward a foreign captive in high office as a king's counsellor, amid
all the trouble incidental to the insanity of the king
and the murder of two of his successors, in that whole
critical period for his people, Daniel continued."

Meinhold concludes his remarks on the chapter
by saying: "On factual and linguistic grounds the assumption that the chapter originated during the period
of the Exile must be rejected." We believe we have
demonstrated to all who are not biased by preconceived
notions that there is not a single statement of the chapter that stands in the way of its being composed during
the period of the Exile by Daniel himself.

This chapter has furnished us with a brief but
satisfactory introduction in which at least the major
characters are given their proper setting.

HOMILETICAL SUGGESTIONS

The entire chapter may be used as an introduction to the book of Daniel if sermons are to be preached on the entire book. In that case the object in mind will be to set forth how, in the providence of God, Daniel came to a position of prominence, and how, in that same providence, he early experienced God's remarkable care.

If the book is not being preached on in its entirety, vv. 8-16 constitute a notable section of Scripture to give men courage to abide boldly by what the Lord demands of His own. Whatever our conscience knows to be the unalterable will of God, by that we must abide, let happen what will. If need be, God can do miraculous things to preserve His own.

Vv. 17-20 are an excellent text for emphasizing that all true knowledge comes from God, the Fountainhead of truth, and also to set forth the superior merit of divine wisdom.

CHAPTER II

I. The Development of the World Power, Chapters 2-7

A. Chapter 2: Nebuchadnezzar's Dream— The Fall of Empires

The first half of the book, extending from chapter two through chapter seven, portrays in a many-sided way how the world power develops. The second half of the book, chapter eight to chapter twelve, portrays how the kingdom of God develops. Yet the development of each is always sketched with reference to the other. We may, then, state the situation more comprehensively by asserting that the first half of the book depicts the development of the world power over against the kingdom of God.

This first vision is basic, for it sketches in a summary way what is to be developed in greater detail by the remaining chapters of the section. Nebuchadnezzar's dream reveals rather clearly what the ultimate fate of kingdoms and empires, constructed by man in dependence upon human strength and ingenuity, must ultimately be: they are doomed to a startling and drastic overthrow. Therefore we have given as a second title of the chapter the caption "the Fall of Empires."

There was need for the revelation of the ultimate fate of the world power, a need that was more pressing at Daniel's time than it had ever been. For, apparently, in the conquest of Judah by Babylon the world power had scored an important victory, a victory that a few years hence was to be made absolutely decisive by the destruction of Jerusalem and the final deportation of the people of Judah. When such deportations occurred, the fate of the nation involved was sealed with finality. So past experience had without exception demonstrated. The prospect of such a fate for the people of God, with whose destinies the future of God's kingdom was inextricably bound up, spelled the end of all hopes and aspirations for the future, in fact, the end also of all Messianic expectations. Such a future would have meant the loss of all faith in *Yahweh*. God had to speak and reassure His people that greater hopes were in prospect than blind human vision was at that time able to discern. At the same time, since no one else could tell them, *Yahweh* had reasons for revealing also to the heathen nations that their conception of what they could achieve by their own strength was utterly erroneous. Facing, apparently, only glorious victory, they were in reality rushing on to headlong ruin.

It was very proper to have human achievement or world power represented in the dream by a human figure, a glorious colossus. For the excellent things that man had achieved by his power were being evaluated; and at Nebuchadnezzar's time and to the Babylonians they certainly appeared enormous, glorious, and enduring. But destruction threatened them from an undreamt-of source.

It was at the same time eminently proper to make Nebuchadnezzar the first recipient of this message. Young though he was, this monarch had already given ample proof of his rare capacities and attainments. Even before he had come to the throne, while still waging war in his father's name, success had attended his every venture. Under him Babylon was being welded into an empire such as the world had never seen. He it was that had with ease administered a crushing defeat to Egypt and to God's ancient people. What was now revealed to Nebuchadnezzar could under the circumstances be spread most readily throughout his entire realm and so serve to prepare the heathen world for the revelation of the gospel of the Christ.

a. The Inability of the Court Interpreters, 2:1-13.

1. **And in the second year of the reign of Nebuchadnezzar, Nebuchadnezzar dreamed dreams; and his spirit was disturbed, and his sleep was done for upon him.**

The first phrase of the chapter as well as the very first letter have been the object of attack on the part of criticism. The first letter is *waw*, the conjunction "and." When it connects sentences it usually is the so-called "*waw* conversive" and is joined to a verb form. Here it is joined to "year"—a noun. Criticism therefore stamps it as a later redactional insertion to bind chapter two the closer to an introductory chapter which, it is assumed, was later prefixed to the book. Such claims are as clever as they are precarious.

Since no man can do more than to voice unprovable claims in regard to matters of this sort, the more reasonable explanation is that the phrase "in the second year" stands first in place of the verb of the normal sentence order for the sake of emphasis, the intention being to show how early in Nebuchadnezzar's reign this event occurred. The "and" is very much in place, for it connects the events of chapter one, which show how Daniel came into a position of prominence in Babylon, closely with the events of chapter two, which show how necessary such a man as Daniel became for the emergency which arose so soon after his acceptance among Babylon's wise men.

Furthermore, the phrase "in the second year" is both harmless and unassailable. According to Jer. 25:1, as already noted in connection with Dan. 1:1, Jehoiakim's *fourth* year was Nebuchadnezzar's first year. If, then (see 1:1), Daniel was deported and his training was begun in Jehoiakim's *third* year, the second year of Nebuchadnezzar's reign would allow for the passing of the three probationary years of Daniel (see 1:5). But very shortly after the three years had elapsed, it would seem, Daniel was already making full proof of the ministry to which God had ordained him.

Another fact may be introduced into the explanation to relieve us of difficulties, the fact alluded to on page 55, namely, that the Babylonian manner of reckoning a king's reign did not regard the unexpired portion of the last year of the deceased monarch as the first year of the new king but reserved that designation for the first full year of the new monarch's rule. Since kings did not, as a rule, die at the close of the last year of their reign, there were usually months intervening between reigns, which would allow just enough latitude to make the initial phrase of our chapter entirely proper. *Farrar* is hardly reasonable when he labels an explanation such as the above inadmissible by the somewhat acrimonious assertion: "The apologists get over the difficulty with the ease which suffices superficial readers who are already convinced." Criticism magnifies surface difficulties into insuperable obstacles and labels its opponents "superficial" because they do not take the same position.

The simplest explanation for the use of the plural noun "dreams," *chalomôth,* is that the king dreamed several dreams, one of which finally roused and disturbed him. The other explanation, that this is the plural of extent and reflects upon the different aspects of the one dream, is not quite so natural. The effect produced by the dreams, particularly by the last one, was deeper than to arouse mere curiosity—the king's spirit [rû(a)ch] was disturbed." "Troubled" (*A. V.*) seems a bit mild as a rendering of *tithpa'em*; *erschrak,* "was frightened," *Luther,* introduces a different concept.

The last clause is difficult because it contains the passive (!) of the verb "to be," *nihyetha,* a form that is simply impossible from our point of view yet quite common in Biblical Hebrew. This must mean—as our rendering somewhat colloquially and inelegantly

reproduces it—"was done for," i. e., was at an end.
The last phrase, "upon him," in our rather literal
rendering makes the English still more harsh; but the
Hebrew point of view is quite simple: sleep is something that descends "upon," *'al*, a man and broods there.
Calvin's and all kindred renderings are without foundation, being based upon a misunderstanding of the
preposition *'al*, for all these construe *nihyetha* to mean
that his sleep again fell upon him.

**2, 3. Then the king commanded to summon the
scholars and the enchanters and the sorcerers and
the Chaldeans that they might tell the king his
dreams. So they came in and stood before the king.
And the king said to them: "I dreamed a dream,
and my spirit is disturbed to know what the dream
means."**

Many instances could be cited to demonstrate the
great importance that was attached to dreams in days
of old. A king who had a whole college of experts at his
disposal, men who were professional dream interpreters, such a king, we say, would naturally summon
a goodly assortment of these courtiers to relieve his
mind, which, in this instance, was unusually disturbed.
The importance the king attached to having his mind
set at ease is apparent in the fact that four classes of
dream interpreters or wise men were summoned to
appear before him. The terms "scholars" and "enchanters" were discussed in connection with 1:20.
Though we are not absolutely certain in regard to the
meaning of any of these terms we know their approximate import. "Sorcerers," *mekhashshephîm*, seems to
be pretty nearly established in its meaning, for the
Assyrian root *Kašâpu* is said to mean "practice sor-
cery," although *BDB* gives the meaning "diviners and
astrologers in Babylon" as well. "Chaldeans," *Kasdîm*,
constitute the most important group in the entire assembly, for as vv. 4, 5, and 10 show, they either spoke

for all, or their name represents the whole group that was called in by the king.

This word has received its share of criticism. As any Hebrew dictionary will show, the word refers first to a people and then to Babylonian astrologers. The latter use causes difficulty. There is ample evidence to prove that already in patriarchal days a *people* by this name lived in southern Babylonia, cf. Ur of Chaldees, Gen. 11:28. They were a warlike group who in the course of time caused the Assyrians much trouble and finally overcame them, it seems, in the person of Nabopolassar, Nebuchadnezzar's father.[1] Though it is not clear how they mastered the Assyrians, the fact as such is historically beyond a doubt. The difficulty involved in the second use of the name is obvious: does it seem natural that a class of astrologers in vanquished Babylon, no doubt a group of ancient standing, should as a group be designated by the name of their recent conquerors? The easiest solution is in harmony with the bulk of the critics to claim that the inapt use of the word betrays a writer of the second century who was not quite "up" on his history. But *Wilson*[2] has shown rather exhaustively that the profane usage of the term "Chaldeans," dating back nearly to the time of Daniel, agrees with Biblical usage, in fact, that the meaning "astrologers" is the more common one. *Haevernick* has what strikes us as being a rather plausible explanation as to how the name of a conquering people came to designate a college of priests and astrologers. He says: "What is in itself more likely than that the Chaldeans as conquerors of Babylon made themselves masters of that group (*Stand*) that exer-

---

1. Pinches, T. G., *International Standard Bible Encyclopedia,*, Chicago: The Howard Severance Co., 1925, "Chaldea," p. 590.

2. Wilson, R. W., *op. cit.* Chapter, "The Chaldeans," pp. 319-366.

cised the strongest influence in the state, the group to which the care of sacred things and of the very religion itself was entrusted?" Though this is conjecture, something of this sort must have happened. *Charles* makes matters very difficult for himself at this point. Instead of assuming with *Haevernick* that very shortly after their conquest of Babylon the conquering Chaldeans made themselves masters of the group of astrologers, augurers, and the like, who occupied so prominent a position in that venerable old empire, he assumes that it never occurred to the Chaldeans to take such a step until the time of the Persian conquest. Of course, if they waited that long, this second meaning of the term could not readily have been used by Daniel, and therefore Daniel is charged with error. Since *Charles* is dealing with assumptions in any case, why not make the equally reasonable assumption that the Chaldeans as a conquering group, coming into Babylon at the time of Nebuchadnezzar's father, Nabopolassar, very shortly thereafter managed to get control of the work and the prerogatives of the astrologer class, and that the term "Chaldeans" would have been used in a twofold sense decades before Daniel appeared on the scene? Why could this practical idea not have occurred to them earlier than the Persian era? In the absence of historical evidence in the matter one assumption is quite as plausible as the other.

Another solution of the difficulty is presented by *Wilson* in the article referred to. He assumes that the noun "Chaldeans" in the second sense is derived from the Babylonian *galdu*, which is used with reference to a type of official that is often met with in Babylonian records and inscriptions, who has the supervision of public projects of every sort. Since such projects were never engaged in nor dedicated unless favorable auguries and prognostications had been secured, the work of these officials would naturally involve astrology and kindred practices. This agrees well with the Biblical position assigned to the Chaldeans. Besides, *galdu* is obviously analogous to *Kaldu*, the Babylonian term for the Chaldeans. In any event, we have here a possibility that can be reckoned with. For the rest of the discussion of "Chaldeans" cf. 1:4 and the suggestions offered at that point. The verb *'amar* is in this verse clearly used in the later sense of "commanded," not "said."

3. With the large group assembled before him, the king announced what occasioned his unusual summons. He has dreamed a dream, *chalôm*, singular. No matter how many dreams preceded, this one takes precedence over the rest to the point where the others are forgotten, namely, the ones mentioned in v. 1. His royal spirit is disturbed. Whereas the Hebrew says "to know the dream," we have translated more freely, "to know what the dream means."

4. **Then the Chaldeans spoke to the king in Aramaic: "O king, live forever. Tell thy servants the dream, and we will make known the interpretation."**

The "Chaldeans" speak. The term is used either to designate the four classes mentioned in v. 3 by using the name of the most prominent group—the most likely view—or the Chaldeans were the acknowledged spokesmen of the Babylonian wise men. As a matter that is worthy of mention Daniel records that these dignitaries spoke in Aramaic. One feels immediately that this would not have been mentioned if they had been speaking the same language that the king spoke. Consequently the king will have spoken his native tongue, which, if he was a Chaldean, some interpreters suppose to have been an Aryan language. The wise men employ their native Semitic tongue, *'aramîth*, "Aramaic." Some commentators suppose that the wise men could have used the king's language but preferred to use a language that was less familiar at court in order not to

·display their confusion publicly. But their confusion arises at a point that is later than this.

The word "Aramaic has received the strangest treatment. It is claimed that "the *'Aramith* here, as in Ezra 4:7, is probably a gloss or marginal note, to point out the sudden change in the language of the book" (*Farrar*). Certainly, such a means of indicating that one intended to change the language in which one was writing would be altogether too subtle. Furthermore, why should the word be under suspicion at all? It makes such good sense and fits so well at this point. It is true, of course, that beginning with v. 4b the Aramaic language takes the place of the Hebrew and continues to the end of chapter seven. But stranger still is the claim that the writer is said to indicate that he purposes to write in the East-Aramaic, which was spoken at Babylon, but ignorantly continues in the West-Aramaic of Palestine. In other words, a claim which he never made is charged against him, then the folly of that claim is proved, and so, it is thought, one of the errors made by the author has been brought to light.

It can be demonstrated that the difference between Eastern and Western Aramaic arose about the first century B. C., if so early.

A few remarks on the major differences between the Hebrew and the Aramaic will put the reader who knows no Aramaic at ease.

One chief difference is that the Aramaic does not use the familiar Hebrew article but employs instead the so-called emphatic state, which is practically nothing more than the syllable *a'* added as a suffix to a noun. Furthermore, the Aramaic no longer uses the construct state but substitutes a phrase introduced by an "of," which is spelled *dî* in the Aramaic. Furthermore, the *waw* conversive, so prevalent in the Hebrew, is unknown in the Aramaic. The spelling of words is peculiar, even the sound of the language is radically different from the Hebrew. The familiar Hebrew roots reappear in many instances, but they have an entirely different meaning. In many other instances, of course, the kinship between the two languages is made apparent by the fact that the roots have the meaning that we are familiar with in the Hebrew.

The salutation is, "O king, live forever." Similar forms of greeting are found in I Kings 1:31; Neh. 2:3; Dan. 3:9; 5:7, 10; 6:7, 22. "Forever" is apparently used here in the sense of "a good long while." Oriental courtesy especially required elaborate forms of greeting. The natural concern of the Chaldeans is to be told the dream so that they might at once busy themselves with the task of interpretation. They feel perfectly sure that they will be able to produce what will be regarded as a creditable piece of interpretative work. So they say, quite confidently, "We will make known the interpretation."

Dibber (*Piel*) is used in the sense of *'amar*—a later usage.

5, 6. The king answered and said to the Chaldeans: "The matter has been fully determined by me; if ye do not make the dream and its interpretation known to me ye shall be cut in pieces, and your houses shall be made a dunghill. But if ye do make the dream and its interpretation known ye shall receive at my hands gifts, presents, and great honor. Therefore show me the dream and its interpretation."

Anxious as Nebuchadnezzar was to know what his dream meant, he must at the time have been equally determined, for reasons not divulged here, to test his boastful Chaldeans to the utmost. It seems almost as though he was determined to be rid of them and their proud pretensions at practically any cost. So he does the unreasonable and tyrannical thing of demanding on the spot that the Chaldeans reveal both the dream and the interpretation. Such utterly despotic behavior on the part of these absolute monarchs of the Orient was witnessed in many instances. Their power was so utterly unlimited as to make such a procedure on their part quite possible. We venture to say that, if the Chaldeans had not made prentence of having access to the deepest and most completely hidden things, the king would never have made this unreasonable request of them. Not that he had forgotten the dream. The mistranslation of our versions encourages this opinion: "The thing is gone from me" (A. V.). Interpreters are quite commonly agreed that the rendering should be something like "the matter has been fully determined by me." For the difficult word *'azda'* very likely means "assured, certain," being a Persian loan word. The meaning is then: "The word is assured from me," and that must mean, "The thing is fully resolved upon by me" (*BDB*). If *'azda'* is taken to be a verb form for *'azal,* "to go forth," "l" being changed to "d," the only support offered for this use is the *Talmud,* which is a late product; and that seems farfetched even though in the Talmud *'azadh* does mean "go forth." The meaning would then have to be: "The word is gone forth from me," and that would be practically our first meaning: "The matter has been fully determined by me."

The king must, therefore, have been in an ugly mood that morning. He announces his irrevocable decision in all its despotic unreasonableness and fixes the most cruel punishment as the reward of failure: "ye shall be made pieces" (so the Aramaic), *haddamin* being factative object or accusative of effect, *K. S.* 113e. Besides, their houses shall be made *newalî.* The meaning "dunghill" is based on the *Targum* and is accepted by *Strack* in his grammar. The *Assyrian* parallel *nam(w)alu* which is accepted by *Buhl* and *BDB* means only a "ruin." But enough instances are on record to show how, after a place had been utterly destroyed, further disgrace was heaped upon it by making it a public outhouse (cf. II Kings 10:27). So in his wrath the king would hardly have hesitated to reduce the ruined homes to places of utter disgrace. *'Aneh*— the participle for the past tense—typically Aramaic.

6. On the other hand, the king wants also to play the part of the munificent ruler. If his request is met, he promises "gifts," *matnan,* "presents," *nᵉbhizbah*—a *Persian* word, singular, collective, and "great honor." Sharp and incisive is the command that concludes his edict: "Show me the dream and its interpretation."

7-9. They answered a second time and said: "Let the king tell his servants the dream, and we shall make known the interpretation." The king answered and said: "Now I know with absolute certainty that ye would gain time. Just because ye see that the matter is fully determined by me, that, if ye do not make the dream known, one law applies to you, and ye have been agreed among yourselves upon lying and corrupt words, to speak them in my presence, until things change; therefore tell me the dream, and I shall perceive that ye can show the interpretation."

The verb "let him tell," *ye'mar,* in place of the imperative used in v. 4, "tell," shows how carefully these men are trimming their sails to the wind as they politely request "a second time" to hear the dream before they proceed to interpret it. Nor do they venture to speak at great length. The situation being as precarious as it is, they dare to do no more than merely to add that they will "show the interpretation."

8. The phrase "of a certainty," *min-yatstsibh,* stands first in the king's answer. This emphatic position adds so much to its force that we have ventured to render it "with absolute certainty." "To gain time" is in the Aramaic "to buy (*zabhenîn*—plural participle) time." In the New Testament, for example, in

Eph. 5:16 it means to make the most of the time. Here its meaning is quite different: it means "to gain time" by a very ready transition in thought. Because you acquire more of the thing that you buy. So also *Luther* translates: *dass ihr Frist suchet;* in not quite the same sense apparently *A. V.* renders "ye would gain the time," which would seem to mean: make yourselves masters of the situation. Whatever bold pretences at deep and hidden knowledge these men may have made in the past, the king sees plainly that in the present instance they are fencing for time.

It may be best, as we have done, to combine v. 8b with v. 9 into one period although in any case the sentence structure is a bit complex. *Kol-qᵉbhel de* can be retained in the meaning *eben wegen* (K. W) i.e., "just because." The king repeats his demand, basing it on two points. First, because they see that the king's mind is fully made up that, if they fail, one law applies alike to all. In other words: you see I mean business; therefore speak up. Secondly, he senses that there is some kind of collusion between them to speak lying and corrupt words until things change. By this harsh terminology the king describes all evasion and temporizing as "lying and corrupt words." For the *Aramaic* idiom "until the time be changed," *'iddana' yishtanne'*, we have substituted the more easy colloquial "until things change," which we feel fully covers it. *Gordon* says about the same thing: "hoping that a change may come." The king resents the fact that they feel, as he has correctly sensed, that this decree of his is an unreasonable whim, which they hope may presently blow over; in the meantime they are talking against time. The expression "one law applies to you" means "to all of you alike." The word "one," *chᵃdhah*, is emphatic. The *Aramaic* says: "One is your law or decree."

10, 11. **The Chaldeans answered in the king's presence and said: "There is not a man upon the**

earth that is able to reveal what the king asks, for
no great king or ruler has asked a thing like this of
any scholar, enchanter, or Chaldean. Besides, the
matter that the king is asking is difficult, nor is there
any other person who could make it known before
the king except the gods, whose dwelling place is
not with mankind."

The answer of the Chaldeans is clearly marked
by a twofold purpose: on the one hand there is the
desperate attempt not to say anything that might
further irritate the despot; on the other hand they are
endeavoring to convey to the king the idea that his
demand is just as unreasonable as it can be. The introductory statement hints gently at their dilemma
when it says: "They answered *before the king.*" They
were very conscious of who it was before whom they
stood. Their first word is an excuse. Whatever bold
claims they may ever have raised, they certainly now
know their human limitations: "there is not a man
upon the earth that is able to reveal what the
king asks." That is tantamount to telling the king,
"You are unreasonable." Though they keep their statement objective they repeat it with the addition of
subtle flattery. They at the same time generalize as
they did at first: No great king or potentate of any
sort ever asked persons such as we are about such a
problem. This implies that the king is, of course, in
the category of the truly great and mighty.

11. Not to refer to the king too directly they
next venture to discuss the king's demand as such, always calling it "the matter," *millah,* "word, thing."
They surely must have been convinced that the king
was asking the impossible, but they presume to assure
him only that it is "difficult." Their boldest statement
finally follows to the effect that, as little as they can
provide the answer, so little can any other person.
Such circumlocution adds up to the statement, "It

cannot be done." Being more or less religious, they were ready to admit that the gods, whose dwelling place is not with "mankind" (*Aramaic: bisra'* = "flesh"), could solve such a mystery. That statement is a milder form of the assertion that the king expects superhuman achievements from poor mortals. Veiled though all these rebukes are, they cannot but further vex the king in his ungracious mood.

The *le* before *kol* (v. 10) is the common Aramaic construction of the direct object with *le, K. S.* 289m.

12, 13. On this account the king was angry, even exceedingly furious, and commanded to destroy all the wise men of Babylon. And the order was published to have the wise men put to death, and they sought Daniel and his companions that they might be put to death.

The king's mounting anger is described by having the verb "was exceedingly furious" follow the expression "was angry." His violent anger reached a prompt decision: he commanded that all the wise men of Babylon be destroyed. In this instance the term "wise men" apparently denotes the four classes mentioned in v. 2, who have since usually been designated as the famous Chaldeans. The choice of the word "wise men" seems motivated by the king's attitude, who wishes to dispose of those who falsely claim to be wise. Since the word *babhel* means either the city or the province of Babylon, in this instance perhaps only those of the immediate city were referred to.

13. The formal publishing of the "order," *dath,* seems to involve that a public mass execution was being contemplated, and that this required a bit of time till all personages involved could be arrested and properly assembled. This would explain how Daniel could find time for his project. The *Aramaic* seems to call for the translation, "and the order was published, and the wise men were slain," in which event

the slaughter would have already been in progress.
To make the participle a gerundive, "that they were
to be slain," for *mithqatt*^{e}*lin* is permissible but not so
good as the simple explanation which puts this statement on a parallel with certain other cases of co-
ordination of clauses where subordination is really
involved. Such cases are "command and" for "command to" or "sent and called" for "sent to call." So
here "ordered and killed" = "ordered to kill," as is
fully substantiated by *K. S.* 3691. The reason Daniel
was not among those summoned before the king
(v. 2) would seem to have been the fact that he was
as yet a novice, though the public tests mentioned in
chapter one had revealed his unusual capacities. Consequently, when the fatal order was issued, Daniel
and his companions had to be sought in the general
roundup.

b. *The Revelation of the Matter to Daniel,* 2:14-24.

14-16. **Thereupon Daniel gave a discreet and
prudent answer to Arioch, chief of the king's executioners, who had gone forth to slay the wise men of
Babylon. He answered and said to Arioch, the king's
captain, "Why is the decree from the king so
harsh?" Then Arioch made the matter known to
Daniel. So Daniel went in and made a request of the
king that he give him time, and that he might show
the interpretation to the king.**

At first glance there seems to be a discrepancy
between v. 14 and v. 15, for v. 14 extols highly the
wisdom of Daniel's word to Arioch, but v. 15, in reporting the word spoken, offers a very ordinary question, which seems to reveal nothing of an unusual
cleverness. Verse 14 does really offer high praise of
Daniel's word: it says (*Aramaic*): "He returned (by
way of answer) counsel and insight," or as we have
rendered above: he "gave a discreet and prudent
answer ("answer" being used in the familiar sense

though no question precedes). But let it be considered that Arioch (a name found already in Gen. 14:1) as "chief of the executioners," or "slaughterers," *tabbāchayya'*, would be intent upon little else than to please the king by a speedy execution. A lengthy question or an attempt to lecture him would have met with little favor. Daniel must have displayed unusual tact also in the way in which he approached the man. He does give the man somewhat of a shock by venturing to put into words what many had thought but had not dared to express: the king's decree is *harsh*. Apparently a good friend of Arioch's, Daniel wants to know: "why this harshness?" Perhaps "harsh" as a translation of *meḥachtsephah* is a bit strong; it does mean at least "peremptory" and more than "urgent" (*A.R.V.*) or "hasty (*A.V.*). In any case, Arioch feels impelled to take time to answer Daniel's inquiry, for the news of what had transpired behind the walls of the royal palace had apparently not begun to spread.

16. The very audacity of Daniel's plan of conduct under the circumstances contributed very largely to make it successful. At the root of it all must have been the prompting of God's Spirit, with whose gifts Daniel was so richly endowed. God's Spirit it was that emboldened Daniel to think and to know that he had been ordained of God for an emergency such as this. Humanly speaking, it was good psychology to venture into the king's presence so shortly after the fatal decree had been issued. For, in spite of all his vindictiveness, the king must still have been extremely anxious to learn what the dream meant. On the other hand, only the strongest faith on Daniel's part that he was called by God to take such a step could have made him assume the risk involved. For failure on his part would have entailed sharper punishment than was involved in the first instance.

The account is quite evidently condensed at this point by the omission of certain obvious details of court etiquette. For everyone still knows, and more assuredly knew in Daniel's day, that it was quite unthinkable that any man should venture into the king's presence unannounced or unsummoned, cf. Esther 4: 11. The step presupposed and passed by as the narrative moves along rapidly is that Arioch referred Daniel's request for permission to enter the royal palace to the proper official, who in turn relayed it to the king. By a similar circuitous route an answer was returned to Daniel. All that Daniel asks after he has been admitted to the royal presence is "time," a stay of execution. The prospect he confidently offers the king is the only one that would have merited consideration under the circumstances—"the interpretation," *pishra'*. Only the interpretation is mentioned and not the dream. That is to be explained on the score of the conciseness of the narrative. For he that can provide the interpretation must needs first know the dream. Another possibility must not be lost sight of. Since the king did not say (v. 5) that he had forgotten the dream, the likelihood is that he remembered it, at least the main features of it. How else could he have had any check upon the correctness of any dream that might be offered by his dream interpreters?

The construction of the sentence seems a bit difficult. What actually occurs is that the second object clause after *be'a'*, "made a request," is not a "that" clause but an infinitive clause, which we have also rendered as a "that" clause. The change to the infinitive seems to have been caused by the fact that the second clause at the same time expresses purpose.

17, 18. Then Daniel went home and made the matter known to his companions, Hananiah, Mishael, and Azariah, that they might ask mercy of the God of heaven in reference to this mystery, so that Dan-

**iel and his companions might not perish together
with the rest of the wise men of Babylon.**

Inspired though he was to believe that God had
raised up him and his companions for this emergency,
Daniel did not venture to expect to receive the needed
revelation without prayer. His companions are so
thoroughly of one mind with him that he needs only
to reveal his intention in order to secure their consent.
We have a mixed construction here exactly as we had
in v. 16: the construction veers over from an object
noun to an infinitive of purpose which is connected by
"and" because, in reality, the purpose was also something that Daniel made known to his companions.
Daniel very aptly designates God as "the God of
heaven" or literally, "of the heavens." This name,
which is found more frequently in the later books (see
Ezra 1:2; 6:10; 7:12, 21; Neh. 1:5; 2:4) had been
used already in Gen. 24:7. It is used in opposition to
the Babylonian and other views of the starry heavens
as spheres of influence that determine man's destiny
(astrology). He who truly exercised such control was
He who controlled the heavens as well as the lives of
men and was truly superior to all things that were
created by Him. That was Israel's faith and the only
correct faith, which was embodied for non-Israelites
in this pregnant designation of the Most High.

Daniel very honestly sets down his own and his
companions' chief objective in presenting their petition to the Lord: it was that they might not perish.
When one is in peril of one's life one will naturally
seek to save himself first of all. That is not always
selfishness but is often necessity. God, indeed, had
higher purposes in mind, which were also ultimately
realized. When it is said that these prayers were made
that they "might not perish together with the rest of
the wise men of Babylon" that by no means proves,
as *Meinhold* claims, that not only the *intention* to slay

them was evident but that the slaughter was already under way. The *Greek* translators, without good warrant, insert the word "fasting" before the word "prayer."

19. Then the secret was revealed to Daniel in a vision of the night. Then Daniel blessed the God of heaven.

The fact that the intended prayer was actually offered is so obvious that it is not recorded. Instead the narrative tells of the answer to this prayer of faith. This answer came in the form of a "vision," *chezwah,* emphative form from *ch^ezû,* not a dream; for dreams are, for the most part, the mode of revelation used for those who are lower in the scale than the theocratic people. Visions usually came during the night, when the disturbing influences from without are reduced to a minimum, therefore: "vision of the night." Daniel's blessing of God can well be attributed to a double cause. Daniel first expresses his gratitude that his prayer was heard. Then the truth revealed by the king's dream is perhaps even the major cause of blessing God, for gracious truths of blessed import were by the dream conveyed to Daniel first so that he might in turn transmit them to others.

20-23.   Daniel answered and said:
"Blessed be the name of God from everlasting to
     everlasting,
For wisdom and might are His!
He changeth seasons and years;
He deposes kings and sets up kings.
He giveth wisdom to the wise and knowledge to
     them that possess insight.
He revealeth the deep and hidden things:
He knoweth what is in darkness;
And light dwelleth with Him.
Thee, O God of my fathers, I do thank and praise,

**For Thou hast given me wisdom and ability
And hast even now made known unto me what we
    sought of Thee;
For Thou hast let me know the problem of the king."**
This is Daniel's psalm. It shows how well-versed in Scripture Daniel was. For if the parallel Scripture passages are examined, it will be seen that he was thoroughly familiar with them though it is not possible in every instance to prove that Daniel was quoting or alluding to familiar passages. The psalm gives proof of Daniel's originality in adapting the material in hand. On 20a cf. Ps. 103:1, 2; Ps. 113: 1, 2. On 20b cf. I Chron. 29:11, 12; Job 12:13, 16-22. On 21a cf. Ps. 31:15; on 21b cf. Job 12:18; Ps. 75:6, 7; on 21c cf. I Kings 3:9, 10; 4:29. On 22a cf. Job 12:22; on 22b cf. Job 26:6; Ps. 139:12; Isa. 45:7; on 22c cf. Ps. 36:9. On 23a cf. Gen. 31:42; Exod. 3:15.

The major theme of the psalm is God's mighty revelation which Daniel has just received and which displays God's transcendent might and power and marks Him as the Source of all wisdom. Daniel bestows all praise upon the "name of God," which connotes, as *Montgomery* says rightly, "God in His self-revelation." He who has truly sensed the greatness of the Lord will be desirous of having His praise sound on to eternity, "from everlasting to everlasting," for only an eternity of praise will begin to show due honor to our God.

In this instance Daniel praises God in particular for the fact that "wisdom and might are His," the "wisdom" that knows how to control this world's seeming chaos, and the "might" actually to do what His wisdom discerns should be done. For Daniel had just seen the most significant instance of this capacity in the dream that had been revealed to him.

To this must be added the general principle of God's control of the *time* element: "He changeth seasons and years." He it is that determines how long one influence shall prevail, and when another shall become operative. "Seasons" are shorter periods, occasions when it is suitable to do a thing; "years," *zimnayya'*, actually "times," the broader term, here perhaps referring specifically to that which we call "years." The reverse order of these terms appears in 7:12 and Eccles. 3:1; cf. Acts 1:7; I Thess. 5:1. *Montgomery* says very properly, "In this expression lies a challenge to the fatalism of Babylonian astral religion."

21b.   There now follow specific instances that are still stated in the form of general principles. He it is that "deposes kings and sets up kings." Rulers owe their tenure of office to Him though on the surface little or nothing of His control may be in evidence. Kings are a kind of puppets in His hands. Another class of important personages is then shown to be in utter dependence upon the good Lord, namely, the wise. If they have true wisdom they can claim to have it only from Him who gives it to "the wise" and "knowledge to them that possess insight," *bînah*.

22.   And now what about the things that are not yet known by man? If they come to light, "He revealeth" them. That was the fact which was most significantly displayed by this momentous occasion. It matters little to the Almighty if these things be "deep and hidden." "He knoweth what is in darkness." And this is again possible to Him, for "light dwelleth with Him."

It may be that an old distinction of terms is to be observed here. *Nehôr*—emphatic *nehora'*—would seem to refer rather to physical, natural light. *Nahîrû* rather to inner light, "illumination, insight." In our passage, where the former would be expected, the latter is written, and so the marginal form (the *Kerî*) has been substituted in the text. This was perhaps quite unnecessary since the second word makes good sense. The word "dwelleth," *shere'*, means as much as "is at home with Him." The Jews stretched a point when they referred the term "light" *in this verse* specifically to the Messiah—though He is indeed the Light.

23. There follows Daniel's thanksgiving because his petition was heard without special mention of the fact that his life was spared, because in the full assurance of faith Daniel had not been in doubt as to this issue. The double verb—"thank and praise"—betokens the full measure of his gratitude. However, to give a keener edge to the expression of this gratitude God's name is made to stand first. This emphasis implies distinctly that there is none other who shares in this honor that is God's. When he addresses Him as the "God of my fathers" Daniel implies that he is having an experience of God's mercy which is analogous to that to which the fathers of old give testimony on the pages of the sacred story. The author and sole source of "wisdom and might" (v. 20) has imparted of His resources to Daniel. However, in Daniel's case the word "might," *gᵉbhûrta'*, had better be rendered "ability," i.e., the ability to solve the problem in hand. In conclusion, Daniel thanks in specific terms that he was granted what he had sought, even to know the "problem (*millah*, 'thing or matter') of the king." By saying "what *we* sought," Daniel acknowledges the part his friends had in this earnest, effectual prayer.

This prayer, though brief, is comprehensive and stands on the high level of the Biblical psalms.

The verb form for "be" occurring in v. 20 calls for discussion. It is *lehᵉwe'* whereas the normal form would be *yehᵉwe'* or *yehᵉweh*, which is the *Aramaic* equivalent of the imperfect of the *Hebrew* verb *hayah*. The explanation for the use of this form that is most in vogue calls the *l* a substitution for the customary prefix *y* and is said to be made because of the over-strong reverence that the later Jews felt for the four consonants that represent the sacrosanct name of *Yahweh*—YHWH. *Montgomery* offers a sturdy defense of this contention, but *König* builds up a stronger case for another explanation in *K. S.* 396 kl. He argues that the Aramaic, especially that of a later date, presents parallels where the prefixes *l* and *n* are used for the customary *y* of the imperfect. His chief argument is that the *l* prefix is also used in the plural where there is no danger of reading *Yahweh's* holy name because the consonants are different. Furthermore, we do not believe that sacred writers ever give evidence of such a superstitious reverence for God's name; neither do we believe that it can be shown that at any period in their history Jews took such liberty with the text of the Holy Scriptures as to venture to substitute consonants.

24. **Therefore Daniel went in unto Arioch, whom the king had appointed to destroy the wise men of Babylon; he went and thus he said unto him: "Destroy not the wise men of Babylon; bring me into the king's presence, and I will make known the interpretation to the king."**

The keyman Arioch must be contacted first, chiefly because in his hands lay the lives of all, and also because his position allowed him to act as an intermediary to bring persons into the king's presence. The chief matter of public concern was whether the wise men would have to perish. Daniel therefore first stops any move in this direction by venturing to countermand the king's orders, and he does that without any danger to himself because in his possession was the much-coveted answer to the great mystery. This brings him to the matter of chief concern to the king, the interpretation of the dream. He demands to be brought into the king's presence, knowing full well that his interpretation will make him a person who is extremely welcome to the royal presence. In this instance the narrative tells in detail how Daniel could not have presumed to step before the king without proper permission. This naturally conditions and explains his previous admission before the king mentioned in v. 16.

c) Daniel's Disavowal of Native Ability, v. 25-30.

25, 26. Then Arioch, much excited, brought Daniel before the king, and thus did he say to him: "I have found a man of the captives of Judah who will make the interpretation known to the king." The king answered and said to Daniel, whose name was Belteshazzar: "Art thou able to make known to me the dream that I saw and its interpretation?"

The statement is a bit stronger than that Arioch brought Daniel "in haste" (*A. V.*), for the verb *bahal* means to *"alarm."* We venture to translate the infinitive *behithbehalah* with the colloquial "much excited." Those who are critically minded have found Arioch's statement impossible under the circumstances: a few hours before this he had secured permission to let Daniel appear in the king's presence; now Arioch says, "I have found a man," as though the former episode had not occurred. Furthermore, Arioch ventures to explain to the king who the man is who a short time before conversed with the king as one who was known to him—an incongruity. However, taking more careful note of the circumstances, we discern that what is said is a normal statement. Arioch is pleased to be a prominent figure in a great drama a second time and makes the most of his share in the event. He slightly overstates his part, making it appear that he found Daniel rather than that Daniel found him, which is not so unusual an exaggeration on the part of an officious person. In the second place, Arioch puts into words what just about all feel on this occasion: it is not one of great Babylon's wise men but one of inconspicuous and almost unknown Judah's captives.

The insertion of Daniel's Babylonian name is a reminder of the fact that, though Daniel prefers his own original name and calls himself by it, yet on this occasion he was being regularly addressed as Belteshazzar. Without further preliminaries the king at once asks Daniel whether this is really so. Whereas only the "interpretation" has usually been mentioned as the vital thing, in this instance the king mentions the "dream" as well, for he himself apparently did not believe it possible that the dream could be disclosed by anyone.

27-30. **Daniel answered and said in the king's presence: "As far as the mystery is concerned that the king is asking about, no wise man, enchanter, scholar, or astrologer is able to show it to the king. But there is a God in the heavens who reveals secrets, and He has made known to Nebuchadnezzar what it is that shall be in the latter days. Thy dream and the visions of thy head upon thy bed were as follows: As for thee, O king, as thou didst lie upon thy bed, thy thoughts arose what it was that should happen next; and the Revealer of secrets hath made known unto thee what shall happen. But as for me, it is not by any wisdom which is in me before all the living that this secret has been revealed to me but for the purpose that the interpretation might be made known to the king, and that thou mightest understand the thoughts of thy heart."**

Daniel was not going to miss so fine an opportunity to proclaim the glory of the true God. Furthermore, it would have led to the most grievous of misunderstandings if he had posed as one who was able to interpret dreams because of some gifts that were resident within him. So Daniel cannot do otherwise than did Joseph on a similar occasion (Gen. 41:

16) : he makes a strong disavowal of gifts that might naturally be his and gives all honor to God. He at the same time indicates in a summary way what it was on the king's part that prepared the king's mind to receive this revelation by means of a dream. In order to make his personal disavowal as strong as possible and incidentally to administer a deserved rebuke to the king because of his unjust decree Daniel makes the assertion that no wise man of any sort can answer questions such as that concerning this mystery. Note the wisdom and the fairness of this part of Daniel's answer. Incidentally, at this point a new class of sages is introduced, the *gaz*^{e}*rîm*, "the astrologers," from a root meaning "to divide," in the sense of dividing off the heavens into spheres or areas of influence. Over against all human impotence Daniel places his God, whom he again designates very aptly as the "God in the heavens," a phrase that is in meaning about the same as "the God of heaven" (see v. 18). This God is described as being the One who has capacity for revealing secrets and has deigned Nebuchadnezzar worthy of being a recipient of a revelation as to "what it is that shall be in the latter days."

This expression *'ach^{a}rîth yômayya'*, "the end of the days," does denote, as *Driver* (quoted by *Montgomery*) says, "the *closing period* of the future so far as it falls within the range of view of the writer using it." But to stop short at this point and to deny Messianic import to the passage as such is misleading. Though the content must determine how much of the future is involved, a careful evaluation of all the passages involved shows that from the first instance of the use of the phrase (Gen. 49:1) onward the Messianic future is regularly involved. In this passage the Messianic element will be seen to be prominent. Yet that does not mean that only the Messianic shall figure prominently and as much of the events leading up to these last days as may at any time be essential to present a well-rounded picture.

The expression "visions of thy head upon thy bed" is an Aramaic way of saying: as your head lay upon your bed these were the visions that flashed before your mind. The phrase "upon thy bed" modifies directly the noun "head." When Daniel says they were "as follows" he really means only that they came under the following circumstances. Only after he has ascribed all honor and all glory unmistakably to God does he enter upon the details of the dream as such.

29. The initial pronoun is either a nominative absolute, as our rendering gives it, or a means to make the following vocative stand out more distinctly, *K. S.* 290b. Daniel recalls what had preceded Nebuchadnezzar's momentous dream: the king had found his thoughts turning to the question, "what it was that should happen next," *'ach^arey dh^enah*, i.e., "after this."

This situation by no means points to the latter part of Nebuchadnezzar's reign as though only after the firm establishment of all his conquests could he think in terms of the future. For Nebuchadnezzar was somewhat of an Alexander: he had made rapid and substantial conquests at the very beginning of his reign, in fact, already during the time of his father's reign. With such a multitude of victories already behind him, the king might well wonder what the future had in store, for he was well-nigh at the top of the ladder already.

Daniel coins a new name for his God; he describes Him as the Revealer of secrets and asserts that He it is who has revealed to Nebuchadnezzar what he had sought to know. Observe how much more effective such instruction about God's hand in the matter must be while the mind is still tense as to the meaning of it all and not yet absorbed in the details of the revelation.

30. Daniel once again humbly disclaims having

any wisdom above other living mortals that had made him worthy to receive such special revelation. For well might the young Daniel wonder that he should have been singled out to receive so unusual a forecast of the future. Daniel discerns clearly that God, for reasons of His own, has chosen to impart certain knowledge of future events to this great monarch, and that he, Daniel, is merely the vehicle that carries the truth. These preliminaries having been disposed of, the approach is clear, the setting right, and the king is enabled to get the correct perspective of things. He now sees in advance that the issues involved are more momentous than he had even remotely sensed.

The verb that we have rendered "might be made known," *yᵉhôdhᵉ'ûn*, is really active and plural: "that they might cause (thee) to know"—one of many instances where the third person plural active functions for the passive in the *Aramaic*; cf. 3:4, 21; 4:13, 22, 23; 5:21; 7:9, 12, etc. (cited by *Meinhold*). *Lahen*, which has a variety of meanings, here plainly means "but," *K. S.* 372n.

d) *The Summary of the Dream, 2:31-35.*

31. **"Thou, O king, wast gazing and, lo, a mighty statue. This statue, which was immense, and whose splendor was extraordinary, was standing before thee, and its appearance was terrifying."**

With consummate skill Daniel reviews the essentials of the dream. He recalls to the king how he was gazing upon a "statue," *tsᵉlem*, and was fascinated by what he saw. The verb "to be" with the participle (*chazeh*) is a distinctively Aramaic way of expressing continued action which is found frequently in this book. It pictures how the king was entranced by the sight, unable to take his eye off what he saw. Abruptly and skillfully, after a deictic "behold," *'ᵃlû*, this sentence with-

out a verb thrusts the statue before the mental vision,
just as it suddenly stood there before the king.

One of the things that fascinated the onlooker
was the size of the thing. This feature is therefore
alluded to a second time: it "was immense." The
second thing was its "extraordinary splendor." One
can well imagine what an imposing sight it must have
presented—huge, of shining metal, no doubt beautiful
and attractive as well, but, apparently because of its
tremendous size, the general "appearance was terrifying." Nebuchadnezzar may have recalled vividly
how the sight of the statue had frightened him as he
beheld it in his sleep.

D^{e}chîl is a passive participle from *d^{e}chal*. We
prefer to render *ts^{e}lem* as "statue" because we believe
this word is more readily understood. The *chadh* after
ts^{e}lem is really the numeral "one" but apparently has
no emphasis here, standing, as it does, between the
noun "statue" and the adjective "mighty" and so merely
appears in a "weakened form" (*in schwaecherer
Potenz*, K. S. 291e) as the equivalent of an indefinite
article. To build deductions on this word, as *Keil* and
Kliefoth do, becomes impossible though the fact they
contend for is indubitably correct, i.e., that "the world
power is in all its phases one, therefore all these phases
are in the vision united in *one* image."

**32, 33. "As for this statue, its head was of fine
gold, its breast and its arms were of silver, its abdomen and its thighs of bronze, its legs of iron, and its
feet part iron and part clay."**

The significant details of the statue are made to
pass quickly in review before the king's mental vision,
whether he had at the time so carefully observed them
or not. "Statue" stands first, nominative absolute; we
say "as for this statue." It must have been apparent
in some way that the gold of the head was "good,"

tabh, or pure. The "breast" or chest, plus the arms, were of silver. The "abdomen" refers, not to the inward parts, but to the "external belly" (*BDB*). The material of which it was made as well as the "thighs," i.e., the upper parts of the upper half of the legs, was bronze, translated "brass" in *A.V. Shaq* refers to the upper half of the leg but must here refer to the major part of the leg from the thighs to the feet. These "legs" were of iron, and the feet were a mixture of two materials: "iron" and "clay." *Chasaph* strictly signifies a product, not a material, namely "potsherds." However, later in the chapter it is referred to as "*ch*ᵃ*saph* of the potter" and as "*ch*ᵃ*saph* of clay"—a kind of superlative, which may signify even "*ch*ᵃ*saph* of mud." We believe that by metonomy, in the list of other materials mentioned, *clay* must be mentioned here. Iron and clay are prominently in evidence at a glance.

Minnehôn, strictly "of them," here used correlatively, must mean "partly" or "part . . . part." The suffix is a bit irregular, being masculine though referring to "feet."

34, 35. **"Thou didst keep gazing until a stone was cut loose without hands and smote upon the statue, that is to say, upon its feet of iron and clay, and demolished them. Then the iron, the clay, the bronze, the silver, and the gold were all demolished together and became as the chaff of the summer threshing floor, and the wind bore them away; and no place was found for them. But the stone which had smitten upon the statue became a huge mountain and filled the whole earth."**

There was no action in the picture at first, it was merely that of a monstrous, immovable figure. The picture now becomes a moving picture. A stone is "cut loose" or merely "detached" from a mountainside, which, by the way, is not introduced into the account until v. 45, most likely because the stone was at first merely noticed as a detached stone rolling swiftly downhill. It is noted that the image lay directly in the path of the moving stone. Yet it is definitely noted that it was not the image as such which was struck but specifically the feet which consisted of iron and clay, that is to say, the most vulnerable part of the whole. These were then "demolished," *haddèqeth,* a Haphel from *deqaq.* Somehow, though not struck by the stone, the remaining metals were demolished as well. They are mentioned in an ascending climax of values. *Daqû* from *dûq* is a third person plural active for a passive, cf. v. 30: therefore "were crushed or demolished" for "they crushed."

It might have been anticipated that the demolition would have resulted in broken *pieces* of metal strewing the scene. Instead the very unusual thing is observed that the entire statue is reduced to the consistency of "chaff of the summer threshing floor." The wind is next seen bearing these dust particles away before the astonished onlooker's eyes until the site of the statue is swept clean. We should have said, "No trace of them could be found" (*Gordon*). The *Aramaic* viewpoint is quite different; it says, "No place was found for them." The sweeping away was so complete that the dust found no visible resting place.

The climax is the visible growth of "the stone which had smitten upon the statue." It grew to such gigantic proportions that it became "a huge mountain and filled the whole earth." "Earth" must refer to the entire visible area that was beheld in the dream. The noun *tûr* (Hebrew *tsûr*) really means a rock mass or rock. In connections such as these a rock that fills the entire earth is surely a "mountain." So the vision begins with a huge statue; it ends with the hugest possible mountain. There is not a superfluous word in Daniel's entire description and account. It is a mas-

terpiece of pithy word painting. We admit a certain
"incongruity" (Driver) in a mountain's filling the
earth, but, as the same author remarks, it is an incongruity "which would not be perceived in a dream."
When v. 34 says "until (*'ad-di*) a stone was cut
loose," the "until" is not used absolutely as if the
writer saw no more thereafter, for the account shows
that he saw more. The conjunction marks "an epoch
or turning point" (*BDB*), cf. Gen. 49:10; Ps. 110:1.

   e) *The Interpretation of the Dream, 2:36-45.*

   36-38. **"This is the dream, and we shall tell
the interpretation of it before the king. Thou, O
king, the king of kings, to whom the God of the
heavens has given the kingdom, the power, the
might, and the honor, and into whose hand He has
given the children of men, wheresoever they dwell,
the beasts of the field and the birds of the heavens,
and has made thee ruler over all of them, thou art
the head of gold."**

   Daniel's statements are arranged in the best order:
the dream is narrated without confusing it with the
interpretation; the interpretation is presented in a
clear-cut way as a coherent unit. Daniel even announces expressly when he makes his transition from
the dream to the interpretation. The narrating of the
dream was a necessity even for the king because,
though he had dreamed and remembered it, the essential details may not have been noted by him with
sufficient clearness.

   Who are the "we" in "we shall tell," *ne'mar*? Is
this a kind of plural of authority, something like the
regal or editorial plural? Or does it refer to Daniel and
God? Or to Daniel and his friends? Or to Daniel and
all the true worshipers of Jehovah? The first suggestion results in a stilted expression. The second
hardly savors sufficiently of humility. The last goes

too far afield. The third—Daniel and his friends—
fits the case best. His friends had assisted him materially by their prayers; besides, these four had been
regularly associated together. Had Daniel failed to
give credit to those who had aided him by prayer in
securing this revelation he would have been extremely
selfish and ungrateful. *K. S.* 206b, basing too strongly
upon v. 30, feels the "we" refers to Daniel and God.

37. Verses 37 and 38 fit together as follows: the
vocative, address to the king, is followed by two relative clauses, the second of which has a double verb;
the conclusion of v. 38 then gives the predicate for the
original subject, which is repeated at this point—
'ant(h), "thou." Though this form is always written
with a final *h*, the *Keri* always ignores this letter,
reading as though it were *'ant*. Daniel shows all deference due to the great king, addressing him by the well-
merited title "king of kings," a title in current use
apparently with reference to Babylonian as well as
later to Persian monarchs and an Aramaic superlative,
cf. Ezek. 26:7; Esther 7:12. *Montgomery* quotes
Prince to the effect that this is "not the customary
Babylonian form of address" without, however, adducing proof. But the Ezekiel passage just referred to
cannot be brushed aside so readily; and, in any case,
Nebuchadnezzar *was* "a king of kings." If it is true
that the fragmentary monumental evidence provides
no instance of the use of this title with reference to
Babylonian kings, that is far from being the equivalent of a proof that this title was not used with
reference to them.

With a very clear-cut confession Daniel ascribes
Nebuchadnezzar's accession to the throne and all his
success to the only true God, the "God of the heavens"
(cf. v. 18). Daniel does not blur issues in order to
curry favor. It must be acknowledged that much had
been bestowed upon Nebuchadnezzar. Daniel's com-

plete list of the several items involved is headed by "the kingdom"; that might mean the rule over the kingdom or the sovereignty. "The power" is the capacity to rule this kingdom. "The might" could then mean the strength displayed in coping with external problems. "The honor" is the resultant glory that comes from ruling a kingdom well. So these terms are seen to be arranged in an ascending series or climax.

In addition, Daniel lists all those over whom the king has authority. The first are "the children of men, wheresoever they dwell." This construction necessitates supplying a noun like "place" after *bᵉkhol*, "in every." "In every place where they dwell" naturally= "wheresoever they dwell." It could be said quite truthfully that all these "children of men" were Nebuchadnezzar's subjects because he actually reigned over all the then-known world. If a measure of hyperbole inheres in the expression, the hyperbole is on the whole not excessive. To make the extent of the king's rule appear as absolute as it must have seemed to his admiring contemporaries, the hyperbole continues to list those over whom his authority extended as including "the beasts of the field and the birds of the heavens." At least this much is true in quite a measure, that God had "given them into his hands" and in reality made him "ruler over all of them."

We see, then, the propriety of the first major item of the interpretation, "thou art the head of gold." That is the equivalent of the statement, "Thy kingdom is the head of gold." But since all that Babylon is finds itself embodied in Nebuchadnezzar, this other form of statement is very proper.

A very fine propriety marks the entire imagery of the dream; and so when we note how the interpretation draws on this deeper symbolism we feel that, without forcing the implied meaning, we may justly interpret this symbolism without going beyond the limits intended by revelation. So, then, if these empires or monarchiès have Nebuchadnezzar as their head, that must imply that the idea of world empires originated with the Babylonians even as the head thinks and plans. Besides, the policies they originated continued to control succeeding empires even as the head controls the body. May, perhaps, even this thought be implied: schemes of this sort emanate from the head, the clever intellect; not from the heart or from sympathetic love that aims to serve and to help? There must have been a measure of intrinsic worth in this enterprise because it is best represented by the most precious of metals—gold. It seems as though interpretation, if it is to stay within reasonable limits, dare go no farther than this.

One matter calls for explanation. On the basis of a comparison of maps representing the empires of the ancient world as offered by atlases the Babylonian or Chaldean empire seems far too small to be matched with the vast Persian, Greek, or Roman empires that followed. But what it lacked in magnitude it more than made up by its spirit, tenacity of purpose, and long endurance. In a sense the empire founded by Nebuchadnezzar was small and endured about a century. In another sense it was the empire that dated back to the great Sargon I and had continued uninterruptedly for well-nigh two thousand years. In reference to it *McCurdy* says very properly: "Whether the controlling dynasty of the River country was North Babylonian or South Babylonian or Elamitic or Assyrian or Chaldean, the purpose and the effort were unalterably maintained."* He refers to the purpose and the effort "of the rulers of the East to subdue and dominate the west-land." Babylon always remained the animating

---

*McCurdy, James Frederick, *History, Prophecy and the Monuments*, New York: MacMillan, 1911, pp. 105, 106. Par. 93.

soul of these imperial designs, of an empire of greater duration by far than any of the others. Or to speak the language of this image of Nebuchadnezzar, she was the head.

Furthermore, in partial support of the contention that a higher value is embodied in Nebuchadnezzar's empire we may point to the character of the king who was singularly religious. *McCurdy* says of him: "Now what is conspicuous in Nebuchadnezzar is the purity and self-abandonment of his adoration, as contrasted with the self-laudatory grandiloquence of the Assyrian kings."* The natural heathen religion had at least retained some of its finer qualities in his day. All in all, his empire is the one that reaches back to those beginnings of empire described in Gen. 10:10 in the days shortly after the Flood. All empires that followed the Babylonian were mere children in comparison with this venerable patriarch.

39. **"After thee shall arise another kingdom inferior to thee; then still another kingdom, the third, of bronze, which shall rule over all the earth."**

The only thing said for the present about the second kingdom is that it was to be "inferior to thee" or, what amounts to the same thing, "inferior to thine" (*Luther*). The word for "inferior" is *'ar'a'* from *'ªra'* meaning "earth," which with the locative ending (*Keri* is unnecessary) means "earthward, lower, inferior." The critic, judging by mere externals, consults the atlas, notices that the Persian Empire had far greater extent than the Chaldean, and concludes: the Persian cannot be meant; this must refer to the kingdom of the Medes. This claim has come to be a commonplace among critics, which they have endeavored to re-enforce with exegetical argument. *Farrar* waxes so exuberant in his claim to absolute

---

ibid. pp. 150, Par. 1054.

and unassailable correctness that among his bold assertions, characteristic of critics generally, may be
read statements such as these: "It may be regarded
as a certain result of exegesis that the four empires
are—(1) the Babylonian; (2) the Median; (3) the
Persian; (4) the Graeco-Macedonian." Or, stigmatizing
the claim that the fourth empire might be the Roman
and, of course, by implication, the second the Persian,
he claims: "Thus to introduce the Roman Empire into
the Book of Daniel is to set at naught the plainest
rules of exegesis." They who know the history of the
great Babylonian Empire which originated shortly
after the great Flood must admit that in point of influence and achievement it outranked the Persian
Empire by far. So "inferior to thee" is a very
correct statement.

But "inferior" or "lower" must include more than
mere size. *Meinhold* says correctly that the sense is
more ethical than local. *Keil* sees the inferiority in the
fact that the Medo-Persian Empire lacked inner unity
"since the Medes and Persians did not form a united
people." *Zoeckler* finds it in the inferior moral worth.
Kliefoth feels that the inferiority lay in this, that the
new empire was not universal in character, it lacked
ecumenicity. For by this time the Greeks had stepped
into the forefront among the historical nations, but
the Medo-Persian power never proved strong enough
to assimilate the Greeks.

Each of these points contains an element of truth,
for, surely, we need not insist that inferiority must
be reckoned on some one score alone. But taken all in
all, the two thousand years of Babylonian culture and
its dominance in western Asia certainly outweighed
the two hundred years of Persian dominion in its effect upon contemporary and later developments so
overwhelmingly that all one can say about the Persian
Empire is that it was "inferior."

If the statue represents the truth of history, the
silver could not refer to a Median empire, for there
never was such an empire. The Medes rendered valuable service in the matter of helping to conquer Babylon. The rulers from Cyrus onward were Persian.
Media had been conquered by the Persians in 550
B. C.; Babylon fell in 538. No historian places Media
among the world empires. To attribute ignorance to
the writer of the book of Daniel by using *Bevan's* explanation: "Of the Median empire next to nothing was
known in the time of the author," and calling it a
"most plausible" explanation is most unique, especially
if it is assumed that some Jew, writing near the middle
of the second century B. C., wrote the book of Daniel.
For by that time the issues were perfectly clear. Men
knew what came after Babylon, and how Alexander
had overcome the Persians. Crass ignorance on this
point coupled with brilliant insight into the prophetic
future on the part of the author of this chapter is an
unbelievable combination. Into such absurdities critics
are thrust by their misinterpretations, which keep
raising their ugly heads and causing trouble. For a
full discussion of the baselessness of the claim that
the Medes are the second empire see R. D. Wilson's
Studies in the Book of Daniel, pp. 128-238.

A few items of interest and profit may be pointed
out as being directly indicated by "the breast and
arms of silver." Moral values are not extinct in the
Persian kingdom. Cyrus is a more or less noble figure.
Even true virtue was at first found among these
people—indicated by the "silver." The two parts of the
empire, which were primarily Media and Persia, are
represented as being joined together as the arms and
the breast are in the human body, yet the two elements
never fused so thoroughly as to become one undivided
whole. Whether any conclusion dare be drawn from
the fact that the breast encloses the heart is more than

we venture to assert though, certainly, Cyrus is reputed for a heartfelt charity that he bestowed on
friend and foe as is attested also by his restoration of
the Jews from their captivity.

39b. The successive deterioration of empires is
indicated as clearly as it can be by the successive
metals that constitute the statue. Therefore the third
kingdom of "bronze," *n^echash*, not "brass," *A. V.*, taken
all in all and not only on one particular count, is of
less intrinsic worth than either of the preceding. This
is the Greek kingdom of Alexander plus the four kingdoms that resulted after the death of Alexander. Something is said about it that is in no wise suggested by
the symbolism of the statue, viz., it "shall rule over all
the earth." This must again be understood according to
the use of the term "earth." Men included no more
territory in the term than was known to them at the
time. It therefore means the "then-known earth."
Alexander's kingdom did include the land of Greece
which the Persians had vainly attempted to conquer
and embodied practically all of the Persian realm.

We do not venture to draw deductions from the
fact that the abdomen is involved. But we must point
out that, as the abdomen and the thighs (v. 33) are of
bronze, at least this essential truth is indicated: what
begins as a unit divides itself into two separate parts
which do not reunite. After Alexander's death the four
resultant parts of his realm amounted to practically
two: Syria and Egypt. These are the two thighs of
the statue. They are still separate when the last empire
appears on the scene.

40-43. **"And the fourth kingdom shall be
strong as iron. Inasmuch as iron crushes and smashes
all things, and as iron was demolishing all these, so
shall it crush and demolish. And as thou didst see
the feet and the toes, part potter's clay and part iron,
so shall the kingdom be divided, and there shall be**

in it something of the firmness of iron even as thou
didst see the iron mingled with the earthy clay. And
as for the toes of the feet being part iron and part
clay, to an extent the kingdom shall be strong, but
a part of it shall be fragile. And as thou didst see
iron mixed with earthy clay, so shall they be mixed
together by the seed of men; but they shall not
cleave together, the one to the other, just as iron
and clay will not mix."

It will be seen at a glance that this fourth kingdom
receives a more extensive treatment than do those that
preceded it. The reason for this may be the fact that it
lies farthest in the future and so is depicted more exhaustively lest its distinctive features be lost sight of.
Generally speaking, the mark of the fourth empire is
strength—"strong as iron." This is at once explained
to be, not the strength of inner cohesion and unity,
but destructive strength: it shall "crush and demolish" as "iron crushes and smashes all things." The
Roman legions were noted for their ability to crush
all resistance with an iron heel. There is apparently
little that is constructive in the program of this empire in spite of Roman law and Roman roads and civilization because the destructive work outweighed all
else, for we have the double verb "crush and demolish."

41. The rest of the description has to do with
the lack of inner unity and the resultant brittleness of
this empire. The division involved in this instance is
quite different in character from those of the second
or the third empires. In the third, for example, the two
thighs stood separately, each a unit in itself: Egypt
and Syria simply could not be amalgamated. Now the
feet and the toes are seen be "part potter's clay and
part iron." Though such a strange blending should be
attempted, the iron and the clay will not fuse. "Something of the firmness of iron" shall be in evidence continually, but this lack of cohesion shall be especially

in evidence in the toes. It shall always be that "a part of it shall be fragile." Since the lowest part of the statue indicates the latest development in the sequence of time, this means that in the latter days of the fourth or Roman Empire, that is to say, down in the feet and the toes, this mixture of "firmness" and frailty shall be most in evidence. The iron is apparently the old Roman stock, the clay representing the more plastic Germanic and other peoples who were at that time not such good material for empire building, whatever virtues they may otherwise have had.

43. This commingling of the two materials is explained as involving that the two elements shall "be mixed together by the seed of men." For the expression "by the seed of men"—less clear *A.V.*, "*with* the seed of men"—*Gordon* substitutes freely but correctly "by marriage." Roman stock and Germanic and other stock intermarried—a melting-pot experiment—but the resultant stock was not the material that enduring empires are made of: "they shall not cleave together, the one to the other." This may involve also that the intermarriage plan was perhaps not carried out on a larger scale but only here and there and also by a marriage of princes and princesses—an expedient that failed, after all, to consolidate the groups. "Seed of men" means also human expedients, contrast Jer. 31:27.

Critics charge this account, v. 40-43, with "redundancy, which is surprising in this compact narrative," and even (v. 41ff) with "insipid repetitiousness." It seems that these commentators cannot sense when a thought is stated with emphasis and plainness. So v. 41 repeats the thought of "crush and demolish," but it says with emphasis that the sturdy, solid qualities of iron are not the only consideration though something of that thought enters into the picture later.

It must also be noted—a fact that might have

been stated already in connection with v. 35—that the stone smites the part of the kingdom that is most vulnerable. The stone comes at a time when the kingdoms are most readily overthrown. The fact that, though the feet are smitten, the other parts of the body are broken as well indicates that, though the sovereignty passes from one empire to another, the preceding empires have not entirely ceased to be. They simply are no longer dominant empires, but their material, their civilization, religion, and culture are left, having been successively absorbed, both in their good and their bad elements. Consequently, when the last monarchy is crushed, they are all crushed. But all this cannot be expressed perfectly by the one figure that is used.

It does not disconcert us when criticism states, "The victory of Christianity over Paganism, so decisive and so divine, was in no sense a destruction of the Roman Empire." All students of history are ready to grant that the Christian Church was able to salvage out of the wreckage of the Roman Empire all elements that were worth conserving. But it is just as true that the Christian Church broke the power of pagan Rome. The disintegrating and corrupt empire crumbled through decay from within as well as through the impact of the sound morals and the healthy life of Christianity that condemned lascivious Rome. Other factors played into the process, not the least of which was the migration of barbarian hordes, who came in countless myriads from the Germanic forests and central Europe. But the deepest and most powerful forces alive in history are moral forces like Christianity in particular. Their influence is most keenly felt and goes farthest. Christianity was in a sense God's judgment upon sinful Rome.

The interpretation does not take note of the ten toes except in a general way when it mentions the fact that the two constituent materials, iron and clay, extended into the very toes. Yet we are, no doubt, correct in saying that the toes, generally speaking, represent the kingdoms into which the Roman Empire broke up when the disintegration set in. Since ten is the number of completeness or totality this would have the toes represent the sum total of these kingdoms. All attempts to name the resultant kingdoms of an earlier or a later date prove abortive and unreliable. For the number ten is definitely a symbolical number as are numbers generally in visions or dreams of this type. There might in reality be nine or eleven or nineteen or twenty. Ten represents the totality of whatever number there is. Those interpreters who attempt to find the fulfillment of prophecy in enumerations in which ten European kingdoms are reckoned as an exact ten in number are seen to have juggled the facts in an unworthy way and to cut the evidence down to suit the preordained pattern. Such attempts inspire no confidence, are misleading, and involve a misreading of prophetic utterances.

Boutflower (*In and Around the Book of Daniel,* Chap. III) has shown in a very effective way that from another point of view the choice of metals which are descriptive of the successive empires indicated by the huge statue is most apropos, especially along the line of the sequence of empires that we have suggested above. His contention is that "gold" was in a peculiar sense the metal that distinguished Babylon, having been used more profusely by her than by other nations in images, shrines, and adornments of the temples of the gods. In like manner "silver," a term that is synonymous with *money* in Hebrew and in other languages, marked in a peculiar way the more commercial spirit of Medo-Persia which sought to acquire wealth and expressed its ambitions and its sense of values in terms of money acquired. "Bronze," the metal used for implements of war, can be shown to have been distinctive of that which the Greeks emphasized and developed above all other nations. Lastly, "iron" is shown to have been a metal that was peculiarly distinctive of Rome, having been used in Roman armor and weapons and being symbolic of the cruel hardness which Rome displayed in dealing with her adversaries.

44, 45. **"And in the days of those kings the God of heaven shall raise up a kingdom which shall eternally not be destroyed, nor shall the sovereignty be left to another people. It shall crush and bring to an end all these kingdoms; but it shall stand forever. Forasmuch as thou didst see that a stone was torn loose from the mountain without hands and crushed the iron, the bronze, the clay, the silver, and the gold, the great God has made known to the king what it is that shall be after this. The dream is certain and the interpretation reliable."**

The phrase "in the days of those kings" must be carefully evaluated. Strictly speaking, no kings have been mentioned by name except Nebuchadnezzar. But "kingdoms" have been mentioned. Kingdoms, however, presuppose kings. The last of the four monarchies was referred to in the words that precede v. 44. Therefore the phrase "in the days of those kings" refers to some time during this fourth empire, whether the rulers be referred to as kings, emperors, triumvirs, or what not. More particularly shall the kingdom of God be raised up in the days when the mingling together of the diverse elements of the Roman Empire was especially in progress. For we do not believe that the expression "in the days of" refers specifically to one day such as the day of the Savior's birth or Calvary or Pentecost but to that whole period of time when the kingdom of God was taking root during the first *centuries of the Christian Era.*

The new kingdom is very plainly called a "kingdom" to show that it, too, has a head as do the king-

doms of the earth; and to show also that the ideal
aspired after in the futile empire building of man becomes a reality in "the kingdom (*malkhû*) of God"—a
phrase that is commonly used in the New Testament
and is grounded in Daniel. The Author of this last
kingdom is again "the God of heaven" (cf. v. 18), who
is so named to indicate that all agencies are under His
absolute control. The outstanding mark of this kingdom over against those that precede it is, first of all,
that "it shall eternally not be destroyed." Though the
expression "eternally" may be used in a relative sense,
the thoughts that cluster about the expression indicate
that it is here used in an absolute sense. This thought
is fully substantiated by the second statement of its
enduring character—"nor shall the sovereignty be left
to another people." That was a characteristic feature
of world empires: they kept changing hands; each had
its day; not one had permanence.

The word that is rendered "sovereignty" is
malkhû, "kingdom," but in this connection means "the
rule of the kingdom" or "the royal authority" (*BDB*),
or "sovereignty." There shall never be a time when
the kingdom of God has to bow to the authority of another. It shall, in fact, be a force that will be operative
in the overthrow of all the kingdoms that the world
produces—"all these kingdoms," for it "shall crush
and bring to an end." The kingdom of God does that
in part by the overthrow of the ancient and entrenched
wrongs which are characteristic of all the world
powers. Note how feudal systems, slavery, and caste
systems—institutions of the world powers—yield before the Spirit of Christ in His church. To some extent this overthrow is still future, for the final victory
of the church coincides with the day of judgment. Then
Christ and His saints shall judge and overthrow whatever of sin or wrong still remains. In this overthrow
there must be included also the gentle victory of the

gospel which makes its gracious influence felt and conquers, but not with violence and bloodshed. Though thus engaged in continually overthrowing what the world constructs, such effort shall not wear out God's kingdom: "but it shall stand forever."

45. This verse seems to lack a conclusion that is in conformity with what the first part of it says shall be explained. Yet if the meaning of the tearing loose of the stone be only this, that "the great God has made known to the king what it is that shall be after this," then this verse apparently means that the activity of the stone points to the one new feature to be looked for in the future. Heretofore all that history seemed to amount to was: kingdom conquering and replacing kingdom. That, however, is not an inevitable, unalterable cycle. For a new power, not conditioned by man's control, shall come into operation and shall break the old order of things and establish a lasting and definite victory. That's the burden of the future, that is "what shall be after this." On this victorious note the interpretation ends. The interpreter speaks with the certainty of one who knows, and knows also when he has said enough. So he tersely informs the king that this dream as such is "certain"—he knows he is not guessing—"and the interpretation reliable," i.e., trustworthy. Throughout the narration of the dream and of the interpretation there were absolutely no hesitancy and fumbling on Daniel's part. Such is the certainty of every word that comes from God.

Thus the dream sketched the course of the history of the world in bold strokes. Since "the kingdom of God is at hand" men have still been blundering along, trying to establish a lasting world power. But each product of human effort shall go the way of all flesh. Christ's kingdom outlasts them all and conquers them. It is the power that has the hardness of stone that endures and yet grows till, mountain-like, it towers

over and fills the entire world. It seems questionable
to refer the mountain from which the stone is torn to
Mt. Zion, which would be a unique way of saying that
salvation is of the Jews. This mountain seems to be
merely a part of the necessary framework of the
dream. For that reason the original mountain was not
mentioned in v. 34. Yet it cannot be denied that Isa.
2:2 seems to point in this direction, cf. Mic. 4:1.

With strange unanimity it is stated by all commentators that the stone, *'ébhen,* signifies the kingdom
of Christ. *Farrar* says: "All alike are agreed that by
the mysterious rock-fragment the writer meant the
Messianic Kingdom." *Montgomery* assures as that the
Jewish commentators *Rashi* and *Aben Ezra* "tersely
state that the final kingdom is that of King Messiah."

The correctness of the details of this interpretation will be further substantiated when the parallel
chapters, viz., 7 and 8, of this book are examined more
closely. Then, too, opportunity will be offered of
proving more fully the groundlessness of the claim
that the second empire is the Median. A similar opportunity will be offered in connection with 5:31, in
examining the name "Darius the Mede."

f) The Results of the Interpretation, 2:46-49.

**46, 47. Thereupon King Nebuchadnezzar fell
upon his face and cast himself down before Daniel
and commanded that oblations and soothing offerings be presented to him. The king answered Daniel
and said, "Of a truth, your God is a God of gods and
a Lord of kings and a revealer of mysteries, for thou
hast been able to reveal this mystery."**

Nebuchadnezzar is so deeply impressed by the
manifestation of the power and the knowledge of the
Almighty that he bestows singular honors upon the one
whom God used to transmit this revelation. He casts
himself down before God's prophet as he would before

God. But Daniel had already in v. 30 clearly asserted his personal inability to do more than any other of his fellow mortals might do. In concluding his interpretation in v. 45 he had again ascribed the revelation to God. This must have clarified the king's thinking and led him to worship God by honoring His representative.

It is quite true that the text says that the adoration as well as the sacrifices were offered to Daniel. Yet we cannot but feel that the religious king intended divine honors for the God of Daniel. Had it been otherwise, we have every reason for believing that Daniel would have refused to permit such homage. The critics point out the writer's lack of discernment in letting Daniel refuse to eat unclean food (chapter 1) but thinking nothing of accepting worship which was due only to God. However, they make little or nothing of the earlier explanations and protestations on the part of Daniel which remove the misunderstandings before they can take root in the king's heart. "Oblation," *minchah*, is any sort of gift; *nicho(a)ch* is something "soothing," calculated to please the deity.

47. Nebuchadnezzar's words prove more clearly than anything else could what he meant by his oblations, for he confesses nothing regarding Daniel but does make rather far-reaching admissions with reference to Daniel's God. He begins with an emphatic "of a truth." He continues by ascribing to Him a position that is higher than that of many other gods. The king discreetly leaves his own gods out of the discussion. For a polytheist to admit the existence of another god is not strange. To the king "Merodach, the healer and protector of mankind, and his son Nebo, the god of revelation and knowledge,"* were still the most important of all. That Daniel's God was in a special way

---

op. cit. p. 150, Par. 1054.

concerned with rulers and their sovereignty is admitted by the words that describe Him as a "Lord of kings." And lastly—it seems somewhat reluctantly— he admits that God is also "a revealer of mysteries" and substantiates this admission by the statement, "For thou hast been able to reveal this mystery." For Nebuchadnezzar is now treading on dangerous ground if, as quoted above, his god Nebo is "the god of revelation and knowledge." This confession seems to have been forced from the king's lips. But in its entirety it was apparently made by one who was overwhelmed by what he had just witnessed. *Thomson* points out rather appropriately that Nebuchadnezzar does not admit that *Yahweh* is *"the* God of gods" and also adduces proof that it was not uncommon in days of old for men to ascribe a sovereign position to several gods, not implying, however, that any one of those mentioned was absolutely supreme.

48. **Then the king made Daniel great and gave him many and great gifts and made him ruler over the entire province of Babylon and chief prefect over all the wise men of Babylon.**

According to v. 6 the king had promised munificent gifts and royal rewards to the man who was successful in giving him an understanding of his dream. The king is now faithful in keeping his promises although all these honors may not have been conferred at once. If he "made Daniel great," that seems to imply that he conferred social standing upon him, or else it is a comprehensive statement that is intended to include the separate honors that follow. He also "gave him many and great gifts," which might have included a palace, a retinue of servants, wealth, and splendid robes—if we care to let our imagination run on for a bit. His official position is to be "ruler over the entire province of Babylon," which, it would seem, must have been the chief of all the provinces of the realm but certainly not the Babylonian Empire itself. As far as the wise men are concerned, over whom he has definitely established his superiority, he becomes "chief prefect" of all those within his own province of Babylon. It is not often that such recognition comes to a man who is so young. But God had occasion to make use of this man for purposes of His own, and such a high station was best suited to make Daniel's efforts effective.

They who seize upon every pretext to discredit the author of the book as though he had been but poorly informed and so wrote many things that are quite inconsistent—these persons, we say, make it appear as being highly incongruous that a man who was so conscientious about contamination by things heathen should be represented as being quite ready to be identified with the wise men of Babylon and, no doubt, share in their religion and superstitious practices. However, the last part of the charge, which is the incriminating element in it, is clearly inserted into the text. Daniel merely becomes "chief prefect" of the wise men. His oversight of them laid no restrictions or demands upon him in matters of believing or practicing as they did just as little as the learning of the wisdom of Babylon, according to chapter one, involved the obligation to practice things that were hostile to the spirit of the religion of Israel.

49. **And Daniel asked the king to appoint Shadrach, Meshach, and Abednego over the affairs of the province of Babylon. But Daniel was in the gate of the king.**

It would have been ungrateful on the part of Daniel not to have seen to it that his friends shared in the rewards which the king was bestowing. They had helped him by means of their prayers. Why should he reap the rewards alone? Daniel also recognized that they were men of parts; the first public tests had demonstrated that quite convincingly. He was merely asking that positions commensurate with their talents be bestowed upon these men. Though he himself was made "ruler over the entire province of Babylon" he apparently did not have freedom in the matter of the appointment of secondary officials. So he prevailed upon the king to appoint his three friends "over the affairs (*'abhidha'* = 'work') of the province of Babylon." These positions were apparently not sinecures. Daniel's position naturally raised him to the rank of one at court, or, as the phrase of that day had it, he "was in the gate of the king."

So we are prepared for the development of things in the next chapter though the things stated in this verse serve more directly as an adequate conclusion of the story of the great peril in which Daniel and his companions had found themselves. Minor details are omitted as being unessential to the purpose of the book. We are not even told that all the wise men were spared because of the revelation that came to Daniel, nor how truly grateful they were.

One impression remains with the attentive reader rather clearly, and that is the thought that it always has been and always will be the lot of the kingdoms that the might of man establishes to go the way of all flesh and to collapse. Each new combination of forces or nations that is tried to achieve the result of a lasting kingdom invariably meets with the same overthrow. So history is a succession of defeats. But for the one who knows the Almighty God there is hope. History cannot be a mere futility to him, for the Omnipotent One will in due season make it apparent, as His own already now know it to be, that He has a kingdom that will never be overthrown, and that will finally stand out as eternal and entirely successful. This kingdom is the hope of mankind and God's vindication in the course of history that He has not labored in vain. The labors of His Christ shall be crowned with ultimate and perfect success.

HOMILETICAL SUGGESTIONS

Attaching to the thoughts suggested in the preceding paragraph, we suggest that, on the one hand, one might dwell on the weakness of earthly kingdoms and empires; how they are being continually built up merely to yield place to the next claimant for supremacy; and how they finally end in a great catastrophe. At the same time a steady process of deterioration of empires is going on as is indicated by the succession of metals mentioned in the dream. The subject is of such moment and so amply detailed and at the same time so little understood that anyone might well make an issue of it. Here we have the folly of imperialism.

The major emphasis, however, should be laid on the enduring character of the kingdom of Christ. Verses 34-45 could be the text. The fate of the empires of this world would in this case merely serve as the dark background for the glorious truth concerning Christ's eternal kingdom.

It should, in this connection, not be forgotten that the things that the Savior teaches concerning His kingdom are based directly on Daniel's presentation of the truth involved.

CHAPTER III

B. The Three Men in the Fiery Furnace:
The World Power Cannot Imperil the Safety
of God's Saints

The second chapter showed the final outcome of the growth and the success of the world power—the world power must crumble. Yet while its power lasts, must the kingdoms of this world not be feared by God's own because of the harm these enemies can and will do to God's saints? This chapter gives the answer, "No"; He that is with us is greater than he that is with them.

In point of style a certain feature may be noted. Though judgments on this question are largely subjective in character, some feel (e.g., *Zoeckler*) that this chapter has an intentional similarity to the style commonly found in monumental inscriptions that record the official decrees of kings—a certain formal dignity, long lists of high officials and musical instruments, repeated even three times in the case of the instruments.

More vital is the question whether we are dealing with an event that is purely historical in character. There is nothing in the narrative as such which savors of unreality, fiction, or untruth. They who approach every miracle with the assumption that, because it is a miracle, it very likely did not take place, can hardly do otherwise than to stress to the utmost every feature that can be made to seem difficult or even preposterous. The list of objections, popular with some since the days of Rationalism, includes matters such as the prohibitive cost of a solid gold image; the instability of so slender a statue; the disorder resulting in the kingdom because of the assembling of *all* dignitaries and authorities at Dura; the unseemliness of the bold taunts of the three confessors; the second miracle that is necessary in order to have the executioners slain by the flames of the furnace; then primarily the miraculous preservation of the three youths; and then even the unbelievable sequel—no smell of smoke had passed upon them. These and other objections constitute the stock in trade of some who treat this subject. Most of these items will be examined in order as we proceed.

Farrar labels the chapter "historic fiction" although he conceives its purpose to be "to inculcate the noblest truths" and says he has "always regarded it as one of the most precious among the narrative chapters of Scripture." But even if such fulsome praise is bestowed upon this chapter as to cause *Farrar* to say that it "is not only superb in its imaginative grandeur, but still more in the manner in which it sets forth the piety of ultimate faithfulness," we cannot regard such a position as satisfactory or correct. A purely fictional deliverance is small comfort to a man who is confronted by a factual peril of death. Solid words of God or solid facts alone avail under such circumstances. To cite as parallel to such "historic fiction" the parables of Christ is a misapplication of the latter.

Equally unsatisfactory is the theory (*Montgomery*) that the author did not invent this story "but drew its materials from popular legends." The situation remains the same as that just described: having no guaranty of the truth of the legend, because legends, in the very nature of the case, are very largely composed of what is neither true nor possible, we have no guaranty of the validity of any deductions or any comfort that we may attempt to draw from the legend.

We must also disapprove those comparisons which place this chapter into the class of later Jewish writings—the *Talmud* and the *Midrash*. It may be true enough in regard to these writings that "the doctrine is everything; the mode of presentation has no independent value," and to claim that "the inveterate tendency of Jewish teachers" is "to convey doctrine by concrete stories and illustrations, and not in the form of abstract thought." But those of us who hold firmly to the doctrine of plenary inspiration as taught by the Sacred Scriptures themselves cannot concede that the Biblical books or any parts of them stand on the low level of the *Talmud* or the *Midrash,* which contain much that is trivial, fantastical, absurd, and utterly worthless.

Our chapter is, therefore, a straightforward account of a miraculous deliverance that is fully on a par with all the rest of Holy Writ as to form and content and is approved by the New Testament allusion to it, Heb. 11:34: "quenched the power of fire."

a) *The Test by Means of the Golden Image, v. 1-7.*

1. **Nebuchadnezzar, the king, made an image of gold; its height was sixty cubits and its breadth six cubits. He set it up in the plain of Dura in the province of Babylon.**

When did he do this? It cannot be important to know the time, otherwise Daniel would have recorded it. The Greek translators venture a guess when they insert at this point "in the eighteenth year of King Nebuchadnezzar." This strikes pretty close to the year of the destruction of Jerusalem (cf. II Kings 25:8) and is a supposition which is apparently based on the idea that the sack of Jerusalem and the overthrow of Judah particularly inspired the king to this act of reverence to his gods. However, Judah belonged to the smaller fry among the nations, and its overthrow will hardly have begotten great joy in Nebuchadnezzar's heart. It would be reasonable to expect that Nebuchadnezzar would not have erected such an image near the beginning of his reign (604 B. C.) when many of his conquests were still to be made. Nor at or near the end of his reign (562 B. C.), when the incentive for such an act would hardly be found; but at some time when he had completed his major conquests and had felt the magnitude and the strength of his empire.

The question arises very naturally, "What did this image represent?" Suppositions range from Nebuchadnezzar himself or one of his gods, particularly Bel or Marduk, to the symbol of the world power or "the symbol of allegiance to the empire." Though much may be said for each of these suggestions, we feel that the second last has most in its favor—"the symbol of the world power established by Nebuchadnezzar" (*Keil*). It would seem so natural to have mentioned the name of the god whose image it was if it had been the image of a god or even of Nebuchadnezzar. It is not quite to the point to call it "the symbol of allegiance" (*Montgomery*) because the allegiance was to be offered by the assembled people, not embodied in the image: the people were not to worship allegiance or its symbol. The image could have taken the form of either the king or of some favorite god of his.

The fact that the image was made of gold may, indeed, have been the result of a remembrance on the king's part of what his own dream image had conveyed (2:36): "thou art the head of gold." We are at once confronted with the question: "Had Nebuchadnezzar forgotten the rest of the revelation that chapter two reports, in particular the claims of the true God as they had come home to him as a result of Daniel's interpretation?" These impressions had apparently become much dimmed, and since no conversion of any sort had resulted on Nebuchadnezzar's part, the dense fog of heathenism had again enfolded him rather closely. He now speaks and acts in a fashion that is typically heathen and does what any king of his type would have felt much inclined to do.

The reader may be startled for a moment when he thinks of the enormous amount of gold that so huge an image would require in case it were solid. Even if we allow for the possibility of fabulous wealth in the treasuries of Nebuchadnezzar—a matter concerning which we possess no authoritative information—the fortune involved would still stagger us. However, Biblical evidence gives ample warrant for concluding that the core of the statue was wood and that gold plates were skillfully laid over the entire surface. Note how the expression "golden altar" is used in Exod. 39: 38; 40:5. Yet Exod. 37:25, 26 informs us that this altar was made of "acacia wood," and that Moses "overlaid it with pure gold." Referring specifically to idols, Isa. 40:19; 41:7 describe the process of over-laying with gold as involving the use of nails and solder. Isaiah is very evidently describing the current method in the manufacture of images. Jeremiah 10:3-9 agrees with this. The Greek term χρύσεα ξόανα implies the same type of image.

The word for "image" is *ts^elem*. This means "image" in the very broadest sense—a figure of a human being, an idol image, for that matter even an obelisk. In this case the proportions disturb us: if a living being, human or divine, was represented, then the ratio 60:6 or ¹⁰.:1 hardly agrees with the proportions of a human figure in which height and breadth are in the ratio of 6:1 or even 5:1. This leads the majority of commentators to assume that the term *ts^elem* is elastic enough to allow for an image that was provided with a proportionately tall pedestal. Many suggest 24 cubits of pedestal and 36 cubits of image proper in order to secure a human figure atop the pedestal in the proportion of 6:1. One might go still farther. Not infrequently in days of old monumental figures were primarily pillars, perhaps more or less square, provided with feet and surmounted by a human bust. *Montgomery* even cites an apt parallel where this same root *ts*ᵉ*lem* appears in the Nerab inscription "where the stone is decorated at the top with the relief of the bust of a human body." Other commentators cite as parallel a certain statue of Apollo, which consisted of a pillar to which feet and a head had been affixed. If this strikes us as presenting a somewhat grotesque though gigantic figure, we must remember that much of the art of antiquity, particularly the Babylonian, sought to impress the beholder by vastness of size. To represent the victorious Babylonian world power only a heroic image would suffice.

The height of the image is not without parallels in antiquity. It is customary to draw attention to a passage in Herodotus (1:183 according to *Montgomery*) in which he describes a great golden statue of Zeus which was found in a temple at Babylon in his day, in the precincts of which temple a statue of a man, also of gold, was found which was twelve cubits high. The statue of Zeus must apparently have been by far the larger, but Herodotus was apparently unable to secure measurements in the temple proper. Later the historian Diodorus Siculus tells of three golden images on the top of the Belus temple, "the first of which was forty feet high, weighing 1,000 Babylonian talents." But even Nebuchadnezzar's image could not quite cope with the famous Colossus at Rhodes which was reputed to have been seventy cubits high.

The "plain," *biq'ath*, really means a "valley-plain." "Dura" is a rather common name in Mesopotamia, being a name that is applicable to any place which is enclosed by a wall. It seems quite likely that a

spot by this name about six miles south of Babylon may
be the one referred to, for a massive square of brick
construction is still to be seen there which is fourteen
meters square and six meters high. This may have
served as a base for the image or have been the
pedestal or a part of it.

2, 3. **Then Nebuchadnezzar, the king, sent to
assemble the satraps, prefects, governors, counselors, treasurers, law-bearers, magistrates, and all
officials of the provinces to come to the dedication of
the image which Nebuchadnezzar, the king, had
set up. Then the satraps, prefects, governors, counselors, treasurers, law-bearers, magistrates, and all
officials of the provinces were assembled for the
dedication of the image which Nebuchadnezzar, the
king, had set up; and they stood before the image
that Nebuchadnezzar had set up.**

In days of old such images were solemnly dedicated. In this instance Nebuchadnezzar reckoned, no
doubt, with the psychological effect that such a dedication would produce. The sight of the whole body of
officials, great and small, civil, military, and judicial,
bowing before this image in unison must have had an
overpowering effect by giving a drastic display of the
power of the empire. But above all this dedication gave
opportunity for all officials assembled to take a common oath of fealty to the empire and its victorious
king. For in days of old practically all nations were
still at least so religious as to believe that success in
arms was attributable to the power of the gods. If a
nation had prevailed over another nation, the thing
that had happened behind the scenes was that the
victorious nation's god· or gods had prevailed over
those of the vanquished. This being a universal conviction, there could hardly be any hesitancy to confess
such a conviction. Such a confession was practically

what Nebuchadnezzar asked. To have all make the confession simultaneously would make the occasion impressive.

From all this it appears that there could be no attempt on the king's part to practice any religious persecution, or to interfere with anyone's worship of his own gods, or to compel men to accept a new god as their own. The king expected men to do what men naturally expected to do, but he wanted them to do it in an impressive setting that would enhance the glamor of the Chaldean Empire.

All this should be borne in mind because the situation is not parallel to that at the time of Antiochus Epiphanes, who did practice religious persecution. Consequently they err who claim that the writer of the book took events from Daniel's time and drew lessons and comfort from them for his contemporaries. We should then have a misfit instead of a parallel.

The old criticism that is voiced at this point scarcely deserves to be mentioned: that the affairs of the empire would have lapsed into confusion in the absence of all heads. But, surely, the organization of the realm could hardly have been so loose that, as soon as the department heads happened to be away from their offices, rank confusion prevailed.

We cannot be too sure of the meaning of the official titles occurring in these verses. For, in the first place, with the differences of administration and office that prevail between those times and ours, we scarcely have exact equivalents even if we should happen to know exactly what offices these officials held. The following listing will show a part of our problem.

1. *'achashdarpenayya'* = "satraps" (Persian: protectors of the realm).
2. *śighnayya'* = "prefects" (Aramaic).
3. *pachᵃwatha'* = "g o v e r n o r s" (Babylonian or Persian).

4. *'ᵃdhargazᵉrayya'* = "counselors" (Persian).
5. *gᵉdhobhrayya'* = "treasurers" (dubious).
6. *dᵉthobhrayya'* = "law-bearers" (Persian).
7. *tiphtaye'* = "magistrates" (dubious).

Three, perhaps four, are terms that are derived from the Persian. One seems to be Aramaic. One could be Babylonian. Two are dubious although *K. W.* derives the last one from the Old Persian. Many of the meanings finally arrived at are partly conjectural. But despite all that, it is a list that is typical in documents of those days. Sargon has left us an inscription that was made after the completion of his new palace Sharrukin: "Sargon established himself in his palace with the princes of all lands, the regents of his country, the governors, presidents, magnates, honorable and senators of Assyria, and instituted a feast" (*Montgomery*). We involuntarily recall the scene presented in Esther 1:3 where a like assembly of officials was made although for a different purpose. Rulers have always loved to stage gatherings that gave them opportunity to display their power and their wealth.

The preponderance of *Persian* names about fifty years before the Persians became dominant might at first glance prove disconcerting in what is supposed to be a list of officials who were gathered by the *Babylonian* monarch. *Meinhold* states the case for this side of the question: "The Persian names make it impossible to assume that this section was composed during the time of the Exile. An exile could not have given Persian names to men who governed Babylonian provinces; even a reference to the Persian period of Daniel's life cannot make the case plausible." However, a little more reflection on the "Persian period of Daniel's life" will show us that the list as it stands is exactly what we must expect. For Daniel will surely have taken pains as nearly as possible to bring his book up to date and to have kept it so in case certain portions had been written earlier in his long life. We know that the gigantic and revolutionary upheaval known as the Persian conquest or the founding of the Persian Empire occurred toward the end of Daniel's life. Such conquests involved a reshaping of the whole of the Babylonian Empire after the Persian pattern. Persian names would naturally be substituted for the old Babylonian terms wherever possible. Being a man of high standing also in the Persian realm (6:2), Daniel would be thoroughly informed as to the details of this reorganization. He would then most likely have substituted the corresponding new terms for the old Babylonian names also in our chapter so as not to leave his book cumbered with a lot of terms of antiquarian interest instead of terms that would be readily understood. This explanation is so plausible that we cannot do otherwise than to suppose that the very nature of this list harmonizes perfectly with what we should have expected Daniel to write.

The scene pictured by these verses closes with the assembled multitude's standing expectantly before the image awaiting the signal to give token of its homage and its loyalty.

4-7. **Then the herald cried aloud: "To you it is commanded, O peoples, nations, and tongues, that at the moment that ye shall hear the sound of the horn, the pipe, the zither, the trigon, the lyre, the bagpipe, and every other sort of musical instrument, ye shall fall down and do homage to the golden image which Nebuchadnezzar, the king, hath set up. And whosoever shall not fall down and do homage shall instantly be cast into the midst of a furnace of flaming fire." Therefore at the time when all the peoples heard the sound of the horn, the pipe, the zither, the trigon, the lyre, and every other kind of musical instrument, all peoples and nations and**

tongues did homage to the golden image which Nebuchadnezzar, the king, had set up.

The royal "herald," *karôz*, makes the expected proclamation. It is true that this word bears a striking resemblance to the corresponding Greek word κῆρυξ. However, as *Haevernick* has shown rather exhaustively, the root involved can with equal facility be traced to Semitic origins because certain types of these terms are inclined to be onomatopoetic.

Into this discussion as to the possibility of the Greek origin of certain words used in Daniel must be drawn the names of some of the musical instruments mentioned in this connection, namely, at least three: *qaythros*, analogous to κίθαρις; *p^esanterîn*, resembling ψαλτήριον; and *sûmponyah*, somewhat like συμφωνία. We are ready to concede the possibility that these words may represent the names of instruments that were originally known to the Greeks, and that they may have retained their Greek names when they were adopted by the Babylonians. For we know with what tenacity the names of foreign instruments will cling to a particular instrument: "violin" has practically displaced "fiddle"; "viola," "cello," and the like are not of English origin; "ukulele" is of Hawaiian origin. But there is another possibility: these names may originally have been Semitic and have been retained in analogous Greek names—in which case, however, the Greek συμφωνία, a compound, would be somewhat unusual.

Nevertheless, even though we concede that the names of these three instruments plus the "herald" are words of Greek origin, we have said nothing that might lend weight to a later dating of the book of Daniel. To assume that Greek words would begin to appear in Hebrew or Aramaic only after Alexander's Greek empire had been established is to ignore historical evidence which points to contacts with the

Greeks before Nebuchadnezzar's time. *Kliefoth* summarizes the available evidence. He says: "If one recalls that reciprocal relations between Assyria and Greece were established already before the beginning of the Assyrian Empire, brought about by the Semitic peoples which were crowded toward Asia Minor by the Assyrians, Semitic peoples such as the Solymians, the Lykians, and the Lydians, on the other hand the Ionian Greeks also established mercantile connections. Then it is to be remembered that from very early times Sinope (on the Black Sea) had been an outpost both of Assyrian trade and of Assyrian power, as well as of Greek commercial settlements. Also that in the Assyrian army of Esarhaddon (682 B. C.) as well as later in the Babylonian army of Nebuchadnezzar, especially in the wars that the latter waged in Syria and Palestine against Phoenicians and Egyptians, Greek mercenary troops were found. Also that the most manifold effects of these contacts appear on the part of the Greeks. Also that the clearest traces of this Semitic, Assyrian, and Babylonian influence appear in the Greek language, religion, her musical instruments and melodies, and in the philosophy of Pythogoras."

We need offer no further explanation for the presence of these Greek words in the Aramaic of Daniel's time. In fact, Wilson has turned the argument as it should be turned when he advances the claim that, if Daniel had been written in the days of Antiochus Epiphanes, it would be very difficult to explain why so few words of Greek origin occur in the Aramaic of Daniel.*

The persons addressed by the herald are the "peoples, nations, and tongues." "Peoples," *'ammayya'*, are the larger national units; "nations," *'ummayya'*,

---

*Wilson, Robert Dick, "The Aramaic of Daniel," in *Biblical and Theological Studies*, New York: Chas. Scribner's Sons (1912), p. 296.

are the smaller tribal groups; and "tongues," *lishsha-nayya'*, are those groups that are affiliated by the use of a common language, whether they be of the same racial stock or not. Though *'iddan* means "time" it must here mean "point of time" (*B D B*) and so may be translated "at the moment."

The sound of such a heterogeneous assortment of musical instruments shrieking, blowing, and thrumming simultaneously would seem truly barbarous to us. But it must be remembered that they furnished only a signal and were designed to impress the hearers by their variety and their volume of sound. Furthermore, symphonic music had not yet developed to any extent in those early days.

The individual instruments can be identified with a fair degree of certainty. The *qe'ren*, from the general meaning "horn" of a beast, comes to signify a "musical horn." The *mashrôqîth*, from the root to "whistle," suggest an instrument with a shrill sound; it is usually assumed that a couple of reeds or Pan's pipe is meant. The sound may have resembled the fife. The "zither" has an analogous name, *qaythros*, which should perhaps have been pointed *qîthros* in the Aramaic. That it was a stringed instrument is certain although we cannot determine the number of strings it had. The "trigon," known also to the Greeks and the Romans, was called *sabkha'*, for which "sackbut" (*A. V.*), an early form of the slide trombone, is an incorrect translation. For the instrument is thought to have consisted of a triangular board with short strings which gave off high-pitched notes. The word we translated "lyre" is *pesanterîn*, which could also have been rendered "harp," being a stringed instrument with twenty strings. The term "psaltery" (*A. V.*) does not usually suggest this type of instrument. It is derived from the analogous Greek word. The "bagpipe" is again a wind instrument— the "dulcimer" (*A. V.*) is a stringed instrument—as the Greek name συμφωνία, a "sounding together," suggests. Whether it bore any resemblance to the well-known Scotch instrument is highly problematical.

Even these names do not exhaust the variety actually found in that orchestra, for the account adds "and every other sort of musical instrument." *Kol z^eney z^emara,* literally, "every sort of music," must mean "every *other* sort" after the preceding enumeration and not just "music" (*A. V.*) but "musical instruments." *Zan,* "sort," is a Persian loan word "adopted early in Aramaic"—fifth century (*Charles*).

The royal edict demands that, when this cacophonic blast sounds forth, all officials assembled at once "fall down and do homage," i.e., not only prostrate themselves but do it in token of submission to the world power that conquered them. Some have drawn unwarranted conclusions from the word "do homage," *s^eghidh,* as though its use must imply that the image of some deity stood before them. The word may be used thus, but it must not be so construed.

6. The combination *man-dî* gives the interrogative "who" the meaning "whosoever." The expression "instantly" resembles "at the moment" (v. 5), for it means "in that hour" but in this connection comes to mean "at once," *sofort, K. W.* The expression "in that hour" has the anticipative use of the suffix (*Stev.* 5, 14), for the Aramaic says "in it the hour." The translation of *A. V.,* "burning fiery furnace," might lead to the conclusion that a definite furnace was in complete readiness with the fire already kindled, a fact that would have lent a certain peremptory touch to the king's edict. However, according to the original this reads "a furnace of burning fire," we should say "of flaming fire." That leaves the question open as to whether the fire had been kindled in advance.

7. At the given signal the huge multitude falls

prostrate. If the added threat seems to suggest that such an empire was built very largely upon the harsh use of power, that is only too correct. Assyrian and Babylonian rulers secured the results desired by the unscrupulous use of power.

In this catalogue of the musical instruments the "bagpipe" is not mentioned separately as it is in the first list. *K*ᵉ*dhî*, "when," is used in this sense in 5:20; 6:11, 15 and in Aramaic papyri of the fourth and the fifth century B. C. (*Charles*).

It should yet be remarked that the *religious* significance of this act of general homage by the assembled officials was largely incidental. It was the *political* significance of the event that stood out. He who refused submission was a rebel. A modern parallel would be requiring an oath of submission and good behavior on the part of a subject group.

b)   The Accusation of Daniel's Three Friends, v. 8-12.

8-12.   **Thereupon at that time certain Chaldeans came near and maliciously accused the Jews. They answered and said to Nebuchadnezzar, the king: "O king, live forever. Thou, O king, didst issue a decree that every man who should hear the sound of the horn, the pipe, the zither, the trigon, the lyre, and the bagpipe, and all other kinds of musical instruments should fall down and do homage to the image of gold. And whosoever should not fall down and do homage should be thrown into the midst of a furnace of flaming fire. Now there are certain Jews whom thou didst appoint over the business of the province of Babylon, Shadrach, Meshach, and Abednego. These men have had no regard for thee, O king; thy gods they do not worship, and to the image of gold which thou hast set up they do not do homage."**

Strange to say, the failure of Daniel's three friends to obey the king's command is not chronicled separately. It is discovered from the report of the Chaldeans. They, the prominent leading class of court astrologers (cf. remarks on 2:2), are the ones who bring charges against the faithful three. The *Aramaic* has the common Semitic expression "devour the pieces of the Jews." Just how this comes to mean "slander or accuse" is not clearly apparent, but the malice of the procedure is in evidence, and so we agree with *B D B*, who translate "accuse maliciously."

From the whole tenor of their report it is clear that jealousy and envy motivate their deed throughout. Their reference to the fact that the king had ventured to place these foreigners "over the business of the province of Babylon" shows clearly how they felt about this appointment. They come just short of reproving the king for such inconsiderate advancement of men who were no better than traitorous rebels. They play upon the king's personal feelings in the matter when they tell him: "These men have no regard (*te͑em*) for thee, O king." Wounded vanity and unreasoning jealousy motivate what looks like a patriotic disclosure. *Gubhrîn*, "men," in this idiom means "certain" (Chaldeans) ; so *Charles*.

As for details (v. 9), the participles are used as regular finite verbs; there is therefore no good reason for a translation such as "they were answering and saying." The entire accusation is patterned after the fulsome style of Oriental pronouncements. In v. 12 the fact that the thought of the service of the gods is coupled with the worship of the golden image does not invalidate our contention that the whole issue was primarily political. For to acknowledge Nebuchadnezzar's sovereignty was in reality tantamount to saying that his gods had gained the upper hand. Consequently the service of the gods was involved at least to this extent. The noun *ᵉlahaykh,* as the "y" indicates, is intended as a plural and is best translated "gods," for Nebuchadnezzar was a typical polytheist.

It would be best here to dispose of the question, "Where was Daniel at this time?" Most important of all is the fact that Daniel did not deem it worth reporting his absence because it did not actually have any bearing upon the case. In the second place, no one knows the answer to the question, consequently no man on either side of the argument can prove anything for or against the contentions that are raised. In other words, the entire discussion must prove futile. Besides, no one can prove that Daniel was among those of whom homage was to be exacted. It might be possible that 2:49—"Daniel was in the gate of the king"— indicates so high a position that an oath of loyalty was not to be demanded of him. But even that we cannot prove though that contention seems very reasonable to us.

From days of old suggestions have been advanced such as that Daniel was sick at the time as he was known to be later; or that he was absent from the capital on official business. Even the assumption that he was among those who refused to fall down before the king's image but was not accused because the Chaldeans sought to dispose of his friends first and could not quite venture to make him the target of their attacks—even this assumption is by no means capable of proof. But, surely, what can be neither proved nor disproved can hardly constitute ground for criticism. No writer is to be faulted merely because he fails to answer a secondary question in which we happen to be interested.

The *yathᵉhon* (v. 12) is the one instance of *yath,* a sign of the accusative (*Stev.* 4, 3), in Biblical Aramaic.

c) *The Steadfastness of the Faithful Three,*
v. 13-18.

13-15. **Thereupon Nebuchadnezzar, in
wrath and hot anger, commanded to bring Shadrach, Meshach, and Abednego. Then these men were
brought before the king. Nebuchadnezzar answered
and said to them: "Is it true, Shadrach, Meshach,
and Abednego, that as far as my god is concerned,
ye are not worshiping him, and as far as the image
of gold is concerned which I have set up, ye are not
doing homage to it? Now if ye will be ready at the
time when ye shall hear the sound of the horn, the
pipe, the zither, the trigon, the lyre, and the bagpipe and all other sorts of musical instruments to
fall down and to do homage to the image which I
have made, well and good; but if ye will not do
homage, in that very instant ye shall be cast into the
midst of the furnace of flaming fire. And who is the
God that can deliver you out of my hand?"**

We can readily understand how the absolute
monarch becomes very much angered at the presump-
tion, as he deems it, of these three men. He is perhaps
aroused all the more because they had, upon Daniel's
petition, been advanced to positions of rare importance.

The form *lᵉhaythayah* is Haphel infinitive of
'ᵃthah. The *heythayû* in the last clause has not yet been
explained in a satisfactory way. To call it a Hophal is
hardly reasonable. It is perhaps a secondary Haphel
form with an indefinite subject.

14. *Hatsᵉdha'* is usually explained as being compounded of the interrogative and *tsᵉdha'* "(malicious)
purpose," for the parallel *Hebrew* root means "to lie
in wait." Therefore *A. R. V.*: "Is it of purpose?" But
an ostracon found by Lidzbarski uses the word in the
sense "true" (*Montgomery*), and so we are taken
back to *A. V.*, "Is it true?" *Luther* has it amount to
the same thing, *wie?*

The king's double question does not conflict with our explanations given above, for it makes a clear distinction between the image set up and the acknowledgment of the gods whose dominion and power it represents. From the king's point of view it is unbelievable that anyone should be so bold as to venture to refuse to obey the king's demand. Yet he purposes to give them another chance. He seems to allow that there may have been some misunderstanding. He will not have been ignorant of the jealousy that motivated the accusers. He will then be guided by the evidence which his own eyes behold. A measure of fairness is apparent in this approach.

15. The first part of the verse amounts to a protasis without an apodosis. Similar cases of aposiopesis are found in Exod. 32:32 and Luke 13:9. We have supplied as the apodosis "well and good" (*Gordon*) ; "well" (*A. V.*) would have been sufficient. We might have used a statement such as "ye shall not die." *Luther* gets a spirited translation by making the initial "if" clause imperative: *Wohlan, schickt euch!*

The king's words are marked by a spurious regal pomp in that, quoting from his own edict, he recites the whole catalogue of musical instruments, the sound of whose rolling phrases seems to please him. His final challenge is not quite downright insolence, but it is at least an impious challenge of the Almighty, concerning whose supreme power he had sufficient evidence to cause him to speak with modest restraint. The *hû'* in this last question is not a copula but reenforces the interrogative so as to yield the meaning "what god, if any, is there," etc?

16-18. Shadrach, Meshach, and Abednego answered and said to the king: "O Nebuchadnezzar, we need not answer you a word in this matter. If our God, whom we worship, is able to deliver us from a furnace of flaming fire and from thy hand,

O king, He will deliver us; but if not, then be it known to thee, O king, we will not worship thy god, nor will we do homage to the image of gold which thou hast set up."

These three men know the blindness of the heathen heart. Lengthy explanations will not be understood; an extended defence will not impress the darkened mind of the king. Therefore their attitude is that, the more resolutely they persist in their refusal and commit their souls to the hand of their faithful God, the more clearly will the issues stand out. They are right, therefore, in claiming: "We need not answer you a word in this matter." They are not insolent. Their words are not tainted by arrogance.

Their answer must be considered as a whole. To stop short with the first sentence would create an unnecessary difficulty. To regard the rest of the answer as explaining why there is no need of answering the king at length puts us on the right track. There is no need of words because either God will deliver them, and the issues will then be cleared up, for God is well able to do it, or else, for reasons best known to Him, He will not be able to deliver them; yet even in that case they cannot alter their position and do anything other than what they originally purposed to do. Even their death will help to clarify the issues. *Gordon* may be right with his rendering: "We need not waste any words in discussing this matter with you."

Some interpreters have considered the direct address, "O Nebuchadnezzar," unseemly and so make the preceding *lᵉmalka'* vocative— "O King Nebuchadnezzar." But a dative with *lᵉ* cannot be regarded as a vocative, and the Jewish accents which put an *athnach*—practically a colon—after "king" are correct. The twofold use of the word "O king" in the rest of the answer seems to offset the failure to use this word in the first address. We know too little about the forms of court etiquette current in those days to be able to advance the claim that a mere "O Nebuchadnezzar" would have been insolent.

Another part of this answer has caused commentators more trouble, the statement: "if our God . . . is able," because the faith of these men seems to be too clear and strong to allow for any doubt of God's omnipotence. In the last analysis, he that cannot believe in God's omnipotence virtually does not believe in God. Yet we have both statements: "if our God . . . is able" and: "but if not." We believe that the simple solution to our problem lies in the fact that these men are thinking in terms of *ethical* ability as some call it. That is to say, if there is nothing else in the way of God's delivering them. Deliverance might in the end not be as conducive to the salvation of the souls of these men as to perish in the flames at a time when their souls are entirely ready for such an ordeal. Furthermore, there are instances when an act of God, done for the good of an individual, has an effect upon others which is not as beneficent as it might be. There are countless situations that modify and determine the advisability of a certain course of action (cf. Gen. 19: 22) also as far as God's attitude is concerned. "If our God is able" therefore means, if it be in conformity with His wise and good plans; if it suits His benevolent purpose; if the higher plans and purposes of God are furthered thereby. In other words, these three men take the only proper and safe position. They have not been inspired to believe that God will work a miracle on their behalf, as v. 17 *A. V.* seems to involve, unless one prefers the forced interpretation that this verse means: "Our bodies may perish, but God will preserve our souls." At least as *A. V.* reads (so also the *Greek*) v. 17 is a word of absolute certainty and v. 18 a word of uncertainty. Such ambiguity is not found in the original. The thought expressed is more nearly that of *Luther's* rendering although *Luther* discarded the initial *hen,* "if," and avoided the somewhat difficult: "if our God . . . is able."

A point which no interpreter seems to have observed may be suggested here: these men do not say, "He is able to deliver us from *the* furnace of flaming fire," but "from *a* furnace of flaming fire," meaning *any* furnace and not implying that any one furnace is standing ready, belching forth flames. *Charles's* labored argument that the Hebrew text as we have it is corrupt overestimates the isolated Aramaic parallels of *'ithay.*

Sheyzabhûth and *yeshezîbh* are *Shaphel* forms after the analogy of the Assyrian and the equivalent of *Haphels,* i.e., causative (*Stev.* 16, 8).

The quiet, modest, yet withal very positive attitude of faith that these three men display is one of the noblest examples in the Scriptures of faith fully resigned to the will of God. These men ask for no miracle; they expect none. Theirs is the faith that says: "Though He slay me, yet will I trust in Him," Job 13:15.

d)   The Punishment, v. 19-23.

19, 20.   **Then was Nebuchadnezzar filled with hot anger, and the expression of his face was changed against Shadrach, Meshach, and Abednego. He answered and gave commandment to heat the furnace seven times more than it was customarily heated. Then he gave commandment to certain ones who were mighty men in his army to bind Shadrach, Meshach, and Abednego for the purpose of throwing them into the furnace of flaming fire.**

The second test is not made; the king discerns that there could be no object in making it. Besides, he will have found it very unusual in a court abounding in flatterers and sycophants to find one who dared to

oppose him to his face. This angered the king to the
extreme—*ch*ᵉ*ma'* = "hot   anger"   (accusative   with
verbs of fulness). The degree of anger felt was visible
in the change it wrought in his features. *Gordon*
renders quite effectively: "His face was distorted
with rage."

The verb *'eshtanniw* is plural, being attracted to
the number of the noun in the genitive, "face," which
is always a plural noun, *K. S.* 34f. The verb "answered" shows that his command to heat the furnace
was the answer to their confident assertion (v. 18).
The *Aramaic* uses the unusual idiom to heat "one
(*chadh*) seven more"— *'al* used comparatively, *K. S.*
308e. *Ch*ᵃ*zeh* regularly has the meaning "to be customary or normal." *Mezyeh* is infinitive from *'*ᵃ*za'*.

20.   We are not told whether any great length of
time elapsed between the command to heat the furnace
hotter and this next command to bind the victims. The
probability is that stores of fuel were available which
were hurriedly dumped into the fire. No man knew or
cared whether the resultant blast of flame was actually
seven times hotter or not. For seven must be regarded,
we believe, as a larger round number as it appears
also in Lev. 26:18, 21, 24, 28. It seems artificial to attribute to it a meaning that involves full atonement
or retribution in judicial matters as *Zoeckler* supposes.
The king was not thinking and speaking as a jurist
but as a very angry man.

These furnaces, we take it, resembled our present-
day limekilns. They were stone or brick furnaces that
were open at the top and approachable by an elevated
path or inclined plane because the kiln was built
against a hillside from which the approach was made.
At the bottom there must have been an opening that
was large enough to enable men to peer into the
very fire.

21-23. Thereupon these men were bound in their boots, leggings, caps, and robes and cast into the midst of a furnace of flaming fire. **Inasmuch as the king's command was urgent and the furnace was burning mightily, those men who fetched up Shadrach, Meshach, and Abednego were slain by the flame of the fire; but those three men, Shadrach, Meshach, and Abednego, fell bound into the midst of the furnace of flaming fire.**

These men had appeared at this occasion of state dressed in their finest apparel. Ordinarily, before criminals of any sort were bound, at least their mantles and their finery would be stripped off. In this instance, due to the urgency of the king's orders, the victims were taken just as they were. This is reported also because the magnitude of the ensuing miracle is enhanced by the fact that these garments constituted just so much more combustible material.

This is another case where the lack of information concerning articles of wearing apparel makes the identification of the different items quite a problem. No two commentators or lexicographers seem to see eye to eye in the matter. A reputable authority (*BDB*) suggests the following three possibilities for the first word: "probably mantle, or trousers, or shoes." Since the fourth word does mean "garments or robes," it is hardly likely that the first will have the same meaning. Since the majority agree that the third means "caps" or perhaps "helmets," it would seem that the description would have made its beginning with things that cover the lower extremities, therefore, "boots." Some kind of leg covering seems to be meant by the second word, for *Luther* renders it *Schuhe; A. V.,* "hosen," i.e., trousers; and *K. W.* "leggings," *Beinkleider.* This justifies the translation we offer. We may be further justified in classing most of these items as finery because "boots" were perhaps worn only on dress occasions. The account, however, wishes to indicate that every last article of wearing apparel was left on the condemned men.

22. Driven by the fury of the king's anger, the executioners had to make all possible haste, and so, it seems, they failed to reckon with the added danger that grew out of the increased intensity of the fire. Since the added precautions were not taken, rushing in as far as the needs of the case demanded to hurl the sentenced men into the fire, they succeeded in their task, but the flames must apparently have been driven back by some sudden wind, and their intensity brought instantaneous death to them. This, of course, serves to make the deliverance of the faithful three all the more marvelous.

It is a matter of debate whether *n*^e*phalû* means "fell" or "were thrown." The fact that the executioners perished does not eliminate the "were thrown" because the very last thing the executioners did in their mad rush to the opening may have been to give these three the thrust that carried them over the edge. To eliminate the very possible meaning "were thrown" brings us too near to the unacceptable idea that, with the executioners dead, the condemned men simply executed the sentence themselves and fell in—an act that borders on suicide.

At this point the *Greek* text inserts the two apocryphal portions, the Prayer of Azariah and the *Benedicite* (The Song of the Three Children—*Der Gesang der drei Maenner im feurigen Ofen*), a hymn that is incorporated in the Morning Prayer of the Book of Common Prayer. That these three godly men went into this ordeal with prayer, perhaps also very confident prayer, in their hearts and upon their lips is quite obvious. But it did not please the Spirit of inspiration to preserve their prayer for posterity. The elaborate indictment of v. 23 by *Charles*, trying to prove it an interpolation, is not very convincing: v. 21 and v. 23 do not overlap.

e) *The Miraculous Deliverance, v. 24-27.*

24, 25. Thereupon Nebuchadnezzar, the king, was startled, and he arose hastily and answered and said to his counselors, "Did we not cast three men bound into the midst of the fire?" They answered and said to the king, "Most assuredly, O king." He answered and said, "Lo, I see four men not bound walking about in the midst of the fire, and they are unhurt, and the appearance of the fourth is like unto that of a son of the gods."

The king is seated at a safe distance from the opening of the furnace, ready to derive a cruel satisfaction from seeing men punished who had ventured to oppose him. Instead he sees a startling sight, so startling as to bring him to his feet in haste and to lead him to ask his counselors in perplexity about a thing so simple, as though he could not trust his own memory in reference to a thing that just happened, whether it had not been three men who were cast into the furnace. They apparently do not see what he sees because he has perhaps the one vantage point from which alone the interior could be viewed. Several things startle the king profoundly: 1) he sees not three but four; 2) they are not bound but free; 3) they are not lying down or standing still but walking about; 4) they are not roasting in the fire but are unhurt (literally: "harm was not upon them") ; 5) the appearance of the fourth was like unto a son of the gods. Any one of the things he observed would have been quite sufficient thoroughly to startle any man. To this we might add a sixth important observation: these men were not scampering with all haste toward a possible exit from the furnace, but, since it was pleasing to God to deliver them, they were submitting themselves to His pleasure and to His mode of deliverance. No doubt, a rare miracle was transpiring, and all such manifestations of the supreme power of God startle and alarm poor sinful man. Read *mᵉhallᵉkhîn*, Pael participle, rather than *mahlᵉkhîn*, Haphel.

The king speaks as a typical heathen when he likens the fourth person to a "son of the gods." The expression *bar-'ᵉlahîn* has also been rendered "the son of God," but that would imply a deep and true knowledge of God on the part of this heathen and would also raise the objection that *Jerome* already stated in his day: "I do not know how the ungodly king deserved to see the Son of God." Besides, the Aramaic does not allow this rendering as Driver has shown. The majority of the church fathers of days of old judged the expression too much as if it had been uttered by an apostle or a prophet and not as though it had fallen from the lips of a spiritually blind heathen king. From the king's point of view the gods had children, either those who were begotten as the result of a union of the high gods, or those who were the result of promiscuous relations on the part of the gods with certain mortals. Such offspring would quite naturally be marked by superior bearing and beauty. Any angel would impress the king as belonging to this class. And certainly, the mighty angels of God were capable of delivering from even a peril as great as this. The mighty Son of God, indeed, delivered His own also in Old Testament times, but His agents or ministers to execute His purpose were the angels: "He will give His angels charge over thee, to keep thee in all thy ways," Ps. 91:11.

It is a pretty Jewish conceit when *Raschi* suggests that Nebuchadnezzar was able to recognize the angel because he had accompanied Sennacherib (702 B. C.) on his expedition against Jerusalem. However, assuming a conservative date for the episode of our chapter, let us say 585 B. C., we see how incongruous this suggestion becomes.

26, 27. Then Nebuchadnezzar approached the door of the furnace of flaming fire, answered and said: "Shadrach, Meshach, and Abednego, servants of the Most High God, come forth and come here." So Shadrach, Meshach, and Abednego came forth from the midst of the fire. And the satraps, the prefects, the governors, and the counselors of the king were assembled together and saw that the fire had had no power upon the bodies of these men, and that the hair of their head was not singed, neither were their shoes affected, neither did the smell of fire cling to them.

It was as apparent as it could be that, from the heathen point of view, a mighty god had wrought a mighty miracle. How could Nebuchadnezzar oppose those whom the gods so signally favored! The king saw but one course open before him under the circumstances and acted with the same dispatch in giving direction for the deliverance of these three as he had in executing their punishment. He approached the door of the furnace in person, as near as circumstances permitted, and cried out sufficiently loudly to be heard above the roar of the flames, "Come forth and come here." This command was an admission of virtual defeat. The three men, who had shown no trace of a rebellious spirit, not even in the matter of seeking deliverance prematurely, now ventured to come forth.

The list of those who crowded about these favorites of their God is not as long as the list of officials occurring in v. 2 *et al.*, for the author does not want to create the impression that the entire body of officials thronged about these three—a procedure which would have been a physical impossibility. But Daniel does want it to be understood that a large and

entirely reliable body of witnesses satisfied themselves
as to the perfect deliverance from most grievous peril
these three had experienced. It seems that in v. 24
haddabherin was a general word for all royal officers;
here in v. 26, where three other classes are mentioned
first, the same word still serves as a summary for all
the rest. "Counselors" is a somewhat dubious meaning
for this word.

Several significant facts are noticed separately.
Generally speaking, the bodies of Daniel's friends were
not affected by the fire. The hair of the head, which
may be singed without a person's being burned otherwise, was not harmed. Their shoes, *sarbalehôn*, in
which they had walked upon the fiery embers were not
"affected" (the *Aramaic* says "changed"). And even
the most subtle test of all, the smoke test, could be
met, for ordinarily the mere nearness to a fire is sufficient to have the smell of smoke pass upon garments.
Here no smoke smell could be detected. On the expression "the Most High God" (v. 26) see the discussion of v. 29.

f) Nebuchadnezzar's Decree, v. 28-33.

28, 29. **Nebuchadnezzar answered and said:
"Blessed be the God of Shadrach, Meshach, and
Abednego, who sent His angel and delivered His
servants who trusted in Him, and who cancelled the
order of the king and risked their own lives that
they might not fall down and do homage to any god
except their own God. And I do issue a decree that
any nation, race, or tongue that shall say anything
amiss concerning the God of Shadrach, Meshach,
and Abednego shall be cut in pieces, and his house
shall be made a dunghill, because there is no other
God who can deliver after this manner."**

Nebuchadnezzar's reaction to his experience is a
word spoken in praise of Jehovah. Yet the manner of

designating Him as the God of Shadrach, Meshach, and Abednego is that of a heathen and polytheist. The king believes that Jehovah has distinguished Himself and displayed power that is greater than any other god was capable of displaying; but it does not even remotely occur to the king to consider Him the only true God and all others mere creations of human fancy. The one whom he had previously designated as "a son of the gods" he now describes as "His angel." No special enlightenment was required to see that it had been the mission of this angel to protect His faithful servants. The king's religion agreed with the religion of Israel on this point—guardian spirits or angels were known to exist.

In this recognition of the God of Israel, Nebuchadnezzar commends these three ministers of his for several things which must originally have appealed to him but were pushed into the background by what he deemed a lack of proper submission to his supreme authority. These things are: 1) "they trusted" in their God—true faith elicits the admiration of even those who have faith only in their own gods; 2) "they cancelled the order of the king"—the inferior law had to yield precedence to the higher law; 3) "they risked their own lives [*Aramaic*: 'gave their bodies'] that they might not fall down and do homage to any god except their own God"—absolute and exclusive fidelity. At least for the present the king sees the justice of the claims to exclusive fidelity to Jehovah, for there are in reality no other gods.

29. The decree that Nebuchadnezzar issues is typical of a heathen king. It is negative in character. The king is not in a position, as far as his convictions in the matter go, to deny his own national deities. He would say nothing that might conflict with the honor due them. He does not think of decreeing that Jehovah is to be esteemed as the one and only God. Nebu-

chadnezzar is too deeply rooted in typically heathen
views to believe that. But he feels that he owes at
least this much to Jehovah, whose marvelous power
has just been displayed before his very eyes, that he
forbid having anyone "say anything amiss" (*Aramaic*:
"speak remissness") concerning Jehovah. Fear may
largely have inspired this decree. After what he saw
the king felt he had better take care lest he offend.
His earlier remarks, when he was confronted with the
steadfastness of his three ministers, may have disturbed him to such an extent that he felt that at least
something should be done that might remove whatever
was "amiss" about them. So he proclaims this decree.
The threat supporting the decree is sufficiently dire
to testify to the king's sincerity of purpose. They that
offend "shall be cut in pieces [Aramaic: 'be made
pieces'], and their houses shall be made a dunghill,"
cf. 2:5.

It still seems strange that the king goes no farther
than he does. For his concluding statement is the
strongest of all and seems to compel certain other
necessary conclusions. The king admits finally: "There
is no other God who can deliver after this manner."
That agrees with v. 26, where he designates Him as
"the Most High God." Conceding that He is above all
and knowing, as Nebuchadnezzar no doubt did, that
He laid claim to being the only God and had taught
His people thus, the king ought to have concluded: He
that has the highest authority has advanced this claim;
it must be true. But such is the blindness of heathenism that its errors cannot be cured by sound logic.

30. **Thereupon the king promoted Shadrach,
Meshach, and Abednego in the province of Babylon.**

Here as elsewhere in the Scriptures material prosperity is regarded as an added token of divine favor
and the normal experience in the case of those who
are true to the Lord. The word "promoted" does not

mean that this position was given to them, for that was a position previously held by them, see 2:49. The verb *hatslach* means "cause to prosper," *Erfolg haben lassen* (*K. W.*). The king supported and favored them so that their position was made easier and their work more successful in spite of the opposition of those that begrudged them their success.

Summarizing, we find that this incident and this chapter teach us "how the true worshipers of the Lord under the dominion of the world power could and would come into difficulties, imperiling life, between the demands of the lords of this world and the duties they owe to God. But we also learn that, if in these circumstances they remain faithful to their God, they will in a wonderful manner be protected by Him; while He will reveal His omnipotence so graciously that even the heathen world rulers will be constrained to recognize their God and to give Him glory" (*Keil*).

A few items may yet be touched upon to show that, if this chapter had been written about the time of Antiochus Epiphanes to teach persecuted Jews and to comfort them, the events recorded in this chapter would be an unfortunate misfit from several points of view. We have already shown in connection with v. 2 that religious persecution was not Nebuchadnezzar's object whereas Antiochus Epiphanes was engaged in what must be termed religious persecution in the strongest sense of the term. For this wicked king not only commanded to have only one type of worship practiced in his realm, namely, the worship of his gods, but also commanded to stop the worship at the Temple in Jerusalem; to desecrate the sanctuary; to set up strange altars, temples, and images; to offer pigs and other unclean beasts; to forbid circumcision; and the like (cf. I Macc. 1:43-51); and all this with the threat of death for disobedience.

To make the issue still clearer we must add that

such an attitude on the part of Antiochus Epiphanes must be called religious fanaticism of the most rabid sort. Such charges cannot be raised against Nebuchadnezzar, for it is very apparent that he expected all officers in his realm to continue in the worship of their own gods as they had been wont before acknowledging his golden image.

In an effort to draw a striking parallel between our chapter and the events of the time of Antiochus Epiphanes it used to be claimed that, as Nebuchadnezzar set up an image of gold, so Antiochus had set up an image of Zeus upon the altar of bronze at Jerusalem. However, that claim has been so successfully answered by *Hengstenberg** that it is to be mentioned only as an instance of misconstruction in support of a dubious issue. For I Macc. 1:54 does speak of "the abomination of desolation" set up upon God's altar in Jerusalem, but even that verse, but more particularly v. 59, show beyond the possibility of doubt that an opposition *altar* was meant, not a statue. That being the case, there is no parallel between these two incidents, for one had been manufactured to establish a parallel.

The lack of agreement finally becomes so pronounced that it must be apparent to all that the very idea of a parallel is a misfit when we note the fact that in the end Nebuchadnezzar acknowledges *Yahwe's* power and might, gives glory to Him, and publishes a decree that none should say anything amiss about the God of Shadrach, Meshach, and Abednego. That decree does not fit the spurious parallel that has been drawn. Antiochus remained a deadly enemy of the God of Israel and died as fiercely hostile to Him as he ever was. He did manifest a certain type of grief when his failure became manifest, but it was a deadly grief that hastened his end. I Macc. 6:8-16.

---

*Hengstenberg, E. W., *Die Authentie des Daniel*, Berlin: Oehneigke, (1831), p. 85f.

HOMILETICAL SUGGESTIONS

It will hardly do to break up the chapter into several texts for separate sermons. It is too much of one piece for that. Yet to take the thirty verses as a text is obviously cumbersome. It would, apparently, be better to let the entire chapter be read as a lesson in the service and then, perhaps, choose vv. 24-27 as a text, drawing upon the entire chapter in the course of the sermon whenever necessary.

We feel that the specific purpose of the chapter within the book should not be lost sight of. This purpose is not merely to set forth God's power in being able to protect His own but specifically the fact that "the world power cannot imperil the safety of God's saints." Throughout the ages the world power has manifested its character of deep hostility against God's people. In certain periods of the world's history this character of the world power had to become quiescent. It may burst into activity at any moment. God's people should be kept aware of this. But far more important is the setting forth of God's marvelous grace and power in safeguarding His own. Not apprehensiveness but quiet confidence should be preached. Again, not so much our attitude as God's all-sufficient power to keep His own in every time of danger.

CHAPTER IV

C. Nebuchadnezzar's Dream of the Great Tree:
The Overthrow of the Pride of Worldly Empires
Hebrew 3:31—4:34

The broader significance of this chapter is often lost sight of, especially when it is dissociated from Scripture passages such as Gen. 11, Isa. 13 and 14, or even Rev. 17:5. For when these prophetic passages present the overthrow of the king of Babylon rather than that of the wicked city, the king is considered only as the personification of what the city itself stands for. The pride and the spirit of the world found their classical expression for the first time in the building of the Tower of Babel, but they also met their first significant defeat at that time. From that time onward Babylon appears in the Scriptures as a symbol of the world power in its most significant and truly representative expression. Even as *its* overthrow is foretold in the prophets, cf. Isa. 13 and 14, so the overthrow of its *king* is sometimes mentioned, cf. Isa. 14: 12ff. In Daniel, too, the head of the empire is considered less as an individual and more as a representative of the spirit of the world power, and, as our double caption of this chapter indicates, the dream portrays that the pride of the world power will receive its just recompense of reward.

We, therefore, regard it as a very unsatisfactory statement of the purpose of this chapter when it is claimed (in line with the supposed late date of the book as this is assigned by critics) that it aims "to show the sheer helplessness of heathen powers over against God. . . . The obvious lesson involved is that the Jews are not to fear the power of Antiochus Epiphanes." This misses the obvious point of the characteristic pride of empires, which calls for the just judgment of God. Nothing in the chapter suggests that the ruler portrayed had any evil designs upon the people of God. That note is not even sounded in the course of the chapter. Not even a subdued reference to it appears.

The chapter division found in the *A. V.* and in *Luther's* translation agrees with our approach, and the numbering of the verses in the German Bible agrees with that of the Hebrew. In the Masoretic text the point at which we begin is v. 31 of chapter three. These last three verses—v. 31-v. 33—are without a doubt the heading of the edict recorded in chapter four, for this edict speaks of signs and wonders that God wrought in the interest of Nebuchadnezzar (4:2 *A. V.*), a statement that is certainly far more applicable to the king's experience in connection with his dream than to his experience in the matter of the deliverance of the three men from the fiery furnace.

On the face of it this chapter is an edict of Nebuchadnezzar's. No doubt, even in days of old such royal edicts could have been penned by the kings themselves or have been written by the royal scribes at the kings' command. In either case the royal edict would constitute a pronouncement of the king. In the case of our chapter it is not improbable that Daniel himself may have functioned as such a scribe and have committed to writing what the king ordered him to express. In any case it is true in every sense of the word that this is a valid and an authentic edict of Nebuchadnezzar's.

Zoeckler argues very sturdily that Nebuchadnezzar himself would hardly have written in the manner in which this edict expresses itself. His chief argument is that the king would not have employed a style that savors of the theocratic viewpoint. But great care must be taken not to involve Daniel in anything that veers toward falsification. For assuredly, had he been delegated by the king to draw up this document, Daniel would have felt conscience-bound to devise an edict that reflected the king's viewpoint correctly: he would not put into the king's mouth sentiments that the latter could not have uttered. Consequently, contact with Daniel as well as the experience of the dream will have taught Nebuchadnezzar to speak as he does in the few instances where points of contact with revealed truth appear. But on the whole it is impossible for us to determine exactly who framed the edict as it now stands. We must, however, earnestly contend for the fact that it was both as to content as well as in phraseology, exactly what Nebuchadnezzar desired to publish.

Montgomery's objection runs as follows: "As an edict the document is historically absurd; it has no similar in the history of royal conversions nor in ancient imperial edicts." This argument would say: since no parallel to such an edict exists, the very matter that it records is an impossibility. But observe how many events recorded in the Scriptures have no parallels in secular history and are yet accepted by us, especially matters of divine revelation. Such an approach makes nonscriptural history the criterion of what may be allowed as possible and reasonable in the realm of revelation.

Farrar disposes of the historical character of the event by a method which would strip everything supernatural from the Bible record. He explains the genesis of this chapter thus: some writer who was familiar with the Babylonian tale of Abydenus, quoting Megasthenes, how "Nebuchadnezzar at the close of his life ascended his palace roof and there received some sort of inspiration, after which he mysteriously disappeared, allows his imagination free play and devises a tale—called by the Jews of that day a 'Midrash'— with a practical lesson and written in the style of devotional literature." Despite the excellent things Farrar says by way of praising such a Midrash, a tale thus begotten unfortunately lacks what it needs most to give it conviction—it is not true. Lessons based on pious fictions are strangely lacking in emphasis even if they are labelled "the stately and striking *Midrash* of this chapter." Finding this chapter in an inspired Scripture, we know it to be true and venture the plausible supposition that the above-mentioned tale of Abydenus may be a legend, distorted as legends are but reminiscent of the things recorded in this chapter.

   a)   *The Superscription of the Edict. v. 1-3*

   1. (Hebrew v. 31 of chapter 3). **Nebuchadnezzar, the king, unto all peoples, nations, and tongues that dwell in all the earth: "Peace be multiplied unto you."**

This is the superscription of the royal edict. It identifies its author and specifies to whom it is addressed. It begins, furthermore, with the formal and customary greeting: "Peace be multiplied unto you." *Meinhold* quotes a parallel that *Rawlinson* found in a similar edict: "May my greeting make glad your heart." The extravagant style of such royal proclamations finds expression in the phrase "in all the earth," which cannot mean "throughout the land," for the Babylonian monarchs actually made claim to being monarchs of the whole world though they well knew that there were unexplored regions over which they exercised no authority. The fact that this edict is designed to be proclaimed universally indicates the importance that Nebuchadnezzar attached to his experience. He saw that it was of moment not merely to himself. He understood that he would be doing wrong to keep it to himself. He recognized that there were many besides himself who needed to take to heart what had been brought home to him under such extraordinary circumstances. He had been entrusted with a wholesome truth which it would have been criminal to keep to himself.

2, 3 (Hebrew 3:32, 33). **"It hath seemed proper to me to make known the signs and wonders that the Most High God hath wrought toward me. How great are His signs, and how mighty are His wonders! His kingdom is an everlasting kingdom, and His dominion is to all generations!"**

The verb "seemed proper" means originally "be fair or seemly" and can with equal propriety be rendered, "I thought it good" (*A. V.*). The things experienced by the king, as he rightly feels, call for an utterance on his part. He has seen "signs and wonders." Signs and wonders usually mark an experience that is designed for the good of many. The "signs" as such are in the Scriptures usually regarded "as pledges or attestations of divine presence or interposition" (*B D B*); they signify that man is dealing with God, whose power far exceeds that of man. The "wonders" are usually regarded "as a special display of God's power," which, as our word "wonder" indicates, causes men to marvel. Though the expression "signs and wonders" occurs elsewhere in the Scriptures (cf. Deut. 6:22; 7:19; 13:1, 2; 26:8; Neh. 9:10; Isa. 8:18, etc.), in the Hebrew the first of these two words is almost the same as the Aramaic word used here (*'ôth* vs. *'ath*), but the second is different (Hebrew *mopheth* vs. Aramaic *temah*). Besides, it would be but natural to use two expressive terms for so impressive an experience as this was.

Already here the critical claim that Nebuchadnezzar speaks too Biblical a language in his edict is seen to be exaggerated. This Aramaic combination appears nowhere else in the Scriptures. And yet, should the combination be patterned loosely after Scripture phraseology, that need not surprise us, for excerpts from Babylonian psalms and the like often remind of Biblical psalms. Besides, Daniel no doubt improved the occasion by speaking divine truth freely to the Babylonian monarch, and that at a time when the king's unusual experience will have rendered his heart and his mind exceptionally receptive. We have good reason for expecting that the king's edict would reflect this contact both as to content and phraseology.

This idea is in part embodied in the name that is used for God, whom Nebuchadnezzar designates "the Most High God." Yet, lest we impute too much to the expression, it seems to imply only that Daniel's God is in the category of the most high gods like Marduk or Bel and Nebo. For this interpretation compare especially v. 6 and v. 18.

3. The king is still deeply impressed by what has just befallen him. He exclaims: "How great are His signs, and how mighty are His wonders!" It was a rare deliverance that the king had experienced, and he still feels very correctly that this experience reflects primarily how God's rule over created things goes on uninterruptedly from generation to generation, for he calls His kingdom "an everlasting kingdom" and says in reference to His dominion that it is "to all generations," *Aramaic*: "with generation and generation." Much as *we* are wont to use such expressions with reference to God in an exclusive sense, the fact must not be overlooked that Nebuchadnezzar could have gone on in the same breath and made similar claims with reference to his favorite Marduk.

At this point (v. 33 Hebrew) the king's words have a kind of poetic fervor and actually take on poetic form, a double parallelism. A similar fact will be noted at different points in the edict. Yet all this amounts to no more than an exalted strain of diction which is often characteristic of words that are spoken with a deeper feeling. The attitude which makes these sections strict poetry, in our estimation, overshoots the mark. The attempt to secure an exact poetic structure necessitates repeated textual alterations, which are nothing other than trimming the evidence employed to make it prove the desired claim. It would be more to the point to call such sections *vers libre*.

They who make assertions as to how the text should be reconstructed inform us that vv. 31-33 have "been wrongly transposed to the beginning of this chapter by the revisers of the Aramaic." They fail to see the naturalness and the fine propriety of having the king, still deeply grateful for his restoration to sanity, begin his proclamation with an outburst of gratitude and praise. Their prosy verdict says: first the date, then a strictly temporal sequence of events, else the text is corrupt.

b) Nebuchadnezzar's Dream, v. 4-18.

4, 5. "I, Nebuchadnezzar, was secure in my house and flourishing in my palace. I saw a dream, and it frightened me; and my thoughts upon my bed and the visions of my head alarmed me."

The matter to be recorded by the edict begins. This did not happen during the time of his campaigns which occurred in the earlier part of his reign, for he tells that he was in his "house" and in his "palace." Here he was "secure," *sheleh* = "be at rest," *sorglos sein,* K. W., and "flourishing," *ra'ᵃnan* = "to be green," spoken with reference to trees, here in anticipation of the dream about to be related. It is usually thought that this dream occurred in the latter half of the king's reign.

5. The abruptness with which this verse is introduced is a literary device to indicate how utterly unexpectedly the dream came. Though the dream was not understood it was felt to be ominous, for the falling of so mighty a tree portends some mighty overthrow; and so the king says, "It frightened me." This refers to the immediate effect of the dream. However, it was followed by other results which heightened this effect in two ways. Apparently awakened by the dream, though he is still lying down, he is alarmed also by his "thoughts" upon his bed, the reflections occasioned by the dream. Furthermore, certain fancies or blurred images reminiscent of the dream, here called "visions of my head," contributed to the same result and also "alarmed" him. All this confirms the impression that the king was highly perturbed.

The verb *yᵉdhachᵃlinnanî* is one of the cases of the rare use of the imperfect for the perfect in the Aramaic.

6-8 (Hebrew 3-5). **"And a decree was issued by me to bring before me all the wise men of Babylon that they might make the interpretation of the dream known to me. Then came in the scholars, the enchanters, the Chaldeans, and the astrologers, and I recounted the dream before them; but they could not make known to me the interpretation. Then last of all there came before me Daniel, whose name is Belteshazzar according to the name of my god, and in whom is the spirit of the holy gods; and I told the dream before him."**

Not only interpreters are summoned, but the matter is of such moment to the king that he issues "a decree" that all the "wise men" be summoned—a collective term for the various classes about to be enumerated. They are said to be "of Babylon" because most of them, at least the more renowned of them, no doubt lived there. The decree apparently contains the purpose of their being summoned—"that they might make the interpretation of the dream known" to their sovereign lord.

L^ehan'ālāh is conceded to be a Haphel form of the type "always found in the Fifth Century Papyri" (*Charles*).

On the list of those who came, according to their classification, see 1:20; 2:2, 27. It must have been quite a sizable group that was assembled before the king and heard him "recount," *'amar*, "tell," his dream. They may have listened with some trepidation when they recalled how a similar occasion, perhaps twenty years earlier, was fraught with grave danger for a similar assembly in which some of those present may have taken part. One additional point of similarity between then and now was most striking—the utter inability of the entire college to produce an interpretation.

It hardly seems fair for *Farrar* to belittle the event by saying: "As usual he [the king] summoned the whole train of *Khakamim, Ashshaphim, Mekashshaphim, Kasdim, Chartummim,* and *Gazerim* to interpret his dream, and as usual they failed to do so." Such a statement involves the thought that the author was overworking the device of summoning this learned body. In any case, since this is only the second instance of their being assembled, it surely is a hasty generalization to say "as usual."

8. It is usually suggested at this point that the author has Daniel brought in last in order consciously to heighten the effect of his superior wisdom. Such an approach savors too much of shaping the material to produce certain effects rather than of giving an entirely correct and exact account, which we decidedly believe Daniel did. Besides, it is usually overlooked that Daniel was not summoned last. He merely came in last, either because he could not come earlier—he may have been busy assembling the wise men—or else because he chose to defer his coming till the learning of

Babylon had exhausted its resources. Such a delay on his part may have been entirely permissible and without offence to the king. For Daniel may have timed his arrival carefully to coincide with the moment when his absence became noticeable. To tell the truth, we know too little about the details involved in this aspect of the matter to say much about it, least of all to criticize it.

If it is asked why the king did not summon Daniel at once, mindful of the distinguished services related in chapter two, and why he did not dispense with assembling the rest, we dare not forget that these wise men were a distinct institution at the Babylonian court, specially trained and kept for services such as these. If the king does not appear sufficiently mindful of the event recorded in chapter two, need it surprise us if a heathen king subordinates what he has heard from the true God? Nebuchadnezzar may have been even a bit apprehensive about soliciting Daniel's assistance, being mindful of the general purport of the early dream. If that is the case, Daniel wisely kept in the background till the need of his presence became apparent.

The word *'ochoren* should be read as a plural and as such is used adverbially, "last of all."

In the matter of the names that are employed for Daniel the critic is wont to object at this point that Nebuchadnezzar would not designate him as Daniel, whose name he, the king, had personally changed; and in particular the etymology of Belteshazzar is assailed. We feel that much may be said in defence of what the text offers. After the lesson that Nebuchadnezzar had learned from the entire experience that is related in this chapter we can readily understand that the king might have been very careful to do or to say nothing that might seem to indicate a lack of reverence for Daniel's God, as for example wilfully to pass by the

original name of the man, "Daniel," which incorporated an allusion to this man's own God (*Dani'el* =
"God is my judge") and to substitute a name that
honored the king's god.

In addition to what we said about the name Belteshazzar in connection with 1:7 we should like to append what seems to us an even more plausible statement of the case. "Belteshazzar" may well be compounded, as is commonly claimed, of *balât,* "life," and
shar-utsur, "may he protect." But the interpretation
of proper names as these are found in the Scriptures
is seldom an etymological study in our sense of the
term. Popular interpretations, *a refined sort of pun,*
are usually involved even as we use many such in our
day. These interpretations were devised by men who
were not students of linguistics or trained etymologists
or lexicographers but men who appreciated a good pun
as the common man still does. The critics view these
simple problems too much from the professorial angle
and forget that such an approach was quite foreign to
the life of men of olden times. So the charge that "this
misinterpretation points to a time after the fall of the
Babylonian empire and to an author ignorant of the
Assyro-Babylonian language" (*Meinhold*) is refuted.

The expression *'elahîn qaddishîn* could be rendered
as a singular according to good Hebrew analogies, cf.
Josh. 24:19. But ,it is equally correct to say that the
terms used could be translated "holy gods"—plural.
We favor the latter because so many other indications
point to the fact that the king never forsook his polytheistic viewpoint and would, therefore, very naturally
refer to a higher spirit such as the gods are wont to
possess, that is, the *holy* or *good gods.* A second re-
cital of the dream becomes necessary for the sake of
Daniel. At this point the king deems it desirable to
recount his dream for the reader.

In connection with the conclusion of v. 8 it is

claimed that the construction used in the expression "I told . . . before him is against the usage of our author," *qodhomohi* being used for *le*. If this argument is correct it would offer proof that some later writer who was not conversant with the original author's style reworked the text and here gives proof of his lack of skill. Now, though it seems to be pretty well established that *qodhom* is used with *'āmar* and not *le* when an inferior addresses his superior, there are other factors that enter into the case. In the preceding verse as well as in this, when the king uses *qodhom* before his college of wise men as well as before Daniel, this seems to us to be very incisive testimony that the perplexed king for the moment felt himself to be in the presence of his superiors when he requested an explanation from them regarding a matter that he was utterly helpless to expound. It would seem to us that there is a most singular propriety about having Nebuchadnezzar address Daniel thus, whom, in a most special sense, he knows to be possessed of "the spirit of the holy gods." We feel, therefore, that this usage argues very strongly for a competent knowledge and use of the Aramaic idiom as it appears consistently throughout the whole of the book. In other words, it proves the opposite of what the critics claim.

9-12 (Hebrew 6-9). **"O Belteshazzar, chief of the scholars, inasmuch as I know that the spirit of the holy gods is in thee, and that no secret is too hard for thee, tell me the dream which I saw and its interpretation. As for the vision of my head upon my bed, there I was looking, and behold, a tree right in the midst of the earth, and its height was great. This tree grew great and strong till its height reached to the heavens, and it was visible to the end of the whole world. Its foliage was beautiful and its fruit abundant, and there was food in it for all. Under it the beasts of the field were finding shade,**

and in its branches were lodging the birds of the heavens, and all flesh was being fed from it."

A man of such importance as Daniel is must be addressed in a manner that is befitting his station— "chief of the scholars." We still claim that "chief of the magicians" is a translation that is less to the point and certainly far more likely to be misunderstood, for in our day magicians are thought of as purveyors of cheap magic, a meaning which, of course, did not originally lie in the term taken from the Greek *magoi*, μάγοι. The king also confesses freely and correctly where the source of Daniel's superior abilities lay: "the spirit of the holy gods is in thee." It was not a matter of natural gifts in the case of Daniel. Yet the statement betrays the king's polytheistic point of view.

The rest of the king's statement indicates his exalted conception of Daniel's ability. Surely, Daniel himself had never claimed that "no secret was too hard" for him. Yet the king could hardly believe otherwise after the events recorded in chapter two. The demand, "tell me the dream . . . and its interpretation," is a looser statement by hendiadys for "tell me the interpretation of the dream." That it was meant thus appears from the fact that the king proceeds at once to declare the entire dream as such to Daniel.

The verb *'anes* means "oppress" or "burden." If the mystery does not burden Daniel it is "not too hard" for him. The resemblance of the thought expressed to Ezek. 28:3 is so pronounced as to suggest that the prophet most definitely had our Daniel in mind and none other.

10. (Hebrew v. 7). The Aramaic expression *hazeh haweth* definitely presents a progressive "I was looking" and includes the thought that the king studied the situation by gazing steadfastly upon what he saw. The outstanding feature was a "tree" whose prominent position in the vision is indicated both by its tremen-

dous size as well as by the fact that it stood "in the midst of the earth," not off to one side or in an obscure corner. The tree definitely held the center of the stage. In addition to being already very tall it continued and "grew great and strong till its height reached to the heavens." All this the king beheld as he kept on gazing in his dream.

The second of these verbs, *teqîph,* does not mean "was strong" (*A. V.*) but "grew strong." The importance of the tree for the whole world is indicated by the fact that "it was visible to the end of the whole world." The *Aramaic* for this reads: "its visibility [was] to the extremity of the whole earth."

12. Hebrew v. 9. The king had leisure to notice other outstanding features with reference to the tree, for everything about it was superlative. First, its foliage was beautiful. Then it was seen to have an abundance of fruit. This fruit again served as food for all. The statement is rather extravagant; but fantastic things are characteristic of dreams. The Aramaic text (by a *maqqeph*) ties the words "for-all-in-it" into a unit and secures the meaning that all who lodged in the tree found fruit upon it. This *maqqeph* is apparently a worthless addition, for it would be out of keeping with the grandeur of the description to have the tree supply food only for the birds lodging in its branches. We therefore prefer to translate: "There was food in it for all." The final statement agrees with this: "All flesh was being fed from it." The picture of the ecumenical importance of the tree is rounded out by two statements that let the beasts of the field find shade and the birds of the heavens lodge in its branches. A really imposing sight!

The last three imperfects describe what was going on in the dream: "were finding," etc.—iterative imperfects.

The Scriptures offer parallels to this description. There is Ezek. 31:3-18, a still more extended description in which Assyria is likened to a mighty cedar. Besides, Ezekiel has 17:22f. and 19:10f. Why writers cannot allow for any originality on the part of Biblical authors has long puzzled us. Many assert that Daniel must needs have borrowed his vision from Ezekiel. But even a superficial reading will detect numerous points of difference that stamp each description as having features that are entirely its own. Furthermore, this dream is not any man's invention; it is a statement of what Nebuchadnezzar saw.

The records of antiquity know of two interesting parallels which grow out of the simple fact that it is very natural to liken a prominent personality to a flourishing tree; cf. Ps. 1:3; 37:35; 52:8; 92:13 ff., Prov. 11:28; Hos. 14:7. The Mede Astyages dreamed that a vine grew out of the womb of his daughter Mandane. This vine spread over all Asia and was none other than the famous Cyrus, according to the report of Herodotus. Not quite so close is the analogy of Xerxes who dreamed that he was crowned with the shoot of an olive tree, "whose branches extended over every land, but afterward the crown about his head disappeared."

13, 14. (Hebrew 10, 11). **"I kept looking in the visions of my head upon my bed and, lo, a wakeful and holy one came down from the heavens. He called aloud and said: 'Hew down the tree, lop off its branches, strip off its leaves, and scatter its fruit; let the beasts be driven away from under it and the birds from its branches.' "**

The king gazed upon the imposing tree with a kind of expectancy, fascinated, as it were, by the spectacle and anticipating some sort of climax. This climax is reached in the appearance upon the scene of a being coming down from heaven, a being called "a wakeful

and holy one," 'îr *weqaddêsh*, literally, "a wakeful
one and holy." Only one being can be meant, for the
singular is used consistently in the following verse,
consequently the *we*, "and" = "namely." For this use
of "and" compare 1:3; 8:10, and *B D B*, p. 252. The
emphasis is upon the word 'îr which the Greek translator (*Theodotion*) merely transliterated, attempting
no translation. "Watcher," *A. V.*, *Waechter*, Luther,
does not quite cover the case, for it is not a sentinel
that is thought of but one that does not sleep, a "vigilant one." Still, of course, even that name implies that
he keeps guard unceasingly. So *Gordon's* translation
"guardian" is not wide of the mark. This vigilant one
is not thought of as sharing human imperfections and
so is called "holy." We at once incline to the opinion
that this must be one way of describing an angel as
the *Greek* translation (*Septuagint*) already suggests—
ἄγγελος. This word is used also by the Book of Jubilees
and the Book of Enoch—pseudepigraphical writings—
to designate *angels*. This fact shows merely that at a
later time men rightly understood what type of being
was meant. Such use at a later date would not in itself
be a safe index of interpretation.

Even though the angels in no other instance in
the Scripture are called by this name, that does not
rule out the possibility or propriety of this designation
in this instance. Especially suitable is the thought that
these are angels if it be recalled that these beings
function as agents of God's judgment. Angels function similarly in other instances. The angel of God
slew the first-born in Egypt (Exod. 12:23) ; he was the
active agent in the pestilence in David's day, when that
king saw him stand with sword drawn over Jerusalem
(II Sam. 24:16). If the term angel is not used in our
chapter, that is due to the fact that that was a type
of being that was unknown to the Babylonians. But
when the king hears this being describe himself (v. 17)

as "a vigilant one" the king readily understands that
a type of being is involved whom nothing escapes. Continually alert, they observe all things, especially the
persistent wrongs of men, and act accordingly. This
does not eliminate or supersede God's omniscience and
omnipotence. His agents are described as noting what
transpires and as being ready to act, and so they are
not mere automata or dull creatures without adequate
understanding of their work and their duties.

This approach to our problem harmonizes with the
use of the term "wakeful ones," *'irîm*, in this chapter.
For the word as such was first used by the "wakeful
one" who gave the command to hew down the tree; see
v. 17. Daniel uses it very appropriately (v. 23) by
building on the use of it made by the heavenly messenger. The king's use of the word (v. 13) is based on the
same fact. Now, surely, the king could have understood
from this name and from the functions this messenger
ascribes to beings of this sort just what their work was
even though Babylonians were not familiar with
angels in their theology. Whether the king then went
a step farther in his own thinking and likened these
beings to the so-called θεοὶ βούλαιοι, "council deities" or
"consultant deities" of the Babylonians, we are, of
course, unable to say.

Commentators tell us that it is Diodorus Siculus
who informs us about these Babylonian deities, whom
some writers describe as "planetary deities, who keep
watch over the affairs of the universe." The question
is raised whether Nebuchadnezzar is speaking according to his pagan beliefs or in terms of revelation.
Or, wording the issue more pointedly: Did God give
this revelation to the king in terms of heathen notions
that were familiar to Babylonians generally or in terms
of revelation of the truth which the king was, nevertheless, well enough able to understand? Even though
Hengstenberg and *Keil* as well as many others favor

the former view, we feel that it involves some dangerous assumptions. One such assumption is that in revealing truth God had to resort to the use of terms of error by speaking of beings that actually had no existence as though they existed. We cannot believe that divine revelation, even in dreams, needs to resort to such doubtful expedients to achieve its ends. Another such assumption is that God could not convey correct conceptions to ignorant man through truth as readily as through error.

14. This wakeful one "called aloud" as being one who is sure of himself and transmits dependable revelation. His summons is addressed to unnamed agents in the plural (*goddû*, etc.), agents who are thought of as being available and entirely competent to fulfill their assignment. But since they do not actually cut down the tree in the vision they are not further identified. Perhaps they, too, belonged to the watchful and holy ones. At least the demolition of the tree is to be complete, for in addition to being cut down its branches are to be lopped off, its leaves stripped off, its fruit scattered, and naturally all birds and beasts driven away from in and under it. As great as is the tree originally, so great is to be its overthrow in the end.

15, 16 (Hebrew 12, 13). **" 'Nevertheless, leave the stock of its roots in the earth with a band of iron and brass in the tender grass of the field, and he shall be moist with the dew of heaven, and his portion shall be with the beasts in the grass of the earth. His heart shall become different from that of a man, and the heart of a beast shall be given unto him; and seven times shall pass away over him.' "**

Whereas it seems for a moment as though the utter destruction of the tree had been intended, it now appears that there will be a prospect of its reviving. At least "the stock of its roots" is to be left in the earth. The word *'iqqar* is a bit uncertain. Some assign the meaning "root" to it. Then "the root of its roots," by a kind of superlative, would be the taproot, *Haupt-wurzel* (*K. W.*). That seems a bit strange. Better would be the other meaning, "stock" of its roots, and that would mean the stump with its roots (so *Luther*), which is surely clearer than the expression "the stump of his roots" (*A. V.*).

But why the "band of iron and brass" on the stump? Some claim that such a band or bands, fastened firmly around the stump, would be a protection against the effects of the weather and would keep at least the stump intact and prevent its splitting. Yet, when has such an arrangement ever been used on stumps; or do stumps usually split in the process of weathering? Do they not rather rot? And would metal bands prevent rotting? In view of the manifold difficulties of this interpretation commentators generally conclude that in this instance the figure and the reality begin to blend. But some go too far in making these "bands" or bonds—for the word may also mean "chains" (see Ezra 7:26)—represent the actual fetters by which the raving maniac Nebuchadnezzar was to be bound. There is nothing to indicate that the king became raving mad. About the most violent thing the poor demented king did was to eat grass. So the more moderate interpretations suggest that these bonds represent the king's malady that held him bound, a point of view that is confirmed also by passages such as Ps. 107:10 and Job 36:8. The "and" before *be'esûr* must be "namely," it is more like the German *und zwar*.

Unfortunately, the king's condition has been pictured by commentators in colors of all-too-vivid hue. His prospective fate involves only what the text states. In the middle of v. 15 the subject changes from the tree to the man, and so we ventured to translate: "And *he* [not it] shall be moist with the dew of heaven." For it would be an idle statement to relate that a stump was bedewed: that's too obvious for record. But this man shall descend to such a brutish condition that he shall not know enough to keep under cover at night, or he shall mind the night dews as little as do the oxen. "His portion shall be with the beasts in the grass of the earth" means: it shall be his lot to share with cattle the grass they eat.

15. When this verse adds the deeper-going fact that "his heart shall become changed," the "heart" appears to be regarded as the center of mental activity (*Denkwerkstaette, K. W.*) or, as *Gordon* says, "mind." When in its stead there is "the heart of a beast," we have all the earmarks of that form of mental derangement which is also called lycanthropy: a man regards himself to be a wolf or some other beast or creature. To all intents and purposes he behaves as such a beast would behave. Numerous parallels to this condition have been found in every age. There is absolutely nothing impossible or improbable about such a state of derangement. The clause "the heart of a beast shall be given unto him" can hardly refer to a physiological transformation of the physical organ called the heart.

This state is to continue until "seven times shall pass away over him." This could mean seven years. But in a book like this, where the symbolical use of numbers stands out so prominently, the emphasis obviously rests on the seven as being the number that marks some work as a divine activity. Consequently we regard it to be far better to translate *'iddanîm* "times" and to take the entire expression to mean: enough time for God to finish his specific work upon the man. This would seem to require more time than a few months. Yet seven years seems too long a time to have the kingdom kept in reserve for Nebuchadnezzar. However, the length of time involved is of no moment; the important thing is that God accomplishes His purpose.

The expression "from that of a man," v. 16 (Hebrew 13), is the equivalent of a negative result clause: "so that he longer was a man" (*K. S.* 406n). For "the heart of a beast shall be given unto him" *Driver* (see *Charles*) suggests: he shall "imagine himself an animal."

17, 18 (Hebrew 14, 15). " ' **By the decree of the wakeful ones is the command, and by the word of the holy ones is the demand, in order that the living may know that the Most High rules over the kingdom of men and gives it to whomsoever He will and setteth up over it a lowly one among men.' This dream did I, King Nebuchadnezzar, see; now do thou, O Belteshazzar, tell me its interpretation inasmuch as all the wise men of my kingdom are unable to make the interpretation known to me. But thou art able, for the spirit of the holy gods is in thee.**"

The king needs to be assured that the dream is no idle and meaningless fancy on his part but a divine revelation of an impending fact. For this reason the words ordering the tree to be cut down are said to be both a "command," *pithgam^a'*, also "sentence or decree," and a "demand," *she'elta'*, also "request." This command or demand is based on a "decree" or "word" of the "wakeful and holy ones." Since we have determined above that these wakeful ones must be angels, does it not exceed the limits of Scriptural revelation to have these angels make decrees about the lot of men? We do not think so. These statements just happen to leave out the part that the Almighty has in the entire proceeding; v. 24 indicates that, in the last analysis, this is, after all, a "decree of the Most High," and they emphasize that the part of the angelic agents is not an idle gesture. This interpretation regards the

initial "by," *be*, as introducing also the second clause—
a double object of a preposition. We read of heavenly councils elsewhere in the Scripture, cf. 1 Kings 22 and Job 1. What part do angels play in such assemblies? Is their participation futile and meaningless? Hardly, if they are beings of a higher order. Though, in the last analysis, God's will must prevail, they find themselves in fullest accord with His plans and will to do what He desires to have done. So from one point of view the decree or decision may rightly be described as being theirs. But since the decision is theirs as well as the Almighty's, it is by no means to be trifled with. That is the substance of their final utterance here. The development of the idea of a heavenly council in later Judaism is extravagant if not blasphemous as Weber, *Jüdische Theologie*, p. 170f. shows.

They then reveal by their statement that the broader purpose of it all is that from what befalls so prominent a monarch as Nebuchadnezzar men everywhere upon the earth may know that there is one Ruler who is higher than the highest among men and therefore the "Most High," *'illaya'*, in whose hand lies the disposal of "the kingdom of men." That is, men do not, in the last analysis, set up whomsoever they please, but He "gives it to whomsoever He will." In fact, in the case of the Almighty the rule prevails not to set up the high-minded in such places of prominence; but He prefers to use "a lowly one among men." For "men" the text, strange to say, has a Hebrew plural (*'ănāshîm*) in the Aramaic text. Since Nebuchadnezzar no longer possesses this attribute (viz. "lowly") he is about to be removed. This conclusion is implied in the statement presented. All this is but another version of the statement, "God resisteth the proud; but giveth grace to the humble." See also I Sam. 2:7, 8; Luke 1:52; I Cor. 1:26ff.

18.   In his concluding statement the king implies that there was no more to the dream than what he has just told. He again asks for the interpretation as he did in v. 9, for that is naturally his chief concern; and he again dwells upon the utter failure of the wisdom of the official dream interpreters and implies that that paves the way for Daniel to display his superior wisdom as he had done on a previous occasion. And that such superior wisdom is present in Daniel he admits a second time as though such an admission might please the "holy gods" whose spirit he knows Daniel to have and induce them to enlighten Daniel. On the expression "spirit of the holy gods" see v. 8 and 9.

The critical remarks of *Charles* on the Aramaic of this verse are instructive but at the same time an indication of the caution with which the results of language study that is based on meagre materials are to be applied. He points out that the expression "this dream" has the demonstrative standing first, over against the Aramaic usage that is observed in the eleven other passages where the demonstrative occurs. We grant that this order must appear as unusual. But, surely, it would be presumptuous to assert that such usage was not good and warranted, seeing that we have such limited Aramaic texts at our disposal. We have a feeling that, had such a usage been observed in an extrabiblical document, it would simply have been labeled as exceptional, and the quality of the Aramaic of the document would not have been called into question.

Similarly the usage "King Nebuchadnezzar" as it appears here differs from the more common usage, "Nebuchadnezzar, the king." We deem it highly unfair to call this usage "rare in our author" when it is admitted that it occurs in but seven of nineteen cases. That hardly allows for the verdict "rare" but for a term like "less frequent." Then to add that "the LXX supports the Aramaic in only three of these seven passages" does not in any sense invalidate the fact that the ratio still stands 7:12. Efforts of this sort to cast a cloud of doubt upon the Biblical text must be branded as what they are, quite unscientific.

c) *Daniel's Interpretation and Counsel,*
v. *19-27; Hebrew 16-24.*

19. **Thereupon Daniel, whose name is Belteshazzar, stood dumbfounded for quite a time, and his thoughts upset him. But the king answered and said to him: "Belteshazzar, as for the dream and its interpretation, let it not upset thee." Belteshazzar answered and said: "My lord, a dream for thy enemies, and its interpretation for thy foes."**

Every reader of the book is by this time aware of the fact that Daniel's name is Belteshazzar, but there is a particular propriety in mentioning it at this point; for he who bore a name that indicates the superior power of Babylonian divinities with the superior power that his own God gives him interprets what the Babylonian sages are powerless to discern. Since the interpretation of the dream is immediately revealed to Daniel, he is completely dumbfounded by the bitter grief about to fall to the lot of the king. In fact, his stupefaction is so protracted as to provoke general comment. It lasted "for quite a time," *keshaʿah chadhaʾ*, which means literally "about an hour," but by synecdoche must mean something like "quite a time." To have the man of God stand appalled for an hour is preposterous. To reduce the meaning of the phrase to "for a moment" is impossible.

In addition to a whole chain of "thoughts," thoughts concerning the consequences involved plus thoughts of pity for the poor king also "upset" Daniel. We cannot venture the explanation that Daniel was afraid to give his message. But who does not dread to be the bearer of evil tidings, and who would not be much disturbed by so tragic an overthrow?

The king, hardly aware of the impending evil, feels impelled to encourage Daniel to speak up. He could sense that evil impended but hardly believed that it could be so alarming. The words "dream" and "interpretation" are regarded as a unit and are, therefore, followed by a verb in the singular. Their emphatic position suggested our translation: "As for the dream," etc. We do not regard the usual interpretation of Daniel's reply as correct or in any wise suitable: "The dream be to them that hate thee," etc. There is an ethical objection to this rendering. It would make as sincere a man of God as Daniel was sink to the level of a flattering courtier who, without regard to the right or the wrong of the issues involved, would simply wish the grievous lot impending over the king upon all who happen to be so unfortunate as to be at enmity with the king. There is fortunately no necessity for translating thus. It has been correctly pointed out by *Kliefoth* that a more proper translation would be: "The dream is for thy enemies (or haters)." That would mean: this is a dream that would please your enemies; what it portends they would surely like to see fulfilled upon you. The second half is parallel in meaning: "its interpretation for thy foes." To catch this different meaning of the remark of Daniel we have ventured to translate the first word "*a* dream" though the article is used because that suggests what we have in mind: Such is the type of dream your adversaries would surely like to have come to pass.

20-22 (Hebrew 17-19).   **"The tree which thou didst see, which became great and strong, and its height reached to the heavens, and it was visible over the whole earth, and its foliage was beautiful and its fruit abundant, and there was food in it for all; and under it dwelt the beasts of the field, and** in its branches lodged the birds of the heavens—it is thou, O king, who hast grown great and strong; and thy greatness hath grown and reacheth to the heavens, and thy dominion reacheth to the end of the earth."

Daniel's recapitulation of the description of the tree is stated almost word for word in the very terms that the king himself had used and so requires no further comment. Yet Daniel was not merely sparring for time. Having once come to the point where he was ready to speak, nothing could have deterred him. But so exact a recapitulation served to impress upon the king the fact that Daniel had correctly heard word for word what his king had told him, and so there could be no room for any misunderstanding and inaccuracy. The substance of the interpretation is as brief and as pointed as it can be. The king wants to know; Daniel must tell. Circumlocution would have confused the issues. Like Nathan's famous "Thou art the man!" so Daniel's interpretation rings out clear-cut: "It is thou, O king," Aramaic: "Thou art he." Practically the only new term used thus far by Daniel is the word "thy dominion," that being a term that naturally belongs to the interpretation as such.

23-25. (Hebrew 20-22). **"And whereas the king saw a wakeful and holy one come down from heaven and say: 'Hew down the tree and destroy it; nevertheless leave the stock of its roots in the earth, namely, with a band of iron and brass in the tender grass of the field; and let him be moistened with the dew of heaven; and let his portion be with the beasts of the field until seven times shall pass away over him'; this is the interpretation, O king, and it is the decree of the Most High which has gone out against my lord, the king: Thou shalt be driven out from among men, and thy dwelling shall be with the beasts of the field, and thou shalt be made to eat**

grass as oxen, and thou shalt be moist with the dew of heaven, and seven times shall pass away over thee until thou knowest that the Most High ruleth over the kingdom of men and giveth it to whomsoever He will."

Again that same fidelity of narration in the original terms with the same purpose that we pointed out in connection with v. 20. A brief summary is given instead of a narration of the separate steps followed in disposing of the tree, namely, cutting off the branches and stripping off the leaves, etc., v. 14; Daniel simply says "destroy it." As he advances to the interpretation he points out how authoritative it is and substitutes by way of explanation that all this is by "the decree of the Most High." In v. 17, Hebrew 14, the decree was ascribed to the wakeful ones. Both points of view are correct. Here Daniel points to the ultimate source; there he indicated the mediate source. Should Nebuchadnezzar have overlooked the fact that what the wakeful ones are allowed to decree is also the decree of the Most High, he at least knows it now and understands that it is not to be trifled with.

25, Hebrew 22. Using terms that are familiar from the previous statement of the case, Daniel needs only to insert the "thou" in reference to the king, and his interpretation is complete. A typical Aramaic construction appears here: the third person plural used impersonally takes the place of the passive, or to be more exact, plural participles represent the third person plural in this use (*K. S.* 324n) ; we have translated these forms freely as passives—"thou shalt be driven," etc. Then there is this difference: in v. 17, Hebrew 14, it was indicated that the lesson involved in this experience was for "the living"; Daniel now applies the point directly to the king, "until thou knowest." In that expression, by the way, there lies an intimation that, when the purpose indicated has been achieved, the punishment may be withdrawn.

26, 27 (Hebrew 23, 24). **"And whereas it was commanded to leave the stock of the roots of the tree, thy kingdom is assured for thee from the time that thou recognizest that the heavens do rule. Wherefore, O king, let my advice be acceptable in thy sight: break with thy sins by dealing righteously and with thine iniquities by showing mercy to the wretched. Perhaps there may a lengthening of thy prosperity."**

The one feature remaining to be interpreted is now disposed of—"the stock of the roots." That is the part of the dream that portends hope. As the stump with its roots remains, and such a stump could quite naturally send forth shoots in which the former comes to new life, so the king can look forward to such a prospect. Since in the case of so great a king as Nebuchadnezzar was mere restoration to sanity without restoration to the kingdom would have been but half a restoration and hardly worth the name, he is now assured that the kingdom shall surely become his again from the very moment (*min-di* = "from [the time] that") that he recognizes "that the heavens do rule." By an obvious metonomy "the heavens" are mentioned for the King of the heavens. In the New Testament the same metonomy occurs; see Matt. 21: 25; Luke 15:18. God asks no more than the recognition of the obvious and the relinquishment of the bloated human pride.

Daniel now offers what he has not been asked to provide—spiritual counsel. It must have taken moral courage to do that because unsolicited advice, which in this case involves a very direct admonition, could not be tendered freely to a monarch, least of all an Oriental monarch. Nevertheless, the interpreter becomes a counsellor and monitor. Daniel, of course, speaks with becoming respect as the Fourth Commandment bids him do.

His counsel is: "Break with thy sins by dealing righteously." A more literal translation would be: "Break off thy sins by righteousness" (*A. V.*). "Righteousness," *tsidhqah,* as a virtue in a ruler must here signify "right doing," *B D B,* or as above, "dealing righteously" in the plain ethical sense. This term takes into account the common fault of monarchs: the failure to exercise perfect equity in their dealings with men or in dispensing justice. Nebuchadnezzar, too, must have been guilty of tyrannical behavior, of violence, of highhanded dealings. All these and similar faults are to be renounced, and the primary virtue of monarchs is to be cultivated—plain, straightforward righteousness. The king's remissness in this direction is plainly labelled "sins," *chatai,* because he had been missing the mark. These he is to "break off" or, as we might prefer to say, "break with." This involves no work-righteousness or synergism because after all these years Daniel must have understood quite well that conversion on Nebuchadnezzar's part was out of the question. Consequently he admonishes his king to do at least what lies within the realm of possibility and within his own powers, viz., to cultivate civil morality, to correct the most flagrant abuses of his reign.

The parallel demand says: (break with) "thine iniquities by showing mercy to the wretched." Impartiality in the administration of justice is advocated, especially over against "the wretched," *ᵃnayîn,* persons who have no influence and none to plead their cause and so suffer much abuse. Kindly dealings on the part of the absolute monarch would do him credit. Yet both these virtues—justice and kindliness— are not thought of as being merely a few choice and appropriate virtues but as evidences that the king has humbled himself because of the rebuke of the Most

High, for throughout the chapter Nebuchadnezzar's fundamental error is his overweening pride.

If the king would correct these most manifest abuses he would be doing only what any right-minded man would do, who had been reminded that a certain practice of his sorely needed to be amended. That would, of course, lie entirely in the sphere of everyday civil righteousness and would have nothing to do with salvation. Neither does Daniel assign any connection with salvation to such a course. He merely asserts that in this life, in the matter of continuing in his present fortunate situation, the king may, perhaps, experience a continuation or "lengthening of his prosperity." By this form of statement ("perhaps") Daniel indicates that he for his part is not sure what it may please God to do; he merely anticipates the possibility of the cancellation of the impending doom of the king. As far as the words themselves are concerned, it must be as clear as daylight that nothing has been said or intimated about forgiveness of sins or about salvation. The prospects held out to the king remain entirely on the level of earthly values—*shelewah* ="rest or prosperity."

This passage is treated in the Apology of the Augsburg Confession, Art. III, p. 131ff. (Mueller's edition), though from a different point of view. The thing that made the passage a matter of controversy was the translation of the vulgate: *Peccata tua eleemosynis redime et iniquitates tuas m'sericordiis paupperum*, "Cancel thy sins by deeds of charity and thine iniquities by deeds of kindness to the poor." This unfortunate translation resulted from the *Greek* which had said about the same thing; and this translation in turn was based on a postbiblical use of the term *tsidhqah* or Hebrew, *tsedhaqah,* which meant "almsgiving." But even *Montgomery* rejects this meaning and suggests: "Rather it is the general expression for good works, in which sense it is used in the Sermon on

the Mount." So, too, a secondary meaning of *peraq*—
the verb for "break off"—is to "cancel or redeem."
But that use of the word would result in an unbiblical
statement. The strangest comment on this contro-
versial issue is Montgomery's, who says: "And indeed
why the Protestants should quarrel with the Catholics
over the Biblical virtue of charity it is hard to see."
"The Biblical virtue of charity" was not at all the
issue at stake.

Going a bit more fully into the details of the issue
as to just what "righteousness" means at this point, we
refer to the position of those who, without hesitation,
claim for it the meaning "almsdeeds." It must be obvious to those who believe even in a measure in the
harmony of the truth revealed in the Scriptures as
well as in the inerrancy of the Scriptures that to accept such a meaning here would place this book into
flat contradiction with the rest of the Scriptures, which
beyond a doubt teach *sola gratia*. This Scriptural position has plainly been abandoned by the apocryphal
books (cf. Ecclus. 3:30, 31; Tob. 4:7-11, etc.), and so
for good reasons the Apocrypha are not included in
the canon. But to claim that "righteousness" here
means "good works," as some unhesitatingly do in
the face of the much better sense that our interpretation offers, has the appearance of being an attempt
to try to prove the canonical Scriptures at variance
with themselves. Where the principle is still held that
Scripture must be interpreted by Scripture, there the
obvious fact carries weight that *tsedhaqah* can nowhere else in the Scriptures of the Old Testament be
shown to have the meaning "good works" as even
critical writers freely concede. The Septuagint merely
reflected a current error when it rendered this word
by ἐλεημοσύνη in Deut 6:25; 24; 13; Isa. 1:27; 59:16;
Ps. 24:5; 33:5; 103:6. Cf. also Weber *System der
Theologie*, p. 273ff, (1880).

We are not told how Nebuchadnezzar received this admonition. It was, without a doubt, heard rather coolly. In fact, nothing is related about the king's reactions to the interpretation as a whole. The sequel shows that he did not take the lesson to heart—a strange hardness of heart after so astounding a divine warning. *Farrar* surmised that "the absence of any mention of rewards or honors paid to Daniel is perhaps a sign that he was rather offended than impressed."

d)   Nebuchadnezzar's Madness, v. 28-37;
Hebrew 25-34.

This entire section is written in the third person whereas all the rest of the edict is in the first person. This need not strike us as strange. In fact, as long as the consciousness of the ego of the king was dimmed, if not entirely submerged, he perceived nothing of what had really happened to him and consequently could not report concerning this period. It matters little, as far as we are concerned, whether the king himself for this reason reported objectively about himself what others told him had transpired, or whether he let his scribe do it for him. The propriety of the change of person is apparent. Besides, such a change is readily understood.

28-30 (Hebrew 25-27).   All this befell Nebuchadnezzar, the king. At the end of twelve months he was walking about on the top of the royal palace at Babylon. The king answered and said: "Is not this Babylon the great which I have built as a royal residence by the strength of my own power and for the glory of my majesty?"

The summary report, covering the whole case, precedes in typical Hebrew or Aramaic style: "All this befell Nebuchadnezzar." The details follow. In point of time exactly twelve months had elapsed since the warning of the dream had come to the king. Within his own heart the king may for a time have given a measure of heed to the warning, but even that effect presently wore off. On this momentous day, on the anniversary of the dream, he might have recalled at least what had been done for him by that revelation. Instead he allows himself to be swept away into an utterance which practically amounts to a defiance of the Most High because of its arrogant self-glorification. We have no means of determining at what point during the magnificent building program carried through during Nebuchadnezzar's reign this episode occurred. The program must have been nearly completed at the very least. The roof of the royal palace is the most natural place for the king to be strolling about, surveying the most recent evidences of regal grandeur. The ancients such as Herodotus and Ctesias have almost fabulous things to tell about a palace's being completed in fifteen days; about walls, gates, and moats; about temples and gardens. Modern excavations have amply sustained all the claims made. Almost every brick that is now picked up is said to bear the stamp of the great builder, Nebuchadnezzar. Well might a proud mortal under such circumstances be moved to respond to a sight such as this—the *Aramaic* naturally reports "answered and said"—as the king did.

Charles offers a very appropriate quotation from *Prince* to this effect: "Nearly every cuneiform document now extant dating from this monarch's reign treats, not of conquest and warfare, like those of his Assyrian predecessors, but of the building and restoration of the walls, temples, and palaces of his beloved city of Babylon." The following illustrative samples are offered: "Thus built I my palace, the seat of my royalty," and, "In Babylon my dear city which I love."

30.   "Babylon the great" is a most apt description in the light of all facts, both ancient and modern.

Scarcely a city has ever impressed nations as did Babylon. After the Babylonians had recaptured the city from the Assyrians they set about with fresh zeal to make it a most glorious city, worthier than ever of its ancient glories.* The results of this expansion program now lay before the king's eyes. He had, without a doubt, been the moving spirit behind the whole project. All this helps us better to understand his exclamation: "Babylon . . . which I have built." It throws light also upon the explanation "as a royal residence." The phrase that follows ascribes the success of the enterprise to his own ingenuity and talents—"by the strength of my own power." We inserted "own" before "power" as helping to convey the very spirit of the claim. The king's last statement shows that his ultimate objective was the glorification of his own name—"for the glory of my majesty." The very language employed is strangely reminiscent of inscriptions discovered at a comparatively recent date. *Meinhold* quotes one bearing the words: "In Babylonia is the palace of my dwelling for the glorification of my dominion," Nebuchadnezzar's own words. *Montgomery* cites: "Then built I [Nebuchadnezzar, of course] the palace, the seat of my royalty . . . the bond of the race of men, the dwelling of joy and rejoicing."

As a whole, whether it is directly intended as such or not, the king's boastful utterance is a defiance of the Almighty who had bidden him to desist from his unseemly pride.

31-33 (Hebrew 28-30). The word was still in the king's mouth when a voice fell from the heavens: "To thee is it spoken, O King Nebuchadnezzar, the kingdom is gone from thee. And away from the presence of men shalt thou be driven; and with the beasts of the field shall be thy dwelling

---

*McCurdy, *op. cit.*, Par. 1055-1064.

place; and thou shalt be made to eat grass as oxen; also seven times shall pass away over thee until thou learnest that the Most High rules over the kingdom of men and giveth it to whomsoever He pleaseth." In that very moment this word fulfilled itself upon Nebuchadnezzar, and he was driven from the presence of men, and did eat grass as oxen, and was made moist by the dew of heaven until his hair grew long as eagles' feathers and his nails as claws of a bird.

The statement recorded in the preceding verse was so stark an expression of the king's ungodly pride that it at once called forth the long-delayed punishment. The verb "fell" is very appropriately used for the statement that was uttered with reference to the king because it involves the thought of a heavy load dropping upon the king "from the heavens," the dwelling place of the Most High. Since this voice is none other than the voice of God it is obviously not to be identified with that mysterious *bath qol* of later Judaism which did not necessarily have to be a direct voice of God. See Weber, *op. cit.*, p. 187ff. The utterance takes the king in hand directly: "To thee it is spoken"—"to thee" being emphatic. The *Aramaic* says "to thee do they say"—impersonal third person plural. The ample warning and the season for grace are past; so the sentence is pronounced at once—"the kingdom is gone from thee," the kingdom that he had deemed his inalienable possession, as long at least as his life should last. What follows in the sentence is practically a literal quotation from Daniel's ominous interpretation, beginning with v. 25. By quoting thus the sentence as it is now announced came to the king's notice more emphatically as the sentence of the Most High, the God of Daniel. This quotation embraces the entire v. 32.

33.   Even as we may use the expression "the same hour" more loosely or more accurately, so it apparently

here means, not "after a while," but practically "in that very moment" as we have translated. His demented state manifested itself so completely that it was no longer feasible to keep the maniac in the presence of men; and since he behaved like an ox he had to be treated as an ox. So he was driven from the presence of men.

Commentators (like *Haevernick*) have done well to draw attention to the fact that even under these unusual circumstances a measure of decorum was preserved by the subjects with reference to the almost sacrosanct person of the king. Although he was demented he was not exposed to the curious gaze of the multitude, or to harsh treatment, or to derision. He did not become the gazingstock of all that passed by but was, no doubt, confined in the precincts of the royal palace; and the affairs of state were carefully taken in hand by his ministers and counsellors by the establishment of a kind of regency, all in the hope that sanity might return. Driver, quoting Farrar, cites a number of historical parallels.

One new feature is added to the description of his state—the growth of his hair and his nails. The abbreviated Aramaic description says: "His hair grew long as eagles'," meaning naturally "as eagles' feathers," which aptly describes the matted, long, unkempt hair. The second comparison is after the same pattern: "and his nails as birds'" = "as the claws of a bird."

34, 35 (Hebrew 31, 32). **"At the end of the days I, Nebuchadnezzar lifted up my eyes unto the heavens, and my reason returned to me. Then I blessed the Most High and praised and glorified Him who lives forever, whose dominion is an everlasting dominion, and His kingdom to all generations. All the inhabitants of the earth are accounted as nothing, and He doeth as He pleaseth with the host of**

**the heavens and with those that dwell upon the
earth; and there is none that can stay his hand or
say unto Him: 'What doest Thou?' "**

The lapse of time involved again seems unimportant, much as we might like to know how long the
king's dementia lasted. Merely its conclusion is referred to by the phrase "at the end of the days." Two
events are reported: he lifted up his eyes, and his
reason returned. Some interpreters feel that this involves a *hysteron proteron*—the latter being mentioned
first—and claim that reason must have returned first
and then the upward look. Others would let the order
given in the text stand. The text is very likely not reporting the order of the occurrence so much as first
what occurred outwardly, then what took place in-
wardly. It is most reasonable to suppose that both
events happened simultaneously. In the very moment
when the king was ready to acknowledge the Most
High, in that very moment his reason returned. We
naturally wonder how much capacity for reflection,
if any, had been left the king, and what dim powers
of reason, if any, still remained. Such psychological
investigations are outside of the purpose of the king's
decree. But it is almost a touching detail to notice that
the outward evidence of the return to reason is the
upward look, the most noticeable feature that differ-
entiates man from the beast. It is significant that from
the Aramaic point of view "reason" is *manda'*,
"knowing."

Such a restoration calls for blessing, praise, and
glorification, which the king willingly tenders, ascribing to the Most High, as he does so, eternity and
everlasting dominion and unchanging rule (cf. Ps.
145:13). This fulsome praise finds poetic expression in
parallelism as it rises in a higher strain. How insignificant the dominion of man is must have come home
very keenly to the king.

35. To express this thought with stronger emphasis the king takes all the inhabitants of the earth together as a unit and avers that they are "accounted as nothing," not in the sense that God puts no value upon them, but in the sense: when they are contrasted with God. God's absolute sovereignty finds expression in the thought that "He doeth as He pleaseth with the host of the heavens"—the angels who are subservient to His will and purpose—"and with those that dwell upon the earth"—as Nebuchadnezzar just experienced to his sorrow.

"As he pleaseth" is the infinitive *mitsbe'* from *tsebha'*, "according to his pleasing." This last thought the king makes still more emphatic by adding, "There is none that can stay his hand." *That* the king had also found to be true when the sentence was finally passed, and he found himself suddenly brought low. In fact, the king is ready to admit that even remonstrance, not to mention opposition, is entirely beyond the pale of what would be permissible to man: "Who can say: 'What doest thou?'" It would be difficult to state the absolute power of the Almighty more clearly and more fully. "Stay His hand" involves the verb *mecha'*, "to smite," i.e., to smite the hand of children in order to restrain them.

36, 37 (Hebrew 33, 34). **"As soon as my reason had returned to me, then my honor and renown also returned to me for the glory of my kingdom; also my counsellors and my distinguished men sought me, and I was reinstated over my realm, and surpassing greatness was added to me. Now I, Nebuchadnezzar, praise, exalt, and glorify the King of the heavens, for all His works are right, and His ways are just; and those who walk proudly He is able to abase."**

The Aramaic, like the Hebrew, coordinates clauses and says: "At the same time my understanding re-

turned and," etc. Since the return of the understanding
was reported in v. 34, the clause should be subordinated here, as *Gordon* suggests, and should be translated: "As soon as my reason had returned," etc. Great
as the favor would have been to be restored merely to
reason, the greater fact is recorded that the former
"honor and renown (Aramaic: *ziv*, 'brilliance') also
returned." And rare had been the renown that the
mighty king enjoyed. The kingdom as such suffered no
impairment but experienced an increase of glory, for
so we construe the phrase "for the glory of my kingdom." Again, without attempting to follow a strictly
temporal sequence, the king reports how his "counsellors and distinguished men" (*Aramaic*: "great ones,"
rabhrᵉbhan) sought him out, and so he had all that
had once been his, in fact, "surpassing greatness was
added to me." The king achieved greater renown than
ever. But he is very careful not to ascribe all these new
honors to himself. He has learned his lesson well.

37.   This verse contains the climax of the edict—
grateful praise of the King of the heavens and the admission that all He does is "right" and "just" (*Aramaic*, stronger—"rightness and justice"), and the
warning conclusion: "T h o s e   who   walk   proudly
(*begevah*, 'in pride') He is able to abase." We feel inclined to hold with *Calvin* that, since God's justice is
admitted but nothing said of His mercy, even though
His goodness is praised, we may well doubt whether
the king's experience led to his conversion.

It behooves us to take issue regarding a matter
of textual import, which, if it had not been advanced
with so much skill and labor by recent scholars, could
well have been ignored. *Charles,* for example, has
raised and elaborately supported the claim that "the
LXX has in the main preserved the true order of the
text and its original character." If it could be shown
that this is true, it would be one of those factors which

tend to break down confidence in the Word of God in the form in which we now have it, as though the sacred text were in a most untrustworthy state. We must, therefore, examine into the matter in connection with this particular chapter at greater length.

It appears to us that *Charles* to a very large extent supplies the major arguments for the refutation for his position when on the next page (p. 80) he concedes "that the order and contents of the prescript [he means the royal edict that constitutes practically the whole chapter] in the LXX are confused beyond conception." This "order" which he claims to be utterly confused is, nevertheless, the "true order" according to the position taken.

Since the matter is argued at length, the individual arguments must be considered. The first is that "the analogies of chapters 3 and 6 support the order into which the matter is cast in the LXX." In other words, in these two chapters we find first "the king's psychical experience, and thereupon follows his royal prescript." We hold that the law of variety is just as valid as the law of similarity in the matter of literary composition. If an author has twice used a certain pattern he may as well choose to depart from that pattern as to be inclined to keep following it. On questions of style such as the present one critics have made claims that have not been substantiated.

Charles next points to the fact that the person of the narrative changes (vv. 16, 25-30) from the first to the third. We believe that our comments in explanation of this phenomenon carry far more plausibility (cf. the verses in question *supra*) than the critic's suggestion that the redactor "has here forgotten to transform these features." This is common critical procedure: first to invent redactors who tampered with the text and then to make them out to be rather incompetent to do their task well, and then to let the whole thing reflect on the state of the text. Have the critics not yet discovered that there ought to be such a thing in the treatment of the text of the Sacred Scriptures as trying to enter sympathetically into the statements of the text, and only when this is an utter impossibility—which it certainly is not in this case—to begin to consider the state of the text? We believe that the consistent good sense that the Hebrew text in its present state makes is its best vindication here as always. We also believe that our interpretation offered above has demonstrated, at least in a measure, this clear good sense that we refer to.

The next critical proof is really only a subhead under the preceding argument. It runs thus: "The LXX alone of all the authorities preserves the date of Section IV [i.e. chapter 4] and that, as is our author's all but universal method, in its opening sentence." We offer a counterargument that we believe is just as reasonable an explanation of the absence of this date in the Hebrew text and of its presence in the Greek. The tendency of the Septuagint text to smooth out difficulties is so well known as demonstrated, for example, by *Koenig* in his *Einleitung* that we can well understand how the early Greek translators, noting the other dates throughout the book, were struck by the absence of the dating of this chapter and sought conjecturally to supply the defect. Equally strong is the argument that the other Greek text available for the Book of Daniel, namely, that of Theodotion, also does not give any date for the chapter.

Then, on the whole, it must be considered that the Jews as a nation and in their leaders always harbored so great a reverence for the sacred writings they possessed that it would be preposterous to ascribe to them the tendency to make alterations of the sacred text as such rather than to the translators of whose conscientious scruples under this head we learn nothing from any available evidence. It may be remarked here that this same Septuagint text which Charles favors so highly at this point offers forty per cent more words in chapter four than does the Hebrew and in the next chapter 30 per cent fewer words.

The next argument for the priority of the Greek text is the fact that it omits vv. 3-7a (6-10a), "which recounts the assembling together of the wise men of the king." The idea involved in the argument is that "the relative positions of Daniel and the wise men during Nebuchadnezzar's reign were settled once and for all in chap. 2." We believe our comments offered above on this situation take care of this argument.

HOMILETICAL SUGGESTIONS

If a series of sermons is being preached on the book of Daniel, the major purpose of this chapter must definitely be kept in mind, the purpose indicated by our caption "The Overthrow of the Pride of Worldly Empires." It is not so much the individual who is under consideration, Nebuchadnezzar, the king, but this monarch in so far as he exemplifies the spirit of worldly empires. Such pride is characteristic of empires and particularly of empire builders. But it is equally reprehensible in all and doomed to an ultimate overthrow. The positive element for the text is supplied by v. 32b, "the Most High ruleth in the kingdom of men."

Especially in days like ours, when imperialistic aims become more pronounced, Bible truths like these serve to orient the thinking of men. Vv. 28-37 would be the portion used. The rest of the chapter would be woven into the picture as needed.

The text may by adaptation be used to illustrate the truth, "God resisteth the proud but given grace to the humble."

CHAPTER V

D. Belshazzar's Feast:
The Overthrow of the Insolence of the Degenerate World Power, 5:1—6:1

Nearly seventy years have elapsed since chapter one (Driver). One note has been rung throughout each chapter since chapter two: the world power will fall or be overthrown and is, therefore, not to be feared. The same thought appears here, with this difference: in chapter four it was the *pride* of the world power, here it is its *insolence* that is to be overthrown. The advance from pride to insolence suggests an increase in degeneracy. There is evidence, therefore, of the successive deterioration of the powers that are hostile to the Lord and to His kingdom. Since these deeper considerations come to the forefront in this chapter, it will be apparent that from certain points of view the otherwise correct title, "Belshazzar's Feast," is inadequate. We, therefore, add the above subtitle.

a. *The King's Insolent Deed*, v. 1-4

1. **King Belshazzar made a great feast for a thousand of his lords and drank wine before the thousand.**

The identity of "King Belshazzar" is the great problem of this verse and one that deserves careful investigation, chiefly because of the sweeping claims of critics that have been made under this head and are still in circulation, at least in part. *Cornill* is still very modest in his assertion when he says that to call the one who was on the throne when Babylon fell Belshazzar, and to say that he was the son of Nebuchadnezzar "contradicts all the rest of the reliable evidence of the Scriptures." *

A number of solutions of the difficulty have been attempted. Some identify Belshazzar with Evil Merodach, king of Babylon, Nebuchadnezzar's son, mentioned in II Kings 25:27, on the very correct assumption that notable persons, especially kings, often bore more than one name, witness Solomon who is called Jedidiah (II Sam. 12:25). Others insert Belshazzar between Nebuchadnezzar and Evil Merodach. In either case it is claimed that 5:30 and 5:31 (*A. V.*) speak of events that lay rather farther apart than a hasty reading might suggest. Still others identify Belshazzar with Nabonidus or with the son of Nabonidus.

In order to facilitate the understanding of the issues involved we shall give in order the kings of Babylon as the Babylonian historian *Berosus* is known to have listed them, as well as their fate:

Evil Merodach, son of Nebuchadnezzar, was killed.

Neriglissar, son-in-law of Nebuchadnezzar, died.

Laborosoarchad, grandson of Nebuchadnezzar, was killed.

Nabonnedus, not related, not of royal blood, died.

The picture becomes a bit clearer when we add the needed dates, beginning with Nabopolassar who came to the throne upon the overthrow of the Assyrian power and set up the empire of the Chaldeans. We shall give the form of the names that is more commonly in use in our day and the date of accession.

625 B. C.—Nabopolassar.

604—Nebuchadrezzar.

562—Amel-Marduk.

560—Nergal-shar-usur.

556—Labashi-Marduk.

---

*Cornill, Carl Heinrich, *Einleitung in die kanonischen Buecher des Alten Testaments* (Tuebingen: 1905), p. 239.

555—Nabunaid.

538—Capture of Babylon by Cyrus.

Berosus must have been a reliable historian, for the monuments and the inscriptions amply confirm his sequence of kings at this point. At first glance the above list, if it is as reliable as we claim, seems quite disappointing, for it contains no reference to Belshazzar. This might drive us back to the position taken by men like *Keil* and *Kliefoth* who belong to the class of those mentioned above, who identified Evil Merodach (Amel-Marduk) with Belshazzar, chiefly on the ground that he appeared to be the son of Nebuchadnezzar in this chapter.

However, since the time of these valiant champions of the truth new evidence has been unearthed, which, to use *Montgomery's* words, has "strikingly demonstrated the existence of a Belshazzar at the end of the Chaldean dynasty by the discovery of his name on the Nabonidus cylinders, in which he appears as Nabonidus' son." In spite of the evidence yielded by this discovery one other supposition was maintained in the face of the statement of the book of Daniel which calls him *"King* Belshazzar," namely, the claim that he could not have been king. However, presently new evidence was discovered which "shows that royal dignity was actually conferred upon Belshazzar." Although these and other statements of the text have been strikingly confirmed, some interpreters still assert unreservedly but without evidence that the account is "unhistorical." The pertinent inscriptions are mentioned by Barton.* When all the extant material in the form of inscriptions is collated, it seems that there is even the possibility of the existence of two men by the name of Nabonidus, father and son, and that Belshazzar may have been the son or the brother of Nabo-

---

*Barton, George A., *Archaeology and the Bible* (Philadelphia: Seventh edition, 1937), p. 481 ff.

nidus II as *Wilson* maintains (ISBE, article: "Bel-shazzar"). We shall not defend this last rather complicated view.

It must at the same time be observed that the un-modified title "King Belshazzar" by no means implies that he was king of the empire of Babylon but merely king of Babylonia, the district, and perhaps of a few adjoining districts. The *Hebrew* and the *Aramaic* do not have a word for "emperor," who is over kings. One word, "king," covers all such and similar relationships; and to this day kings function under other kings, es-pecially when their father happens to be monarch over several countries.

It may be well in this connection to dispose of the allied problem: "Who was the 'queen' mentioned in v. 10?" At least, "What was her relation to Belshazzar or to Nabonidus?" Frankly, no man knows exactly. But our ignorance does not impeach the veracity of Daniel. Since, as indicated above, Nabonidus was not related to Nebuchadnezzar, there are several possibilities as to what this usurper might have done to ally himself with the line of the renowned Nebuchadnezzar. Since only seven years had elapsed between Nebuchadnezzar's death and the accession of Nabonidus to the throne, it could have easily been possible that a young widowed queen of Nebuchadnezzar was available for Nabonidus. Compare the parallel situation mentioned in I Kings 2:13. Such a marriage gave a newcomer social or royal standing.

There is also the other possibility that Belshazzar, a true descendant, even a son of Nebuchadnezzar, may have been living at the same time. When Nabonidus married the widow he may have adopted the son and thus secured an heir for himself, a scion of the illus-trious family of Nebuchadnezzar. Such a situation, which is entirely possible from any point of view, would throw light on the words spoken to Belshazzar by this mysterious queen mentioned in v. 10. There are, of course, many other possibilities, the very number of which should make any interpreter cautious to assert that the author of our book is in error. *Wilson* has shown how among the Arabs and the Babylonians the word "son" lent itself to no less than twelve separate uses, including "grandson" and "adopted son"; and the word for "father" has seven separate and distinct uses.*

So it must be evident on the basis of thorough and scientific historical investigation that the criticism raised against the book on the matter of the reference to this King Belshazzar was both premature and ill-advised.

Belsha'tstsar is the preferred spelling; *Bel'shatstsar* (7:1) is less correct. The name means "Bel guard the king."

Against a case such as we have assumed, i.e., that Nabonidus married a widow of Nebuchadnezzar, *Charles* makes the counterclaim that, if Nabonidus had done anything of this nature, the records available in tablets and in inscriptions and the like would undoubtedly have made mention of so important a fact. But it dare not be forgotten, as every student of archæology knows, that the records of the past are very fragmentary and leave great gaps practically everywhere. It is only during the past twenty years that Belshazzar has been discovered in these records. The claims that were made on that score concerning the accuracy of the Biblical record ought to teach men caution.

Quite a bit more impressive is the other claim made by the same author that Daniel seems to regard Belshazzar as "absolute sovereign." That means, of course, that he did not hold the rule of merely the little district of Babylon but was ruler of the whole Baby-

---

*Wilson, Robert Dick, *Studies in the Book of Daniel* (New York: Putnam's Sons, 1917), p. 117 f.

lonian Empire even as Nebuchadnezzar had done. As proof for this the fact is pointed to that in 7:1 as well as in 8:1 the author of our books dates events according to the years of the reign of Belshazzar. This would be in obvious conflict with what the tablets record concerning the events of the reign of Nabonidus, which extended over a period of seventeen years.

We feel that a clear distinction must be made between the tablets and the Biblical record. If it was customary to date events on Babylonian tablets according to the years that had passed since the accession of the reigning monarch, that does not mean that such a procedure must be followed by a writer of a book like Daniel's. For the thing that is of importance is that the matter about to be recorded stands in relation to the king mentioned in the opening words of the record. In some cases it might be the supreme monarch; in others it might be the local king. Though the Biblical writers, without a doubt, have many things in common with the secular writers of their day they never followed such literary patterns rigidly. They manifested rather a freedom and an originality which showed them to be in advance of contemporary literary procedure. In other words, the argument: Thus and so did contemporary writers, therefore the Biblical writers must be judged accordingly, has, we say, been used again and again beyond the measure allowable by the standards of exact criticism.

Strangely, the same author, though he concedes that the question whether Belshazzar is the son of Nebuchadnezzar is "one of the unsolved problems of history," regards the position taken by the book of Daniel as involving a "historical misconception of our author." In other words, even when the evidence is not yet clear, the *Biblical* book cannot be correct. We cannot call this a case of keeping one's mind open on an unsettled question.

Of this king it is said that he made a "feast,"
léchem, originally meaning only "bread," for a thousand of his lords. That cannot strike us as being unusual when we recognize that Persian and Babylonian
courts were proverbially large establishments. Commentators refer to the report of a historian Ktesias
who informs us that the Persian monarch provided food
for 15,000 persons daily in his royal menage. Though,
as a rule, these monarchs dined by themselves, on state
occasions, especially as the degeneracy of the Oriental
courts grew apace, the king and his most renowned
men of state sat on an elevated dais in the very banquet
hall. The drinking of wine followed after the meal as
such had been eaten; it signifies the procedure that
might be termed a "drinking bout."

2-4. **When the wine was beginning to taste
good, Belshazzar commanded to bring the vessels
of gold and silver which Nebuchadnezzar, his father, had brought forth from the Temple in Jerusalem that the king and his lords, his wives and his
concubines might drink out of them. Then they
brought the golden vessels which had been brought
forth from the Temple of the house of God which is
in Jerusalem; and the king and his lords, his wives
and his concubines drank out of them. They drank
wine and praised the gods of gold and silver, bronze,
iron, wood, and stone.**

2. It will be noted that the Biblical record does
not report much about this insignificant king, whose
reign was brief, and whose deeds were apparently not
worthy of record. The only thing that distinguished
him was one superb act of insolence which is set down
as a notable matter of record. The connection in which
this deed is reported is highly suggestive: he committed this misdeed under the influence of wine. The
wine devil breaks down wholesome restraints.

The *Aramaic* says: "When he tasted the wine."

This apparently indicates what we have rendered: "When the wine was beginning to taste good." It cannot mean: at the very first sip of wine. The wine had already produced that well-known boldness and pseudocourage. In this case this unwholesome frame of mind led to a deed that is unparalleled in the records of antiquity. Temples may have been destroyed and sacked, but such vandalism would be compensated for by the erection of new temples for the deities of the conquered nations. For the gods were venerated; a man respected his own gods as well as the gods of others. They might have been vanquished for a time by more powerful divinities, but they were still to be treated with extreme respect and deference.

When Belshazzar "commanded to bring the vessels of gold and silver, which Nebuchadnezzar, his father, had brought forth from the Temple in Jerusalem (cf. II Kings 24:13; 25:15) that the king and his lords, his wives and his concubines might drink out of them," this was plainly an act of open defiance, calculated to insult the God whose Temple had stood in Jerusalem. Why should Jehovah have been singled out thus? Belshazzar had apparently had no contact with Judea or Jerusalem, which had now lain in ruins for almost seventy years. The only explanation we can offer is that, seemingly, the king had heard of the truth as it is in Jehovah, the one true God. The stubbornness of the malevolence of sin, which is not disturbed by religiousness or religions as they are commonly practiced by men, is much perturbed by the truth. The hidden depths of iniquity stir up the basest of passions when they face God and His kingdom. This fact it was that led Belshazzar to commit an act of arrogant defiance against the Most High and, as it were, to challenge Him to avenge His honor.

As the sequel shows, the king had had ample opportunity to know better than to venture upon such a course. Nothing is related about the reaction of the lords and the others present at the time. Since no sentence is pronounced upon them, it hardly seems likely that they had much zest for this type of drinking bout but hardly dared to oppose the absolute monarch.

Haythayah is Haphel infinitive from *'athah*. On the word *'abhûhî*, "his father," see v. 3. *Mā'ney*, "vessels," is acknowledged to be old Aramaic.

3. The carrying out of the king's orders is reported in almost the very words that were used in the command in order to indicate that they were obeyed to the letter. One slight addition indicates the writer's feelings on the subject—to the word "Temple" he adds the words "of the house of God." This was the Temple of the only God and His only Temple. This addition suffices to indicate the heinousness of the offense. The report of what was done with these vessels is again stated in the very words of what was previously recorded as having been the king's purpose in calling for these vessels. All this is an effective rhetorical device for indicating that up to this point everything was going strictly according to schedule and so preparing for the sudden interruption of the contemplated course of procedure. The presence of the king's "wives" and "concubines" was usually not tolerated at banquets. It was, however, permitted when degeneracy began to run rampant.

The form *'ishtîw* comes from *shetha'* and merely has a so-called prothetic *'aleph*, which in no sense indicates an *Aphel*.

The word *'abh*, "father," which is used in this connection with reference to Nebuchadnezzar is still referred to by critics in order to make out a case against Daniel's reliability. *Pusey's* words may be cited because the critics affirm that this word scarcely makes sense unless Belshazzar was the very son of Nebuchadnezzar in the commonly accepted meaning of the term. *Pusey* says: "These men teach the old prophet, that he ought to have said, 'Nebuchadnezzar, thy grandfather,' 'and thou, his grandson.' Most accurate advice! Daniel would doubtless have followed it, had he been speaking in English. But what if, in Chaldee [we should say 'Aramaic'], it was impossible without coining a new word? Neither in Hebrew, nor in Chaldee, is there any word for 'grandfather,' 'grandson.' 'Forefathers' are called 'fathers' or 'fathers' fathers.' But a single grandfather, or forefather, is never called 'father's father' but always 'father' only."* Still, for all of that, we hold that Belshazzar may have been a true son of Nebuchadnezzar as explained above.

4. The spirit of their undertaking is characterized in a very concise way. Their drinking of wine is accompanied by praises of their own many idols. They evidently meant it all in the sense that they glorified their own gods and challenged Him whose Temple vessels they were putting to unholy use to prevent this and to punish them if He could. We again remark, how much enthusiasm the throng present had for this venture we can hardly say. We feel that *Zoeckler* is quite on the right track when he points to the number six as being the number of the types of man-made idols listed ("gold, and silver, bronze, iron, wood, stone"), for "six, generally speaking, is the number of the world destined for judgment and hostile to God."

Already at this point a contention of the critics is seen to be groundless: the contention that Belshazzar typifies Antiochus Epiphanes, that bitter foe of the Jews. In the first place, there is nothing on record of his ever having profaned sacred vessels of Jehovah's Temple. Note to what extremities the critics resort in order to make out a case for their view by

*Pusey, E. B., *Daniel the Prophet*, (New York: Funk and Wagnalls, 1885), p. 346.

inserting into the evidence the claim they desire to
prove as though it were actually a matter of record.
Says *Farrar:* "The story . . . is really suggested by the
profanity of Antiochus Epiphanes in carrying off, and
doubtless subjecting to profane usage, many of the
sacred vessels of the Temple of Jerusalem." Note, no
man has as yet adduced evidence of his "doubtless subjecting to profane usage." That supposition is an invention pure and simple. Besides, there is a peculiar
impropriety about having Antiochus Epiphanes represented at one time under the guise of Nebuchadnezzar,
at another under the guise of Nebuchadnezzar's "son."
Meinhold admits this. *Montgomery* goes so far as to
say: "Belshazzar is not the type of the arrogant
despot Antiochus Epiphanes; he does not appear as the
destroyer of the Jewish religion, only as the typical
profligate and frivolous monarch. . . . The story . . . is
doubtless far more ancient than the second century B. C."

b. *The Dreadful Handwriting on the Wall and
the Inability of the Wise Men to Interpret
It,* v. 5-9

5. **At that very time there came forth the
fingers of a man's hand, and they wrote over against
the candlestick upon the plaster of the wall of the
king's palace; and the king saw the tip of the hand
that wrote.**

The banquet has proceeded far enough to allow
the king to reveal plainly what was in his mind and
to offer insult to God Most High. "At that very time"—
for so the Aramaic "in that hour" is meant—the terrible prodigy appeared: "there came forth" within the
range of the king's vision, perhaps at the very point
upon which his eyes rested, "the fingers of a man's
hand." No more needed to be seen. The fingers suggested the presence of the rest of the body of the one

who was writing, and that what was being written was not an optical illusion but was caused by an intelligent agent.

To see the fingers and no more may have served a double purpose. On the one hand, seeing only the fingers may have served to terrify still more because the imagination would have free scope to think of all manner of beings. Again, had, let us say, an angelic agent appeared, his very presence might have drawn attention away from the thing he was delegated to write. It seems very likely that this event was held at night. It is for this reason that attention is drawn to the fact that the writing appeared over against "the candlestick," *nebhrashta'*—probably a foreign word and so hardly a reference to the seven-branched candlestick from the Temple at Jerusalem.

An interesting sidelight is thrown on this episode by the discoveries of the archæologist. The chief royal audience chamber which was more than 50 feet wide and more than 160 feet long has apparently been identified. There is a niche in the center of one of the long sides, and it would seem that the throne must have stood there. Perhaps, if this was the scene of the banquet, the niche might have been the place where the royal table stood. Here "the walls were covered with white plaster," which is recognizable to this day as surfacing a coarser material that was used as a base and thus coincides with the expression used in our text, "upon the plaster (*gîra'*) of the wall" (*kethal*).

Many must have simultaneously witnessed the same sight as they discovered afterward when they compared notes. Of the king, who must have been as near as anyone to the fatal spot, it is definitely said that he "saw the tip [*pas*—so rendered by *K. W.*, but 'palm' by BDB] of the hand that wrote." This suggests vividly that everyone tried to see more of the unseen agent, but none succeeded.

Certain rationalistic explanations must be rejected as untenable in the light of this plain narrative. It was not a case of some prank being played on the king by hostile lords at court who had their plans laid to assassinate the king this night and were now playing upon his forebodings. It was not a case of some strong light falling upon a few chance but ominous words that had long ago been inscribed on the palace walls but now suddenly stood out in this clear light with a new meaning. But it is a significant contrast that the inscription should appear on the palace walls which usually abounded in records that glorified the royal achievements and heroic deeds.

6, 7. Then, as for the king, his face changed color, and his thoughts perturbed him so that his very hips shook, and his knees smote one upon the other. The king called aloud to fetch the enchanters, the Chaldeans, and the astrologers. He answered and said to the wise men of Babylon: "Whosoever shall read this writing and make its interpretation known he shall be clad in a robe of purple with a, gold chain about his neck and shall occupy the position of 'talti' in the kingdom."

Whereas attention has for a moment been centered upon the handwriting, by setting an independent nominative in the forefront Daniel draws our thoughts exclusively toward the king. The Aramaic word *zîv* means about as much as "healthy color" or "brightness." The statement, "his healthy color changed for him," is covered pretty well by *Gordon's* rendering, which we have followed, his "face changed color." The suffix on *shenôhî*, "changed *for him*," shows the latitude possible in the use of object suffixes, which may even be datives (*K. S.* 21).

The sequence of the things reported about the king is, no doubt, exactly what an onlooker might have observed. He grows pale; it then becomes manifest that painful thoughts are perturbing him; those standing near by then observe a violent trembling which affects more than the knees: "his very hips shook." By the use of "very" we have tried to reproduce an unusual Aramaic expression: "the knots or joints of his hips were loosed." The paralyzing effect of excessive fear seemed to dissolve his strength up to the point of the ball-and-socket joints as *K. W.* renders the expression. What a pitiful spectacle of a king who had a few moments before ventured to defy the Almighty! Luther renders very effectively: *dass ihm die Lenden schuetterten, und die Beine zitterten.* The general idea is found elsewhere, cf. Isa. 21:3; Nah. 2:10; Ezek. 21:11; Ps. 69:23.

7. Unable to sit down because of his agitation, hardly able to stand because of his overpowering fear, the king calls with excessive loudness, *becháyil,* in order to mask his trembling voice. His thoughts have moved along the traditional lines: supernatural manifestations are within the special province of the wise men of the courts, three classes of whom, who are representative of all classes, are mentioned. See 2:2 on these names. Those who begin to arrive are from this point onward referred to by the collective term "wise men." To understand the sequence of events correctly it is necessary to bear in mind the very obvious course followed by the king. He would hardly have waited till every last one of the wise men had come in. As soon as a sizable group was assembled, he will have made his request known, which course would appear all the more natural since everybody was still staring at the mysterious handwriting. Those first arrivals will quite naturally have conveyed the king's demand to the ones that came straggling in later.

The words of the king do not make clear the exact nature of the difficulty, for the king mentions both the reading of the writing and the making known of the interpretation. This may mean that the words could neither be read nor be interpreted. It might mean that the words as such could be read but could not be construed satisfactorily, and so even the reading seemed doubtful. These questions are of little moment, and all attempted solutions are conjecture. We cannot even surmise in what language the handwriting appeared, whether in the ancient Sumerian, the current Babylonian, or the Aramaic.

The king's promises of reward for an interpretation are bountiful: "he shall be clad in purple," 'arg^ewana, resembling the corresponding Hebrew word and meaning, no doubt, "a robe of purple," a color that was reserved for royalty or near royalty (cf. Esther 8:15). The gold "chain," hamnîkha', apparently of Persian origin and closely resembling the Greek μανιάκης, is also a mark of rare distinction, cf. Gen. 41: 42. It has been pointed out that chains could be worn only "when presented by the king."

The last reward promised is usually rendered, "And shall be the third ruler in the kingdom." It reads literally: "And shall rule in the kingdom as talti." It has been granted since *Haevernick's* time that talti is not the ordinal numeral "third," which would have to be telîthî. So some interpreters translate the word "triumvir" or dritter an Rang (K. W.). That view, of course, always led to speculation since the king was, no doubt, first. Who was the second? The queen mother or Nabonidus II or someone else? The simplest solution appeals to the parallel Hebrew form shalîsh (the Aramaic substitutes t for sh), which, though also apparently involving the root for "three" or "third," has the meaning "adjutant or officer" (BDB). It, no doubt, involves a very high dignity here, but no man is able to determine exactly what dignity. *Montgomery* lists several English words which have, in a similar way, completely lost their root meaning: "tetrarch," "chamberlain," and "knight."

We must again reckon with the question of the corrected and improved text, with which we are so frequently confronted in our days, and which has impressed some men so profoundly that they have freely conceded that the proof offered for the corrupt state of the Hebrew text is overwhelming. One such effort is submitted by *Charles* who gives his improved version of vv. 5-8 and prefaces it with the remark: "We are now in a position to give a translation of a text superior to that of the MT" [i.e., the old standard Hebrew text]. We shall refrain from attempting a complete refutation of the separate critical arguments advanced by the learned author. We believe it to be quite readily demonstrable that the whole effort moves almost entirely within the realm of conjecture and opinion or is of the type that follows the maxim: "Had *I* written this account, *I* would have written it so and so." In the nature of the case such results cannot be called "scientific."

The sequence of events as given by the Septuagint is followed in the main in this rearrangement of the text, and for this sequence it is claimed, "We have here . . . the rational order of events." However, the advocate of this claim has overlooked the most obvious fact that the very thing that was taking place was occurring in the midst of a scene of utmost confusion. Who knows what the "rational order of events" was at such a time? This observation alone shows how precarious are all such efforts at trying to make a better text. Here, as usual, as our interpretation attempts to show, the very order of events given in the Hebrew text makes very good sense.

8, 9. Then all the wise men of the king kept coming in, and none were able to read the writing or to make its interpretation known to the king.

Then the king Belshazzar was utterly upset, and his face changed color, and his lords were sorely perplexed.

The very natural sequence of occurrences as reported at this point elicits the attacks of criticism. It is claimed that the preceding verse had already introduced the wise men and had them hear the king's demand. Now the wise men are said to be pictured as entering in v. 8. An obvious matter is overlooked by such criticism, namely, as pointed out above, that the king would lay his request before any larger group as soon as it was assembled. All that is required is to translate the participle (*'allilin*) used in v. 8 as a progressive—they "kept coming in." Finally, when they were all assembled, it was found that not one could offer the least bit of help.

9. When it became apparent that from this quarter help could no longer be expected, the king's confusion increased, and he again paled visibly as he did in v. 6. The expression differs but slightly in this repetition of v. 6 in that here the suffix is attached to a preposition rather than to the verb. The perplexity of the lords is mentioned separately because the king was now apparently about to appeal to them for aid, and they were as much at a loss as was the king.

We cannot but remark how utterly human wisdom collapses when the Lord sets about to display its shallowness. "He that sitteth in the heavens shall laugh; the Lord shall have them in derision," Ps. 2:4.

c. *The Queen Mother's Suggestion, v. 10-12*

10. **Now by reason of the words of the king and his lords the queen came into the banquet house. The queen answered and said: "O king, live forever; let not thy thoughts perplex thee, and let not the color of thy face be changed."**

We have discussed the identity of the "queen," *malketha'*, in connection with v. 1. It seems reasonable to us to believe that she may have been the widow of Nebuchadnezzar. Such queen mothers enjoyed rare authority which exceeded even that of the chief wife or queen of the reigning monarch. She had not been present at the banquet board, perhaps as a protest against a profligacy and an indifference to duty of which she could not but disapprove. The "words," *millah,* of the king as well as the remarks of the lords had been conveyed to her, no doubt by the ever-active and curious servants. To render this word "cries" goes beyond the things recorded and makes too much of a baby of the king. To render it "matter"—*Luther:* *Sache*—is not foreign to the meaning of the word but conflicts with its number. Having a truly helpful suggestion, the queen mother ventures to come "to the banquet house," a name that suggests not only a separate hall but even a separate house. She uses the conventional form of address (cf. 3:9; 6:6) and then exhorts the king to pull himself together. She speaks as one who has a suitable remedy to propose.

11, 12. "There is a man in thy kingdom in whom is the spirit of the holy gods. In the days of thy father there was found in him enlightenment and insight and wisdom like unto the wisdom of gods; and King Nebuchadnezzar, thy father, did appoint him chief of the scholars, enchanters, Chaldeans, and astrologers, thy father, O king, I say. Because there is to be found in him pre-eminent capacity and knowledge and insight, interpretation of dreams and solving riddles and unravelling knotty matters—namely in this Daniel, whose name the king appointed to be Belteshazzar—therefore now let Daniel be called, and he will make known the interpretation."

The queen ascribes to Daniel more than she ascribes to the rest of the wise men. She sums up his rare gifts in the phrase, "the spirit of the holy gods," (cf. 4:8, 9). She lists separately the gifts that grew out of the possession of this rare spirit: *nahîrû* = "light or enlightenment"; *sokhlethânû* = "insight"; and *chokhmah* = "wisdom." This last is so superlative as to be like that "of gods." She remembers also what Belshazzar may have never been aware of, that Nebuchadnezzar, having put this man to the test thoroughly, had made him chief of all his wise men. The subject, "thy father," is repeated because the subject had gotten so far removed from the predicate. *Malka'* is better regarded as a vocative.

12. A better rendering results when v. 11 is definitely closed with a period. The first clause of v. 12 is then regarded as a protasis of the second half, and in this way cumbersome repetition of the thoughts of v. 11 is avoided. The listing of Daniel's gifts is now most detailed. First there is mentioned the all-inclusive "pre-eminent capacity," *rû'ach yattîra'* (*A. V.*, "an excellent spirit"; *Luther, ein hoher Geist*). "Knowledge" appears in this list. The remaining terms indicate what his rare attainments can achieve: "interpretation of dreams and solving riddles and unravelling knotty matters." In his day Daniel had apparently engaged in all these mental tasks and had been known to excel in them. The queen prefers to call him Daniel, remembering, it seems, 4:8. She avers confidently that Daniel will supply the needed interpretation. "Knotty matters," *qitrîn*, literally, "knots," should not and need not be translated "magic knots." That was not Daniel's province.

It will hardly seem strange to note that Daniel had not appeared before this time if it is remembered that with the coming of a new king, especially when usurpers arose, wholesale dismissal of the men in office was the rule. Daniel may have been demoted even before Belshazzar appeared on the scene.

But could a man of Daniel's reputation actually

have been forgotten by the time of Belshazzar? *Farrar* states his view of the case: "He must have known of the Rab-mag Daniel, whose wisdom even as a boy, had been found superior to that of all the *Chartummim* and *Ashshaphim*; and how his three companions had been elevated to supreme satrapies, and how they had been delivered unsinged. . . . Under no conceivable circumstances could such marvels have been forgotten." Such a statement hardly agrees with the facts of the case. For, in the first place, heathen Babylonians will not have been any too eager to perpetuate traditions which told of the overthrow of heathen world power. In addition, men have frequently been known to forget what it was convenient to forget, all the more so, as all men know, truths which involved God's revelation; and all that was known about Daniel was tied up with divine revelation. Lastly, it dare not be forgotten that many a man has forgotten the most obvious things under the stress of a strong emotional strain. Especially v. 13 and 14 indicate that Belshazzar had heard quite a bit and still remembered it.

d. *The King's Request*, v. 13-16

13-16. Then Daniel was brought before the king. The king answered and said to Daniel: "So thou art Daniel, who art of the number of the captives of Judah, whom my father, the king, brought up from Judah! Now I have heard concerning thee that the spirit of the gods is in thee, and enlightenment and insight and excellent wisdom is found in thee. Now there were brought before me the wise men and enchanters that they might read this writing and make its interpretation known to me, and they have not been able to disclose the interpretation of the matter. Now I for my part have heard concerning thee that thou art able to give interpretations and to solve knotty questions. Now if thou be able to read this writing and to make its

interpretation known thou shalt be clothed with a robe of purple and have a golden chain about thy neck and shalt hold the position of 'talti' in the kingdom."

It may be possible that the king's first statement is a question as most of the versions render it, although there is no interrogative word in the original that indicates this. Even if it is a question, the king apparently did not expect an answer, for he proceeds with his request at once. The result is almost the same if the words are rendered as a statement of surprise: "So thou art Daniel" or even, "So thou art that Daniel," the man about whom he had heard but whom, in his profligate and frivolous life, he had never taken the trouble to consult. The aged Daniel, no doubt, presented a venerable appearance and had a countenance that elicited the king's admiration. It is significant that, by contrast, Belshazzar seems to remember much better the record of his father's conquests, and that this Daniel belonged to those captives who were brought up from Judah. The expression we rendered "number of the captives" has a truly Semitic flavor in the original, namely, "children of the captivity." "Daniel" he calls him, perhaps with the intent of not displeasing the God whose name he bears.

The rest of the words of the king are quoted mostly from what the queen mother had said, except that Belshazzar, having a bad conscience, prefers to say "spirit of the gods" rather than "of the holy gods" as his mother had said (v. 11). In v. 16 the king displays the only bit of authority that he ventures to assert over against Daniel when he begins, "I for my part," as much as to say, "I for one know you can interpret." The "knotty questions" are called merely "knots," *qitrîn,* in the original. This word, of course, has no reference to enchanters' knots, so-called. For the current Aramaic form *tikkul,* "thou art able," the text offers a Hebrew equivalent *tukhal,* which, after the fashion of the Masoretes, is pointed as the form should be read (*keri*) and not as it is printed (*kethibh*).

e. *Daniel's Admonition to The King,* v. 17-24

17. Then Daniel answered and spoke in the presence of the king: "Keep thy gifts for thyself and give thy rewards to another man. Nevertheless, I shall read the writing to the king and make the interpretation known to him."

A certain brusqueness marks Daniel's words. This is to be explained primarily by the fact that the king's conduct is offensive to God and must necessarily be offensive to Daniel. The smooth, flattering courtesy of the man at court would certainly have been out of place on this occasion. Yet Daniel cannot be charged with disrespectful behavior. The gifts of the king must be refused (cf. II Kings 5:15, 16) because Daniel dare not appear as being on the same level with the mercenary wise men of Babylon who traffic in their wares. He has received very special and undeserved revelation from the only true God and cannot appear as one who derives personal profit from God's revelation. When Daniel later (v. 29), nevertheless, accepts certain royal honors, the situation has by that time become different. He can then no longer be suspected of retailing divine revelations for profit. His plain speech to the king had put that misconstruction of his position outside of the realm of possibility. Refusal of recognition at that point would have amounted to an insult.

We feel that we have not imparted a tone of undue brusqueness to Daniel's words by our rendering, for the Aramaic says: "Let thy gifts be to thee and thy rewards to another." The rest of the statement, "Nevertheless, I shall read," etc., indicates conclusively that in this case gifts have nothing to do with Daniel's

course of conduct. It goes without saying that such a
stand, so plainly stated, required real courage in facing
Oriental despots of those days. The form *lehewyan* is
feminine third person plural from the verb "to be."

**18, 19. "O thou king, God the Most High gave
to Nebuchadnezzar, thy father, the kingdom and
greatness and honor and glory; and because of the
greatness that He gave to him all nations and
peoples and tongues feared him and trembled at his
presence; he slew whom he pleased, he kept alive
whom he pleased, he exalted whom he pleased, he
humbled whom he pleased."**

These verses are the beginning of one of the finest
sermons delivered by a court preacher under the most
trying circumstances. The preacher is not found re-
miss in a single item. He tells the whole truth, and tells
it with unmistakable clearness. He cringes before no
man; he uses no evasion or circumlocution; and he
maintains a respectful attitude throughout. Withal he
aims at the moral restoration of his hearer or hearers.

Nebuchadnezzar's greatness as well as his pride
are presented in detail in order to indicate that, in the
case of this king at least, there was a semblance of
reason for his pride, an excuse which, by contrast,
Belshazzar could hardly advance. Yet with perfect
truth Daniel ascribes even all this greatness of Nebuchadnezzar's to "God the Most High," a most appropriate designation at this point to show the one God's
supremacy over all those whom men called gods.

The things bestowed on this king were first the
kingdom, then ability to manage the kingdom, which
is well rendered, "greatness," then the "honor" that
results from successful administration of office, and
lastly the well-deserved reputation that grows up
among men—"glory." Quite an array of gifts! Outside
of his own realm all other nations "feared" him whenever they thought of him and "trembled" when they

stood in the presence of the illustrious monarch. History has verified the fact that the picture is not overdrawn.

Besides, in his day there were no powerful ministers who overawed him or favorites who covertly controlled him. There was no power behind the throne: the king did exactly as he pleased without regard to men. That is the idea conveyed by the fourfold statement, "he slew whom he pleased," etc. The emphasis is on "whom he pleased" as the repetition indicates. Consequently these words are not designed to convey the idea of arbitrariness but rather the idea of unhampered, unrestrained power. Every day men were moved up or down, consigned to death or to pardon, as the king might be minded to decree. Under the circumstances Daniel could hardly have ventured to overstate the case because that would have impugned his position as the herald of truth.

The form *mäche'*, pointed with a long *ä*, represents "the fiercer construction" (*K. W.*) of the Masoretes, for it would then come from the root "to smite." It is rather to be pointed *măch(ch)e'*, Haphel from *chaya'* = "to keep alive."

20, 21. "But when his heart was lifted up, and his spirit became proud and arrogant, he was thrust down from the throne of his kingdom, and his renown was taken from him. And he was driven away from the sons of men, and his heart was changed to be like that of a beast, and his dwelling place was with the wild asses, and he was fed grass like an ox, and his body became wet with the dew of heaven until he learned that God the Most High has dominion over the kingdom of men and sets upon it whomsoever He pleases."

The point remains that such a man as Nebuchadnezzar was, with the honors and the achievements that were his, might seem to have just reason for pride; but even in his case such an attitude called forth divine correction. The conclusion *a maiori ad minus* is now drawn: how much more deserving of punishment are you proud and haughty wastrel, who has not even won his spurs and has no ground for legitimate pride? All the thoughts expressed in these verses are found in chapter four; a few expressions are different. The "wild asses" are mentioned particularly. They are particularly shy creatures (cf. Job 39:5-8). "The king would avoid all contact with mankind as much as they" (*Charles*). The expression we rendered "became proud and arrogant" reads thus in the *Aramaic*: "became strong to become insolent." The *'im* before *chêwtha'* is the equivalent of a *ke*, "as" (cf. *K. S.* 338e).

22-24. **"But thou, O Belshazzar, his son, hast not humbled thy heart even though thou didst know all this. But thou hast lifted thyself up against the Lord of the heavens to have the vessels of His house brought before thee; and thou and thy lords, thy wives and thy concubines drank wine out of them; and thou didst extol the gods of silver and gold, bronze, iron, wood, and stone, who neither see nor hear nor understand. But the true God, in whose hand thy breath is and who controls all thy destinies, Him thou didst not glorify. On this account the tip of a hand was sent out from Him, and this handwriting was inscribed."**

This is a plain-spoken indictment, which is uttered with a forthrightness that had, no doubt, never before been experienced by the king. "His son" need not be understood in the most literal sense though we believe that this meaning is entirely allowable here. The statement is, of course, more emphatic in such a case but would still be very effective if a grandson or an adopted son were involved. The record of such an experience as Nebuchadnezzar's was could not have perished so soon. Belshazzar is not to be excused on any score. He is now told exactly what his deed amounts to in the matter of fetching and using the Jerusalem vessels.

Despite the plain-spoken bluntness of these words there is nothing unseemly or insolent on Daniel's part. He states his charges in a purely objective way: the king became arrogant; he sinned against God; he led others to do the same; he defiantly extolled his dead and dumb idols. This charge against the idols is particularly effective; and it must have required remarkable courage to deliver it (cf. Ps. 115:5ff; 135: 15ff;; Deut. 4:28; Rev. 9:20). By an effective litotes ("Him thou didst not glorify") Belshazzar's sin is evaluated as failure to do what so obviously ought to have been done, and for the doing of which the king had ample knowledge and incentive. This part of the king's guilt is a sin of omission. This explains why God sent agents to transmit a message to the king.

This preliminary explanation was, in a sense, more necessary for Belshazzar than was the interpretation of the handwriting. Or, to be more exact, this was the initial part of the explanation; this explained the broader purpose. The handwriting was the climax of the divine message.

f. *Daniel's Interpretation of the Handwriting*, v. 25-28

25-28.   **"Now this is the writing which was inscribed: ME-NE, ME-NE, TE-KEL, U-PHAR-SIN. This is the interpretation of the matter. ME-NE: God hath numbered thy kingdom and determined its destruction. TE-KEL: thou hast been weighed in the balances and hast been found wanting. PE-RES: thy kingdom is broken and given to the Medes and the Persians."**

There is something designedly striking about the handwriting. This is the so-called lapidary style in its perfection. The words, strange though they seem, are no sooner heard than they are remembered. Equally

clear-cut and just as readily remembered is the interpretation. The brevity of the message plus the
terseness of the interpretation at the same time have
a note of unquestioned authority.

Furthermore, this is the verdict on all human
pride and achievement apart from God. This sentence
contains an irrevocable doom that is ringing to eternity.

As to form *mene'* is the passive participle of
menah, "to number." There is a kind of double meaning in the verb "to number." It means not only, "to
count" but "to fix the limit of" as is also the case in
our common expression that a man's days are "numbered." Here it is the kingdom that is numbered: a
count of it, so to say, has been made, and it has been
found to equal its total assignment, and so God "hath
determined its destruction," *hashlemah*, a Haphel,
literally = "caused to be completed." The "kingdom"
signifies the Chaldean Empire, which, like all empires,
was a conglomerate of many smaller kingdoms, princi-
palities, or states. This human handiwork was destined
to destruction. Others will come along and will re-
assemble the parts after a different pattern. It seems
that the repetition of the word is an indication of the
double meaning to be sought in the term. After the
key to the treatment of the words has been given, the
remaining words are not repeated.

27. *Tekel* is a passive participle form that is
built after the analogy of or is fashioned to conform to
the vowels of *mene'*. As to form it is the Aramaic
equivalent of the Hebrew root *shaqal* (*t* regularly
takes the place of *sh* in Aramaic). Since it means to
"weigh," the thought is that the king has been weighed
in the balances to test, as it were, whether he is of full
weight, or whether he fully conforms to the standard.
A double meaning quite naturally suggests itself here,
for weighing may result in detecting inadequacy, which
is the verdict pronounced with reference to the king:

"Thou hast been found wanting." The king does not measure up to the divine specifications for a man who is to fill this responsible position. On God's weighing compare I Sam. 2:3; Job 31:6; Ps. 62:9; Prov. 16:2, etc.

28. *Peres* is used as the third word although *upharsin* had been used in the first reading. The *u* of the original form is the customary conjunction "and." *Pharsin* is merely the plural form of *peres*, which again, as to vowels, is patterned after *mene*. The two forms used here suggest a double meaning. The verb *peras* as such means "break or divide." If we then render *peres* "divided" (*A. V.*), that means, of course, "broken up" into its constituent parts; and so we have translated "broken." But *paras* as such also means the "Persian"; *parsin* or *pharsin* is merely a plural, "Persians." It is given to Daniel to discern that this means that the kingdom is to be "given to the Medes and Persians" after it has been broken up.

This sequence: "Medes" first, then "Persians," indicates a point of historical accuracy that fits in beautifully with the idea of Daniel's authorship of the book. The supremacy in this dual kingdom remained but a short time with the Medes and that while Daniel was still on the scene, and then passed permanently to the Persians, a fine point that a writer who lived in the Maccabean age would hardly have thought of recording. Yet the form *upharsin*, "Persians," gives the emphasis to the much longer Persian supremacy.

Though this interpretation is convincing, and though no man apparently doubted it when Daniel spoke it, yet it is like divine revelation generally in this respect, that no man can discern it by himself, but after it is given it is found to be simple and clear.

Another interpretation of these oracular words finds much favor in our day, an interpretation that adds a new element of perplexity to the first im-

pression that the words might have conveyed. This
interpretation is built on the observation that the
letters of the first word are the same as the letters of the
words for the Babylonian and Hebrew coin, the *"mina"*
or *"maneh,"* worth about $34, if it is of silver, and con-
taining fifty shekels. Of course, *tekel* has the consonants for the word "shekel"—worth roughly about
75 cents. What brought this approach particularly
into favor was the discovery of an inscription which
K. W. calls the "Sendschirli—Panammu Inscription,"
on which the consonants of *peres* occurred apparently
in the sense of a "half-mina." The three terms would
then seem to bear the names of three coins, a fact that
would, indeed, add to the perplexity of the reader: a
mina, a half-mina, a shekel. *K. W.*, however, seems to
be well justified in counseling caution, for he points out
that the meaning only of "mina" is supported and
justified by inscriptions. The one instance of *peres* as
"half-mina" is not yet substantiated as correct; and
for *tekel* used as "shekel" no support is offered by
Babylonian inscriptions. Consequently this new interpretation is still two-thirds a guess. Besides, nothing
is really gained by the new interpretation except that
it would make the issue still more complicated. *Charles*
claims that *Cowley* offers substantiation of the use of
tekel as the equivalent of *shekel*. Even so, if the interpretation offered by Daniel is to be regarded as having
any value, it certainly does not even in the most remote way allow for this strange construction.

g. *The Sequel,* v. 29—6:1

**29-6:1. Then Belshazzar gave commandment
that Daniel should be clothed with a robe of purple,
and that a golden chain be hung about his neck, and
that proclamation should be made with reference
to him that had been given the position of TALTI
in the kingdom. In that night Belshazzar, king of the**

Chaldeans, was slain; and Darius the Mede received the kingdom, being sixty-two years of age.

The king was duty-bound to keep his promise of giving a reward. Whether he fully believed the interpretation or not is of little moment at this point. The circumstances had been so extraordinary that it seems impossible that the king could still doubt. Weak characters like Belshazzar might be expected to be all compliance and acquiescence. He will have been grateful in a measure that at least the suspense was at an end. He, no doubt, hardly expected so swift a retribution as he actually met.

Though all these rewards were carefully ordered, it cannot be a matter of great moment to us whether the orders were ultimately carried out or not. It is more than likely that a public display had been planned for the next day. The purple robe and the golden chain may have been placed about Daniel at once. If the sudden death of the king intervened, and the proclamation had to be cancelled, that is a matter of little concern to the writer or to us.

As for Daniel's not refusing these honors, it has been suggested that they were in a sense at least an acknowledgment of the power and the wisdom of the true God, whose servant Daniel was. From that point of view it was hardly permissible for Daniel to refuse the acknowledgment and what it involved. His position had been made sufficiently clear in the first words of his address to the king.

30. In this instance judgment struck very swiftly because the insolence had been so very daring, beyond even what heathen standards might have allowed; and, without a doubt, the king had given no tokens of repentance. Swift punishment could be a wholesome lesson for the whole nation, for these unprecedented occurrences would very shortly be blazed abroad throughout the entire realm.

The historical records available from inscriptions are not in any way at variance with this account. The so-called "Nabuna'id—Cyrus Chronicle"* tells of a peaceful capture of the city by Cyrus, but, unfortunately, the text cannot be read at the very point where the name of Belshazzar could have appeared. They who read into Daniel's account the thought of a siege or an attack and a bloody capture of the city do violence to it as much as they who insist that some internal revolution made by Chaldean lords was the cause of the king's death. They who insist that an interval (of perhaps twenty-one years) should be thought of as occurring between v. 30 and 6:1 do so only in the interest of their theory that Belshazzar was Evil Merodach. But these two verses belong so naturally together that only an unfortunate chapter division (rectified by *Luther* and *A. V.*) has prevented interpreters from seeing the obvious fact.

6:1. At this point another major problem crowds into the forefront: "Who was Darius the Mede?" The monuments do not happen to know him by that name, at least the monuments discovered thus far. Over against that fact the other well-established fact should be remembered, viz., that in those days men often went under more than one name. We believe that the evidence points convincingly to the person of Gobryas of Gutium, the man who was appointed by Cyrus to rule Babylon after he himself (Cyrus) had entered the city. *Wilson*† has given the most exhaustive and satisfactory treatment of the subject that we have. From him we cull the following major items that remove the bulk of the difficulties. Though Darius is called the Mede, that need not conflict with the fact that the "Chronicle" calls him "gov-

---

*cf. Barton, *op cit.*, p. 483.

†Wilson, Robert Dick, *Studies in the Book of Daniel* (New York: Putnam's Sons, 1917), chap. VII-XII.

ernor of the land of Gutium," for Gutium and Media were adjacent to one another, and he who ruled the one land may well have come from the other. Furthermore, when 6:1 tells us that he received "the kingdom," this is defined in 9:1 as "the realm of the Chaldeans." This Chaldean realm is, however, in no sense identical with the Medo-Persian Empire but merely a segment of it, over which Gobryas (Darius) ruled under the supreme ruler, Cyrus.

It is surely significant that it is not asserted of Darius the Mede that he secured this kingdom in his own right. He merely "received" it (*German: ueberkam*), and that at the hands of Cyrus as we read elsewhere. This verb *qabbel* does not eliminate Cyrus but rather makes room for him.

When we say this we do not advance the claim that the phrase "received the kingdom" *necessarily* means that another gave it to him. It merely allows for this interpretation. *Charles* has offered proof that the expression may be used when a regular succession to the throne is involved, or when an individual gains possession of the throne by force. But it must be admitted that the phrase as such merely points to the fact that one gave or had to give the rule of a certain domain to his successor. In itself the phrase indicates neither whether the predecessor gave it reluctantly or cheerfully, nor whether the recipient took or merely received it. Our claim still stands that the expression used is not out of harmony with the idea that Cyrus appointed Gobryas king over Chaldæa.

It should be pointed out also that we are not dealing with a writer who does not know his history and so is perhaps guilty of confusing Darius the Mede with the later Darius I called Hystaspis, who, as is well known, came to the throne in 521 B. C. and reigned till about 485, and not from 538 on, when Babylon was captured by Cyrus.

Most of the difficulties have arisen from attempts to impute to Daniel's book certain thoughts that are surely not contained in the words used, and so do not deal fairly with the evidence submitted. One reason Daniel may have preferred to use the designation "Darius the *Mede*" seems to have been the fact that that name most strikingly confirmed what he had predicted, viz., that the kingdom would pass into the hands of the "Medes and Persians" (v. 28). This would have been all the more fitting if Belshazzar is regarded as king only over Babylon and not over the whole realm.

The claim advanced at this point that the author of the book of Daniel had erroneous conceptions of history must be regarded for a moment. Here it is, of course, the claim that he believed that a Median Empire succeeded the Babylonian. We point out the fact that the repeated use of the term Median in this book in no sense warrants this conclusion. In every instance this is a conclusion that criticism thrusts into the plain meaning of words.

Just as unwarranted, though it is advanced by *Charles* with a positiveness that is worthy of things better established, is the claim that the kingship of Darius the Mede is "a supreme, not a delegated kingship." This author assumes that appointed kings had no power over life and death and could not divide their kingdom into districts according to their own discretion. For all this he offers no proof. We for our part have found nothing that indicates that in these early days subordinate kings were shorn of all such powers.

Our treatment of the details of the chapter will show how unwarranted is a claim such as the following: "From the above it is simply incontestable that our author honestly believed that Darius was the sole and independent sovereign of the Babylonian empire after its conquest by Cyrus." Daniel is first charged with what he never claimed, then his claim is rejected as being preposterous.

From all this we see quite readily why it is very proper to append this verse to the conclusion of chapter 5. It is only when one acts on the supposition that a later Darius like Darius Hystaspis, who came to the throne some twenty years later is meant, that one feels any need of setting this verse apart from what precedes. But if the truth of the matter is, as we very strongly contend, that on the night when Belshazzar was slain, Cyrus actually took the city and then very naturally as a direct sequence of this gave the rule of the Chaldean kingdom (9:1) to this subordinate of his, Darius the Mede, then, we say, chapter 5 should close with the report concerning this adjustment. The Hebrew chapter arrangement, as well as the German, is therefore not the happiest. In German the numbering of the verses is correct.

Boutflower's suggestions on the subject of the peaceful entry of Cyrus into the captured city merit attention. The Annalistic Tablet, which advances this contention, would seem to have the prior claim to veracity in considering all the evidence. However, as he also points out (p. 130), these as well as other official records have been edited "to a degree of which it is difficult to conceive." Therefore "the pride of the Babylonian priesthood" must be regarded as having prevented them from making a faithful record of the stratagem whereby the city was captured and as having induced them to chronicle the event in as harmless a color as possible. Since Cyrus apparently had to engage in no further carnage than that of the memorable night of capture, this element of the record is passed by briefly; and so the impression is created that the conquest was less marked by carnage than it actually was.

At the same time we see the reason for the in-

sertion of the age of Darius. Since he was sixty-two
at the time, we realize at once that he cannot have
continued in office very long. Yet as the favorite of the
conqueror Cyrus he deserved this recognition, to be
given a distinctive position of honor in the new imperial setup. Incidentally, the original does not say
"*about* sixty-two" but just "sixty-two."

So v. 30 and 6:1 furnish a striking conclusion of
the whole episode: the insolence of a king, who very
aptly represents the degenerate world power, is
effectively overthrown.

HOMILETICAL SUGGESTIONS

When preaching on this chapter, the broader purpose
should be remembered: Belshazzar is not so much an individual
as the exponent of the ungodly world power. He is merely the
representative of a larger class. From time to time such ungodly braggarts will arise and hurl defiance at the Almighty
and His church. They who do this will not always be overthrown in as startling a way as was this king. But they amount
to as little as he does, and from time to time the overthrow that
occurs will be so striking a parallel to that of Belshazzar that
men will be compelled to see the finger of God in the matter
—as when Hitler and his crew of brutal thugs were brought
low. At the same time two other features usually appear in such
characters: they represent a certain degree of degeneracy, and
they manifest unusual insolence.

The section vv. 17-31 ought to be sufficient as a text; and
again the rest of the chapter would be woven into the picture

As far as the vexing critical questions are concerned, thoroughly as the preacher himself may be informed on them, he
need never introduce anything other than assured facts into the
sermon. Let the assumption be: the Scriptures speak with
authority and are correct also in matters of history.

As an independent text the portion vv. 25-28 could be used
to show how God, the eternal Judge, appraises the acts of men
and deals with the evildoer according to his deserts.

In any case, the emphasis should not be on the negative: the
overthrow of ungodly insolence, but on the positive: all this is
merely a part of God's just and sovereign rule of His church
and His kingdom.

CHAPTER VI

E. **Daniel in the Lions' Den**

or

The Safety of God's Saints in Persecution, 6:1-28

"Daniel has hitherto been uniformly prosperous
. . . But, in his old age, his trial also comes" (Driver).

There is no denying the fact that this chapter has
points of similarity with chapter 3. If in both instances
the danger which the members of God's kingdom must
encounter is under consideration, the reason is that,
when such seasons of danger come, the church needs
an abundance of assurance in order to be prepared for
the trying nature of such times. But the manifest difference between the two chapters lies in the fact that
in the former it is not directly persecution as such that
is involved. Nebuchadnezzar had not intended to persecute; the fundamental difference between the nature
of the two opposing kingdoms merely became so
sharply accentuated that a threat to God's saints resulted. In the present chapter the situation is clearly
a different one. Actual persecution is under consideration. It is in this case prompted by envy. But it is
persecution with the avowed purpose of disposing of
those who are hated and envied. Such situations arise
periodically and especially the nearer we draw to the
end of all things; and God's saints may well thank Him
for the hope that passages of this sort engender
and sustain.

We remind again that the Darius mentioned here
is the one whom we at the close of the last chapter
identified with Gobryas of Gutium as he is called in

other records. Since one major objection to this identification has not yet been touched upon, we wish to dispose of it before we proceed. It is claimed that there is no proof available that Gobryas can be said to be a "Mede" because he is described as being of "Gutium." Wilson* offers the following to show how Media may well be included in this term: "Gutium was a country of undefined extent but probably embracing all the territory between Babylonia on the one side and the mountains of Armenia to the north and Mt. Zagros to the northeast on the other, and perhaps even the country beyond Mt. Zagros whose capital city was Ecbatana." After the thoroughgoing refutation that Wilson has offered of this as well as of all other current objections on the question of the identity of Darius the Mede we believe that serious questions as to the correctness of our account can hardly trouble any man who is ready to weigh all the sound evidence submitted by this able scholar.

Before we proceed at least a brief statement should be made about the character of this Darius the Mede. Because he allowed himself to be entrapped into issuing a decree that was unnecessarily tyrannical and also dangerous to Daniel in particular and found his wishes overridden by his lords, the king is sometimes represented as being a very weak figure and is otherwise derided. We believe that the evidence found in this chapter points to at least a moderately capable monarch, who undertakes a reorganization of his kingdom, displays some courage and positive conviction, has a measure of administrative ability, but was, perhaps, not always as alert as he might have been against the wiles of conniving courtiers. In brief, he was a pretty fair monarch as Oriental monarchs of those days went.

---

*Wilson, Robert Dick, *Studies in the Book of Daniel* (New York: Putnam, 1917), p. 201.

We may append an investigation into the peculiar position which *Charles* takes on the entire question of the Medes and their position in the Book of Daniel. Though he does not believe that the Medes ever actually arrived at the point where they may be said to have controlled an empire he yet believes that the Biblical writers, at least Daniel and the apocalyptical writers, were definitely of this mistaken opinion. The title "Darius the *Mede*" is to him one of several indications of this position. This is obviously a case of inserting a preconceived view into terms and phrases used by a given writer, except, of course, in the case of nonbiblical apocalyptic, which is as different from the Biblical position on this and many another matter as day is from night.

The argument used by the above-mentioned writer to substantiate his position should be evaluated briefly. He claims that earlier Biblical prophecy told of the conquest of Babylon by the Medes. He correctly refers to passages such as Isa. 13:17; 21:2; Jer. 51:11, 28. We hold that already here the point is that these prophets designate the conquering nation as the Medes because in those days the Medes were known, and the Persians were comparatively unknown. But the claim is then advanced that these prophecies gave rise "to the tradition that the Medes had in fact conquered Babylon." Later writers, it is claimed, like the author of our book, being none too sure of their history, went on the assumption that the Medes were the conquerors and wrote their history accordingly. Since much of what is offered is then fabrication, this title "Darius the Mede" is just a bit more of such inaccuracy.

Without attempting a complete refutation we merely point to the well-substantiated fact that the Book of Daniel does not give any evidence of supporting the mistaken historical opinion that there ever was a Median Empire. Neither does the passage in question. Neither is any man now in a position to disprove the accuracy of this designation, considering the scant information that we possess on this and many other of the details recorded in this book.

Note: We follow the numbering of the verses as found in *A. V.*

a. *Daniel's Position in the Realm under Darius,* v. 1-3

1-3. It seemed good to Darius to set over the kingdom one hundred and twenty satraps to govern the entire kingdom. Over these there were three presidents, of whom Daniel was one; that these satraps might give report to them, and that the king might suffer no losses. Then this Daniel distinguished himself above the presidents and satraps because there was a remarkable spirit in him, and the king intended to set him over the entire kingdom.

Defining issues a bit more clearly, let us note first that we are unable at this point to follow such otherwise very safe guides as *Keil* and *Kliefoth* who identify Darius with Cyaxares II because they assume that a regent who was ruler over the entire empire is referred to whereas 9:1 tells us that he ruled over only the kingdom of the Chaldeans.

We assert also (although that should be evident from our entire position) that we regard what is recorded in this chapter as being a historical account which is correct and reliable in all its parts. We believe that to consider these accounts mere parables, perhaps even "powerful parables, rich in spiritual instructions, but not primarily concerned with historic accuracy," is an untenable position. For this attitude is not only a contradiction of the clear truth of plenary inspiration but also seeks to build up solid comfort and instruction on the shifting sands of mere fables. Every reader would be obliged to feel with reference to the lessons here taught: "How nice! Would that they had a real basis in fact!" When the basis is dubious, the comfort offered is dubious.

The arrangement made by the Chaldean king, Darius, according to this verse, seems to have been put into operation shortly after he became king. It appealed to him as a feasible plan to have "over the kingdom one hundred and twenty satraps." If the kingdom which had been assigned to him included, as some reasonably suppose, "Chaldea, Babylon, Accad, and Susiana," then, certainly, a goodly number of officials could well be used if the affairs of this rather large realm were to be administered efficiently. If all these were in turn directly responsible to superiors, this arrangement argues for a system of government that was compactly and efficiently organized.

Because of certain preconceived views many interpreters scarcely take note of this important fact but merely draw attention to what they deem a historical discrepancy. They point to Esther 1:1 and the 127 provinces of the realm of Ahasuerus, who was Xerxes. But Xerxes divided the entire empire of Persia thus. Darius reigned over only the kingdom of Chaldea. Whatever administrative districts Darius was pleased to inaugurate, his arrangement cannot conflict with what in his day Xerxes did with a much larger realm. Or if Darius, not Darius the Mede, created twenty satrapies, according to Herodotus, that still leaves our statement correct. For the term "satraps" was manifestly used in a broader and a narrower sense. No one knows just exactly how narrow or how broad the implications of this term may be.

On this point Wilson* has given most exhaustive proof for the contention that we advance. Strangely, Daniel is charged with an inaccuracy. In fact, it is said, "The same technical inaccuracy is found in the Greek historians, who use 'satrap' of lower officials, e.g.,

---

*op. cit., pp. 175-186 and 200-220.

Xenophon, Appian." This use of the term by the Greeks, we feel, should rather be regarded as a strong indication of the fact that "satraps" was used with reference to higher as well as to lower officials. We may go even so far as to say that for a realm as large as that of Darius 120 officials was in no sense an exorbitant number. Josephus asserts, with more plausibility than interpreters usually concede, that the number of officials employed by Darius was 360. There is even the possibility that at a later date that number of men may have been utilized.

Charles offers the very good note that "some sort of division of Babylon is recorded on the Annalistic Tablet of Cyrus, where it is said that Gubaru, governor of Babylon under Cyrus, 'appointed governors in Babylon.' " Since we identify Gubaru with Darius the Mede we regard the note in question as extrabiblical confirmation of the fact involved.

We regard the last infinitive phrase, "to govern the entire kingdom," as an indication that this plan of the king's was inaugurated in order to take care of every part of his realm. *Luther* loses this more emphatic statement of the case by merging this infinitive phrase with the preceding adverbial phrase.

A typical Aramaic construction appears in this verse: "It seemed good . . . and he set" for: "It seemed good . . . to set." Cf. *K. S.* 361f.

2. In order to effect an efficient organization there were three "presidents" or "prefects" or "chief officials" over the 120 satraps. For the present nothing more is said about Daniel than that he was "one," not "first" (*A. V.*). In order that we might not be under the necessity of using our imagination regarding the question of the interrelation of presidents and satraps we are told that it was the business of the latter to "give report" to the former. This, no doubt, involves that a certain number of satraps was assigned

to each president. To add still more to the material needed to form the required concept it is indicated that the primary objective of the arrangement was "that the king might suffer no loss." Financial considerations were behind the whole scheme. It was not for the purpose of effecting a more adequate administration of justice but rather that the overgrown royal establishments might be amply supplied with revenues. But not to scale our evaluation of the arrangement too low, efficient governmental administration is always to a large extent closely tied up with a sufficiency of revenues. But note that it is "the king" who is to suffer no loss—an indication that we are dealing with an absolute monarchy of the most pronounced type. Darius is safeguarding the interests of Cyrus.

3. The narrative, which is not concerned about details of a merely historical character, comes to a point at once in defining the prospects that developed for Daniel. Though Daniel is writing, his presentation is so objective that he refers to himself as any other writer might have done as "this Daniel." The critics make a point of a merely personal opinion when they say: "Daniel would not have expressed himself thus." Our personal feeling in the matter inclines to the opinion that there is nothing in the way of his using such an expression.

The feature that became prominent very shortly when this gifted and trained statesman began to take up his administrative duties was that "he distinguished himself above the presidents and satraps." When one considers his unusual gifts, which are described in chapter one, his training under such an eminent ruler as Nebuchadnezzar, his experience extending over a period of perhaps sixty years, and the fact that all these advantages were seasoned and balanced by a ripe and strong faith in the Lord, there is hardly any ground for surprise. This is a historical fact that was as plain to all men as it could be. Yet Daniel reports it with becoming modesty and in the very statement of it uses terms that direct attention away from himself and to God who gave him this "remarkable spirit," which *Luther* renders far more appropriately, *"Es war ein hoher Geist in ihm* ("a high spirit"). In 5:12 and 14 the same expansion *(ru(a)ch yattira')* is used with reference to the divinely given spirit; and therefore those interpreters are correct who claim that Daniel here ascribes the glory to God and does not sing his own praises. Daniel had to say something that was accurate if he was to make a presentation of the case that actually made the situation plain. Yet the critics charge that this statement ill comports with the assumption of Daniel's authorship. Again the criticism employed appears too trivial for us to attempt further refutation.

Special note should be taken of the fact that divinely given equipment far outstrips ordinary human talent. This is especially the case when God has designed a man for some position of prominence that he might represent the interests of the kingdom of God before the world as was the duty of Daniel. What makes the contrast all the more remarkable is the fact that in this case the pre-eminent figure was a venerable old man of approximately eighty years, a veteran of sixty years in a public office of great prominence under a succession of monarchs. The equipment God gives wears remarkably well when God has a long tenure of office in store for a man.

Newcomer though he was in the kingdom of Chaldea, Darius, nevertheless, soon discerned that particular distinction which marked the man of God. So we can readily understand why "the king intended to set him over the entire kingdom." This intention will have become manifest in such a way that others at court soon detected the trend of the king's purposes.

We now have all the information that is needed to understand the ensuing developments. With consummate literary skill and in the characteristically terse Scriptural style all needed preliminary details have been laid before us.

In the phrase "above the presidents," the "above," '*al,* is not the customary preposition used in marking the comparative (*K. S.* 308d).

b. *The Decree for Daniel's Overthrow,* v. 4-9

4, 5. Then the presidents and satraps sought to find ground for charges against Daniel in the matter of the kingdom business; but they were unable to find any ground for charges or any fault because he was faithful, and error and fault could not be found against him. Then these men said: "We shall not find any fault in reference to this Daniel unless we find it against him in connection with the law of his God."

A common situation develops at this point: jealousy leads men to attack a colleague who is more competent than themselves. In this case the ordinary feelings are sharpened by another factor that is noticed frequently in this book of Daniel. Because a man is of the kingdom of God, therefore the kingdom of this world drives its members to display a bitterness in their assault that surpasses anything that might have been in evidence had the issues been between men outside of God's kingdom. Speaking more plainly, the devil stirs the fires of natural hatred to a fiercer heat as soon as God's children are involved. Finding themselves outdistanced by this venerable and experienced statesman, the "presidents and satraps" make common cause and seek to find "ground for charges," '*illah,* against their distinguished rival.

They confine their seeking, first of all, to "kingdom business," for so we feel that the word *malkhutha',*

"kingdom," should be translated. With good reason
they first scan the field of the regular duties of this
official. For very naturally, in an office where such a
multiplicity of detail must be taken care of, there is
likelihood that at least some oversight might be detected and made a ground for accusation. With good
and simple emphasis the next statement shows the
futility of this first approach: the opponents were able
to find no "ground for charges," in fact, not even "any
fault." Every phase of his department of the work
soon appeared to have been managed with exemplary
skill. At every step they must have run across evidences of efficient management that made them wish
their own department had been run equally well. At
this point the investigation was promptly deflected lest
the critics find themselves impugned for not having
done as well.

The explanation offered for Daniel's safety from
this type of attack is couched in the terms "because he
was faithful." The man had sought to do what his God
expected of him in this responsible position. That, we
feel, lies behind this modest statement of the case.
Knowing Daniel as we do by this time, we feel that
this interpretation of his statement is entirely in
keeping with the tenor of his ethics. The concluding
statement that "error and fault could not be found
against him" is not "tautologous." Why can interpreters not see that simple repetitions are sometimes
used for the sake of emphasis, here the emphasis
on modesty?

5. The lengthy discussions of the plotters as
they met in secret session are passed by. The ultimate
conclusion alone is worthy of notice because it is essential to the understanding of what follows. Ineffi-
ciency will not be detected; it is completely out of the
question. In the area of his religious life they feel they
can fabricate some snare for him. The expression

bedhath, "in the law," here best regards the preposition "in" as being used in the sense of marking the sphere, *beth sphaerae* (K. S. 279a). For in no case can a man of God live a consistent life in the world without making apparent the fact that his life is separate from what the world does and countenances. And whenever the world becomes aware of this difference she resents it and finds her animosities stirred.

Here the critical attempt to find a reflection of the situation of the times of Antiochus Epiphanes again collapses. For that wicked monarch attempted (I Macc. 1:41ff) to inaugurate one type of worship throughout his realm and, to accomplish his purpose, used religious persecution of the most vicious sort. Our chapter reflects no such thing. This is not so much religious persecution as an attempt to bring an individual to fall on a religious charge that is specially trumped up because no other type of charge is available.

6-8. Then these presidents and satraps came thronging to the king and addressed him as follows: "King Darius, live forever! All the presidents of the kingdom, the prefects, the satraps, the counsellors, and the governors have taken counsel together that the king should establish a statute and should strongly set forth an interdict that anyone who shall make a petition of any god or man for thirty days, except of thee, O king, shall be cast into the den of lions. Now, O king, establish the interdict and sign the document that it may not be changed according to the law of the Medes and Persians which remains fixed."

The rest of the deliberations of the plotters is cut short in the preceding verse. Instead they are represented as coming before the king with their scheme fully hatched out. Dramatically we are apprised of what it is as we hear them present it in the king's august presence. They are shown to us as they "came thronging" in, *hargishu*. The verb is a rather strong one, and it has been discussed at great length. Its original meaning is to "be in tumult." In Ps. 2:1 it may be translated "assemble tumultuously." But here and in the other two instances of its occurrence in this chapter allowance has to be made for attendant circumstances. There certainly cannot have been a riotous storming into the king's presence. None knew better than Daniel, the author, the strictness of the provisions of court etiquette in the days of these mighty monarchs of old. So the verb will hardly imply more than that, after all due ceremony was followed, men came along, so eager to implicate an envied colleague as to border on unseemly conduct in the very court of the king. "Came thronging" (*BDB*) is a very acceptable rendering.

The accusers come with the customary form of salute of the king upon their lips. The "forever" implies no more, as the Hebrew also often does in such connections, than "for a good long while." There follows a clever lie. It takes the form of what looks like a plausible hyperbole. The unanimity of the request for such a decree is the matter about which the king must be deceived. So in addition to the "presidents and satraps" who are the ones involved three further classes of officials are named in order to make the array more impressive. There is the possibility, of course, that the general title "satrap" did not exclude the fact that quite a number of the officials that bore this title may also have been "prefects, counsellors, and governors." If that was not the case in this instance, there is still the possibility that some of these other officials had "sat in" on the sessions of the plotters and had been of one mind with them. There is at least one further possibility, and that is that the report is "padded," and that those additional names do not at all represent the truth.

We need not assume that these nefarious plans were made at the very time when all the satraps happened to be present at Babylon to turn in their annual reports (*Haevernick*), for we possess no knowledge to the effect that such reports were rendered simultaneously and in person by the satraps. That thought seems a bit farfetched. The schemers have reckoned with the fact that the subtle flattery offered will throw the king off his guard, and so there will be no detailed inquiry into every statement that they make in presenting the contemplated piece of legislation.

To gain their end these officials make the most plausible statement of their deliberations; they say: we "have taken counsel together." They label their wicked plot by the fine terms "statute" and "interdict." They give the whole device a pious and religious cast. They make it appear that nothing but the finest loyalty is behind their project.

The law that is to be passed involves that "anyone who shall make a petition of any god or man for thirty days, except of thee, O king, shall be cast into the den of lions." In our day and from our point of view we cannot but be amazed at the seeming preposterousness of it all. It seems to argue for an impossible degree of infatuation with himself on the part of a king that he should have even ventured to entertain such a thought.

This aspect of the case is stressed by the critical approach. The whole situation is described as being utterly "improbable," or the decree as being "so preposterous" because it "might be violated by millions many times a day, without the king being cognizant of it"; this, in fact, "would be proof of positive imbecility in any king who should dream of making it." These are strong indictments. Only a full investigation of the case can serve to give us a balanced judgment and offer a reasonable estimate of the case. Least of all dare we let ourselves be dismayed by the rather positive claim that "far more improbable than this material marvel [the miracle involved] is the alleged edict demanding that no request be made of god or men but of the king for a whole month, an improbability all the greater under the devout Darius. Even the insensate Antiochus Epiphanes, the 'Manifest God,' never made such a claim, and if we desired a historic parallel we should have to come down to the still madder Caligula." This claim contains a particle of truth, but it is based on the assumption that a decree that was drafted by the king and was planned by him is under consideration whereas a somewhat preposterous edict is being foisted upon the king in an unguarded moment. He himself, no doubt, saw the preposterousness of it all, but too late. But the case requires a more extended investigation.

In the first place, some writers regard the deification of the kings too lightly. They do not reckon with the actual historical evidence involved. The idea that kings were representatives of the deity came to the forefront among the Ethiopians. From them it went over to the Egyptians. On this point compare *Haevernick*. Wilson* sums up available evidence under this head by saying: "The kings of Egypt were worshipped as such from immemorial times." Such attitudes naturally passed from one nation to another. He adds: "That kings should be called gods is witnessed by Pharaohs, Ptolemies, Seleucids, Herods, and Cæsars." What did the ancients mean when they raised what seems to us to be so entirely impossible a claim? In the first place, they had a rather inferior conception of what a god was. Consequently they could conceive of mortals as being sons of the deity, for according to old legends in many a case a god, or at least a demigod appearing as a mortal, had been about on the earth, consorting with the daughters of men.

To this approach on their part must be added the

---

*op. cit., p. 312.

proper thought that authority on earth emanates from
God on high; men in high positions have received their
rank from the gods that rule the earth. Whatever
priestcraft may have done to enhance this conception
of the regal office, or to what extent the times were
particularly propitious to all such construction, we
may not be able to determine fully. But the fact remains that nations thought in these terms and approved of such doctrines.

What would such a decree as this be interpreted
to mean from the strictly heathen point of view? In
so far as the position of the king was concerned, it
would give strong expression only to what each one
as a heathen already believed. This decree merely gave
formal definiteness to it all. That part of the implications of the decree none could be opposed to. The decree as such meant much the same thing that the image mentioned in chapter three had expressed in
another way.

As soon as he heard of the decree everyone would
see that it constituted a kind of hyperbole, and yet a
hyperbole that was after the analogy of Oriental court
language generally. In other words, everyone would
make a manifest reservation in his own mind; he
would say: "This is to be taken only in the religious
sense; this does not apply to the asking for things that
are entirely outside of the sphere of prayers." This
interpretation is granted even by those who are
critically minded. They concede that the "position is
an entirely sensible one that the implication of the
story means a petition of religion . . . and that this king
was to be regarded for the time being as the only
representative of the Deity" (*Montgomery*). Driver
takes the same position.

The other interpretation, that every possible request was denied by the decree, is on the face of it so
impossible that it could not have been intended by the

intriguers, nor have allowed for any hope of prevailing upon the king to sign the interdict, nor have entered the thoughts of the king's subjects when they heard of it on every hand.

What if we then encounter the claim that there is no analogy from times of old for a decree that went quite as far as this? We answer that this claim is without a doubt true because the situation upon which it is based is quite without parallel. The decree was the outgrowth of an unusual attempt to bring a hated rival to fall. To argue that this decree represents the convictions current at the time is true only in part. Since no historical situation is quite on a par with what our chapter records, the prerequisites for so unusual a decree, issued at another time and by another monarch, are lacking. Yet that cannot stamp our chapter as unreliable or untrue. It will simply have to be granted that in this particular instance the rivals of Daniel made a very dexterous move to trap the king in his own pride and so to bring a man whom they envied down from his high dignity. We must grant that, to an extent, a kind of diabolical cunning was displayed by Daniel's foes.

One further objection should be answered. It is claimed that the edict here described is out of harmony with the character of Darius as history reveals him to us. He is said to have been too religious and reverent to issue so daring a decree. But when that claim is advanced, interpreters are thinking in terms of Darius Hystaspis and not of Darius the Mede, who ruled only Chaldea. For that matter, the edict under consideration is not in harmony with the character of this Darius the Mede. That can hardly be expected under the circumstances, for the king was not the originator of the petition, nor was it designed to express the king's religious position. This was a decree with an ulterior motive.

Haevernick's remarks on the subject of the place of prayer in the Persian religion throws an interesting sidelight on the whole situation. Prayer was the chief factor in worship; a great part of the holy writings (the Zend-Avesta, etc.) contains only formulas of prayer and a certain type of litanies. Prayer is regarded as irresistible, as operating with a certain magic power. To omit prayer would mean the collapse of the world. Such an explanation can help us to understand why the opponents of Daniel centered their attention on the matter of prayer.

The expression that we have rendered that the king "should strongly set forth an interdict" is not to be interpreted to mean that he was to "make a strong interdict" (*A. R. V.*). The Aramaic does not say that; it places the emphasis on the vigor with which the decree is to be set forth. The preposition *'adh* in this case means "for" and not "until." The capture of lions for the purpose of housing them in dens is referred to also in Ezek. 19:8ff. The purpose may have been, as some suggest, to keep them for the chase.

8. The plotters make it appear that they are motivated by a solicitude for the king's honor and position and so use persuasion upon him. All that seems to be needed to "establish the interdict" seems to be that the king "sign the document." This somewhat unusual attitude that what the king has made to be a law "may not be changed" seems to be an entirely logical deduction from the high position that the Persians were wont to attribute to their kings. If they were the earthly representatives of the deities and themselves divine, then their decrees ought to be irrevocable. The Bible makes further reference to this Persian conviction in Esther 1:19 and 8:8. A historical parallel is found in a case reported by Diodorus Siculus (see *Montgomery*) where King Darius III passes a sentence of death upon a certain Charidemos

but immediately regrets having rendered the verdict
but is unable to revoke his own decree. Of course, they
who were scheming and plotting against Daniel had
taken this feature into account and were banking on
it to help them to achieve their purpose when the king
should later discover their treachery.

On the word "Medes" in this connection see v. 15.

c. *Daniel's Courageous Prayer*, v. 9-15

**9, 10. Therefore King Darius signed the docu-
ment and the interdict. Now when Daniel perceived
that he had signed the document, he went to his
house (now windows stood open for him in his upper
chamber facing Jerusalem), and three times a day
he continued to fall upon his knees and pray and
praise before his God, exactly as he had been wont
to do previously.**

Suspecting nothing, pleased with the flattery of
the decree, glad to have such obsequious nobles, the
king affixes his signature. A matter in which so many
persons had figured could hardly be transacted without having the report thereof spread abroad through
all circles of the court. Least of all could so well-in-
formed an executive as Daniel long remain in ignorance of what had transpired. He acts very
promptly, not with a desire to court danger, or to
tempt God, or to express his contempt of his foes, or
to make a boast of his religion. There was no other
course open to him. Any attempt on Daniel's part to
evade the issue by continuing his prayers in secret or
at such times when he could not be detected would have
been a confession of fear and of unbelief. He would
then at once have appeared as serving his God only
as long as outward circumstances proved to be agree-
able. He would have stamped himself as a man who
was ready to serve his God and to be known as His
follower and worshiper when there was no price to be

paid and no penalty to be feared. In other words, to fail now to make the confession that he had been so ready to make till now would have amounted to an outright denial of his God. So "he went to his house" deliberately and of a purpose to make one, perhaps last, bold confession of his allegiance to his God, who had throughout a long life safeguarded him remarkably against all harm and danger.

The parenthetical remark injected at this point serves to show what made detection so easy and unavoidable—"windows stood open for him (i.e., arranged for this very purpose) in his upper chamber facing Jerusalem." Such an upper chamber, *'ali*, would be constructed upon some corner of the roof or even upon a special tower and, having latticed windows in its sides, would allow a free circulation of air and would thus be a place sought out for rest and meditation. The insertion of a lattice in no sense made these windows spy proof. Other Scriptural instances of the use of this upper chamber as a place of prayer are found in I Kings 17:19; Acts 1:13; 10:9. The suggestion that prayer be made facing Jerusalem seems to have emanated from passages like I Kings 8:33, 35, 38, 44, 48. There, however, the thought is that the *mind* be directed to the holy place that God had ordained. It is a natural second step to let the outward posture in prayer correspond to the inner attitude. So other passages like Ps. 5:8 and 28:2 seem to point to the corresponding outward posture. In any case, they would have supplied the needed suggestion. Ps. 55:17 does not necessarily suggest that such prayer, made three times a day, was universally practiced. But this passage might well serve to lead to a particular practice in the matter of the frequency with which prayer was made. We do not know definitely whether this custom which was practiced by Daniel had already been in vogue in David's day. In any event, it shows that even the best of God's saints found that their devotion could not thrive without regular and fixed prayer habits.

Rather than to translate with a plain imperfect, "he kneeled," we feel that the participial construction here employed together with the verb "to be" should yield the rendering "he continued to fall upon his knees and pray and praise." This is not a statement of what he had formerly been in the habit of doing, but of what he now continued to do. Note that the element of "praise" is not absent even under the pressure of threatening danger. God is so much deserving of praise that danger encountered by us cannot alter that basic feature of all true devotion. But how solemn and devout will have been the words of praise on this occasion! Since the last clause indicates that Daniel's present conduct is meant: "exactly as he had been wont to do previously," we feel that this is an added reason for making the preceding part of the sentence also refer definitely to the present emergency.

11, 12.   **Then these men came thronging in and found Daniel making petition and supplication before his God. So they approached the king and spoke to him concerning the royal edict: "Didst not thou sign an interdict that, if a man were to prefer a petition to any god or man for thirty days save to thee, O king, he was to be cast into the lions' den?" The king answered and said: "That is surely the case according to the law of the Medes and Persians which remains fixed."**

As unseemly as was the procedure of the enemies of Daniel above in v. 7 it is in this case where they are also described as "coming thronging in." It does not require a great measure of imagination to see the propriety of the use of that word. They neglected to observe the caution and the courtesy that would ordinarily be expected, especially, perhaps, after some spy of theirs had told them what they might expect to find. It was certainly not a mode of procedure that was worthy of gentlemen of their standing.

Whether they heard the words spoken by Daniel or not is of little moment. They knew that prayer usually involved making petition. Merely to see the man upon his knees would serve as an indictment. The earnestness visibly displayed in his manner of prayer will have led them to conclude that this might rightly be termed "making supplication before his God." With this evidence assembled through the agency of so many witnesses, though, indeed, not every last one of these officials played the part of a spy, these men felt sure that their testimony would hardly be called into question.

The only possible approach to the king that would make it appear as though their concern was just plain justice and nothing personal was to base everything on the now-famous edict. So they raise the question about the edict. They rehearse its substance. The king unhesitatingly commits himself, just as they had hoped, by referring to the immutability of the document. The words that could be rendered "that matter is certain" are expressed far more correctly in the idiom of our day: "That is surely the case."

13, 14. Then they answered and spoke before the king: "Daniel, who belongs to the captives of Judah, hath no regard for thee, O king, or for the interdict which thou didst sign. Three times a day he makes his petitions." When the king heard this thing, it displeased him exceedingly, and he set his mind on saving Daniel and strove till sundown to deliver him.

Daniel cannot be openly slandered, but one thing, it seems, these foes felt could be said with impunity in an attempt to cast at least some aspersion upon the man: he was of the "captives of Judah." That statement emphasized the fact that he was a foreigner.

Perhaps even already then the Jews were at least to
some extent the *odium generis humani*. At least the
apparent disloyalty of the man has been hinted at.
What he does is given the worst possible construction;
yet the words are entirely slanderous. Daniel certainly
did not continue in prayer because he had no regard
for the king or for his interdict as they claim. Being
a man of God and aware of the fact that government
was God's ordinance and the powers that be ordained
of God, he will have held his king and the king's commands in high esteem. Of course, if these men have
caught Daniel in the act of prayer they seem to speak
with a show of truth. When they say: "Three times a
day he makes his petitions," we feel impelled to conclude that their statement is a hasty generalization.
They hardly waited, according to the preceding account, to obtain proof of more than one instance of
prayer. Knowing Daniel and his fearlessness and his
fidelity to his God, they felt sure that, if further tests
were to be made, the "three times a day" would be
fully established as correct.

14.　The king's reaction is not at all what they
had hoped for. For when these words of theirs were
spoken, it immediately became apparent to the king
what the recent petition had involved, and what its ultimate purpose had been. To have the life of his favorite
minister imperiled, and to see himself made a dupe of
his other ministers, is surely enough to displease any
man exceedingly. Darius was enough of a man and an
independent monarch to attempt at once to extricate
Daniel out of the danger into which his own lack of
alertness had cast him. Since Oriental justice moves
swiftly, the king had only till sundown to attempt this
delivery. How he "strove" to achieve his objective we
can hardly say. The summary account of it all seems
to be the next verse.

15. Then these men belabored the king and said to the king: "Know, O king, that it is a law of the Medes and Persians that no interdict or statute which the king has established may be changed."

The same word that appeared in v. 6 and in v. 11 appears again, this time with a slightly different coloring. The verb is *hargishu. K. W.* suggests the meaning *jemanden bestuermen.* We have sought to catch this thought by the use of the verb "belabor." One feature of the connotation of the verb remains the same: the importunity, the crudeness of their approach. This is further indicated by the double use of the word "king." It was the *king* whom they unceremoniously took in hand. Of course, that inviolability of the Median and Persian law is their one stronghold from which they can never be driven.

Our interpretation, therefore, agrees with those who are of the opinion that verses 12-17 describe a single scene. Since we do not translate *hargishu* "came tumultuously," nothing implies that the enemies of Daniel left the court of the king. Consequently the struggle for Daniel's release must have continued uninterruptedly throughout a day.

In connection with the use of the word "Medes" in this famous quotation (cf., v. 8) it is claimed that it presents a situation that is out of accord with historical fact. Whereas some interpreters try to prove that a Median Empire preceded the Persian and do so in an endeavor to get a different sequence of the four kingdoms mentioned in chapters 2 and 7, and so eliminate the Roman Empire as lying beyond the ken of the prophet's vision, other commentators, also of the rather negative school, assert more correctly that a Median Empire never appeared on the scene before the Persian. Even though this assertion is correct, that does not stamp the phrase "law of the Medes and Persians" as unhistorical. For if Cyrus is the actual conqueror of Babylon, and Darius the Mede is the historical figure Gobryas, it is quite proper in the presence of the latter, being a Mede, to describe a certain Persian law as also good Median usage, for the latter statement would emphasize the fact that Darius was entirely familiar with the irrevocability of such a royal edict.

d. *The Reluctant Sentence by the King,* v. 16-18

V. 16-18. **So the king issued the command, and they brought Daniel and cast him into the lions' den. But the king said to Daniel: "Thy God, whom thou servest unremittingly, may He deliver thee!" And a stone was brought and set upon the mouth of the den; and the king sealed it with his own signet and the signet of his lords, that no one might tamper with Daniel. Then the king went to his palace and spent the night fasting, and no diversions were brought to him; and sleep fled from him.**

The first sentence is typical Hebrew or Aramaic narrative: the whole story relating to a certain incident is told in a summary statement after the style of newspaper headings. So the result is seemingly that Daniel is first cast into the den and is then addressed by the king. But that is in no sense intended. No doubt, while Daniel was being taken past the king, these words of comfort were spoken. The king's pious wish proves him to be a man of some piety and faith in the gods. No one seemed to be ignorant of Daniel's fidelity in serving his God—fine testimony to Daniel's fine confession! It imputes too strong a faith to the king to use the rendering: "He will deliver thee," as *A. V.* has it. Hardly more than a wish or a prayer seems to be intended. How could the king know that Jehovah would deliver? The imperfect allows for both renderings.

From all this it appears that the king's concern was motivated by true regard for Daniel. Darius was not merely peeved because he had been outwitted by clever men at court. He recognized his responsibility in the matter and knew what he owed to Daniel.

17. The word *chadhah*, "one," is used in a weakened sense. It is much like the indefinite article, "*a* stone," as *K. S.* 291e indicates. It seems most reasonable to suppose that this "mouth" of the den will have been in the side of the structure. It seems that the stone was not usually placed over the mouth. This suggests that ordinarily a strong gate, perhaps of iron, may have closed the entrance. The stone seems to have been held in reserve for special occasions. In this instance the special purpose of using the stone is to guard each party in the controversy against the other. For it seems that royal seals were still highly respected. With the stone properly sealed, the king would hardly venture to attempt the deliverance of Daniel, and the nobles would hardly venture to "tamper with" him. To express this thought the Aramaic uses the construction, "that nothing pertaining to Daniel might be changed." We have tried to follow Luther more closely in the use of an idiomatic rendering: *dass niemand an Daniel Mutwillen uebte.*

18. The king's sincere grief over his blunder as well as over the loss of a personally esteemed co-worker manifests itself in the manner in which he spends the night. All desire for food has left him as will often be observed when men are under the stress of very deep emotion. What the next term—*dachawan*—means no one really knows. The conjectures range all the way from "food" (*Luther*) and "instruments of music" (*A. V.*) with the marginal rendering "table" to "dancing girls" (*A. R. V.m.*) and "concubines." We have followed the Jewish Version—"diversions"—as being sufficiently "noncommittal" to include any variety of possibilities and yet to include the general tenor of them all. Some customary form of entertainment seems to be under consideration. Even so it

was not merely a moody moroseness but a deep disturbance of spirit that possessed the king, for "sleep (Aramaic: 'his sleep') fled from him." Considering the callousness of the average run of Oriental monarchs of days of old, this is evidence of a trait of conscientiousness on the king's part that lets him appear in a far better light than do many others.

e. *Daniel's Deliverance,* v. 19-23

19-23.   Then the king arose very early in the morning and went in haste to the lions' den. And as he drew near to the den he called out to Daniel in a pitiable voice; and the king answered and said: "Daniel, servant of the living God, thy God, whom thou servest unremittingly, was He able to deliver thee from the lions?" Then Daniel spoke with the king: "O king, may thy days be many! My God hath sent His angel and hath shut the lions' mouth, and they have done me no harm, inasmuch as I was found innocent before Him, and also before thee, O king, have I done nothing amiss." Then the king was exceedingly glad, and he commanded in reference to Daniel that he be drawn up out of the den. So Daniel was drawn up out of the den, and he was found to be entirely uninjured; for he had trusted in his God.

The expression "at dawn when it became light," which reminds of Matt. 28:1, is rendered quite acceptably by "very early in the morning" (*A. V.*). The king's one concern was whether the one hope in ten thousand was realized. He was religious enough to believe in the possibility of a miracle. He is still approaching the den when he begins to cry out. The distress of his heart is touchingly reflected in his voice; that is what "with a pitiable voice" means. Some interpreters have suggested the translation, "With a voice full of anxiety." Instead of asking a very brief question such as one might have expected under the circumstances, the king makes a fuller statement which at the same time expresses the ground for hope that the king has in mind—Daniel's faithful service of his God. This more elaborate question is explained by the fact that it is poured out of the fulness of emotion which agitated the king's mind at the moment. Although it sounds rather pious the question is typically heathen. When men fulfilled their obligations to their gods they stood a fair chance of being rewarded by their gods— out-and-out work-righteousness! The long question is psychologically explicable on the basis of our suggestions above. The question, as it is put, suggests weakness of faith rather than strength. It implies that if God should not have delivered Daniel He was not able to do so. This is suggested by the words "was He able to deliver."

22. The use of the word "spoke," *mallel*, instead of "said," *'amar*, suggests that, whereas the king was under great tension to hear whether a man's voice would *speak* by way of answer, Daniel actually did *speak*. Respectful as ever, he uses the full courtesy of address commanded in court circles even in this trying situation, showing the full composure of faith that possessed him. We have translated the familiar, "O king, live forever" (*A. V.*), in a manner that suggests the thought implied far more accurately, as *Luther* always does: *Gott verleihe dir langes Leben*, "may thy days be many." "Forever" often has this connotation. With the same calm composure Daniel proceeds to furnish the king with an adequate statement of what had actually transpired. Whatever erroneous notions about such things the king may have had, the truth of the matter is: "My God hath sent His angel." The Scriptures abound in revelation concerning the activity of the angels of God as "ministering spirits sent forth to minister for them who shall be heirs of sal-

vation," Heb. 1:14. It is not very likely that either Daniel or the lions saw the angel. But such service God is wont to render through these ministers. That one angel is able efficiently to restrain a den full of lions is also entirely clear to Daniel. If the king did not know about angels, this was a good time to inform him.

Daniel adds the deeper cause that led God to do such a thing. From one point of view it was the undeserved mercy of God. The mention of that fact was less in order at this time than to clear up another important issue that had arisen because of the foolish edict. Daniel's conduct, his integrity had been impugned. Had there been a manifest wrong in him, God could not have taken his part. The fact that God sent His angel demonstrated the fact that the deliverance was primarily a declaration to the effect that Daniel "was found innocent before Him." This deliverance was God's vindication of Daniel.

Gently but firmly Daniel administers a rebuke to his king, a model retort courteous, namely: "Also before thee, O king, have I done nothing amiss." That is to say: "You knew that I was above reproach, yet you suffered me to be exposed to this extreme danger." In that respect the king had erred; but Daniel was not going to make any more ado about the king's lapse. This was, no doubt, the first and only reference to it on Daniel's part. By translating thus rather than "also before thee have I done no hurt" (*A. V.*) we at least have a better idiom. The whole episode is a good illustration of the passage: "Let the righteous smite me, it shall be a kindness; and let him reprove me, it shall be as oil upon the head," Ps. 141:5.

23. How strongly the king had felt on the whole matter of having Daniel's life endangered thus appears from the fact that when he heard Daniel's voice he "was exceedingly glad," *Aramaic,* "It was exceedingly good to him." The requirements of the stern and un-

yielding law of the Medes and Persians have now, in the king's estimation, been entirely met. He ventures to act vigorously and justly as he should have done in the first instance. He now appears as a resolute monarch who knows his mind, discerns all issues very clearly, and is ready to assert his royal prerogatives.

He first commands that Daniel be "drawn up out of the den." The infinitive *lehansaqah* strangely comes from the verb *selaq*. The fact that Daniel is removed by being "drawn up" indicates that both the lions and Daniel must have been in some sort of pit. This could have been the case if the door and the stone were on the side of the enclosure. The pit would in that event come up to the very door at one side. But all our suppositions are based on conjecture.

In full confirmation of Daniel's words it now appears that he was actually "entirely uninjured." The Aramaic says: "No hurt was found in him." Daniel's explanation for what had happened was that "he had trusted in his God." This man of God was also great in this regard, that he had faith and knew the intrinsic importance of faith. He understood that the chief requisite for a godly man was the having of faith. As for us to this day the greatest essential of the Christian life is faith, so it was in the days of old, and true men of God understood the principle: "According to thy faith, so be it done unto thee."

It may also be noted that in v. 22, where the statement is made that the angel "shut" the lions' mouth, the Aramaic verb for shut is *seghar*. It was this fact that gave a name to an angel found in the letter of *Hermas,* namely "Segri."

f. *The King's Reaction to the Deliverance,* v. 24-28

24. **Then the king commanded, and they brought those men who had slandered Daniel and cast them into the lions' den—them, their children, and their wives—and the lions overpowered them**

and broke all their bones before they ever touched the bottom of the den.

This is surely a bloody sequel. But since it is not invented by Daniel and is an objective record of what was done, we need not attribute any gloating over the fate of his foes to Daniel. If an element of divine justice appears in this, that all the plotters experienced the very fate that they had designed for Daniel, that may well be recorded as a rather striking thing, a startling proof of divine retribution. Daniel himself, no doubt, shuddered at the thought of what had befallen his foes. All commentators claim that this was an instance of typical Oriental justice. From the standpoint of plain justice it can hardly be denied that the death penalty is in many cases just retribution for those who are guilty of attempted manslaughter. The Mosaic law was far more lenient in that it would have exempted the wives and the children of the guilty men. See Deut. 24:16.

When Daniel records how ferociously the lions pounced on these persons, that is told only to corroborate the fact that the lions had certainly not spared Daniel because they had been fed but recently. Their ferocity was so great that it led them to assault each new victim as he came within reach, not even allowing him to reach the ground first. No one who interprets the account reasonably would venture to assert that all the 120 satraps plus their wives and their children are to be thought of as having perished so miserably. Perhaps the active agents numbered only a handful, and they were recognized as the prime movers of the assault upon Daniel.

The Aramaic together with other early languages has a singularly strong idiom for "slander," namely, "eat the pieces of a man"—an expression that is found in the Assyrian and in the Amarna letters.

25-27. **Then King Darius wrote to all peoples, nations, and languages who dwelt in all the land: "Peace be multiplied unto you. I make a decree that in all the domain of my kingdom men tremble and fear before the God of Daniel, for He is the living God and steadfast forever, and His kingdom one that shall not be destroyed, and His dominion shall be unto the end. He delivereth and saveth and worketh signs and wonders in the heavens and on the earth, who delivered Daniel from the power of the lions."**

This decree is not out of harmony with the claim that an appointee of Cyrus, Gobryas, published it. For we do not have to translate "peoples . . . that dwell in all the *earth.*" For as all students of the language admit, it is just as correct to translate "that dwell in all the *land.*" We have, therefore, not necessarily a ruler who had world-wide dominion. He issues a decree that is to be obeyed merely "in all the land" that is his. For the general tenor of the decree compare what was said above on chapter 4.

If the tone of this heathen king's decree appears to be too nearly Scriptural, we need merely think of it in the terms of *Ellicott* who says: "The language is remarkably Scriptural. This is due, no doubt, to the share which Daniel had in the composition of it." It will be noted that the decree asks no more of Darius' subjects than that they show due respect—"tremble and fear"—to the God of Daniel, whom they had perhaps heretofore regarded as only a second-rate deity. It asserts further that He is a "living God"—not the only living God—that His kingdom endures unto the end; and that He is capable of working mighty signs and wonders and has even now delivered Daniel. All heathen would be perfectly ready at any time to admit the deity of one who had wrought signs and wonders. All this is said to safeguard against reading into this decree what it certainly did not intend to say. Darius no more experienced a conversion to the true faith than did Nebuchadnezzar despite the fine tone of his edicts.

28. So this Daniel prospered in the reign of Darius and in the reign of Cyrus the Persian.

Here, as in v. 3, the expression "*this* Daniel" is most appropriate. *Keil* says: "By the pronoun 'this' the identity of the person is accentuated: *the same Daniel*, whom his enemies wished to destroy, prospered."

If it pleased God to extend the limit of the usefulness of His servant so that he served even under the great Cyrus, who, no doubt, after the death of his appointed ruler of Chaldea took over the reins himself, then it is surely a thing that is worthy of record. And since Daniel states it with such brevity and becoming modesty, no one should find fault. Daniel is telling what God allowed him to do. We need to know this fact in order to be able to judge rightly the remainder of the activity of Daniel. With his deliverance from the lions' den his work was not yet finished. That is all Daniel seeks to indicate. Even the great Cyrus was to have the blessing of having Daniel serve under him and direct his attention to the true God and His purposes.

HOMILETICAL SUGGESTIONS

The difference between the kindred chapter (3) and this one is that the former writes in terms of situations which arise without particular design on the part of men who are strangers to the kingdom. Situations fraught with danger for God's saints spring up, as it were, of themselves, yet, of course, not without the clever design of the evil one. It is just as obvious that the enemies of the kingdom sometimes plot and plan against God's own. Chapter 6 deals with issues of this sort. Since Daniel's book is a comfort book, it is quite reasonable that it offers help for both types of cases. It should, however, be made plain that there is no duplication of purpose.

The chapter is again too much of a unit to be broken up into separate texts. Here, too, in order to keep the texts from being altogether too long, vv. 16-23 may be deemed sufficient for a text, and the rest may be used as lessons or be woven in incidentally.

As in chapter 3, the object should not be to make men afraid of the evils which may at any time come upon the earth but rather to reassure them that their God is equal to any emergency, and the free confession of His name is an obligation never to be avoided.

CHAPTER VII

THE FOUR BEASTS AND THE ETERNAL KINGDOM OF THE SON OF MAN, 7:1-28

We consider this chapter to be the conclusion of the first half of the book. We have several valid reasons for doing so. In the first place, this is the last chapter in which the Aramaic language is used. If chapters two to seven present an unbroken section of Aramaic in an otherwise Hebrew book, surely the first thought of those that note this fact must be that the Aramaic section comprises a unit. We add the observation that chapters two and seven are very obviously parallel; both treat the same general theme though the point of view is strictly not the same throughout. This would suggest that the section in which certain fundamental notes are struck at the beginning closes with a re-affirmation of the same truths and so presents a well-rounded whole.

From another point of view this chapter serves very well to round out the first section, for it yields a fitting climax to the first half. This chapter very evidently offers a very glowing testimony to the eternal nature of the kingdom of the Messiah. Chapter two had touched on the subject without actually bringing the Christ into the picture. Our chapter has such a fine statement regarding the place that the Messiah occupies in the design of God that we cannot but see that by this means the major truth of this first half of the book is dealt with in a manner that is commensurate with its importance.

The objection that may be advanced against our view is the fact that, if chapter seven, being a vision, is grouped with the visions that follow, then all visions are appropriately combined. That view considers the subject from the formal angle only: keep all visions together as a unit. It disregards the deeper material consideration: what is the substance of the vision? It also ignores the important feature offered by the language used.

Another significant consideration is tied up with these: the world language, Aramaic, is used in that part of the book that contains the message that is more directly designed for the world at large. In chapters two to seven the world can learn what *her* kingdoms amount to, and where true rule and empire are to be found. The sacred language, Hebrew, is used when the more particular destinies of *the kingdom of God* are referred to. And so the second half of the book is more directly designed for the church or for those who are of and in the kingdom of God.

Since we have spoken of the close relation between the second and the seventh chapters we must make this relation a bit plainer. The vision of the metal image shows what might be regarded as the more human aspect of the world empires, for the image is that of a human being. We should expect to see the better traits brought to the forefront. But it at once becomes apparent that such a mode of delineation gives but half of the picture. The supplement is added in chapter seven where the baser and more cruel aspects of the world powers are set forth—their beast nature. Holding these two halves of the description side by side, we have a more nearly adequate picture.

There must be added the fact that these two chapters agree very noticeably in the sequence of the kingdoms referred to: the two series of four each are parallel in that respect at least. In spite of all efforts to the contrary this agreement must be postulated on other grounds. To let one and the same book have two series of four empires in analogous chapters but to have different kingdoms represented is after all confusing. In an endeavor to maintain its position criticism raises this charge of confusion against the author or redactor of Daniel.

We might state the relation between the two chapters in question also after this manner: chapter two presents the more external aspect of the case without being in any sense superficial; chapter seven probes deeper into the nature of the two contrasted kingdoms. This is again an indication of the fine order that prevails throughout the book: first the summary inspection is made; then, when readers are familiar with the whole territory, the deeper investigation follows.

This would be the place to evaluate the relation of this chapter to the following. Whereas chapter seven aims to give in summary form the course of history from Daniel's time down to the consummation of the kingdom of the Christ, it is the specific design of chapter eight to outline no more than a brief portion of history, running from about 350 B. C. to about 165 B. C. Why such a narrow bit of historical development is treated will have to be determined when the eighth chapter is examined.

What about the contention of those who state that the subject matter, the substance as a whole as well as the manner of presentation, are inferior to the type of material found in the earlier parts of the book? Before taking issue with this claim we must see exactly how it is phrased. One of the critics of the book says: This second division "is unquestionably inferior to the first part in grandeur and importance as a whole, but it contains not a few great conceptions." More damaging seems to be the claim that "in no previous writer of the grander days of Hebrew literature would such symbols have been permitted as horns which have eyes and speak, or lions from which the wings are plucked." Another writer says, "The introductory scene . . . tastes of ancient mythological poetry." Such criticisms are, of course, subjective in character. We, on our part, feel nothing of the sort. Neither the general tenor nor the mode of presentation is in any sense inferior to other grand Biblical scenes of revelation. For all interpreters must admit that, no matter what figures are employed to represent or illustrate truth, they all have their shortcomings. Taken as a whole, the presentation found here makes distinct sense and good sense. Other figures that might have appealed more to the esthetic perceptions are not used because they do not happen to be as adequate in reflecting the thought to be portrayed. There are bound to be occasional points of contact with heathen literature because fragments of truth have been retained here and there in heathen tradition. But such accidental coincidences do not stamp divine revelation as having been derived from these outside sources.

It is a good thing to view the chapter as a whole before examining the particulars. Four beasts arise successively to occupy positions of prominence. These portray the historical development of four nations. Their receding out of the picture successively is scarcely noticed because as each new beast forges into the forefront, the preceding beast is forgotten. These beasts represent successive empires. After the fourth one has come to power, a horn of major proportions on this beast begins to dominate the scene. When this point of the vision is reached, and before an interpretation is offered, the judgment pronounced upon the beasts is presented, especially upon the fourth beast and the horn. A new power appears on the scene, the kingdom of one who is called "the Son of man." This kingdom is to be universal and eternal. Since up to this point Daniel's conception of what was signified was uncertain, he asks that a reliable interpretation be granted to him. This he receives plus an intimation that the little horn will endeavor to persecute the saints of God but shall not prevail against them. Then, since Daniel's interest was attracted especially to the fourth beast and the little horn, he concentrates his questions on these matters. The final interpretation emphasizes especially that the ultimate victory belongs to the kingdom in which the saints shall have a part.

Consequently it should be noticed from the outset that from one point of view the whole vision is a judgment vision, but the term judgment is taken in the sense of implying the destruction of the powers of evil as well as in the sense of establishing God's final victory and eternal kingdom.

a. *The Four Successive Beasts; the Horn with Eyes and a Mouth Speaking Great Things,* v. 1-8

1-3. In the first year of Belshazzar, king of Babylon, Daniel had a dream and visions of his head on his bed. Thereupon he wrote the dream and told the sum of the matters. Daniel answered and said: "I was beholding in my vision in the course of the night, and lo, the four winds of the heavens were whipping up the great sea; and four beasts rose up from the sea, each different from the other."

Belshazzar was last mentioned in chapter five. We there showed how he might well have been a son of Nebuchadnezzar as well as Nabonidus. There was at that point no need of assuming that he was king of Babylon more than a short time. It now appears that that short time was at least four years. That does not imply that at any time during those four years Belshazzar administered the affairs of the entire Babylonian Empire. The city or state of Babylon alone came under his jurisdiction. Besides, it is highly probable that this fourth year was also the last year of his life when, as 5:30 reports, he was slain at the time of the capture of the city.

We agree with those commentators who find in this very specific remark of the date of the vision more than a mere date. This fourth and last year of his was most probably also the last year of Babylonian dominion. When Belshazzar fell, the hour of the doom of that ancient empire as well as of that ancient kingdom had sounded, and a new order of things began to prevail. The statement of our verse therefore implies that this significant year was the year when God gave this signal revelation of the doom of the world powers or empires in general. It is for this reason that the apposition "king of Babylon" is added to "Belshazzar."

Heretofore others had had dreams. It is now none other than the author himself who has them, and he has them at a time when he was far advanced in years, in other words, at a time of life when men are not wont to have such things as significant dreams and relevations. Daniel's dream is described as was Nebuchadnezzar's (4:5), as being also visions of his head upon his bed. It was not merely a haunting "dream" of some sort in which dark premonitions or vague feelings came upon a man, but everything was clearly seen in the form of "visions" that took definite shape in his head as he lay abed. Despite all that it was primarily a dream experience and is therefore designated by that name first of all.

The statement about the writing, being attached to what precedes by a "thereupon," must mean that at once, after having had this significant dream, while the whole matter was still fresh in his mind, the prophet committed it to writing. This, of course, describes merely the human precaution and presupposes as self-evident the more important factor of divine inspiration during the course of such writing.

What he wrote, Daniel describes as being "the sum of the matters." The Aramaic term *re'sh* must here mean "sum" in the sense of "essential content" (*BDB*), for "beginning" (*K. W.*), though a possible meaning, is a rather pointless expression in this connection. Why only the "beginning"? Why not tell the whole experience? By this term "sum" the author appears to say that the essential features were culled out of the great variety of details that a long dream presented so as not to present a bewildering array of detail. For even the prophet needed angelic assistance before he was able to construe aright the multitude of things that he had seen. This word contains a significant reminder that every word is carefully chosen and to the point; unessential items are passed by.

This is a typical example of how the critical treatment of the text follows arbitrary procedures. We are informed that the "he told (*'amar*) must be rejected with the LXX and Th." because "Daniel does not first write down and then tell his visions." May not a conscientious author, after having received a revelation, first sit down to write what he received before he tells it to others?

2.   It is quite customary at this point to find fault with what the author wrote. He is said to use redundant expressions. If, according to the first verse, he "told" what had transpired, why have him here "answer and say"? Or the explanation is offered that a part of what is said here was affixed by a later hand to what was Daniel's or some other author's original draft of the dream story. Yet the mode of presentation employed is not only above reproach but even very fine and accurate. Commentators are often too reluctant to think themselves into a given situation in a sympathetic way. The preceding verse had recorded that the writer had promptly committed his experience to writing, in which writing he aimed to give the essential

content. We might have gone on to say: "Now this is what he said." The Hebrew idiom for our form of statement happens to be, "he answered and said," with this difference, that the verb "answered" suggests that he had in mind the unasked question of all who heard that he had had a dream: "What was your dream?" Whenever the charge is raised against parts of the Hebrew Scriptures that they contain doublets or manifest redundancies, the implied suggestion is always that we can readily detect the evidences of clumsy composition on the part of the Hebrew writers; they on their part somehow never noted how crude the original writer's or the redactor's efforts were.

The rest of the chapter continues in the first person, a feature that is characteristic of this book only from this point onward. This again offers no proof for the contention that Daniel, for example, might have written from v. 2 onward, and that some redactor prefixed v. 1. Such claims ignore that freedom in matters of composition that all writers claim for themselves.

The expression "I was beholding" occurs eight times in this chapter. Being the verb "to be" plus a participle, it emphasizes the continued action and implies a continued gazing, a studious examination of the scene presented. It also suggests that the action involved in the various scenes may have consumed quite a bit more time than the condensed account would seem to suggest. Since this "vision" came during the night in a dream, Daniel must have been asleep, and the ordinary activities of a busy life must have ceased. At such a time the mind of man is far more receptive to higher influences and impressions.

The preposition *'im* must in this instance mean "during" or "in the course of" even though *Charles* fails to find this temporal use substantiated by the Aramaic papyri.

The very first thing seen was significant as the particle *'aru,* "lo," indicates. The "great sea" is seen. Nothing indicates that the Mediterranean is referred to. It was rather merely an expanse of the ocean, it matters not what part of it. The "four winds of the heavens" are in action. Looking at the versions, we find it difficult to determine what the winds were said to be doing. *A. V.* tells us they "strove," *A. R. V.,* they "broke forth," *Luther,* they "dashed against one another."" The Aramaic verb (*BDB* does not list it) means "to break forth"; in the *Haphel* this would involve the meaning "cause to break forth." If the object is "the great sea," this must involve some such idea as "were whipping up the great sea." *K. W.* renders *emporfluten, aufschaeumen lassen.* The disturbed state of the surface of the sea is apparently not due to certain creatures within it who are about to come to the surface but are for the present still churning up the deep but to the winds themselves. If the *four* winds are represented as being in action simultaneously, we may well claim that this is not a presentation from the strictly physical point of view but a poetic description of what was seen in a dream, and it has often been observed that dreams have little regard for the laws of physics. That does not mean that wild disorder prevails in the vision but merely that the figurative mode of presentation betrays, as is always the case, some shortcoming in the figure employed and so a seeming irregularity from the literal point of view.

The world powers that are hostile to God and to Israel are in the Scriptures often represented as mighty waters, see Isa. 8:7f.; Jer. 46:7,9; 47:2; Isa. 17:2f. This point of view is confirmed by Rev. 17:1, 15: "The waters . . . are peoples and multitudes and nations and tongues." This figure reflects the mighty power of these hostile forces. The continual restlessness of the sea corresponds to the state of unrest in which the nations continually find themselves. The waters, roily with filth, present the picture of the continual iniquity and filth that the unrest of the world brings to light.

But do the winds actually represent the heavenly agencies, and is the resultant commotion the result of the clash of the earthly and the heavenly forces? There is something rather inapropos about this view. For that would yield the result that disturbances in the world are attributable to heavenly forces whereas they are more correctly termed the result of purely earthly causes. The unhappy plight and the unrest of the nations are caused directly by the iniquity of these nations as such. We prefer to regard the winds as a second earthly factor in the picture and a rather appropriate one at that. For the heavier disturbances among the nations are periodic even as are the storms on the sea. When, in v. 17, the four beasts are said to come up "out of the earth," the point of view is practically the same. The "sea" is not the Mediterranean but just the ocean in a very general way though elsewhere it may refer to the Mediterranean, cf. Num. 34: 6, 7; Josh. 9:1.

When the "four beasts" appear as rising from the sea, that clearly indicates that the disturbed state of the world gives origin to the successive world powers that appear on the scene of history. We may well maintain that the number "four" has symbolical significance. It is always the number of the world. Four empires represent the sum total of the powers that the world produces in the course of its development. If these are found to coincide with four historic empires, that would be one of those rare instances where the reality happens to coincide with the symbolic representation. Besides, this mode of delineation explains why nothing goes beyond the creature that represents the Roman Empire. This last creature rounds out the account; and after it nothing radically new appears as far as empire development is concerned.

We must note how far the verb "rose up" allows us to go in the matter of interpretation. That is all the beasts did as far as their initial act is concerned. We are not free to add that they came out and stood upon *terra firma*. As far as the dream was concerned, they merely came up from the waters and appeared on the screen of the dream vision. Nor need we be unduly alarmed because nothing more specific is said with reference to where they took their stand. That is quite unessential and is, therefore, disregarded in the dream which the prophet is given to see. What is of importance is the fact that these beasts are "each different from the other." Each of these four world powers has distinct traits of its own. There is regal Babylonia, voluptuous Persia, cultured Greece, and imperial, victorious Rome. That set of distinctions alone makes each of these stand out sufficiently from the other.

To catch the full import of these revelations we must dwell at greater length upon the basic fact that the most adequate figurative representation of these world powers is four "beasts," *chewan*. There may be something of human greatness about empires as chapter two allows. There is just as much justification for the point of view that in their relation to one another and in their mode of acquiring power the world powers are rapacious beasts of great strength and are no longer human. As long as a nation makes no bid for imperial control it may preserve a more humanized attitude and character. As soon as it enters the lists to become a leader among the nations, all resemblance to the finer human traits is laid aside, and the beast comes to the forefront. This flatters human vanity but little but is one of the truest facts ever revealed by the Scriptures. All subtle self-flattery of the nations to the contrary, this is still the most telling and accurate description of the outstanding trait of the nations that aim to exercise control over other nations.

4. **"The first was like a lion, and it had the wings of an eagle. I kept looking until its wings were torn out, and it was raised up from the earth and made to stand upon two feet like a man; and the heart of a man was given to it."**

Before any details in these descriptions of the four beasts are examined, we quite naturally ask, "Are these four beasts counterparts to the four major parts of the metal statue of chapter two?" A number of considerations point in that direction. If one and the same author has recorded both these visions, we may well assume that the same point of view prevails. Probing deeper, we are justified in saying, "If God inspired Nebuchadnezzar's dream and Daniel's vision, there is all the more reason for expecting a correspondence." There is also a striking inner correspondence: each one of the four in each series corresponds with its parallel representation in the other series, that is to say, the first part of the statue corresponds with the first beast, etc.

We shall not consider the question of the sequence of the four that is offered by chapter two. We are more firmly convinced than ever that they are Babylon, Persia, Greece, and Rome. The arguments advanced in support of Media as being the second in both series are not convincing. In fact, this chapter establishes the sequence which we advocated in connection with chapter 2.

We are not impressed by the claims of those who represent the critical approach to this question. Rejecting our view, they tell us that "the former view [i.e., that the fourth empire is the Greek] is now accepted by the whole world of scholarship." This is an exaggeration even from their own point of view. For he that makes it (*Charles*) had just conceded (p. 172) that "some modern scholars advocated this view." But our objection is chiefly that this critical view does not do justice to the facts set forth in the chapter. Then we also know that its background is the fact that to admit that the writer, even had he lived somewhere about 165 B. C., is uttering nothing less than outright prophecy if he predicts the fortunes of the Roman Empire is, in the opinion of these writers of the critical school, simply impossible. Their attitude toward such prophecy is the determining factor in their exegesis even more, than they themselves often realize.

From this it follows that the lion must represent the Babylonian Empire. To tell the truth, imperial developments first appear in Babylon (cf. Gen. 10:10). The only other rival claimant to this distinction might be Egypt. But we hardly need to prove the manifest fact that Egypt never actually came near to achieving world dominion as far as the world of that time was known. Babylon actually did come first.

But even as in chapter two a singular distinction was predicated with reference to Babylon—there it was the "head"—so it is here likened to two beasts of truly regal character: the eagle plus the lion. Both creatures are recognized as being dominant in their own sphere; one is the king of the beasts, the other of the birds. Though it was beastlike, it was still the nobler type of beast. The wings signify that greater swiftness of movement was characteristic of the beast in its conquests than would be expected of a creature that was only a lion.

Another fact that contributes to make the identification of this creature certain is that the nations generally were familiar with such figures as the winged lions that guarded the gates of royal palaces among the Babylonians. Daniel had seen these figures ever since his deportation to Babylon. They were practically emblems of the Babylonian power.

Add the Biblical comparisons that appear in the prophets in many passages (cf. the lion: Jer. 49:19; 50:17, 44; and the eagle: Jer. 48:40; 49:22; Ezek. 17: 3, 12) and it will be seen that there was sufficient material available to point toward a correct beginning of the interpretation. But it becomes equally clear that two approaches are blended throughout the chapter. The creature is sometimes thought of as representing the world power; sometimes as representing the king. But that is an easy and a natural transition. For the king may be so completely identified with his kingdom as to be mentioned instead of it, especially if the traits of the nation are in an unusual manner present in the character of the king as was certainly the case with Nebuchadnezzar. This explanation is not "rather forced," neither have we two "really incongruous sets of ideas."

After Daniel beheld the creature he "kept looking"; the verb is progressive and does not mean merely "beheld." The picture must have fascinated him. He must have studied it closely so that no feature might escape him. He seemed to expect that something would happen. It did. Its "wings were torn out." We are not told by what agent. That feature of the vision is apparently quite secondary. It was then raised up from the earth. This does not necessarily imply that after the creature had come out of the water it took its stand somewhere on the shore. Rather, wherever it stood, that was in the picture "the earth." For the feature that was emphasized was that it was made "to stand upon two feet like a man." To make the humanization of the creature still more prominent we are then told that "the heart of a man was given to it."

This is undoubtedly an allusion to the experience of Nebuchadnezzar which is related in detail in chapter four. The incident signifies that, as nearly as it is possible for a beast to become like a man, so nearly did Babylon lose its beastlike nature. For as far as Nebuchadnezzar was concerned, his proud nature and his lust of conquest were taken from him when God brought him low. Babylon itself, however, shared the king's experience, for he proclaimed and sought as much as possible to induce the nation to cultivate the type of spirit that had been begotten in him. The entire fourth chapter is evidence of that. When the king gave up his desire to conquer other nations, his own nation followed suit. That was a national process of humanization that characterized only Babylon. Whatever may have been the attitude of other kings who succeeded Nebuchadnezzar is not to be considered, for all his successors were men of inferior calibre, and the history' of Babylon practically ends with him. To sum up, when the empire relinquishes its unseemly and arrogant pride, it gains the distinction of becoming more nearly human. Babylon is marked by that experience.

5. **"And, lo, another beast, a second one like unto a bear, raised up on one side; and it had three ribs in its mouth between its teeth; and a command was given to it thus: 'Arise, devour much flesh.' "**

There are several instances on record where the bear appears in conjunction with the lion or follows it. Note Hos. 13:8; Amos 5:19; Prov. 28:15; I Sam. 17:34ff. They just happened to be two beasts of the same category that were nearest alike: after the lion came the bear among the rapacious and dangerous creatures. One major difference between the Babylonian and the Persian Empires is indicated by the differences between the lion and the bear. The latter is without a doubt less regal and more slow and heavy-going. The double expression, "another" and a "second" one, says with emphasis that this was not a metamorphosis of the first creature but the appearance of an entirely new creature. Strictly speaking, this was not a bear any more than the first creature had been a lion. For this beast is only "like unto," *dameyah,* a bear; the creature most nearly resembling it was a bear.

The statement that it was "raised up on one side" has given rise to a diversity of explanations. Some have this signify that the creature had just half lain down or was in the act of lowering its one side. The marginal translation suggests: "raised up one dominion." Still others regard the lower part as the front half of the beast, as though it were crouching for a spring. Still others have it rise up on its front paws as if coming out of a prostrate position. But if one half is down and the other up (for that is what "raised up on one side" must mean according to a reasonable interpretation), then the two original sections of the Medo-Persian Empire are most likely under consideration. The Median half of these two sections was the more passive, the part inclined to lie down. The more aggressive Persian part of the empire will then be signified by the side that is raised up. Nothing more than this is indicated by this part of the vision, and this is a factor that was historically true.

Some make out a case in behalf of the aggressive character of the Medians on the basis of passages such as Isa. 13:17 and Jer. 51:11, 28. But both of these passages were written at a time when the Persians were not yet in the forefront, in fact, were scarcely known. Then the Medes, who were later to become a dormant factor, were still active. But that does not warrant the claim that the Medes had left a tradition of their destructive power. No historian lists the Medes among those who set up a world empire. But those really dominant world rulers are the only powers under consideration in these visions.

"The three ribs in its mouth between its teeth"

point to the conquests of this nation. "Three" appears to be a number that signifies rather substantial conquests and is not to be taken literally. For the Medo-Persian Empire conquered more than Babylonia, Lydia, and Egypt. Such enumerations of three definite powers are more or less arbitrary. Three does sometimes signify nothing more than a fairly large number and has no reference to God or the Holy Trinity. That is especially true in a case like this. Someone has rightly remarked that "the three ribs constitute a large mouthful."

The expression "a command was given to it" reads in the Aramaic, "they commanded to it," a construction which some interpreters did not recognize as involving the impersonal plural subject and so determined that the "they" involved angelic beings. That is surely more than this simple expression seeks to convey. We have, therefore, translated the statement as a simple passive.

The question arises whether the command, "Arise, devour much flesh," implies that the flesh on the ribs is to be eaten, or whether, after substantial conquests have been made, further conquests are to be attempted. The latter seems to be the more reasonable interpretation. When a beast has a generous portion of prey between its teeth it will hardly need to be encouraged to devour this part or the meaty part of its prey. Or is it thinkable that a beast of prey, having secured a huge portion of meat, might stand with the meat in its jaws and forget to dispose of it? The Persian Empire was voracious; it deyoured quite a bit more than did Babylon. This fact is emphasized by these last features of the vision, the three ribs and the command to devour. Summing up, the vision emphasizes a greedy voraciousness over against the royal dignity that marked the first beast.

6. **"After this I kept looking in the night visions and, lo, another one, like a leopard, and this one had four bird wings on its sides; and the beast had four heads; and dominion was given to it."**

We conclude from v. 12 that, as the new beast comes into the forefront of the scene, the preceding beast recedes into the background without having anything in particular happen to it for the time being. There is another aspect of the case: one kingdom overcomes the other. That is substantiated by the presentation that the eighth chapter gives. Though the one vanquishes the other, the vanquished kingdom continues to live on: "their lives were prolonged for a season and a time."

We again have the familiar expression, "I kept looking." The successive visions must have had a fascination all their own. The man of God studied each new one that arose with close scrutiny. Besides, the visions were not of such a character as to frighten the beholder so much as to awaken him, for he again says: "I kept looking *in the night visions.*" The successive visions were one grant and complete vision. Attention is again directed to the new apparition by a "lo." The creature is again only "like a leopard" and not actually a leopard. Leopards may not be quite the equal of lions and bears in point of strength, but they may be compared with them at least in ferocity and may excel them in swiftness and in lightness of movement. Note Hos. 13:7; Hab. 1:8; Jer. 5:6; Rev. 13:2. It is especially this last feature that is under consideration in this instance because this creature is equipped with "four bird wings." A creature that is agile by nature and at the same time has not merely two wings as did the first beast must surely be designed to convey the impression of being marked by the greatest rapidity of movement. The fact that this creature has these wings on its sides and not on its back would seem to point to the fact that these wings are designed for propelling the creature forward but not for flight.

This is without a doubt a representation of the Greek kingdom of Alexander. The speed of that great general's conquests is the marvel of all who study history. He undertook his conquest when he was still a mere youth. When he was scarcely more than a youth the world lay prostrate under this feet. Each stage of the conquests made was accomplished with astonishing rapidity.

It is also readily apparent why the creature is said only to have been "like a leopard," for this creature is known to have neither wings nor four heads. This last feature aims to convey the thought that this kingdom at one time actually had four heads. This happened, as all students of history can readily recognize, at the time when Alexander died at an early age, and no one appeared on the scene who was able to wield his mighty sceptre; and so the empire disintegrated into four major sections which were ruled over by Alexander's chief generals. Each of these generals practically founded a kingdom that continued as a prominent factor in world politics until the next empire appeared on the scene and amalgamated the parts into a new whole.

At this point the last feature recorded must be evaluated, viz., that "dominion was given to it." All the others that preceded certainly also had dominion given to them, but no mention is made of that fact. Therefore in this instance something must be implied that is different from the dominion that can justly be ascribed to the preceding beasts. We believe that the distinctive feature lies in this fact, that the conqueror Alexander did not actually achieve by ordinary conquests the victories that were his lot, but that he had been singled out by divine province to have the world dominion come into his hands. He was, in a very particular way, a man of destiny. It is more appropriately said of him that his dominion *"was given"* than that he actually *earned* and *achieved* it.

The weakness of the position of those who regard the preceding empire to be Media and the leopard to represent Persia is obvious. The difficulty of their position becomes apparent when they interpret the four heads of this beast. These, they say, signify the four Persian kings noted in the book of Daniel. It is their opinion that Daniel knew only four Persian kings although history lists many more. In fact, even these four are arrived at by charging the author with having identified two whom he keeps strictly apart. Their argument is practically this: If in a given writing a man mentions only four kings of an empire over which quite a few more are known to have reigned he *actually knows of only four*. That is rather weak logic, to put it mildly. But the difficult position taken is so precarious that such arguments must be resorted to.

In this connection we may note a similar argument that is advanced to uphold the contention that the preceding beast represents the Median kingdom and the leopard the Persian. It is claimed that an "indication" in the book itself that "the author regards the Median and Persian Empires as distinct" is to be found in the following passages in Daniel: 5:28, 31; 6:8, 12, 15, 28; 8:20; 11:1. If any interpreter can discover indications of such a distinction in the passages cited he is welcome to accept them. An examination of them will yield the result that they are silent on the question as to whether these two empires are "distinct" from one another. All they offer is a reminder of the fact that in this new empire there were two co-operating factors, Medes and Persians. One king is, however, called a "Mede," not because of any distinction of empires, but because he *was* a Mede.

7. **"After this I kept looking during the night visions and, lo, a fourth beast, terrible and frightful and exceedingly strong. It had great teeth of iron; it devoured and broke things in pieces and stamped upon what was left with its feet; it was quite different from all the beasts that were before it; and it had ten horns."**

The prophet's attention is again riveted on what is presented to him. "I kept looking in the course of the night visions," and an entirely different and startling type of creature appears on the scene. The familiar categories of wild beasts fail to yield a suitable specimen for comparison, for something is to be typified which is "terrible and frightful and exceedingly strong." There is apparently no beast sufficiently fierce and terrible to portray so abnormal a type of nation. Everything points to the Roman world power as being the empire typified by this beast. It borders on the absurd to state that the Syrian kingdom is referred to. For, in the first place, no one has ever ventured to assert, if he had an adequate knowledge of history, that Syria, roughly a fourth part of Alexander's empire, deserved to be mentioned in the same breath with Babylon, Persia, and the Greek empire of Alexander. Syria was definitely a second-rate power.

Besides, such an interpretation runs head on against the point of view of this vision which represents the fourth world power as being the most terrible of all. Historically Syria is known to have been the least terrible. We venture to say that, if the beasts had been presented from the American point of view, a good beast for representing or symbolizing the Syrian kingdom might have been a fox or a coyote. For it should be noted that among the characteristics that are enumerated is "exceedingly strong." That must signify greater strength than the preceding beasts possessed, otherwise this characteristic would not have been deserving of mention. That, as well as the "terrible and frightful," fits admirably in the case of the Roman Empire and is inapplicable in the case of Syria.

The third major discrepancy in this interpretation (Syria) appears in connection with the ten horns, noted at the end of the verse, but with which we may very properly take issue from this point of view. This interpretation lists ten separate Syrian kings. Unfortunately, only seven, who actually held the office, are a matter of historical record. Consequently three men who were potential heirs to the throne or pretenders must be included in the count.

That is certainly not sober interpretation. These three are Demetrius, the son of the brother of Antiochus Epiphanes, Heliodorus who laid claim to the throne in Syria, and Ptolemy Philometer. That seems to agree very excellently, however, with the fact that is also mentioned in v. 8 that three of the first horns were plucked up by the roots before the horn that starts to grow as a "little horn," but that is only a surface resemblance which is offset by the above-mentioned fact that the ten horns are ten kings (v. 24), not potential kings.

The features of the vision that are calculated to meet the eye in describing the beast as to its character are three: "great teeth of iron," the fact that it "devoured and broke in pieces" in the sense which we have included in our translation: it "broke things in pieces"; and thirdly, "it stamped upon what was left with its feet." That must surely signify a singularly voracious, cruel, and even vindictive world power. Rome could never get enough of conquest. Rivals like Carthage just had to be broken: *Carthago delenda est.* Rome had no interest in raising the conquered nations to any high level of development. All her designs were imperial; let the nations be crushed and stamped under foot. And the adequate means for achieving such re- sults were the well-trained Roman legions.

It is surely correct to say of such a power that "it is quite different from all the beasts that were before it," and the differences were mainly those which have been enumerated. An added difference is yet to be worked into the picture: "it had ten horns." This, as we already had occasion to indicate on the basis of v. 24, refers to ten kings. But, as we must also keep re- iterating because it is being consistently overlooked, it matters little whether we say the ten horns signify ten *kings* or ten *kingdoms*, for 2:37 makes allowance for both points of view. Since we shall have ample op- portunity to interpret this part of the visions when it becomes an issue in v. 24 we shall reserve our detailed investigation for that time, merely noting the se- quence of events in the vision as they are given in v. 8.

8. **"I kept observing the horns and, lo, another horn, a little one, grew up among them, and three of the first horns were torn out from before it; and, lo, in this horn there were eyes like the eyes of a man and a mouth speaking great things."**

The prophet seemed to sense that the horns were somehow the significant feature about this beast as far as future developments were concerned. It is not the customary "I kept looking" that is used here but "I kept observing," which could also have been trans- lated, "I kept contemplating." The new development in the vision is what is at first a little horn. To begin with, it is not uncommon in the Orient to find sheep that have several horns. "Ten" are, however, unheard of even as it is to have one smaller one come up later and to have it make room for itself, or better, to have room made for it by the tearing out of three of the first ten. For the present let it be remarked that no *special* significance is attached to the *three* horns. They are not to be counted literally; they bear no relation to three rulers of three kingdoms. The three is here, as it was in v. 5, merely a convenient number for conveying the idea of a sufficiently large measure of success. The whole thought is comparative. If *one* replaces *three* it becomes comparatively quite a bit larger than any one of the others. Yet it does not grow as strong as the whole empire—the ten. That may suffice by way of interpretation at this point.

The last significant features are that this horn has eyes that attract attention, also a mouth speaking great things. We are somewhat at a loss to determine just how far we may venture to go in interpreting these features. Eyes and a mouth seem to suggest a human personality so very directly that we are led to wonder whether the horn continued to look like a seeing and a speaking *horn,* or whether it seemed primarily to take on the appearance of a *human being.* For the fact that a human being is symbolized by the horn is made clear by v. 24.

Why should attention be drawn to the eyes? We feel that that problem is cleared up by the fact that the eyes are described as "eyes of a man" or, as we might be inclined to express it, "eyes of a human being." This draws attention away from the beasts that preceded to the human intelligence and character of this new personality. The mouth uttering great things will be seen to speak against God as the sequel shows and also against God's saints, who are to suffer persecution through the agency of this horn. That a coarse type of speaking is involved is suggested by *Luther's* rendering, who uses *Maul* for "mouth." The details receive full consideration from v. 23 onward.

b. *The Judgment by the Ancient of Days; the Consuming of the Beasts and the Horn,* v. 9-12

In a glorious vision the destruction of the beasts and the horn is now shown to be very sudden and thorough. This section is one of the glorious judgment scenes of the Scriptures.

9.   **"I kept looking until thrones were set and an Ancient of Days took His seat. His garment was white as snow and the hair of His head pure as wool. His throne was flames of fire and its wheels burning fire."**

Every item presented in the visions must have had a fascination for the writer, for "he kept looking" time and again. The vision will, no doubt, have been cast in a form that was worthy of so great a theme when it was presented by the Almighty Himself, though in a dream. It matters little on what scene the following took place, and so this detail is not mentioned. These are in reality scenes that are above such limitations as time and space. First "thrones" appear, which are put into place for an impending scene of royal splendor. The thrones themselves will without a doubt have been of rare beauty. The term used is *korse'*, the equivalent of the Hebrew *kisse'*. This term never means anything less than a seat or settle of a very special type which is reserved for very special occasions and personages, here for "the angelic assessors of the Judge." How some interpreters can conjecture that cushions are meant in view of the wheels mentioned in this verse is inconceivable—cushions with wheels! *A. V.* missed the point when it rendered "thrones were cast down." This implies that the thrones that were overthrown are those of the world powers previously referred to. But we were not told that any thrones appeared previously. In any case, beasts on thrones would be rather incongruous. The verb used (*remiw*) does in the Piel mean, "to be cast," but here that is merely a strong term for setting in order quickly. Such paraphernalia as thrones is essential for those who think in terms of human institutions in order to convey the idea of a judgment, not as though God required such trappings for judgment.

After the courtroom is, as it were, properly arranged, the judge enters, who is here called the "Ancient of Days." This name for God, which is used only in this chapter, v. 9, 12, 22, signifies, not one who is marked by the infirmities of old age, but one who has evidently lived for a long time. For it is of moment to emphasize that the judge is the Eternal One who has witnessed all the deeds and acts of men and of kingdoms and is, therefore, well able to pronounce an equitable judgment. To motivate the choice of this name by the suggestion that this term is chosen to eliminate the idea of the more recent gods that Antiochus Epiphanes had sought to foist upon the Jews is an idea that is cancelled by the wrong dating of the book which is made by its proponents. An almost adequate translation of this unusual name of God would be the "Eternal One." The translation the "Venerable One" substitutes appearance for basic fact.

To be strictly exact regarding the term it should be said that it does not express the idea of eternity though it leads up to it in a measure and may be regarded as a popular representation of that idea. Even so, the emphasis lies more upon the long time that He has been able to view the doings of the children of men. Surely, there is nothing irreverent about the name as such. All human designations have their limitations when they are applied to God and are accepted as involving certain shortcomings.

The truly venerable appearance of the Judge is heightened by the further fact that "His garment was white as snow and the hair of His head pure as wool." It seems to be less age and more purity that is indicated by the snow-white garment and the white hair. For it is eminently fitting that the Judge of all mankind be Himself free from every taint of the sin for which He must condemn the sinful among mankind, especially the aggregate total of their sins.

Even this part of the vision of the Almighty presents a scene of superlative heavenly glory, one of the grandest word paintings done by the prophets. Such a one is our God, the One who has redeemed us and will confirm upon us His verdict of justification which is spoken regarding all that believe on Him. The remaining features that are added to this brief but marvelous description further enhance the picture of glory. The throne itself, though it is at a glance recognizable as a throne, is, nevertheless, composed of that ethereal substance, "flames of fire," as being the only matter that is worthy to constitute such a throne. Whereas that might seem to represent a more substantial type of fire, though, of course, only in the vision, the "burning fire" that constitutes the wheels would seem to represent a more active type of flame that is in harmony with the more mobile character of the wheels, though these wheels of the throne do not seem to be in motion as were those in Ezekiel's vision (Ezek. 1). Ancient royal thrones were sometimes represented as having wheels; and so God's throne has them, which is to convey the impression of its not being a throne that is bound to one place. For God's judgment, as is He Himself, is omnipresent. On fire and the Almighty see Exod. 3:2; Deut. 4:24; I Tim. 6:16; Heb. 12:29.

Two additional matters should be mentioned in regard to the name "an Ancient of Days." First of all, it is in the construct relation whereas the accusative of specification would be more commonly used (*K. S.* 336k). Then the term is not *"the* Ancient"—with the definite article. The name does not refer to *the* One who has familiarly appeared thus but is used without the article in order to stress the quality "Ancient." *Luther* writes better German without detracting from the force of the term when he says simply *der Alte.*

The Hebrew accents would suggest the translation: "His garments were as white snow and the hair of His head as pure wool." We feel that our translation is more natural. If in the first instance we render "white as snow" then we must also in the second render "pure as wool," the assumption being that only clean, pure wool is to be thought of

Thus far we have only One sitting on a throne, yet "thrones" were set. For whom were the remaining thrones intended? As far as Daniel's account of the proceeding is concerned, he does not venture to place anyone on these thrones. It seems best to let it go at that. It is true enough that Ps. 89:7, 8 indicates that angels help to constitute a heavenly council. Though that fact is true, the inference is unwarranted that the heavenly hosts play their part every time judgment is pronounced. We are not sufficiently informed to make such a claim. It seems that a number of judgment seats appear in the vision because courts are usually represented thus. It serves no good purpose to seat certain ones on thrones that Daniel himself has left vacant.

10.   **"A stream of fire poured forth and came out from before Him; a thousand thousands ministered unto Him, and ten thousand times ten thousand stood before Him; the court went into session, and books were opened."**

Because of the fire which is said not only to compose the throne and its wheels but also to stream forth so copiously from His presence, one is inclined to think in terms of fiery judgment. That interpretation is, however, only partly correct, for the fire shares in the judgment. It is unwarranted to refer the judgment to negative, destructive work only, for the vision shows us also the positive, constructive side of the judgment.

In like manner the fire should be thought of as typifying also a constructive side of the zeal of God

and not only the consuming of all ungodliness. This
stream of fire "pours forth" as it seems to emanate
from God Himself and then "comes out" as the broad
stream of it flows on. To construe the *minqadhamohi*
as with its suffix referring to the throne of God would
give an undue and unnatural importance to the throne
as the source of the fire. It is, therefore, not "from
before it" but "from before Him."

The scene now enlarges before our mental vision
to an almost inconceivable extent. An innumerable
host is seen before the throne of the Most High. If it
is first described as "a thousand thousands" (cf.
Deut. 33:2) and thereafter as "ten thousand times ten
thousand," the purpose of the double description is to
rectify the first impression by the latter. Only as he
gazed did the author perceive that the host was even
much greater than he had at first discerned. In a word,
it was a host that could not be counted. If they "minister" unto the Lord, that indicates that they know
His divine claims upon them for praise and worship.
If they "stand before Him," that indicates that they
have committed themselves to His service and await
His commands at all times. The implied thought is that
in none of the empires pictured thus far is there so
devoted a host of men that is completely consecrated
to one purpose. The innumerable hosts are without a
doubt the angels of God, of whatever order or character they may be. For *men* in their relation to the
Almighty are described in v. 14.

The statement, "the judgment was set" (*A. V.*)
is not clear. But *dina'* apparently refers not to the
"judgment" but to the "court"; and when those who
constitute a given court formally take their seats, that
is a sign that the session has begun. We therefore
translate: "The court went into session." We might
have rendered a bit more freely still: "The session began." As an indication that the session had begun

"books are opened." Since the books appear to be used for no other purpose than to mark the opening of the session and the beginning of the court's transactions, it might be well to stop short at that point rather than to attempt to determine the purpose of the heavenly books. The situation is similar to that in the preceding verse where attempts are made to seat some characters on judicial chairs that were left vacant by Daniel. If anyone wishes to go farther in determining the exact character of the "books," the following should be borne in mind. The rest of the Old Testament knows of only one book of this sort. That is properly the Lord's book, and in it are written the names of those who are God's own, cf. Exod. 32:32; Ps. 69:28; 139:16. It is also called a "book of remembrance," Mal. 3:16.

To have one's name inscribed means to be saved. To have it blotted out means to be lost. So as a figure it implies that God has an accurate record of all that are His own. Though it cannot be a material book, yet it embodies a reality and has to do with God's saints. But, as becomes apparent from Rev. 20:12, there are also "books." In them are written, not names, but *deeds* of men, a record of their ungodly acts, on the basis of which they will be judged. To claim that in this instance the "books" just mentioned are without a doubt referred to would be looking only at the judgment feature of this great scene. For if two types of books are not mentioned as is the case in Rev. 20:12, the term as such may include both the "books" as well as the "book of life."

A further reason for going no farther than to emphasize the opening of the books is the grammatical fact that "books" appears without the article. Yet it can readily be conceded that books also typify the idea that heaven's record of man's deeds is available and, of course, accurate.

11.   **"I kept looking until as a result of the sound of the great words that the horn spake, I kept looking, I say, until the beast was slain and its body destroyed and given to the fire to be burned."**

As a result of further careful observation the writer discerns that the great horn has not passed out of the vision. It is still doing what it was seen to be doing at the conclusion of v. 8, it was "speaking great things." The nature of these "great things" will be revealed when we consider v. 25. But it now becomes apparent that there is something ungodly about these words, for they provoke action against the beast and against the horn and call forth their destruction. As for what the prophet saw, on the higher level there appeared what v. 9 and 10 portray; on the lower, the horn still speaking great things.

To depict the ease with which the Lord overcomes His adversaries no agent appears to execute His wrath upon the beast, at least not as far as the vision is concerned. This is another way of saying: "He wills, and it is done; He needs no agents as helpers." The beast is simply slain. When its body is destroyed, that marks a step beyond the slaying. After this stage in the punishment has been completed, the body of the beast is no longer a body. That points to something like dismemberment. The body is then "given to the fire to be burned." The complete overthrow of the beast could hardly be indicated more fully. But the question still remains: "Does this burning with the fire convey the idea of annihilation, or does it point to eternal punishment?" The Aramaic original (see margin), correctly rendered, says, the body was given "to the burning of fire." This form of the statement does not point so much to annihilation as to perpetual punishment, especially since other Scripture passages indicate with ample fulness the eternal character of the sufferings of the damned.

The repetition of the introductory remark "I kept looking" is merely a more informal mode of speech that is often used by men when they begin a certain construction. Because of intervening modifiers between the opening clause and its logical continuation one feels the necessity of beginning again lest the construction become blurred. This is neither a vice nor a virtue grammatically but a necessity.

12. "And as for the rest of the beasts, their dominion was taken from them, and length of life was given to them for a time and a season."

Those interpreters are correst who say that this verse is to be understood as constituting a contrast to the preceding verse. For the end of the fourth beast was different from the end of those that preceded. The fourth had a terrible destruction meted out to it. The preceding three had been obliged to demit their position of supremacy, but they had, nevertheless, been permitted to continue under the new regime, not, indeed, as the power that they had once been, but it could not be said that they had been annihilated.

In the expression "a time and a season" the former is the more general term. This leads some to translate *Zeit und Stunde*. *Keil* says that the former is "the more general expression for time—circumstances of time"; the second is "measured time, the definite point of time." Both together imply: for quite a while, depending on the circumstances involved.

c. *The Son of Man Receives Everlasting Dominion,* v. 13, 14

13, 14. "I kept looking in the visions of the night, and, lo, with the clouds of heaven there came one like unto a son of man. He proceeded to the Ancient of Days and was brought into His very presence; and to Him was given dominion and glory and a kingdom, that all people and nations and

tongues might serve Him. His dominion is an eternal dominion which shall not pass away, and His kingdom one that shall not be destroyed."

This is the climax of the visions of the night. The goal of all history is presented. This is the victory of the kingdom of the Christ over all other kingdoms that aspire to universal rule. A figure emerges. Surprisingly little is said about this figure. No glorious and resplendent personality is described in glowing colors. There is no dramatizing in an effort to produce an effect upon our minds. But the essential truth stands out all the more clearly as a result in this sober account.

First of all, it is significant that He appears "in the clouds of heaven." There are many passages in which clouds regularly accompany Him who is the heavenly King. They are His carpet, His mark of identification. The clouds which are seen in the heavens so regularly are reminders of Him who comes from heaven. *Koenig* (*MW*) lists the following passages where clouds appear as an indication of the presence of God: Exod. 13:21ff; 19:9ff; I Kings 8:10ff; Isa. 19:1; Jer. 4:13; Nah. 1:3; Ezek. 10:4; Ps. 18:10, 12; 97:2-4; 104:3ff. But we feel compelled for this reason alone to go farther than Koenig and the majority of the commentators of our day do. The clouds are the mark of both the heavenly and the *divine*. It is for this very reason that the New Testament repeatedly represents Christ as coming in the clouds of heaven, see Matt. 24:30; 26:64; Mark 13:26; Rev. 1:7; 14:14. "*With* the clouds" is a less exact way of stating it, compare the passages just referred to.

But other issues must first be disposed of. It is most obvious that this One who comes in the clouds of heaven follows as the fifth in the sequence that presented four beasts. The beasts represented kingdoms; He represents a kingdom. In this connection the basic thought is without a doubt the fundamental difference between beasts and a man. As different as these two classes of beings are in character, so radically different is the fifth kingdom from all that preceded it; by so much does it excel in glory. Everything good, noble, and excellent that man as a being represents finds fullest expression in the kingdom of the Christ.

Shall we stop at this point and see no more in Him who is said to be like unto "a son of man"? Does He represent only the saints or the church or the kingdom of God? In other words, is this passage Messianic only in this sense as many others without a doubt are which portray the Messianic *times* or the Messianic *kingdom* without specifically bringing the Christ into the picture? We believe that such an interpretation offers a misleading and a false evaluation of the expression "one like unto a son of man." True enough, those who present it point with seeming proof to v. 22 where it is said that the judgment was given "to the saints of the Most High" and to v. 27 where the expression is: "Given to the people of the saints of the Most High." In neither statement do we find a word about the Messiah as such. His *saints,* His kingdom are said to appear exclusively according to the valid interpretation of this chapter. Convincing as that view seems at first glance, it is invalidated by the consideration that v. 14b informs us that "all the peoples and nations and languages should serve Him." That certainly applies more directly to the Christ and only in an indirect manner to the kingdom. But the reason for the use of this particular form of statement that we find in both v. 22 and v. 27, where the saints are spoken of as receiving the kingdom, is readily seen as soon as we note the context, where in each case the sufferings that the saints were to undergo are described in the preceding words. In lieu of this suffering there shall be granted to them a kingdom at the time when the Christ receives His kingdom. In fact, they share in His kingdom.

This leads us back to the expression, "One like unto a son of man." It must apply to the Christ. Further support is lent to this contention by the manner in which Jesus applies the term "Son of man" to Himself. Since all of Christ's speaking and thinking was steeped in Old Testament terminology, it is hardly possible that He should have used so significant a term, that so strongly suggested this expression in Daniel, without intending that it should be considered as being derived from that source. In fact, the "like unto" implies that the One in question was not strictly a man as other men are but appeared as do the sons of men. As it does in the New Testament, so in the Old this expression points beyond itself to the divine nature. As remarked above, this divine nature is, of course, reflected in the fact that He appears "with the clouds of heaven," not standing upon the earth as we earth-born mortals do. In fact, this aspect of the claim is fortified still more when we consider that the term "Son of man" is used by Jesus repeatedly when He refers to His coming in glory. Matt. 16:27, 28; 19:28; 24:30; 25:31.

There is still another aspect of the case that is of great importance. If it were true that this expression were used merely for the saints of God or the kingdom of God over against the preceding kingdoms, it would be passing strange that this one who represents God's saints is said to come with the clouds of heaven. Far more to the point would be a statement to the effect that they or the figure that represents them come from the earth, for they are from the earth. In other words, the claim so frequently made by conservative scholarship is correct when it contends that the expression "Son of man" as used by Christ is based upon the book of Daniel.

Already here the purpose of the use of this mild and humble term is the same as it was on Christ's part when He designated Himself thus, in fact, it is that same purpose which originally prompted Him to appear as man: it is not His desire to astound, frighten, and overwhelm man by His glory as would have been the case had He come in the fulness of His divine majesty. He takes on Himself the humble form of a man that He might be near to us, win us, and gain our confidence. Is not the manner of statement used in these visions reminiscent of the humble appearing of the Son of man on earth, quiet, mild, and gentle?

In the vision this modest Figure "proceeded to the Ancient of Days," drawing nearer step by step. This is the great day prepared for from the foundation of the world. For this the Son had been chosen that in this triumph of His, so very modest and yet so unspeakably glorious, all history, even the history of the kingdom of God, should reach its consummation. When the next statement tells us that He "was brought into His very presence," we are, no doubt, to think of the attendant hosts of angels as forming an honorable escort and solemnly and very naturally conducting Him with every show of reverence and honor until He stood before the Ancient of Days.

14. At this point the symbolical representation that was characteristic of the vision until this point gives place to reality. For how could Daniel have seen that "dominion and glory and a kingdom" were given to Him, or that "all people and nations and tongues might serve Him"? Or how could He detect that His "dominion is an eternal dominion which shall not pass away"? It might have been possible that He heard words that conveyed this thought and believed these words to be full and effective truth. But it is then likely that the account that the writer gives would have stated that such words were spoken, for such

words would surely have been the grandest and most solemn music that ever fell upon the ears of man. Somehow, we say therefore, in a manner that cannot be discerned by us the vision conveyed the fact that such honors and dignities were conferred upon Him.

The first set of terms employed is reminiscent of the familiar doxology or the Conclusion of the Lord's Prayer, in fact, these terms are, without a doubt, derived from this passage. "Dominion" becomes His. Till that day a measure of dominion will have been bestowed upon many who dwell upon the earth, that is, dominion in the broader sense of the term, even as dominion was given to the four empires that preceded the establishment of His own rule. All who attempted to use such dominion apart from the Lord made a most wretched failure of the attempt. This dominion shall now be taken from them. God's saints may share in it, but they shall rule in and through Him, and so He shall rule through them. "Dominion" shall now become a success. He knows how to administer it.

He further receives "glory"—and surely there was never one who was worthier to receive it than He. His achievements are such that He must receive that higher measure of honor that we are wont to term "glory," for to Him must be attributed the salvation of the world, the greatest work that the tongue of man can name. "Worthy is the Lamb that was slain to receive . . . glory." To this is added as a well-deserved gift "a kingdom," that He might govern it as a contrast to all the kingdoms of the sons of men that preceded and show it to be the everlasting kingdom which cannot pass away because under His perfect rule, in the consummation of all things, no flaw shall ever be found in either His rule or His kingdom.

The universality of that which is committed to Him is indicated by the words "that all people and nations and tongues might serve Him." We recognize,

of course, that only those are left who are of a mind
to serve Him. The impenitent and ungodly have been
removed by the judgment; and the scene of this new
kingdom is laid in the new heavens and the new earth,
wherein dwelleth righteousness. Whatever differences
might appear in His subjects, as to their being so great
a number of "people," or as to their being descended
from various national stocks or "nations," or as to
their speaking various "tongues"—this diversity is
described in terms of diversity as we know it and does
not allow us to claim that in the restoration of all
things there shall appear such things as national and
racial differences. The contrast with the four kingdoms that preceded is again prominent. They strove
to achieve universal dominion and could not. To this
One is given what the others could not achieve. But
He is competent as well as worthy to receive it.

The contrast with the four kingdoms is also apparent in this fact that after all the variations and
fluctuations of rule and dominion among men there
shall finally come that which is permanent because it
is perfect. This thought is conveyed by the statement:
"His dominion is an eternal dominion which shall not
pass away." We have a double statement: "eternal"
and "which shall not pass away." This is further re-
enforced by the parallel remark: "and His kingdom
one that shall never be destroyed." Our finite thoughts
can hardly conceive of a perfection so absolute that
change and decay can never again set in. For that
reason the statements used mutually support one another to the point of an absolute assurance.

All of this leaves another question that should be
dealt with before we conclude our consideration of this
section. Why does the sequence of historical kingdoms
in this vision extend no farther than the Roman whereas we know that many developments came after the
Roman Empire and have continued to come before the

judgment? We can venture only opinions under this head, opinions that we believe are reasonable and conform with the situation as it is outlined. One suggestion to be borne in mind is the fact that prophets generally, barring the conclusion of chapter 9 in Daniel, never see the interval of time lying between the first and the second coming of Christ. In the matter of history, therefore, Daniel does not see beyond Christ's days in the flesh and perhaps the persecutions that came upon the early church.

In the second place, it may be correctly argued that the pattern of empire development adopted by the Romans has been followed by practically all the succeeding world powers. Roman law is said still to be the pattern of jurisprudence. Roman classic literature dominates the literature produced since that time. In fact, the powers that can be said to have anything like world dominion are segments of the old Roman Empire, and so the fourth beast is still in a sense alive though Rome was overthrown.

It flatters our vanity but little that the Bible does not seem to deem our modern achievements, inventions, and forms of progress in sciences and arts worthy of separate mention. They are really something that was latent in Roman achievement and are now coming to the surface. These considerations at least help us to appreciate the point of view taken in these visions.

d. *A Summary Interpretation: the Four Beasts; the Four Kings; the Everlasting Kingdom for the Saints,* v. 15-18

15, 16. **"As for me, Daniel, my spirit was shaken within me, and the visions of my head disturbed me. I approached one of those that stood there and sought to get an authoritative interpretation concerning all this. And he told me and interpreted the things for me."**

We have thus far been told merely what Daniel saw. His report was entirely objective. At this point the climax had apparently been reached, and action came to a standstill. Daniel now realizes how he himself feels, and how the revelation has affected him. He emphatically draws attention to himself by letting the pronominal suffix on the word "spirit" be re-enforced by the personal pronoun "I," i.e., "as for my spirit, —I," an unusual construction which we must reproduce somehow as we have above: "as for me, Daniel, my spirit," etc. His perturbation was apparently great, for Daniel says that he "was shaken" as well as "disturbed." To tell the truth, who would not be thus affected? To receive revelation about the future, which no man had ever been privileged to discern, was an experience of the first magnitude. The visions, too, were, no doubt, shot through with a heavenly glory and a realistic character that made them startlingly real. A dullard and fool alone could have remained cold and undisturbed by such visions.

Hardly an item in these statements passes unchallenged by the critics. They find it quite improper for Daniel, if he was the writer, to manifest interest particularly about the fourth empire as he is about to do after the initial revelation and explanation. They regard that interest as proof of the fact that the writer must have done his writing at a late date and must have known the fate of the first three empires and therefore does not inquire about them. Their claim is that, if Daniel himself had been writing at the time when the Babylonian Empire was in power, he would have been far more keenly interested in the destinies of the Babylonian realm and would never had thought so far ahead as to the fourth kingdom. But that is a purely subjective opinion. It is perfectly natural for Daniel to display an interest in regard to this fourth empire because during the time it is in power the church suffers the most trying persecutions. Who of those who love the church of the living God will not display most concern about such times and situations? Besides, this was the point in regard to which the most extended revelation had been made through the vision. Lastly, Daniel had in the vision in chapter two already presented the essential facts concerning the overthrow of Babylon. Since this new vision confirmed already known facts, why inquire more diligently with reference to such? But to inquire about that concerning which God reveals the most—that is both natural and the part of wisdom.

16.   There follows an experience that all who have not had visions must be at a loss to explain: Daniel interviews one of the characters in the vision and gets a response from him. Or to state it from the other point of view: Daniel himself enters into the vision and becomes one of the active figures in it. In any case, after this pattern the God-given vision continues to unfold itself, and the unfamiliar items are made plain.

Daniel approached "one of those that stood there." We prefer to render thus, following *BDB* rather than the familiar version, "one of them that stood by." For this latter rendering suggests that there were also bystanders in addition to the innumerable host that stood before the throne. Who, pray, would they be? Curious onlookers in heaven? In the vision Daniel waxes bold to address one of the host of angels present, trusting that this heavenly being will be informed as to what it all means and authorized to divulge what he knows. On the basis of what Daniel had seen in chapter two in Nebuchadnezzar's dream Daniel might well have construed the bulk of this vision aright. He is, however, under the circumstances not going to be content with fairly reasonable surmises. He wants "an authoritative interpretation." We have thus rendered the word *yatst-*

sibha' which means literally "the certainty" and followed *K. W.* who translates *sichere Kunde*. Whereas we say: "And he told me and interpreted the things for me," the Aramaic says: "And he told me and caused me to know the interpretation of the things." Thus Daniel secured what he sought.

17. **"These great beasts, of which there are four, represent four kings that are destined to arise from the earth."**

It will be well at the outset to note a fact to which we have repeatedly drawn attention: just as certainly as, on the one hand, we may say that the beasts represent kings, just as properly, on the other, we may say that they represent kingdoms (cf. v. 23). The approach to our verse which insists that kings may be referred to supports our interpretation of v. 13 that there, too, the king of the heavenly realm is referred to. If they are here said to arise "from the earth," this statement merely presents the other side of what in v. 3 was said to be a rising "from the sea." In this latter instance the expression was figurative because it occurred in a vision that portrayed the truth symbolically. The same thought is here expressed in a more literal form and conveys the idea that these kings are of the earth, earthy.

We involve ourselves in a measure of difficulty if we take the imperfect verb *yequmun* to mean "shall arise" (*A. V.*), for at the time when Daniel is writing the first of these kingdoms, Babylon, is no longer future, for it has practically run its course. The situation is improved if we use the perfectly legitimate rendering for the imperfect: "are destined to arise." Everything in the interpretation is stated in summary form. It is therefore sufficient to say here that the beasts are kings. That furnishes a valid key to a great part of the chapter. Sufficient details may be gathered from other passages in the book.

18. **"But the saints of the Most High shall obtain the kingdom and shall control it forever, yea,
forever and ever."**

This is the other major factor not to be lost sight
of in interpreting the vision: the saints shall have a
lasting kingdom. The implied contrast is that the four
kingdoms that preceded it are ephemeral; they shall
attempt to achieve what by the grace of God the saints
shall make a reality. Their kingdoms are for a brief
time; this one kingdom is for all time.

Who are these "saints of the Most High"? They
have not appeared in the vision heretofore. That agrees
well with the position they seem to hold in the world
at large. They are deemed insignificant and are
scarcely noticed. Since the term "saints" always
implies those who have been separated from the world
unto God, the term is appropriate here in that they are
such who have not shared in the imperial aspirations
of the world powers. The saints were consecrated unto
higher ideals than to subjugate others. They are, therefore, the true people of God of all times, whether Jew
or Gentile, the Israel of God. It is appropriate that
God should be designated as "the Most High," for He
stands above all kings and has the disposition of kingdoms in His hands. The plural used for "the Most
High" is the plural of potency, cf. Prov. 9:10 and
Josh. 24:19.

It is significant that these saints of God are said
to "obtain" the kingdom. It is bestowed by Him whose
it is to give it. They, on their part, have not striven
after dominion as the rulers of this world do. Yet their
having it is not a trivial something as though it were
in reality hardly theirs. They actually "control" it or,
as *A. V.* states it, "possess" it. In either case the
thought is much the same. A measure of control and
authority is theirs. They really count for something in
the kingdom and are not puppet possessors. The

heaviest emphasis rests upon the eternity of this new relationship. It is absolutely eternal. All things prior to this development were temporal. This shall suffer no interruption or change.

e. *A Question concerning the Fourth Beast, especially concerning the Little Horn,* v. 19-22

19, 20. **"Thereupon I desired the authoritative interpretation in reference to the fourth beast, which was different from all the rest of them, exceedingly terrible, having iron teeth and bronze claws, which devoured and broke things in pieces and stamped upon what was left with its feet. Also concerning the ten horns which were upon its head and concerning the other horn which grew up and before which three fell. And as for this horn, it had eyes and a mouth speaking great things, and in appearance it was sturdier than its fellows."**

The clear summary given in vv. 17 and 18 had supplied the basis for all that followed. But, as we indicated above, the matter that intrigued the prophet was the fourth beast. This he himself now specifically asserts. When referring to the fourth beast he repeats in part the description previously given and thereby indicates what things roused his further inquiries, and he adds a few details that had not been mentioned. The reason for holding a few items in reserve seems to be to allow the writer a bit of variety lest, by stereotyped forms used repeatedly, he weary the reader. One feature is abbreviated: instead of "terrible and frightful and exceedingly strong" we have the condensed description "exceedingly terrible." We again have a statement to the effect that this beast was "different from all the rest of them." Its accessories for destructive work present one added feature: it had "bronze claws." Since all this has been amply expounded in connection with v. 7, we need not again enter into this matter.

20.   The account varies but little from the matter that was offered in v. 8. One minor omission is noticeable: the horn that grew up later is not at first called "a little one." To compensate for that the new feature is added that "in appearance it was sturdier than its fellows." The emphasis naturally rests upon the superior size of this later horn. Why emphasize its smaller beginnings?

21, 22.   **"I kept looking, and this horn made war with the saints and prevailed against them until the Ancient of Days came, and the verdict was rendered for the saints of the Most High; and the time came for saints to possess the kingdom."**

In every instance where the expression "I kept looking" appears we found that the action of the vision continued, and that was the feature that engaged the attention of the prophet. Here, strangely, after an interruption by Daniel in which he accosted one of those in the vision and got an answer, he is again able to take up the thread of action at a given point, namely, just where he had been particularly interested, and where he felt that he should have further information. It is, of course, possible that he is now merely stating what he had already observed then.

But the most unusual feature of the whole development is that which now comes to light: that last horn used its unusual intelligence and its boastful words against the saints of the Most High and actually prevailed against them. What saint of God would not under those circumstances be anxious to know more about what this means? For the particular object of the hatred of this little horn are "the saints." To be more exact, in the Aramaic the word appears without the article, and so the thought expressed really emphasizes merely the quality of these persons; and the idea is that whatever comes under the category of "saints" as such is repugnant to this great horn.

Strangely, God allows this evil power to have a measure of success in these unholy endeavors: the horn actually "prevails." How often this has proved itself true in the history of the church! Saints perished; their cause seemed lost. The opposition seemed to carry the day.

22. But it only "seemed" to do so. For v. 11 had already indicated that the court, presided over by the Ancient of Days, had been convened for the very purpose of taking the case of the horn in hand, and that the beast was slain and its body destroyed. With the beast of course went the horn. By stating the case thus the writer indicates that he was interested in both the persecution caused by the horn as well as in the destruction of the horn.

Whereas the *A. V.* says, "Judgment was given to the saints" we have rendered, "The verdict was rendered *for* the saints." The preposition is *le*, which is here construed better as introducing a dative of advantage. Strangely, the word "saints" in the last clause is again without the article. It has been pointed out that a similar usage is found in 8:24 and in Ps. 16:3. The idea then takes this form: Whatever goes under the name of saints is destined to receive the kingdom.

f. *The Answer to the Preceding Question*, v. 23-28

23, 24. **"He spoke thus: 'The fourth beast will be a fourth kingdom on earth, which shall be different from all other kingdoms, and it shall devour the whole earth and shall stamp upon it and crush it. As for the ten horns—out of this kingdom shall ten kings arise; and another shall arise after them and shall be different from those that were before him; and he shall put down three kings.' "**

The essentials of the interpretation, as far as this fourth kingdom is concerned, have been presented in connection with v. 7. We showed that this must be Rome, not Syria. We feel that we may safely ignore the charge that this interpretation is the outgrowth of "dogmatic bias," as well as the other charge that it "would scarcely have occurred to any unsophisticated reader" as *Farrar* asserts.

24. In connection with the interpretation of the ten horns we should yet like to point to this feature: the horns are not represented as arising consecutively; they are simultaneously upon the head of the beast. They do not, therefore, aim to picture any ten consecutive kings or kingdoms that grew out of the Roman Empire. They present the totality of the power of the fourth empire as it appeared at any time after it was fully grown. Of they may just as well portray the total number of those kingdoms into which the Roman Empire ultimately broke up.

All endeavors to enumerate the resultant ten kingdoms at any one time are to be rejected as never having entered the purpose of this passage. If even the good *Vitringa,* as *Vilmar* reports, interpreting Revelation and referring to this passage, made such an attempt, we present it here as a sample, one of the very many that unsafe guides have offered. He listed the ten kingdoms as follows: France, Spain, Germany, England, Scotland, Denmark, Sweden, Hungary, Bohemia, and Poland. The arbitrary listing that has to be made, no matter what period of history is chosen, discounts every effort of this sort.

There are, indeed, certain features of this prophecy in regard to whose interpretation we must exercise the greatest caution. We agree that the "great horn" mentioned in these verses is the New Testament Antichrist. We also believe that in this figurative presentation the horn is designed to include all manifestations of the Antichrist that may be expected after Christ's resurrection. We believe furthermore that, after the analogy of what preceded in the chapter where the beasts represented both kingdoms and kings, the horn represents both the kingdom of the Antichrist as well as a personal Antichrist in whom all previous manifestations shall culminate. We also hold that in stating that the pope is the Antichrist the Lutheran Confessions were correct much as some men have derided and belittled that view. Such belittling grows out of forgetting how thoroughly the reformers understood the papacy. Present-day shallowness of understanding in this respect leads to shallowness of interpretation. Though the papacy may be the outstanding manifestation of the Antichrist to date, that does not exclude other possibilities of fulfillment of this passage.

We merely indicate another problem without venturing to offer a solution. Since the Roman Empire had the scene of its activity primarily in Europe, and since the remnants of that empire are still in Europe, does that indicate that the Antichrist shall come out of developments as they are yet to occur primarily on European soil? We feel that nothing sufficiently definite is offered by this chapter to allow us to render a conclusive verdict on this question.

25. " 'And words against the Most High shall he speak, and the saints of the Most High shall he harass continually; and he shall intend to change times and law; and they shall be given into his hand for a time, times, and a half time.' "

The new features in regard to the Antichrist or the great horn that are found in this verse are first the fact that the "great things" spoken according to v. 8 are now found to be spoken "against the Most High." The Aramaic expression has an expressive phrase at this point; for "against" it uses a compound preposition *letsadh,* "at the side of." This indicates that in its own esteem the horn elevates itself as high as the Most High Himself.

The second new feature is that the Antichrist's attitude toward God's saints not only leads him to

make war upon them (v. 21) but also to "harass them
continually." It is his continual purpose and design to
do harm to God's saints, if not by war then at least
by continual harassing. There will be nothing that
vexes him so much as the existence and the prosperity
of these saints. Harmless and good though they are,
they shall arouse all his latent fury.

The third new feature disclosed in reference to
the Antichrist is that "he shall intend to change times
and law." This shall, however, not meet with the desired realization as is indicated by the verb "intend."
The "times and law" mentioned cannot be restricted
to "festival times" and the "law of God" as many interpreters prefer to render these terms. There is
nothing to indicate these limitations, for both words
refer to ordinary times and law. The reason for this
restriction of the terms to the Jewish festivals and
laws is the desire to have everything in this passage
point to Antiochus Epiphanes, of whom it is known
that he made an attempt to abolish the sacred festivals
(I Macc. 1:45ff; II Macc. 6:2, 6, 7) and certainly
aimed at the overthrow of every distinctive ordinance
that the Jews observed in accord with their sacred laws.

Since the expressions used are in a measure indefinite, no one knows just how far these attempts at
change will go. By way of illustration we think of the
attempts made by men who were actuated by the spirit
of Antichrist in the days of the French Revolution to
abolish the seven-day week in favor of a ten-day week.
We recall also the same attempts manifested in Russia
at present by men who are motivated by the same
spirit. Russia has added such revolutionary efforts at
overthrowing government, property, and marriage
laws that basic laws and ordinances have undergone
most radical changes. All such attempts are an outgrowth of the fact that the Antichrist is, above all,
against Christ and all that Christ has sanctioned. But

we remind again that all this shall prove abortive, for he shall only "intend" (*A. V.*, "think") to achieve these changes; he shall not actually succeed in bringing them about.

The same thought is in part expressed by the next statement: "They shall be given into his hand for a time, times, and a half time." There is a difficulty in the meaning of the unusual measure of time used. What can it mean? Some commentators translate: "A year, two years, and a half year." That is too definite and is the outgrowth of the desire to give the expression the same meaning which the half week mentioned in 9:27 has, where the week is said to be a "year-week," and half a "year-week" would be three and a half years. Or reference is made to Luke 4:25 and Jas. 5:17, where a similar period is mentioned in passages that have no relation to the expression occurring in this verse. In Rev. 12:14 the same expression occurs but without an indication as to its meaning.

Then, too, it should be remembered that the alteration to "years" is again an attempt to fit this passage into the pattern of things that were done by Antiochus Epiphanes. For he did succeed in devastating the Temple for a space of three years. But three years are not three and a half years. For it is admitted that the rededication of the Temple occurred in the month Chislev, i.e., December of the year 165 B. C., the very anniversary day of its profanation three years before. So First Maccabees testifies, cf., I Macc. 1:57; 4:52. In his *Antiquities of the Jews* (xii, 7, 5), Josephus arrives at the same result by making the time an exact three years. But the original expression is "a time, times, and a half time." It is for that matter also a guess, inspired by the desire to arrive at a certain result, that prompts *Koenig* to interpret the plural of the second term ("times") as a dual (*K. S.* 266d).

A very satisfactory explanation of this unusual expression is available. This explanation lets the literal meaning of the words stand. When Antichrist begins to dominate the scene and to attempt his radical changes, his success shall at first be for "a time." That is intended to be a vague expression, for it does not matter much how long a time it is. It may for various reasons be difficult to compute the time exactly. But after a modest beginning there shall suddenly come a seemingly more permanent success that shall continue for "times," without our being informed just how many. It might be just two times, but the expression is vague. But just as he seemed to have success everything will suddenly collapse, and he will have but a "half time" of success. In other words: a slow beginning with modest success; then a seeming outburst of successful endeavor; then a visible collapse; and by that time the whole project will have run its course and be at an end. This is just another instance where attempts to make an accurate count according to terms that are not even given results in misleading interpretations.

There is a bare possibility that there is something symbolical about this mode of reckoning time. If "times" means "two times"—a construction, the possibility of which must be conceded—then the total would be three and a half times, which is again half of seven. This would then be a broken seven, not a full seven, which is the mark of a work of God. But it hardly behooves anyone to be too positive about assertions in regard to matters that are as uncertain as this is. In Rev. 12:14 the same expression is used; either of the above interpretations may be applied also to this passage.

26, 27. **" 'Then the court shall have its session, and his dominion shall be taken away to be destroyed and consumed forever. And the kingdom and the dominion and the greatness of the kingdoms under** the whole heaven shall be given to the people of the saints of the Most High. His kingdom is an everlasting kingdom, and all dominions shall serve and obey Him.' "

These two verses offer nothing new. They merely reassert with reference to the horn the things that were previously asserted about the beast and confirm the establishment of the everlasting dominion of the saints and their Lord. So v. 26 makes the fact plainer that the occasion for the last judgment shall be the arrogance and the persecution on the part of the horn. To translate, "the judgment shall sit" (*A. V.*) or "shall be set" (*A. R. V.*) is hardly as clear as, "the court shall have its session."

It will be observed that in this instance the destruction of the *beast* is not again mentioned but is taken for granted as following at this point because the fourth beast and the horn are inextricably bound together in their destiny. It had also not been asserted before that the "dominion" of the horn was to be "taken away to be destroyed and consumed forever." To conclude that such would be the case would have been easy and very natural. But to leave nothing to conjecture in so important a matter we have the assurance of a downfall that is as permanent as the establishment of the kingdom of the One like unto a son of man was to be.

27. To tell the truth, it has not been fully established what the nature of the verdict that was to be rendered for the saints of the Most High (v. 22) was to be. They were, indeed, it was said in v. 22, going to possess the kingdom. How much that involved remained to be told. We have it here. They do, indeed, possess the kingdom (v. 22). But we now learn that this kingdom is to be of a universal character. For "the kingdom and the dominion and the greatness of the kingdoms *under the whole heaven* shall be given

to the people of the saints of the Most High." What manner of possession and rule this shall be we cannot as yet fully comprehend. But it is certainly more than a sham possession. If this includes all "under the whole heaven," then nothing shall be exempt, and surely never again shall this glorious achievement of the good Lord be imperiled. "Shall be given" is perfect to express absolute certainty.

At this point another attempt is made to eliminate the Messiah from the picture by letting the pronominal suffixes—in English *"His* kingdom" and "obey *Him"*—refer to the antecedent, "people," *'am.* This could well be possible grammatically in the original. But the attempted construction founders on the verb "serve," *pelach.* For in every other instance where this verb occurs in Biblical Aramaic—that is to say, nine times—this verb is used with reference to service that is rendered the deity. If, then, the second clause must be construed with that fact in mind, namely, "all dominions shall serve and obey *Him,"* that is, God, then in the preceding clause, "His kingdom is an everlasting kingdom," the reference is unmistakably to God Himself or, in the light of v. 14, to the Messiah Himself. So our interpretation of v. 14 finds repeated substantiation in this chapter.

28. " 'Here is the end of the matter.' "As for me, Daniel, my thoughts troubled me greatly, and the brightness of my countenance was changed; but I kept the matter in my heart."

Daniel might have concluded his account of the vision with v. 27 and gone on to speak of the troubled state of his thoughts. The addition, "Here is the end of the matter," says with emphasis that nothing more, absolutely nothing more was divulged to him at this time. If anyone should, therefore, desire further information in regard to what was seen in the vision, he for his part has no more to give. By enclosing these words in quotation marks we indicate that they may be considered as having been spoken by the interpreter. Whereas he recorded in v. 15 that he was grieved, the effect produced upon him personally is now greater in that his thoughts still trouble him, and that to the extent of making "the brightness of his countenance to be changed." We might say that the color of his face was changed, or that he lost his healthy color as a result of the disturbance caused in him by this revelation of the future. All this goes to show how deeply such revelation affects man, who is happiest if the future is not disclosed to him. Here even the revelation from on high, given by the wisdom of God with an abundance of comfort, creates great disturbance of a man's peace of mind. But Daniel did not try to forget. He kept all these sayings and moved them in his heart as being both terrible and precious.

HOMILETICAL SUGGESTIONS

An excellent text on the "eternal kingdom of the Son of man" is offered in vv. 13, 14. To present the full glory of the vision the entire passage, vv. 9-14, may be used. Verses 11 and 12 could in that case be used as a summary statement of how the mighty empires that man builds shall fare. The fate of the Antichrist is also brought into the picture. If the text is further rounded out by the addition of vv. 26, 27, the supplementary truth will receive emphasis that God's saints, too, will share in the rule of the kingdom in eternal glory—a truth not to be made light of. Skillful handling of the context could utilize vv. 1-8, but only as background material and with a brief but positive interpretation.

A definite and glorious note of victory should pervade the entire treatment. On the basis of revelation such as this chapter offers God's people know how history must run its course, and how the history of the kingdom alone will eventuate in a glorious consummation. Only the Christian outlook on the future is sure and hopeful but at the same time inexpressibly glorious.

CHAPTER VIII

II. The Development of the Kingdom of God, Chapters 8-12

A. The Vision of the Ram and the He-goat, 8:1-27

The second half of the book begins at this point. Though it deals with the conflict of the world powers with the kingdom of God, the heavier emphasis lies on the development of the kingdom of God, its victories and its successes.

The fact that a major division of the book begins with this chapter is apparent from the change in language, for at this point the Hebrew is again used for the first time since it was employed in chapter one. This change in language at the same time points to the specific needs of God's people. The first section, chapters two to seven, was written in Aramaic, the world language, and was designed for the world at large. The sacred Hebrew language is reserved for the people of God. By this observation we do not imply that by this change of language the one or the other group was eliminated from using a portion of this prophetic book. But there is certainly a fine propriety about having at least that part of the book which contains very particular revelations about the world empires and their character and their fate written in the language of these empires so that God's revelation to them might be seen to have actually been made available to them. On the other hand, the world empires would have cared little for the special fate of God's people, and therefore, in writing about such a subject, a different medium may be used.

To be sure, there is nothing original about our division of the book into these two sections. Others, like *Keil* and *Kliefoth,* have made it. But it is so apropos that there is no need of devising anything new or different. It just happens to be so much more to the point than to let the second half begin with chapter seven just because the first of the visions is found there and therefore to give the heading "Visions" to this second half. Such a grouping ignores the change of language and besides reckons with a purely external factor.

To be more specific as far as the purpose of the second half of the book is concerned, it aims to prepare the saints of God for the time of suffering that shall presently be encountered. This period of suffering happens to be of a rather extreme sort; and to have Israel experience it without having anything to guide it would have meant to expose the totally unprepared nation to about the worst trial that the Old Testament saints ever had to undergo.

Or to speak in terms of the revelations presented in chapters two and seven—there the fourth empire and the glorious victory of the divine kingdom had been revealed. To look forward to that fourth empire as the time of glorious triumphs would in itself have meant reckoning with a fact that was true enough. But to be ignorant of the great tribulation that must intervene before that fourth empire becomes reality, is to be but poorly equipped for the trials in store. Chapter eight, therefore, fills a need by teaching men what to expect before the days of the Messiah can come. At the same time, to know that the persecutor of the church shall not prevail gives the church some much-needed reassurance.

Before considering the details of our chapter we should also like to point out that this chapter agrees admirably with the interpretation that we have given the two significant chapters, two and seven. In each case we discovered that the sequence of empires was the same—Babylon, Persia, Greece, Rome. We could give no serious consideration to the views that had Media and Persia appear separately or to the attempt to regard the last two as being Greece and Syria. Such attempts did not agree with historical fact, with the plain statements of these chapters, and with the unity and the harmony of this book. It now appears very clearly that the ram typifies Media and Persia (v. 20) as a unit even as the he-goat typifies Greece, again as a unit (v. 21). Attempts to introduce either Media or Syria into the picture contradict the interpretation offered in plain terms by our chapter. Of course, the unwarranted alternative offers itself, viz., to claim that the author had no unified conception of the course of history, or that the book contradicts itself in its various parts—claims which negative criticism makes.

This chapter takes a smaller section of the area covered by preceding chapters and considers this smaller portion more intensively. The more immediate future is subjected to a more microscopic examination.

The claim that this chapter "is notably weaker in poetic force than its predecessor" is subjective opinion that evaluates revelation chiefly by the figurative language in which the truth happens to be cast. We feel that the vision of the four beasts and the vision of the ram and the he-goat are equally clear and equally attractive as far as visionary representation of revealed truth is concerned.

a. The Ram, v. 1-4

1. **In the third year of the reign of Belshazzar, the king, a vision appeared to me, even to me, Daniel, after the one which had appeared to me formerly.**

In many instances the prophets remembered clearly the very time when a certain vision or revelation was given to them by the Lord. To be regarded as worthy to receive such communications from God was so signal an honor that any man might well have marked the day that was thus distinguished. Besides, God's prophets seem to have attached much importance to keeping correct and adequate records of all revelations that came to them.

We do not, however, possess sufficient information in every instance to determine exactly what the date indicated means. The preceding vision (7:1) occurred in the first year of the same king. On the basis of chapter five we might conclude that Belshazzar did not reign long. That is again merely a supposition. In any event, in point of time the matter revealed in our chapter seems to have occurred but a short time before that revealed in chapter five, for Belshazzar's reign seems to have been rather short. *Wilson** is of the opinion that the "third year" refers to the third year of his rule as "king of Chaldea" whereas in 7:1 the "first year" must refer to the "first year as king of Babylon." Within one and the same book, for that matter, even in two successive chapters such divergence in the use of designations of time would seem strange indeed. At any rate, since time is reckoned according to the ruling monarch, it was, as Daniel distinctly recalls, Belshazzar's third year.

The strange emphasis on the fact that it was Daniel himself who received the vision—"even to me, Daniel"—seems to point to the fact that Daniel was much surprised that *he* should be honored a second time by being the recipient of a vision. The same thought seems to be implied in the last impression, "after the one which had appeared to me formerly." We might say: "After I had already once been honored

---

*Wilson, Robert Dick, *op. cit.*, p. 116.

by the good Lord by being granted a divinely wrought vision." Such revelations were momentous events in the lives of these men of God. Each made a distinct impact on the whole inner life.

The expression "which had appeared" offers two possibilities as far as the Hebrew is concerned. If the pointing of the text is considered as it stands, with a long *a* in the last syllable of the word, the article preceding must be regarded as the equivalent of the relative pronoun (*'asher*) as is also the case in Josh. 10: 24; I Kings 11:9, etc. On the other hand, leaving the consonant text as it is but altering the vowel of the last syllable to *seghol,* we have the article with the participle, a construction which yields the same sense and is perhaps to be preferred. See *G. K.* 138, h, i.

2. And I saw in the vision, and it happened as I saw that I was in Shushan, the castle, which is in the province of Elam—and I saw in the vision, and I for my part was by the river Ulai.

The sentence structure is a bit unusual. It could have been simplified with the result that the distinctive nature of the thought conveyed would be materially altered. We believe that, when the Holy Spirit induced men to use an unusual sentence structure, it was because the desired thought could thus be expressed most adequately. Critics speak of glosses. But why should men have inserted glosses, which, as they are commonly viewed, merely impede the thought? The critical procedure of our day strikes the phrases it deems unnecessary. Luther, unfortunately, followed a similar procedure in his translation. The thought this somewhat involved sentence conveys is this: The vision had already begun, and he was beginning to behold things in the course of it, when, first, the fact came home to his consciousness that this vision was taking place in "Shushan, the castle," (on the expression see Neh. 1:1; Esther 1:2, 5; 2:3, 5) and secondly he observed that he personally was "by the river Ulai." And then—to tie up with the third verse—he began to give closer attention to the details of the vision proper. That our approach to this verse is correct is attested to also by the fact that an emphatic "I"—rendered above, "I for my part"—plus another emphatic "I"—which we did not render above—appear in the verse.

Why was it of moment to record these items? Because the setting of the vision was unusually significant. God chose "Shushan, the castle," because this was later to become the seat, or at least the summer capital, of the Persian Empire. When the vision appeared to Daniel, nothing concerning the future importance of this site was known. But since the fortunes of Persia were involved, the future center of Persian life and activity was the best background. The Spirit of prophecy here bears witness to the clear foreknowledge of God. When this city is described as being in the "province of Elam," this fact is added because the yet unknown Shushan no doubt needed to be located for many readers. This explanatory phrase does not, however, say that at the time this province of Elam was considered a province of the Chaldean Empire. This was clearly not the case, nor does the author say so. He must have thought of the province as being a Persian district.

The testimony of the ancients in regard to the river mentioned is not unanimous. Some, like Pliny, call it the Eulaeus, which must be the "Ulai" mentioned in this verse; but Herodotus relates that the city Shushan was located on the Choaspes (see *Farrar*). Possible solutions of the difficulty lie along two lines. These are either two names for one and the same riven or are names for two branches of the same river. In no case is the correctness of the Biblical statement impugned.

Of what nature was the presence of the prophet

in the province of Elam? Was he there in spirit or in body? If he had been transported to this distant land in body, this would have been so notable a miracle as practically to demand a statement to that effect. Since we are repeatedly referred to the fact that this was a vision, the evidence is practically compelling that the prophet was present there in spirit only. There are two Scripture passages which are parallels to this experience: Ezek. 8, which tells of the transporting of the prophet to Jerusalem, and yet there, too, nothing points to actual bodily presence; and Rev. 17:3 which asserts that John was carried into the wilderness "in spirit."

3. **And I lifted up my eyes and saw and, lo, a single ram was standing in front of the river; and it had two horns, and the horns were tall; and the one was taller than the other, and the taller one came up last.**

Having gotten his bearings as to his location, the seer begins to take note of what the vision presents— he "lifted up his eyes." A challenging sight greets him as he looks (note the "lo") and sees "a single ram." We believe that in this instance the numeral is more than a mere indefinite article, in fact, it means just a "single" ram. The common spectacle would have been a whole herd of sheep. This ram stands all alone. The next noticeable feature is that it "was standing in front of the river." This would seem to mean on the side on which the prophet found himself and not on the farther side. Closer inspection reveals two horns standing out prominently on the ram. Both are tall, but the one was noticeably taller than the other, and "the taller one came up last."

We cannot speak of these things without at the same time presenting the essentials of the interpretation which the latter half of the chapter offers. Combining both halves at this place will save us needless repetition as we go along. The ram is Persia or, according to v. 20, Medo-Persia. That being the case, the two horns offer no difficulty. They are the two component parts of the empire, Media and Persia. Of these, too, it is true that the "taller one came up last." For Media had enjoyed supremacy earlier, but not the notable supremacy that came about under the hegemony of Persia. As all men know, we now usually refer to the empire as "the Persian" for that very reason. Another feature of the vision is appropriate, and that is that here, as always, horns typify strength, and both these portions of the Persian realm can certainly be said to have been strong.

But why a "ram"? There must be some similarity between the ram and the Persian Empire. There is, and it lies largely in the realm of the comparison between the ram and the he-goat. For as the ram and the he-goat are related to one another, so did Persia and Greece compare the one with the other. The ram has a certain sturdy strength (on rams as symbols of might cf. Ezek. 17:13, 39; 39:18). It thrusts at that which opposes it and casts it down and, by the way, usually displays quite a tendency to butt things. Yet there is about the creature something of a staid and sober character. It is not superlatively strong like the lion nor as aggressive or wild as are certain other well-known beasts.

4. **I saw the ram butting westward and northward and southward, and there was not a beast that could stand before it, and none could deliver out of his power; and he did as he pleased and wrought mighty things.**

The history of the Persian Empire is sketched briefly. Beginning from its native Persia, the conquests made, especially under Cyrus the Great, extended in three directions: to the west, the north, and the south. The fourth point of the compass is not mentioned because, under the circumstances, it was not feasible for Persia to make conquests toward the east. She herself was the eastern part of her empire. That being the case, it is fanciful to offer the explanation for the omission of the east countries among the Persian conquests that a ram standing in one place could butt in only three directions and not behind itself. For what can lead us to believe that this ram had its feet so tightly glued to the earth that it could not have shifted its position to butt also in the direction of what was originally behind it?

It is true also that, as long as it had its day, this empire was so successful that "not a beast could stand before it." The opposing nations are spoken of as beasts, *chayyoth,* in order to keep all kingdoms on the same level. This is so obvious as hardly to require explanation. It has been pointed out that the expression "he did as he pleased" was in a special sense true of the Persian Empire, in which in a singular measure tyrannical procedure prevailed. Whatever rulers and people wanted in the course of their conquests, that they did, no matter how irregular or strange it might seem to others.

We think the imperfect *ya'amdhu* is the potential "*could* stand," but it is at the same time not like a past tense in the Hebrew but rather conveys the idea: as time went on, none could stand, which is the progressive idea of the Hebrew imperfect.

He "wrought mighty things" correctly draws attention to the fact that the conquests on the part of Persia were of no mean sort. Yet we must revert to the fact that these conquests extended only to three points of the compass. Four would have been the number that is indicative of that which is world-wide, ecumenical. Three signifies that the achievements of this empire were not so ecumenical in character as were those of other empires. This agrees well with the

fact recorded in the preceding chapter (v. 5) where
Persia has "three" ribs in its mouth. This helps to demonstrate the harmony that exists between the various
visions of Daniel and their consistent agreement with
one another.

b. *The He-Goat,* v. 5-8

5. **And as for me, I was giving close attention
when, lo, a he-goat came from the west over the face
of the whole earth without touching the ground. And
the he-goat had a prominent horn between its eyes.**

The seer knew that there was a deeper signification involved in what he saw and also realized that
any word of God that might be revealed to any of the
sons of men was deserving of the closest attention; so
he records that he "was giving close attention" when
a new and significant feature suddenly claimed his interest. Sudden and startling as had been the appearance of the ram (v. 3), just so surprising ("lo")
was the appearance of the "he-goat," *tsephir ha'izzim,*
literally, "buck of the goats." The vision seemed to be
presented in such a manner that directions and points
of the compass stood out. So the prophet was able to
notice that the point from which the he-goat came
forth was the west, *ma'arabh,* "sunset."

When he noticed further that this creature came
"over the face of the whole earth," that would seem to
suggest that, though the general direction was from
the west to the east, he yet seemed to weave his course
over all the intervening land in such a way that all
these lands were traversed or at least touched upon.
The speed of the progress of the beast is made prominent by the statement "without touching the ground."
He literally skimmed along. This Hebrew expression
cannot mean as some have translated it, "No one could
touch him," for the word order would then have to be
different. In any case, that idea is expressed later in a
different way.

The most distinctive mark of all was perhaps the fact that the "he-goat had a prominent horn between its eyes." The expression *qeren chazuth* might mean "horn of vision" as *Kliefoth* renders it, but *chazuth* can by metonomy also mean "conspicuousness" and so "horn of conspicuousness," that is to say, "a prominent horn." What made this phenomenon unusually outstanding was the fact that the horn grew out between the eyes, which is certainly not the usual position of a horn. Still, no particular significance attaches to this feature of the vision. It serves merely to make the horn unusual and distinctive.

As to the meaning of these symbols v. 21 states that the rough he-goat is the king of Greece, not any one king but kings generally or, for that matter, even the kingdom of Greece, for the great horn between the eyes is Alexander, "the first king." Compared with a ram a he-goat has greater strength and agility. These qualities were manifested by Alexander as he moved against the Persians. Small though his armies were, they had far greater toughness.

Furthermore, the Greeks came against the great monarchies of antiquity from the "west." All territory intervening between Greece and Persia, "the face of the whole earth," was completely subdued by Alexander. Never before had a conqueror moved so swiftly and so relentlessly, that is to say, "without touching the ground" (cf. Isa. 41:3). And certainly, since horns typify strength, Alexander was the great strength of the Greek advance.

6, 7. And he came toward the ram, the two-horned creature that I had seen standing in front of the river, and he ran against it in his great anger. And I saw him come close to the ram, and he was enraged against it and butted the ram and broke its two horns, and there was no strength left in the ram to stand before him. So he cast it down to the ground

and trampled upon it, and there was none that could deliver the ram from his power.

A certain suspense is created by the fact that the he-goat is headed for the ram and is seen coming closer and closer. This confirms our earlier observation that the he-goat did not, perhaps, come against its adversary in a straight line. But when in a somewhat detailed statement it is said again that his objective was "the ram, the two-horned creature that I had seen standing in front of the river," we are given the impression that it was evident enough to the seer that quite a bit of time was involved in the processes of history which he was describing, and so he himself had the impression that what he had said about the ram lay rather far in the background. So he recapitulates by describing the ram a bit more fully with reference to its chief characteristic. The expression "the two-horned creature" is a freer rendering of the peculiar Hebrew idiom "the master of two horns," *ba'al haqqerānáyim*. But in all such combinations *ba'al* is merely a relation word, cf., *BDB,* p. 127.

The entirely new feature entering into the description is the fact that the he-goat "ran against it in his great anger." The creature must have displayed a certain ferocity that reminded one of the attitude of anger on the part of human beings. The Hebrew expression "in the hot anger of his strength" means "in his great anger." There is a certain significance in the fact, which is emphasized by repetition, that the ram was "standing in front of the river." This pictures the historic clash of the Greeks and the Persians at the Granicus, for it was at a river that these two great foes first met in these Asiatic wars. The "great anger" that marked the he-goat points also to a historical reality. For after the several earlier assaults of the Persians upon the Greeks the Greeks were very angry at the attempted subjugation, and Alexander's

Greeks went about their task of conquest as though it were being done to avenge a great wrong.

7. In fact, this anger grew to the point where it was nothing less than rage—"he was enraged against it." This fury at the same time represents the nature of the separate attacks that were made upon the Persians in the course of the war. There was an irresistible impetuosity about them that created panic in the hearts of the more timid foe. The first result of the impact of the he-goat's butting was that he "broke its two horns." This cannot refer to the separate conquests of the Medians and the Persians but refers to the breaking up of the empire as a whole. For, since horns typify strength, this breaking of the horns refers to the crushing of the Persian strength. This is verified by the following statement, "There was not strength left in the ram to stand before him."

To make the idea of thorough conquest still more vivid the he-goat is represented as casting the ram down to the ground and trampling upon it. Alexander's conquest were nothing less than as complete an overthrow of Persia as was thinkable. His conquests put a new complexion on the whole Asiatic world and set in motion ideas and principles that were to dominate the conquered areas for centuries to come. If anything were needed to make this thought of most complete conquest still more emphatic, there is added the thought that "there was none that could deliver the ram from his power." No matter what vast hordes were opposed to the young Macedonian in his conquests (though these numbers may have been exaggerated by some historians), nothing could bolster the decaying strength of the decrepit Persian Empire.

In *ure'ithi* we have a weak, not a consecutive, *waw*.

8. **And the he-goat was extremely successful; but just as he had become strong, the great horn was broken, and there came up a strange sight—four**

horns in its place toward the four winds of the heavens.

It is doubtful whether the *A. R. V.* has translated the first verb accurately—"magnified himself" as a translation of *highdil*, for the basic meaning of the causative stem is "to cause to be great." It is not reflexive. *A. V.* is nearer the truth when it renders "waxed very great." We believe that our translation "was extremely successful" does better justice to the idea. For nothing less than so strong a statement can express the phenomenal success that crowned all the undertakings of this military genius. Of course, with this success there came unlimited strength. But just at the moment when this he-goat "had become strong, the great horn was broken." Alexander died unexpectedly and prematurely, partly as a result of his strenuous exertions, partly as a result of his intemperance, having arrived at the age of only thirty-three years. This feature of the visions may have been indicated by nothing more than perhaps a breaking of the horn and its falling off the head of the creature.

What followed was certainly "a strange sight." For it was rather contrary to nature to have "four horns" in the place of one that breaks and falls away. Such a "sight" no man had ever seen. It was contrary to nature. Critics place no confidence in the Hebrew text and have difficulty with the word for "strange sight," *chazuth*, which shortly before (v. 5) meant "conspicuousness" and had to be translated "prominent" in connection with the noun "horn." They do not accept the easy solution offered by *K. W.*, which we have adopted in our rendering—*Phaenomen*. Yet ideas such as "vision, conspicuousness, sight" merge into one another. Attempts to alter the text are an indication of not having thought the problem through.

The natural meaning of the four horns "toward the four winds of the heavens" is that the entire area of the empire conquered by Alexander ultimately came under the dominion of four rulers who practically quartered the territory among themselves. Such minor details as the fact that some twenty years elapsed before they could get control of the situation and parcel out the empire among themselves, need not be recorded in a vision which is throughout marked by a certain lapidary style. History knows about these four. To Lysimachus went Thrace and Bithynia, some say practically all of Asia Minor. Cassander took over Macedonia and Greece. To Seleucus went Syria, Babylonia, and the eastern countries. Some say Asia and Syria. Ptolemy became master of Egypt, to which some add Palestine and Arabia Petræa.

All this has been told in a summary fashion because it is preparatory and leads up to the next section, v. 9-14, for the sake of which the chapter was written.

c.   *The Little Horn that Waxed Great,* v. 9-14

9.   And from one of them there went forth a single horn, very small at first, but it grew exceedingly great toward the south and toward the east and toward the glorious land.

We are confronted by the main issue of this chapter. In the vision there appears a "single horn" that comes forth from one of the four horns previously mentioned. A horn sprouting from a horn—a strange sight, to say the least. It must mean, as v. 23 also indicates, that one of the four component parts of the old Greek Empire will produce a new dynasty, more particularly, a notable king. The phrase "of them," *mehem,* uses the masculine as the more common gender or in place of "horns" "kings" are being thought of as the ones who are represented by the horns. Also here, as in v. 3, the numeral "one" seems to mean "single" and is not merely the indefinite article. The Hebrew expression *mîstse'irah,* "from small," hardly seems to have the *min* comparative, which would give it the meaning "less than small." The meaning "from small (beginnings)," or as we have rendered more freely, "very small at first," appears to be more natural here and is more commonly preferred.

When this horn first appears, no one seems to sense that it has an unusual future; but "it grew exceedingly great." Already at this point the figurative representation is made to bear almost more than the figure allows for, for the horn is said to grow "toward the south and toward the east and toward the glorious land." It is difficult for us to visualize what the horn did, or how the vision conveyed the idea of its growth in these three directions. But almost all commentators regard it as a reference to that one of the Seleucidæ, a king of Syria, who in history has the name Antiochus Epiphanes, who happened to be the eighth king of his dynasty.

A brief summary of his development, as given by *Farrar,* may serve to supply the needed historical background. "But he was a man of ability, though with a taint of folly and madness in his veins. By allying himself with Eumenes, king of Pergamum, as we shall see hereafter, he suppressed Heliodorus, secured the kingdom, and 'becoming very great,' though only by fraud, cruelty, and stratagem, assumed the title of Epiphanes, 'the Illustrious.' He extended his power 'to the South' by intriguing and warring against Egypt and his young nephew, Ptolemy Philometor; and 'towards the Sunrising' by his successes in the direction of Persia and Media; and towards 'the Glory' or 'Ornament'— i.e. the Holy Land. Inflated with insolence, he now set himself against the stars."

The expression "the glorious land" reads in Hebrew *hatstsebhi,* "the ornament." But since in this series the vision mentions regions or lands, this must refer to a land as the use of the same word in 11:16, 41 clearly shows, cf. also Jer. 3:19; Ezek. 20:6; Zech.

7:14. Without a doubt, the land on which God had bestowed so many blessings and which had been the
scene of so many gracious manifestations of God well
deserves to be called "the glorious land." It is mentioned last by a kind of climax, for the attention of
Antiochus was directed against it in a very special way.

**10. And it grew great toward the host of
heaven, and it cast to the earth some of the host,
namely, of the stars, and trampled on them.**

We must remember that this was a vision. In the
vision the prophet saw the horn actually raise itself
against the stars and cast some of them to earth. According to v. 24 this meant that some of the holy people
would be destroyed. That stars should signify God's
holy people is not strange when one considers as a
background the words that were spoken to Abraham
concerning the numerical increase of the people of
God, Gen. 15:5; 22:17. To this may be added Dan. 12:
3, where a starlike glory is held out to those who "turn
many to righteousness." Compare also Matt. 13:43.
If the world calls those men and women stars who excel
in one or another department of human activity, why
should a similar statement not be still more appropriate with reference to God's people? The Hebrew phrase
"and of the stars" involves the epexegetical use of
"and" and should be translated "*namely* of the stars."
On this usage see *G. K.* 154a, note b. They are the ones
of the "host" that are referred to. Plain persecution
must be involved if some of the "mighty ones" (v. 24)
and of the "holy people" are not only cast to the earth
but are actually trampled upon. The individual who
does that must harbor a peculiar aversion to God's
people and treats them with unusual malice.

**11. It even magnified itself to the prince of
the host, and from Him it took away the regular
daily offerings, and the place of the sanctuary
was defiled.**

In connection with v. 8 we contended that the translation "magnified itself" for *highdil* was unacceptable. Here this meaning is, however, demanded by the context. The thought is not exactly that he magnified himself "against" the Lord. That meaning is not conveyed by the preposition *'adh,* it is rather a plain "to." That must then mean that this proud ruler sought to arrogate to himself equality with the Lord on high. That was what was suggested by his name Epiphanes, for the Greek word ἐπιφάνεια was "often used by the Greeks of a glorious manifestation of the gods" (*Thayer*). To enjoy divine honor, as mighty monarchs of days of old often had, was the ambition of this proud king. Yet it cannot be denied that Antiochus directed his hostility against the Lord God of Israel in a special way because the true God is always more hated by those that oppose Him than idol deities are.

This hatred manifested itself thus: "From Him it [the horn] took away the regular daily offerings." The Hebrew pointing wavers in regard to the verb "took away." The consonants call for the Hiphil form *herim.* The marginal reading and the pointing of the vowels call for *huram* (Hophal). This latter form, a passive, was apparently chosen to conform with the next verb, which is a passive, or the text had not been understood. The original form found in the text may well be retained, and the translation will be as we have given it above. The "from him" then refers to God, the *min* being a *min* separative, not one of agent (*K. S.* 107). For when the Syrian king took away the daily offerings, it was an attempt to rob God of what was due to Him in the worship of Israel. "*It* took away" refers to the "horn" and thus to Antiochus.

The Hebrew *tamidh* means a bit more than "the regular daily offerings." The word means "continuity" and is applied to all those practices of the Hebrew cultus which were to recur regularly, such as the daily offerings, morning and evening sacrifices, incense, meal offerings, as well as the showbread. "The daily sacrifice" (*A. V.*) is better than "the continual burnt offering" (*A. R. V.*), for the former involves more. That Antiochus did actually proceed thus against the cultus at Jerusalem is indicated by I Macc. 1:45, 46.

For the statement "the place of the sanctuary was defiled" the Hebrew has only "was cast down"; but this verb usually implies some form of insulting treatment, and so we are justified in translating as we do above. Not the least of the things that Antiochus did was to pour the broth of offerings of swine's flesh about in the sanctuary and to substitute an altar to Jove for the altar of burnt offering. That was, of course, the crowning abomination. No wonder that the Jews felt the necessity of a rededication of the sanctuary when the Temple again came into their possession.

12. And a host was given over together with the regular daily offerings for transgression; and it cast truth to the ground, and he both wrought and also had success.

The following picture has thus far unfolded itself: this ruler made mighty territorial conquests (v. 9); he then concentrated his efforts upon persecution of the people of God (v. 10); he then sought to insult and oppose the Lord Himself (v. 11). In the beginning of v. 12 these last two achievements are now recapitulated. For "a host was given over" refers to the fact that God allowed a large number of His people, "a host," to come into his power, yet not their entire number, for we do not read "*the* host." The seeming successes against the Almighty also did not come without His permission, for that is implied in the passive verb which is to be supplied when it is said that "the regular daily offerings" were also given over. The phrase following is not as obscure as it seems to be at first glance because "for transgression" means that the transgression was the thing for which the regular daily offerings were given over. The "transgression" took the place of the daily offerings. Now this "transgression" apparently refers to the opposition altar, which was sacred to the heathen deity, that took the place of Jehovah's altar. For every sacrifice that the Jews allowed themselves to be persuaded to offer was a transgression.

In summing up the extent of the damage that this proud king did our verse adds the statement, "He cast truth to the ground." It is manifest that the cultus and the revelation that Israel enjoyed were the truth. This was allowed to be cast to the ground as long as a heathen cultus flourished in the place that had been ordained for the true sacrifices. To every truehearted Israelite such a state of affairs must have been deplorable indeed.

Still in the nature of a summary statement are the words, "he both wrought and also had success." This amounts practically to the expression which is current in our day that, whatever a man attempts, succeeds. Nothing seemed to miscarry, though, when the act and the motive were considered, every project ought to have collapsed as soon as it was undertaken. Whatever of all this Israel may have deserved is not stated in this vision. Other parts of the book, like the ninth chapter, make an issue of that aspect of the case.

It is usually suggested in connection with v. 12, in some instances already in connection with v. 11, that the vision proper must have terminated with either v. 10 or v. 11. It will hardly do to be too apodictic about such a matter. We on our part fail to see why *all* this might not have been revelation in the form of a vision. We know too little about visions to be able to define their limitations.

Thus in v. 11 some proud attitude on the part of the small horn, which by this time might have begun

to appear as a proud man, indicated that it had set itself against the Almighty. It might even have appeared
as entering the sanctuary and there putting aside the
regular daily offerings and defiling the sanctuary. That
this may well be called casting the truth to the ground
must be admitted; and no man would venture to claim
that the prophet saw this mortal cast truth as such to
the ground. So at least this statement and the one following, that he both wrought and had success, lie in
the realm of interpretative statement and not in the
realm of direct vision. Yet the vision as such has not
come to an end as v. 13 at once shows.

13. **Then I heard a holy one speaking, and
another holy one said unto that certain one that
spoke: "How far does this vision reach, that is to
say, the regular daily offerings and the crime causing
horror, the giving over of both the sanctuary and
the host to be trodden under foot?"**

Angels speak or discuss the matter under consideration so that the one seeing the vision might
through their words arrive at an authoritative interpretation. This is not merely a device resorted to by
later prophets in furnishing an interpretation as some
interpreters believe. A deeper and very proper motive
is involved. We are made aware of the truth that these
matters of revelation are things that the angels "desire" to look into as I Pet. 1:12 so aptly states. For
the "holy one" speaking to another "holy one" must
mean that one angel spoke to another. The Hebrew
says: "one—a holy one." It is as though the interest
that angels take in such matters as they speak of them
among themselves is utilized in that they are allowed
to appear on the scene; and one of the angels, who
knows less, hears from another, who seems to be initiated more fully into the counsels of God. When Daniel
hears such a one speak he knows that these servants,
who stand in the presence of the Most High, have re-

ceived their deeper knowledge from Him. In the book of Zechariah, the prophet, this method of procedure has been developed to the point where one who functions as *angelus interpres,* the interpreting angel, regularly acts as the prophet's direct guide and informer.

As Daniel notices these heavenly beings in the vision, they are seen to be engaged in conversation, apparently with reference to the vision. What they had been saying up to this point is irrelevant. What clearly and distinctly now reaches Daniel's ear is a revelation that bears upon the very point in regard to which he would have raised a question if he had had the opportunity to do so. The angel who is not so well informed wants to know the same things the prophet desired to know. The problem centers on the point: "How far does the vision reach?" We prefer thus to translate the interrogative particles *'adh mathay,* literally, "unto how long?" The thing that gave rise to this question was the fact that the prophet would naturally build up on what he had heard. The last revelation he had received had spoken of similar things, especially of the persecution of the saints by a bitter opponent and of opposition to the Most High (7:25). But in this earlier instance this was connected with developments that came out of the fourth empire, not out of the third as this vision will show very shortly. Who would not be anxious to know just how far this persecution would extend, and how long it would last?

To make his inquiry more specific the angel that asked the other angel adds several explanatory terms that are in apposition with the general term "vision." By these terms he indicates what portion of the vision is causing him trouble. And we dare not forget that Daniel's problem was exactly the same as the angel's. These appositional terms we have introduced by the phrase that is customarily used in English in such instances—"that is to say." Four things are in ap-

position to the word "vision." They are: a) "the regular daily offerings," b) "the crime causing horror,"
c) "the giving over of the sanctuary to be trodden
under foot," and d) "the giving over of the host to be
trodden under foot." These last two could naturally be
combined into one, and there might be three items in
place of four. That these four coincide and occur simultaneously, or nearly so, is apparent enough to the
questioner. Therefore he practically wants to know
how long the suffering of the saints and the humiliation
of the sanctuary will last. If he knows that he will
know whether this is the same suffering that was
spoken of in the preceding chapter.

All this points to a matter that will later have to
be examined in greater detail, and that is: Just what
relation does this Old Testament tribulation bear to
the times of tribulation of the New Testament that
precede the last coming of Christ?

Since these four items of the inquiry refer to
events already mentioned in the vision, the question
naturally arises: "Since the other three items are clear
enough, to what precisely does the expression 'the
crime causing horror' refer?" This would be easier to
answer if we had noted that the same Hebrew word
occurs here that was used in v. 12, where we translated the word *pesha'* "transgression." We preferred,
nevertheless, to use two different words because it is
difficult to find an exact equivalent for the Hebrew,
which means literally "rebellion" and thus any form
of sin or misdeed. Above we interpreted the term
"transgression" (v. 12) as referring to the altar of
abomination that Antiochus set up together with other
idolatrous practices in the Jerusalem sanctuary. That,
and just that, is the "crime causing horror" as *BDB*
translates. We are following the lead of many interpreters and grammarians who construe the participle
shomem, not as a *Kal,* but as a *Polel* with the usual

initial *mem* omitted, cf. *G. K.* 52s. We can readily visualize what "horror" such a heathen desecration must have caused pious Israelites who knew that their worship was divinely ordained, and that such interference would call forth the just anger of *Yahweh.*

The "host" to be trodden under foot is the same as that mentioned in the preceding verse, the host of the people of God who are oppressed by the "horn." So v. 13 speaks, not of the conquests made by the horn throughout the wide world, but of the oppression brought upon the people of God only.

In this connection an illustration of the critical method employed to amend the traditional Hebrew text may be offered. The remark is made: "No scholar is satisfied with the MT [Masoretic text], and few scholars agree as to its exact meaning" (*Charles*). This remark follows in the wake of the claim that the word "host," *tsabha'*, appears five times in vv. 10-13 in different meanings, referring to Israel, the angels, and in v. 13 to the "service" in the Temple. Apart from other considerations, such changes of meaning or different meanings of words do occur. Our translation and interpretation consistently referred the word to the people of God in an explanation which we believe makes good sense without forcing the meaning of terms. Since the objections raised by criticism can in this as in so many other cases be removed without difficulty, we offer this example in addition to the many others already presented to reassure those who are unduly impressed by the claims of criticism.

K. S. regards *hechazon* as a case of the leading noun in the construct state having the article (303f). As we indicated above, the noun following is not in the construct relationship but is a noun in apposition. It need not be considered strange that *teth*, an infinitive, occurs in a series of nouns, for infinitives are used as nouns.

14. And he said to me: "Unto two thousand three hundred evenings-mornings; then shall the sanctuary come into its right."

Several matters in regard to the text require investigation. Most commentators object to the word *'elay,* "to me," because they feel that "to him" would be more logical and even claim that "to me" is an absurdity, for the inquiring *angel* would not have received an answer, but the *prophet,* who had not yet asked, would be getting a reply. Yet the matter is simple: the angels are speaking in the vision for the prophet's sake; what the one says to the other is in the last analysis intended for Daniel. Why cannot Daniel then say: "He said to *me"?* The "unto," *'adh,* involves a verbal idea like "it shall last," and so the construction may continue with *waw* conversive, *K. S.,* p. 376.

We have here one of the major cruxes of the whole book: What do the "two thousand three hundred evenings-mornings" mean? The compound expression is so unusual that it perplexes the reader. Besides, in v. 26 the equivalent expression inserts an "and" between "evening" and "morning" and prefixes the article to each of these words. Consequently v. 26 reads, *ha'erebh wehabbóqer;* v. 14 *'érebh bóqer.* Yet both refer to the same period of time. Though we can cite no Hebrew parallel, the Greek suggests something analogous, namely, the word νυχθήμερον, which means "a night and a day" (II Cor. 11:25) in the sense of a period of twenty-four hours. This is the simplest and most feasible interpretation.

The alternative would be to think especially of the morning and the evening sacrifices and to claim that evenings and mornings—both terms are used collectively as they are in our translation above—are mentioned as the times when sacrifices were to be offered. Then 2,300 evenings-mornings would be the equivalent of 1,150 days. At this point those interpre-

ters who apply the one or the other mode of calculation begin their historical computation according
to First Maccabees and try to find a period of either
2,300 days or 1,150 days. But these computations offer
grave difficulties. Reckon as you will, there is no clear-
cut period of either the one or the other length. Then
the juggling of facts and figures begins. But the very
fact that neither the longer period of almost seven
years nor the shorter of almost three-and-a-half can
be made to tally with known historical facts should
serve to cause interpreters to cease continuing along
this line. *Meinhold* has said rightly: "An entirely
satisfactory computation has neither been found here
nor for the kindred periods in chapters nine and
twelve." He is absolutely correct.

We do not deem it important to show the unsatisfactory nature of the different computations that have
been made. Anyone who is sufficiently interested may
make a computation according to the first ten chapters
of First Maccabees and see what the issues are. Here
is a brief digest of the pertinent events as they are
recorded in First Maccabees. We give the years according to the Greek era, as they are given in this
apocryphal book. The year 145 in the following
schedule corresponds to about 167 B. C.

137.   Antiochus begins to rule, conquers Egypt.

143.   Antiochus comes to the Temple in Jerusalem, plunders it and slays many.

145.   Antiochus sends a captain to Jerusalem
who gains entrance under false pretexts and fortifies
David's citadel; interferes with worship; the sanctuary is desolate; commands that one religion be practiced throughout his realm, abolishes all sacrifices and
festivals, lets sow's meat be offered, forbids circumcision; on the 15th of Kislev "abomination" is set on
the altar*; altars are erected in Jewish cities; books
of the law are burned; on the 25th of Kislev he sacri-

fices on a new altar; revolt of Mattathias; Judas defeats Appolonius.

147. Antiochus advances to Persia to raise revenues, appoints Lysias captain from the Euphrates to Egypt; Lysias chooses three captains: Ptolemy, Nicanor, and Gorgias; Jerusalem is desolate; the sanctuary is removed to Mizpah; Judah defeats Gorgias at Emmaus; Lysias gathers a great force at Beth Zur (Edom) ; Lysias is defeated, withdraws to Antioch; Judah restores the sanctuary and the altar.

148. On the 25th of the ninth month (Kislev) sacrifice is again offered;* the feast of dedication is decreed; Antiochus attacks Elymais in Persia, is defeated, and returns to Babylon.

148. Antiochus dies in Babylon; Antiochus Eupator, his son, is made king; Lysias assembles a great army, no decisive encounter occurs; Lysias besieges Jerusalem without success.

151. Demetrius becomes king, slays Antiochus and Lysias; Alcimus, the high priest, slanders Judah; Nicanor is sent with an army, blasphemes in the Temple; Nicanor is defeated and slain on the 13th of Adar (twelfth month.*)

We have marked with an asterisk the key dates that are usually used in the prevailing computations.

There is something basically wrong with such computations. They go on an assumption which does not apply to the book of Daniel. None of the numbers that occur in its visions are in the nature of exact arithmetical calculations. What *Zoeckler* calls the "ideal prophetic value" of the numbers (*den prophetisch-idealen Wert*) is the consideration to be reckoned with. We could also designate it the symbolic use of numbers. From this point of view the number 2,300 can be interpreted in but one way. Divided by 365 to determine the number of years, it resolves itself into six years and 110 days. In other words, not into a complete period of seven years. If there had been seven years, since seven is the mark of a divine work, this period would have been characterized as a *divine* period of judgment. As it now stands, this number signifies *not even a full period of divine judgment.* *Keil* compares Judg. 6:1, where the Israelites were delivered into the hands of the Midianites seven years. Construed thus, this figure has a very distinct meaning as do those other figures that are found in Daniel. The fact that it is expressed in days reminds the troubled Israelites that the Lord will not let this period extend a day beyond what they can bear.

When *Kliefoth* gives the number also a literal and not only a symbolical signification he cannot point to any period in which the 2,300 days coincide with the historical realities. Such an attempt means to carry water on both shoulders. It is not in itself an impossibility, but it involves shutting one's eyes to definite facts and using the available evidence to advance one's ends.

When these days or the period that is not even a full period of divine judgment shall have come to an end, "then shall the sanctuary come into its right." This result makes it plain that what is really marked is the period of the desecration of the sanctuary. Such a period would be coterminous with the time of the affliction of God's saints. Since everything centers about the sanctuary, it alone is mentioned.

Since, however, we expressed our preference for the interpretation that regards "evenings-mornings" as a compound expression that means "days" we cannot accept the interpretation that makes this period equal to about three and a half years and then interprets that to be not even a *half* period of divine judgment. Such an interpretation would convey the impression that the judgment involved would be nothing to be greatly concerned about whereas the impression that the chapter as a whole makes is that this would, indeed, be as serious an affliction as the people of God ever encountered.

One recent critic comes to within about 45 days of the 1,150 and claims that this verse was written before the dedication of the new altar of the Lord, the date of which dedication he used in his computations. So he believes he can salvage the idea that this is a *bona fide* prediction, that is to say, honestly made in good faith before the event took place. The fact that it is an erroneous prediction by about 45 days does not trouble him.

d. *The Interpretation of the Vision,* v. 15-27

15, 16. Now it came to pass as I, Daniel, for my part was still looking on and was seeking to understand that, lo, before me stood a figure like that of a man. And I heard a human voice between the banks of the Ulai, and it called and said: "Gabriel, make this man understand the vision."

It must be borne in mind that, though in the exposition of the chapter we have thus far, for convenience' sake, inserted the interpretation of the major features as they were gathered from the later verses of this chapter, Daniel had only one piece of general interpretation, and that was the fact conveyed in v. 14, that the overthrow of the sanctuary and the sufferings of the saints were not to last even through an entire divine judgment period. So we can well understand why Daniel now draws attention to himself and to his immediate reaction to the vision as a whole by using the emphatic personal pronoun *'ani,* "I for my part." He was still gazing at what remained of the vision, for its major elements may have still stood before him—"I was still looking"—and he was also "seeking to understand." Whether this last verb— *'abhaqshah*—involved the idea that he sought by prayer, as *Haevernick* claims, is almost immaterial. For the issue is whether he sought by *formal* prayer. The eager desire of a man of God is, without a doubt, a prayer, whether it is uttered in words or not. We can well understand Daniel's great perplexity, for nothing quite like what he had seen had ever been granted to any man, with or without a vision.

He is further amazed ("lo") by the sudden appearance of a figure before him. It cannot have been a man because a man would not be described as having "a figure *like* that of a man." It must have been a superior being, without doubt an angel, who had been sent in the guise of a man so as not further to terrify the prophet who had already been put under the most severe strain by these divine revelations.

16. In like manner the command spoken by the Almighty Himself is also presented in a form that is convenient for the hearing of man, for it is spoken in a "human voice." If the voice of the Almighty had been heard in its natural accents it would have been distinguishable from the voice that was here heard as being something that was far above the human level. For "human voice" the Hebrew has "the voice of a man." The expression "between the banks of the Ulai" (cf. v. 2) also has a different form in the Hebrew, for it reads "between the Ulai." This would seem to be a shortened expression for "between *the banks* of," for it is very obvious that rivers have two banks. The sixth verse of chapter 12 is usually cited as a parallel because it represents one who is an interpreter and also stands above the waters. In this case it is, however, the voice of the Almighty, for He alone is able to give commandments to His angels. But just why He should have spoken from that point must remain a mystery.

Our supposition that the one who had taken his stand before the prophet was an angel is confirmed here, for this one is called "Gabriel." This angelic name ap-

pears again in Luke 1:19, 26 as well as in Dan. 9:21.
The only other angel whose name the Scriptures record
is Michael, found in 10:21 (cf. Rev. 12:7). These two
are rightly called archangels, a term that is taken from
Rev. 8:2, 7. Other names such as Uriel and Raphael
are apocryphal. It seems that in v. 15 the unusual
name for "man," *gébher*, was used because this term
contains the first half of the name Gabriel, and besides,
gébher means a "hero," and angels are truly heroic
beings, cf., Ps. 103:20.

Gabriel must be the *angelus interpres* (interpreting angel) in this instance, for the command is
given him to "make this man understand the vision."
Not that the angel needs a command, but Daniel is to
be made aware of who it is that interprets, and at
whose behest he does this interpreting.

17, 18. **So he came near the place where I
stood; and as he approached, I was overcome by
fear and fell face downward. And he said to me:
"Understand, O mortal, that the vision pertains to
the time of the end." And as he spoke with me, I
fell into a swoon to the ground face downward; and
he touched me and set me upon my feet where I had
been standing.**

Direct contact with a heavenly being has always
wrought great fear and dread to the heart of mortals.
Our book offers several parallels: 10:9, 15, 17. See also
Ezek. 1:29 and Isa. 6:5. With good reason men feared
that death might overtake them, for the full sense of
one's sinfulness comes home to one under just such
circumstances. See Judg. 13:22 and Exod. 33:20. So,
as Gabriel comes near, Daniel is "overcome by fear,"
nibh'atti. "I was afraid" (*A. V.*) or "I was affrighted"
(*A. R. V.*) are hardly strong enough, for he also "fell
down face downward." How great must the sinfulness
of our human race be that at the mere presence of a
sinless being man should be so completely overcome!

Yet Daniel had not lost consciousness, nor did his fear prevent him from understanding the first cue to the vision that he had seen. For he is told that "the vision pertains to the time of the end." This is an important fact concerning the entire interpretation, and a fact that no man could have discovered by himself. It marks a general approach to the contents of the whole chapter that should be uppermost in the mind of those who busy themselves with this chapter. We have reserved the discussion of this aspect of the case till now because it fits most conveniently into the present connection.

This statement means that, aside from the obvious relation that the vision has to the events that lie in the near future, namely, in the time of the Persian and the Greek Empires, this whole vision also serves as a type of what shall transpire at the time of the end of the present world order. So the "end" referred to the absolute end. And so the noun *qets*, referring to a special event, comes to have the character of a proper noun and is used without the article (*K. S.* 294c). In other words, summing up, King Antiochus is seen to be a kind of Old Testament antichrist like unto the great Antichrist; the overthrow and the defilement of the sanctuary shall correspond to similar experiences of the church; the suffering of the holy people corresponds to suffering in the last great tribulation. When this is borne in mind, the chapter loses its isolation from present-day events and is seen to be typical in a very definite sense.

Two of *Fausset's* remarks may be considered here. He says: "Antichrist, like Christ, has a more immediate future, as well as a more remote." We take it that this is written from the standpoint of the Old Testament times and is a reference to Christ's first and second comings. He then remarks (on v. 9): "Greece with all its refinement produces the first, i.e., the Old Testament antichrist." From this we should be inclined to draw the inference, based on the typical character of the vision, that the refinement of the culture and the civilization of the last days shall help very materially to bring forth the great Antichrist. The more ungodly and antichristian this culture becomes in our day, the more should we reckon with the possibility here involved and not be surprised at such developments.

We could have translated Gabriel's first statement: "Understand . . . *for* the vision pertains." But our rendering seems to contain the distinctive character of this guiding principle in a clearer way. The address that is used by the angel is also very appropriate: "O mortal." Daniel is feeling more keenly than he ever did that he is a mere mortal—Hebrew: "a son of man"—and it is good for him to keep this fact in mind. As *Jerome* says, (see *Haevernick*) this form of address, "son of man," is used to address also Ezekiel and Zechariah with the same purpose in mind, namely, to remind these prophets that they were but men and were marked by all human frailties.

18.   The longer the angel speaks, the more is the feeling of human impotency borne in upon Daniel, till he actually "fell into a swoon." Though the root of the verb involved means "to fall into a deep sleep," that would hardly be an appropriate rendering here. The completeness of his helpless state is in this case also indicated by the fact that strength left the man so entirely that he was not in the least able to control his fall but simply toppled "face downward." Now angels seem also to possess great powers for strengthening the weak, even as one of them did our Savior in Gethsemane. So the mere touch of the angel imparts to the prophet the strength needed to arise and to pay the required attention.

The form *'omdhi,* though originally the infinitive, is here a noun and means "standing place."

19. **And he said: "Lo, I am instructing thee with reference to the things that shall transpire after the period of wrath is ended, for an appointed time has an end."**

"The period of wrath" is the Babylonian captivity, during which God's wrath against His chosen people was continually in evidence. The Hebrew states the matter thus: "I am instructing thee about the things that shall be in the latter end of the wrath," *be'acharith hazza'am.* This must denote, as *Keil* says, "the time which will follow after the expiration of the *za'am,* i.e., the period of anger." The word *'acharith* means literally "afterpart" and therefore in prophetic language "the final period of the history so far as the speaker's perspective reaches" (*BDB*). The last part seen is then the period immediately after the wrath period. The typical meaning that this has according to v. 17 is not for the present being touched upon by the angel. He merely interprets the more immediate future. Upon this bears also the statement: "For an appointed time has an end." That refers, of course, to the *za'am,* the wrath, for the disconsolate Israelites were not to believe that the present divine displeasure under which they happened to be living would continue forever.

This closing statement is, therefore, different in meaning from the conclusion of v. 17. Some overlook this fact as a result of their wrong translation of the words. *Luther* makes the predicate the subject and gives it the definite article. *A. V.* keeps the subject but gives the predicate the article. *A. R. V.* inserts two articles and goes farther off the track. Yet the simple meaning of the words is very literally, "To an appointed time there is an end," or as we render, "An appointed time has an end." Why should the statement made in v. 17 be repeated here? But to indicate that the appointed period of wrath has an end that is appointed by the wisdom of God, that makes good sense and is very much in place for those who are troubled as they experience this great wrath.

20-22. **"The ram which thou didst see, the one with the two horns, it represents the kings of Media and Persia. The shaggy he-goat represents the king of Greece. The tall horn which grows between its eyes is the first king. And as for its being broken and four arising in its stead, that represents that four kingdoms shall arise out of the nation but not as strong as he was."**

20.   The substance of this verse was discussed above. The expression "the one with the two horns" is the same as that which in verse 6 we rendered "the two-horned creature," but we ventured to use a different translation here to indicate the various possibilities of the original. It again appears that two points of view predominate in the interpretation. The symbols involved represent either the kings or the kingdoms even as we regularly substitute the one for the other. The ram is here said to represent "kings." That does not conflict with our approach which claimed that this creature represented the kingdom or empire.

21.   The point of view is the same as it was in the preceding verse. It may be noted that the Hebrew word for Greece is *Javan* or *Yavan*, a form that is related to the other name for the Greeks, "Ionians." For "tall horn" the original has "big horn."

22.   The construction is typically Hebrew: it begins with the participle *Niphal* with the article and uses this absolutely as a participial sentence. The construction is continued by the verb which is connected by the *waw* conversive, *K. S.* 366i The verb *ya'amodh-nah* should have a feminine prefix—*t*. See *G. K.* 47, **3 3.**

23. **"And in the latter time of their kingdom, when the transgressors are come to the full, there shall arise a king, bold and crafty."**

The first phrase used above is ambiguous, in fact, it seems to point directly to the time when these four kings are still reigning, for the term *'acharith* is very difficult to translate. It may mean, and here does mean, the time following their reign. When these four kingdoms have just about run their full course, and the situation is already materially different from what it was when the new regime was established after Alexander, then this new king will put in his appearance. His time is marked a bit more fully by the second clause (an infinitive phrase in the Hebrew) "when the transgressors are come to the full." Though most of the older versions—not *Luther*, nor *A. V.* nor *A. R. V.*— prefer to point the word for "transgressors" to read "transgressions," the Hebrew text may well be left as it is. Driver translates well: "When the transgressors have completed (their guilt)." There are, indeed, expressions that refer to the filling up of the iniquities (cf., Gen. 15:16), yet certainly *transgressors* themselves may "come to the full," that is to say, may achieve a measure of development in their sins that cannot allow the Almighty to suffer them to go on any farther. That thought certainly fits well here.

In determining the time when this very wicked king shall arise, the interpretation shows that he comes in a season when wickedness generally is rife. Other men who are renowned for excessive wickedness shall also be on the scene. They shall also have been carrying on their iniquitous devices to the point where their insolence calls forth the interference of the Almighty. This new character shall be one of this group of wicked rulers. His distinguishing mark, however, shall be that he is "bold and crafty." The Hebrew for this is quite a bit more intricate, it is somewhat like

A. V's., "of fierce countenance and understanding dark sentences." But that again requires a bit of interpretation. For he that is "strong of countenance," *'az-panim,* is, as we might say, "bold-faced." This expression occurs also in Deut. 28:50. We have rendered "bold," following Luther's example who translates it *frech.*

The second double expression does not say much in English if it is rendered "understanding dark sentences." What are the "dark sentences"? They are "intrigues" (*K. W.*). Briefly, the man is "crafty" or "skilled in double dealing." The fact that his craft is of a wicked sort is well expressed by *Luther* with his translation *tueckisch,* but that again loses the basic idea of cunning. A cruel fellow, bold in his enterprises and a past master of all the intrigues that the bold political upstart is wont to employ—such a one will this dreadful enemy of the people of God be as far as his character is concerned. The next two verses picture his career, both his seeming success and his ultimate overthrow.

24. **"And his power shall become mighty, yet not by his own strength; he shall bring about remarkable destruction and shall have success in his undertakings; and he shall destroy mighty men and a number of the holy people."**

The fact that his power must became mighty indicates that his beginnings will be small, cf., v. 9, the "little horn." But in his endeavors to achieve greatness he shall have success beyond the measure that is granted to others who have similar ambitions; "his power shall become mighty." Two thoughts may be implied in the restrictive phrase that is added. "Not by his own strength" could mean either by the strength of God, or, if it be not by strength then by craft. Since the latter thought was conveyed already by the remark that he was "crafty," it seems more likely that the impression to be made is that God allowed this man to achieve what his measure of talents would never have warranted. The original makes the contrast rather strong by using the same word twice over: "His *power* shall become mighty, but not by his own *power*." That is a bit unusual, so the critics say that the second use of the word "power" is a gloss.

This great power shall not be put to good and constructive uses, for "he shall bring about remarkable destruction." *A. R. V.* is far more literal but less clear: "He shall destroy wonderfully." *Niphla'oth, Niphal* feminine plural participle, is here used adverbially; it means literally "wonders." *Marti* says that such an interpretation is impossible. This implies that the king will overthrow and kill and destroy on an unusual scale. He will be one of those monsters that wade through history in a welter of blood.

Another matter that shall cause men to wonder at his career will be the fact that, no matter what he undertakes, whether it is great or small, for the time at least "he shall have success in his undertakings," Hebrew: "he shall cause to prosper, and he shall do."

The destruction of human life implied in the above is now expressly added so that all that is to be expected is made entirely clear: "he shall destroy mighty men and a number of the holy people." Not only the people of God, "the holy people," shall suffer, but in his career he shall remove relentlessly such strong men as may oppose themselves to him. Since a contrast is implied between "mighty men" and "a number of the holy people," this involves that the saints, as usual, will appear to be weak and defenseless, at least to the worldly-minded who do not know that the Lord is their strength. Besides, this indicates that his opposition will not be directed exclusively against the people of God. Our reason for not translating the last expression "the holy people" but "a number of the holy people" is that in the original the article is omitted, it is not "the holy people" but just "holy people." That necessarily means "a number of the holy people." It may have been his ambition to destroy the nation as such. He shall succeed only to a very limited extent.

Thus far the account dealt mostly with his success. It now dwells more on his methods and purposes and collapse.

25. **"And by his cunning he shall cause craft to prosper in his undertakings; and in his own opinion he shall be great and shall destroy many unawares; and he shall stand up against the prince of princes; but he shall be broken without hand."**

This is, in fact, a very skillfully condensed account of the checkered career of one of the most remarkable men that strutted across the stage of history. Its very conciseness makes it ambiguous or difficult to understand if one skims over it too readily.

Verse 24 is in a sense a commentary on what the trait described as "bold" in v. 23 accomplishes. Verse 25 may similarly be considered a commentary on at least the first part of the term "crafty" in v. 23. The noun *sekhel* does not connote a *wicked* cunning; it could even mean cleverness of a good sort. But it must here refer to that which is evil, for *mirmah* is "craft" or even "deceit." The Hebrew preposition *'al* implies that the whole structure of the man's success is built "upon" this cunning. Cunning again furthers craft. Solid achievement is out of the question. For "in his undertakings" the Hebrew has "in his hand." This expression apparently refers rather to the undertaking that he has in hand than to the hand itself. Therefore our translation.

A personal characteristic that shall stand out as the man develops his career will be that "in his own opinion he shall be great." There were plenty of indications of the high regard this man had of himself especially in the tokens of respect that he demanded from those conquered although the first book of Maccabees indicates that this pride was severely shaken before his end. Still along the line of his crafty dealings is the remark: "And shall destroy many unawares." When they deem themselves "in safety (*beshalwah*)" or as we should say "unawares," he comes upon many in his career of destroying his opponents.

This sense of mistaken greatness which causes him to attempt to wipe out all that oppose themselves finally leads him so far that "he shall stand up against the prince of princes." According to 10:13, 21; 12:1 the "princes" are the chief of the angels. Their "prince" is none less than the Almighty Himself. If v. 11 indicated that this arrogant prince among men sought to be classed with God, this verse indicates another side of his ambitions: he aims to set himself *against* God. Such defying of the Almighty Ruler of the universe calls forth His vengeance. So we can hardly be surprised at the conclusion: "But he shall be broken without hand." This naturally refers to the hand of *man*. When the overthrow comes, it is apparent that man himself did not put this arrogant mortal out of the way, but He whose mills grind slowly but exceedingly fine did it. The account in I Macc. 6:8ff tells how this monarch was smitten by God and duly humbled before his death. Besides, "broken" implies that God will make the object of His wrath appear as utterly shattered and impotent, it is a strong verb. The verb involved is often used in the Old Testament with reference to the overthrow of kingdoms, armies, and individuals (cf., Jer. 48:8; II Chron. 14:12; Jer. 17:18; Dan. 11:26).

26. **"But the vision of the evenings and the mornings which was told thee is truth. But do thou preserve the vision, for it pertains to a time far in the future."**

The disclosures concerning the future are at an end. Daniel's attitude toward the revelation as a whole is now to be touched upon. In the first place, since the revelation as such is quite without parallel, he is, on that account, not to question the truth of what God permitted him to see. So we first have the assurance that this vision is true. Rather strangely the designation that this interpreting angel himself gives to this vision is that it is "the vision of the evenings and the mornings." That unusual title does not necessarily imply that the kernel of the vision is found in that term. This may merely have been the most convenient designation because Daniel himself had somehow been particularly intrigued by that statement concerning the mornings and the evenings. We remark again that in this instance the particular expression involved connects the two nouns by "and" and prefixes the article to each.

The verb that follows has received various interpretations. It is *sethom,* which basically does mean "shut up." But it cannot here mean "keep it a secret" or "hide" or the like. To "hide or conceal" is a different verb—*sathar.* The shutting up is here done with the purpose of keeping the vision intact, and we have therefore translated "preserve." For a similar New Testament thought see Rev. 22:10. The reason advanced agrees with this: "for it pertains to a time far in the future." From the setting that had been given at the beginning of the chapter Daniel was able to discern that the vision pertained to a not very remote future. But he was unable to note that this more immediate future was typical of the remote future of which the angel now also tells him. As far as the more immediate future was concerned, Daniel might have transmitted the truth heard to faithful men by word of mouth; and it might have lived on by sound tradition until the times for which it was intended. But in that case it

would have been completely lost for the "time *far* in
the future." So Daniel was to take such precautions
about the preservation and manifolding of the manuscript as might be necessary so that the document
could be preserved for a long time to come. Nothing
about it was intended to be kept secret. God's revelation is never of such a sort in any case. God reveals
so that what He has given may be revealed. There
would be no good sense in revealing for the purpose
of keeping secret. But the critics give this meaning to
this harmless word to make it appear that when men
of the time of Antiochus Epiphanes discovered this
pseudo-Daniel they might have an explanation as to
why this book was seemingly kept secret so long, and
so they might be kept from inquiring into the origin
of this apocryphal book. This feature of the book was
to help to gain it a place in the Old Testament church.
Here would be the basis for the *pia fraus* that is supposed to have helped the book of Daniel, though not
written by Daniel, to be accepted as though it had been.

27. **But I, Daniel, was exhausted and became
sick for several days. Then I arose and tended to the
king's business. But I was appalled by the vision,
and there was no man that understood it.**

The recipient of the vision had already in vv. 17
and 18 been overcome by contact with heavenly beings
and supernatural revelation and had required strengthening before he was able even to receive what was to
be communicated. It need not seem strange that at the
close of this particular revelation his earlier weakness
should again befall him—"I was exhausted"—and that
a further reaction should set in in the form of a temporary sickness "for several days." It is because of the
frailty of man that God does not appear to him directly
or reveal Himself to man more directly. Daniel records
this part of his physical reaction especially, for it is of
moment in establishing the sin-weakened state of man.

But being a man of great fidelity to duty, as soon he has recovered sufficient strength, Daniel again attends to the king's business. Nothing indicates that Daniel held a position under Cyrus that was as high as that which he had held under Nebuchadnezzar or under Darius. Nor does this statement make any such claim. There still seemed to be important work that he was able to do, in which he could further the interests of the ruler as well as of the people of God. So he that had been above reproach (6:4) in his previous administration continued with the same fidelity though his position was no longer what it had been, that of prime minister.

The way in which Daniel's weakness, the faithful performance of his work, and his being appalled at the vision are grouped together in this verse shows how apparently, even in the midst of the performance of his tasks, the thought of the unusual revelations that had been committed to him kept arising continually. Nor was that in the least strange. Here was one individual who alone of all mortals had been given a glimpse behind the curtain shrouding the future. He alone knew of the crumbling of empires and their successive downfall. But this did not merely amaze him or cause him to wonder. It actually "appalled" him. Such knowledge about the crashing of human structures and the suffering of God's saints was no light thing to bear. We see more clearly in the light of this fact and in Daniel's reaction why God has not revealed more of the future to the sons of man: they would be unduly disturbed and grieved by such disclosures.

We are ourselves rather perplexed by the concluding statement of the verse: "There was no man that understood it," viz., the vision. It would seem as though Daniel must have understood because he received an interpretation at the hand of a competent instructor. It would seem equally simple to conclude that Daniel could readily have imparted what he understood to others who were of like mind with him. For, as we saw in the preceding verse, there was no injunction laid upon him in the matter of keeping this revelation secret: Daniel could tell others what he had been told.

The clue to this particular perplexity on Daniel's part lies in the simple fact that every prophecy, no matter how clearly it is given, has an element of the mysterious in it so that the mind of even an enlightened saint is quite unable to grasp more than the merest outlines of the truth till the fulfillment comes. What seems overwhelmingly clear to us now in the light of the historical fulfillment as we know it simply was not understood by Daniel. Witness the parallel experiences of Christ's disciples concerning His predictions of His death and His resurrection and the tragic perplexity with reference to even His plainest statements: "They understood none of these things; and this saying was hid from them, and they perceived not the things that were said," Luke 18:34. In the face of his perplexity Daniel carefully retained the very words that had been given even though he did not understand their import. That fidelity was still the primary duty of God's prophets.

HOMILETICAL SUGGESTIONS

This chapter obviously has a double purpose. In so far as it outlines events soon to come upon the Jews it seems to have fulfilled its purpose and to be of no further use as far as our day is concerned. Yet a section like vv. 1-14, interpreted in the light of the rest of the chapter, could serve as a basis for the truth which is still to be preached, that the future course of history is not hidden from the Almighty. A corollary of this truth is: He that foreknows how history shall run also controls its course with absolute sovereignty. God's foreknowledge and His omnipotence are both still operative, thank God.

In the second place, v. 17b very pointedly says that "the vision belongeth to the time of the end." Among the cycles of history that keep repeating themselves is the Antichrist cycle. Antiochus Epiphanes is merely a type of what shall be in evidence when the present world era comes to a conclusion and Jesus comes again. With this in mind, vv. 15-27 may be used as text, and the truth concerning the overthrow of the Antichrist may well be preached. Care must again be taken to make the negative factor—Antichrist's success and tyranny—secondary and the positive factor, his being broken "without hand" (v. 25), the chief concern. Verse 26 serves a good purpose in this connection in that it recommends keeping the truth revealed in the chapter in reserve for the evil days to come.

CHAPTER IX

B. DANIEL'S PENITENTIAL PRAYER AND
THE VISION OF THE SEVENTY HEPTADS

In the two preceding chapters a rather full account has been given of the future developments through which the kingdom of God was to pass. First the contrast was marked between the manner in which the "One like unto a son of man" acquired the kingdom and the manner in which the rapacious, beastlike powers of the world came into positions of authority; yet the latter would vent their bestial spite on the ones who were in God's kingdom, particularly before the final judgment. Chapter eight covered a more limited territory, sketching the development up to the time of the Old Testament counterpart of the New Testament Antichrist, this Old Testament persecutor being Antiochus Epiphanes.

Necessary as it may be to prepare God's people for trying times that must be encountered when Antiochus is ruling, there are more important revelations than these, revelations that reach all the way to the final consummation of all things, when all that is evil shall be overthrown, never again to rise, and when all that is good and righteous shall be established, never again to be overthrown. That glorious victory should be in the forefront of the thinking of God's people. Chapter seven alluded to it with predominant emphasis on the persecutions that were to precede the glorious consummation. Though already then the note of victory was struck very decidedly, there were things of a very glorious sort that were yet to be revealed, and they are the things that are predominant in our chapter. They are given in a setting which unfolds God's entire plan of development from Daniel's day to the end of time. They unroll a panorama of history that is without parallel even in the sacred Scriptures. This revelation was the glorious answer to Daniel's humble prayer that the Omnipotent might bring His promises to pass. Since the things that were about to happen in Daniel's time were to be of so very humbling a sort that the courage of many a saint might well have failed him, God reveals the glories that a more distant future has in store.

a. *The Circumstances*, v. 1-3

1, 2. In the first year of Darius, the son of Ahasuerus, of the race of the Medes, who had been made king over the kingdom of the Chaldeans, in that first year of his reign I, Daniel, observed in the books the number of the years which constituted the word of Yahweh unto Jeremiah, the prophet, in reference to the desolation of Jerusalem—seventy years.

We examined the question of the identity of Darius, the Mede, in connection with 6:1 (5:31 A. V.) and found ample evidence for regarding him to be Gobryas of Gutium. Though conclusive proof of his Median extraction could not be offered, all who deny this identification are equally at a loss for evidence to prove that he could not have been a Median. He had now been advanced by Cyrus to the rank of ruler of the Chaldeans. The statement made by our verse agrees admirably with that fact—he "had been made king," *homlakh*. That is hardly a statement to be made with reference to a conqueror who makes himself king. It assigns Darius no more than the Chaldean kingdom. No one knows how far that extended. It certainly was hardly more than one of the many constituent kingdoms that made up the realm. This allows, of course,.

for the other well-established fact that Cyrus was the ruler over the Persian Empire. He it was who had made Darius ruler over "the kingdom of the Chaldeans."

It was in the first year of the reign of this Darius that the events recorded in this chapter took place. Daniel emphasizes this fact by repeating the words *bishnat 'achath,* "in the year one," which we have therefore ventured to translate in v. 2 as "in that first year." "Ahasuerus" is the individual whom the Greeks called Xerxes.

2. It is plain that Daniel wanted to mark the year as being a significant one. In truth, a significant thing had happened: Babylon had fallen before the victorious advance of Cyrus. It was the year 538 B. C. This was the overthrow that Isaiah had prophesied (Isa. 13). Daniel, who was thoroughly familiar with the sacred Scriptures, was moved to investigate further. He knew not only of statements that dealt with the downfall of the adversary of God's people but also of words of restoration. This led him to take in hand "the books," *hassepharîm,* that dealt with this case and to look more carefully at the years involved before this restoration could take place, even as Peter points out (I Pet. 1:11) that the prophets searched "what time or what manner of time the Spirit of Christ which was in them did point out."

How much is involved in the term *bassepharîm?* BDB goes so far as to suggest the translation "by means of the Scriptures [canonical books]." We happen to know why critics usually construe the phrase thus: they give as late a date as possible to the composition of Daniel and so claim that the canon of the Old Testament was already complete (300 B. C. or later as some claim), and that Daniel had a complete Old Testament in his possession. Surely, the expression does not suggest anything of the sort. The article before "books," according to Hebrew usage, need imply nothing more than the idea of the books requisite for the passage involved, i.e., "Jeremiah." In fact, the plural *sepharîm* may refer to a single letter, cf., II Kings 19:14; Isa. 37:14. The requirements of the Hebrew are fully met if Daniel had had only the roll of the book of Jeremiah, as well as if a few other books had been written on the same roll.

In the prophet Jeremiah the passages that could have been involved are 25:11, 12 and 29:10, for both speak of the seventy years. Since Daniel says distinctly that the word involved spoke "in reference to the desolation of Jerusalem," the reference must be to 25:11, which states that "this whole land shall be a desolation, and an astonishment, and these nations shall serve the king of Babylon seventy years." The passage 29:10 refers to the *restoration* of Israel.

Note also that we have translated the relative *'asher*, not "whereof" (*A. V.*, etc.), but simply "which." By letting the relative serve as the subject of *hayah* we believe we have a very reasonable rendering: "which constituted the word of *Yahweh* unto Jeremiah."

How shall we reckon the "seventy years" of Jeremiah? The Scriptures do not happen to mark the starting point for our computation, and so different calculations are proposed, several of which are so very much to the point as to seem equally suitable, strange as that may seem. According to 1:1 Nebuchadnezzar had made an initial deportation of captives and of Temple vessels in the third year of Jehoiakim. The capture of the city had surely preceded this deportation. So that could well be regarded as the beginning of "the desolation of Jerusalem." Josiah had been slain in 608 B. C.; Jehoahaz had reigned but three months. So 608 might be regarded as the first year of Jehoiakim, and 606 as the just-mentioned third year. Now it is well known, according to one mode of computation, that the actual first return of captives occurred in 538 B. C. Many others, however, give this date as 536 B. C. In that event we have an exact figure for the years in question: 606-536 = 70 years.

Others prefer to use 586 B. C. as a starting point in their computations, the year of the *destruction* of Jerusalem. Certainly, "the desolation of the city" can very correctly be said to date from this year. However, 586 minus 70 = 516, the date of the completion of the second Temple. Now it is without a doubt not improper to regard the city of Jerusalem as being desolate as long as not even the Temple is restored. So this computation has its justification. However, "the first year of Darius" was 538 B. C. This would involve that Daniel "observed the number of the years" and saw that they were all but complete—assuming the correctness of the date 606. Should the return from captivity actually have occurred in 536 B. C., the seventy years would have been entirely fulfilled at the time Daniel "observed . . . the years."

To tell the truth, our verse says nothing more than that Daniel "observed . . . the years . . . seventy years." *Bînothî,* from *bûn* or *bîn,* means no more than "consider, mark, or observe." We are not told whether he found the years completed or nearly so. He tells us merely that he was giving attention to the seventy years. As a result he turned to God in prayer. But even this prayer does not reveal exactly how Daniel felt about the matter of the reckoning of these seventy years. Other things were more important.

3. **So I set my face unto the Lord God to seek Him by prayer and supplication for favor with fasting and sackcloth and ashes.**

Daniel apparently discerned that a crisis in the fortunes of Israel was impending. Since God had indicated that a deliverance was at hand, Daniel addressed himself to the task of prayer for its consummation. Godly men, believing God's promises, do not become passive because of such faith. Prayer comes so naturally in such cases and fits, they well know, so aptly into the scheme of things that God has ordained, that they must needs approach God in prayer that He might do what He has promised. To "set (Hebrew: 'give') the face unto the Lord" implies conscious turning to God, who is about to be addressed. Whether such an act on Daniel's part involved also a physical orientation toward Jerusalem, that we can only surmise. Since the double name "Lord God" is used, this indicates that Daniel consciously thought of Him as Lord of all as well as the true God. The fact that he employed both "prayer, *tephillah*, and supplication for favor, *tachanûnîm*," shows the earnestness of his petitions.

Our translation supplies a pronoun object after *biqqesh*, which frequently has the object "God" or "*Yahweh*." Since *'adhonay ha'elohîm* preceded, it would seem that the writer thought it unnecessary again to express the commonly used object. "Prayer" and "supplication for favor" are adverbial accusatives. "Fasting and sackcloth and ashes" are employed as auxiliary means to aid devotion. Fasting helps to keep the mind unencumbered and also reminds him who practices it that he has not deserved even food from God. To remove clothing and to substitute a coarse wrap strongly remind the suppliant that not even the comforts of good clothing are his right and due reward. "Ashes" were put upon the head as a token of grief since Daniel sincerely grieved over his and his people's sins (cf., Ezra 9:3).

c. *Daniel's Confession*, v. 4-14

The entire prayer of Daniel (v. 4-19) deserves to be ranked with the finest of the psalms but usually receives rather scant treatment on the part of commentators, chiefly, we presume, because it is overshadowed by that difficult *crux interpretum*—the vision of the seventy weeks (v. 24-27). Anxious to take the avowedly perplexing passage in hand, the commentator hurries through this prayer. True enough, the prayer is not marked by any unusual difficulties.

It has been criticized, however, on the score of not being original. As we proceed we shall show the points of contact between it and Ezra 9 and Neh. 1 and 9. A third parallel is furnished by the apocryphal book of Baruch, whose analogous prayer runs through most of the first three chapters. Where there is a pronounced similarity, the mere claim that Daniel must of necessity be the borrower does not prove the case. The obvious solution of the problem is this: Daniel was, no doubt, the first to offer such a prayer; Ezra and Nehemiah learned from him but yet offer original prayers; Baruch plainly imitates all three. Nehemiah 9 is not a parallel, for it is a composite prayer that summarizes what the Levites had said on that occasion. The point is usually overlooked that these prayers very manifestly differ, each prayer being the outgrowth of a very distinct situation.

To understand why Daniel comes to the point suggested by Jeremiah's prophecy so slowly, we must note what the prayer plainly discloses, that Israel's spiritual unreadiness stands in the way of having the Lord do for His people what He had promised. Israel is still largely impenitent. She may be in distress and deeply humbled by God, but she has not humbled *herself* under the mighty hand of God. Consequently her exaltation is being deferred. As a true teacher of God's people, though this is only incidentally the work of Daniel—a distinction that marks Daniel over against the other prophets of Israel—he leads the way in the confession of sins and points the way to repentance.

Very significant is Daniel's attitude in the matter of dealing with the sins of the nation: they are, as it were, one unit, one mass of guilt, to which the fathers contributed their part and Daniel and his contemporaries their own part. But when confession is made, the whole mass must be confessed. Daniel is caught in the sins of his day and age as much as were the preceding generations who committed the sins that brought about the existing situation.

The rush of emotion that leads to the outpouring of this confession does not, however, as some, including *Haevernick,* claim, produce "a sequence of thought none too clearly articulated or logically arranged." It may be true, the progression of thought is less clearly marked than is sometimes the case. But when intensity of feeling pervades a passage, as is most evidently the case here, emotion pushes logic farther into the background.

On the whole, this is really a touching prayer. It breathes a spirit of deep humility, sincere confession, and a true and living faith. Daniel appears as a man who is deeply rooted in the knowledge of God's dealings with His people in the past and one who is thoroughly familiar with the sacred Scriptures. As a result his understanding of the way of salvation is soundly evangelical. He solemnly disavows every thought that might savor of work-righteousness and builds his every petition on the mercies of his God. The Lutheran reformers clearly understood and strongly appreciated this fact and made an issue of it by pointing to the prayer as a whole and to v. 18 in particular.

4-6. **And I prayed unto Yahweh, my God, and I made confession, saying: "Ah Lord, the great and awe-inspiring God, that keepeth the covenant and mercies for them that love Him and keep His commandments, we have sinned, have gone astray, have dealt wickedly, and have rebelled; we have also departed from Thy commandments and ordinances. And we have not hearkened unto Thy servants, the**

prophets, who spoke in Thy name to our kings, our princes, and our fathers, and to the people at large."

4. The general term "I prayed" is followed by one that more accurately describes the main portion of this prayer, "I made confession." It is a bit out of the ordinary to have a particle like *'annah,* "ah" or "please," followed by the indicative as is the case here (cf. *K. S.* 351g) ; but it is not unnatural. The penitent sinner is impressed by the power and the majesty of God; therefore he uses the name *'el,* "the Strong One," which we translate "God." The attributes "great" and "awe-inspiring," *nôra',* *Nifal* participle from *yare',* "to fear," are quite aptly appended. To this is added a reminder of God's faithfulness in displaying mercy to them that love Him (cf. Exod. 20:6) and in keeping His covenant. On such fundamental things as God's strong covenant the prophet bases his approach. As is done in the passage Exod. 20:6, he associates the love of God with faithfulness in the keeping of God's commandments. This verse corresponds to Neh. 1:5.

5. The confession begins here. It is straightforward and without reservations and offers no excuse or palliation of the guilt of which its author is only too conscious. In the sentence structure the verbs present a somewhat unusual feature in Hebrew, a feature which we have sought to approximate by leaving out the conjunctions and translating: "We have sinned, have gone astray," etc. For the unusual thing in the Hebrew is a succession of unconverted perfects, connected by *waw,* a construction that is used only in the case of synonymous expressions (cf. *K. S.* 370f).

The different verbs used, at least the first three, have derivative nouns which are in common use in Hebrew as various designations of sin. *Chata'* involves "missing the mark"; *'awah* means "turning from the right way"; *rasha'* involves "becoming weak" as a result of having lost one's hold, i.e., God. Add to this the

idea of "rebelling," and surely the sum total of the
confession is: all forms of expression that are characteristic of sin are acknowledged to have been found
in Israel. This is an essential mark of true repentance
—guilt is not minimized.

A further bit of clear insight into the nature of
Israel's plight is contained in the last word, which
traces all these various manifestations of sin to their
actual root, which is departure from God's Word,
which is here designated as "commandments" and "ordinances" because they had both spoken with authority
(*mitswah*) and had also given final decisions for
doubtful cases (*mishpat*). Departure (*sôr*) from God's
Word is the beginning of all moral disorders. The absolute infinitive (*sôr*) is here used after the four finite
verbs of the series—a rather common construction in
Hebrew (cf., *K. S.* 218b) and not an indication of the
later degeneracy of the language as some claim. In fact,
the construction is quite appropriate. It generalizes and
shows the fundamental wrong by the less specific
infinitive form.

6.   The law of Moses had, of course, been fundamental in Israel's life. But historically another factor
had appeared: the prophets had expounded and applied this law according to the needs of successive
generations. Daniel confesses that here, too, a sad
oversight had occurred: he and his people had not
hearkened unto these prophets who had spoken in
obedience to a divine behest ("Thy servants"). In this
instance the guilty persons were primarily the "kings
and the princes," who had been warned more specifically than others, and whose example helped very
largely to determine the course of conduct of the
multitude.

To these Daniel adds "our fathers," the godless
generations preceding his own, who by their example
had directly promoted further godlessness. Last are

"the people at large" to whom the example of the higher-ups always finally descends. Practically the same words are found in Jer. 44:21. Prophets and priests were not as guilty as the other groups referred to and are, therefore, passed by in the enumeration of the guilty.

7-10. **"Thou, O Lord, art righteous, but we must be ashamed, as this day proves in reference to the men of Judah and the inhabitants of Jerusalem and to all Israel, those near by as well as those afar off in all the lands to which Thou hast driven them because of their treachery which they practiced against Thee. O Lord, we are the ones who must be ashamed, our kings, our princes, and our fathers who sinned against Thee. To the Lord, our God, belong mercies and forgivenesses, for we have rebelled against Him; and we have not hearkened to the voice of Yahweh, our God, to walk in His laws, which He set before us through His servants, the prophets."**

Having confessed the manifold sinfulness and disobedience of Israel, Daniel proceeds to claim that Israel's situation is such as to cause her to be ashamed of what she has done. He introduces this claim with the assertion that Israel's sad lot can in no wise be charged against 'Adhonay, the Lord of all, who deals with nations as He sees fit, for He is "righteous." Our translation follows *Luther's* and preserves an English idiom. The *Hebrew* is a bit stronger, it is as *A. V.* translates: "Righteousness belongeth unto Thee." The next Hebrew expression, "to us [belongeth] confusion of face," means, of course, "we must be ashamed" (again *Luther*), for *bósheth* means "confusion" or "shame."

At this point the confession indicts all who belong to God's people, not according to their difference in rank and station, but rather according to their geographical locations, where those who enjoyed the advantage of living in Judah or in Jerusalem are as guilty as those who were less fortunately located in Israel. (cf., Jer. 14:4; II Kings 23:2). He reflects in particular on that experience which put Israelites to shame in a very special sense—the dispersion resulting from the captivity, which the Lord, their God, had suffered them to undergo so that some were still "near by" and others "afar off" (cf. Jer. 16:15; 23:3, 8; 32:37). In either case they were still "in all the lands to which" He had "driven them because of their treachery which they practiced." In other words, God is right, and Israel is all wrong and has no excuse.

Kayyôm hazzeh, "as this day," is elliptical; we supply "proves." Cf., *K. S.* 402u.

8.   When Daniel repeats: "we are the ones who must be ashamed," we are made to feel that he has in mind more than mere embarrassment. He refers to the shame of guilt and consequently does not mince words: sin, SIN, is the direct cause of all these misfortunes.

There is only one thought that affords comfort: God is merciful. At this point our translation which still follows *Luther's,* veers into the pattern of the *A. V.* because no suitable adjective seems to be available to express the concept of the noun "forgivenesses."

The *kî* clauses that follow—"for we have rebelled," etc.—do not, of course, involve a *kî* causal but a *kî* explicative and show more loosely, not why God is merciful, but why there is need for His manifesting mercy. The writer's thoughts revert to the abandoning of the word that came to the people through the prophets. These free admissions of sinfulness are not evidence of a morbid state of mind but of sincere and deep repentance which is ready to take all blame upon itself.

Note that in v. 9 the prayer abandons direct address and speaks about God in the third person in the

manner of reflection. Also for "Thou" there is substituted "the Lord, our God," a more formal and dignified statement which reflects the majesty of God
more fully.

**11-14. "Yea, all Israel has transgressed Thy
law and turned aside so as not to hearken to Thy
voice. And so Thou didst pour out upon us the curse
of the oath which was written in the Law of Moses,
a servant of the true God, because we sinned against
Him. And He hath fulfilled His Word which He
spoke over us and over our judges who judged us
by bringing upon us the great disaster, the like of
which was not done under all the heavens as was
done to Jerusalem—exactly as it was written in the
Law of Moses, just so did all this disaster come upon us. Yet we have not appeased Yahweh, our God,
to turn back from our iniquities and to behave wisely
in Thy truth. Therefore God was careful to bring
the disaster upon us; for Yahweh, our God, is
righteous in all the things that He has done; but we
have not hearkened to His voice."**

The confession becomes more specific. In a sense
it intensifies itself. The thoughts that receive greater
prominence are: Israel's bitter experience is entirely
in the form that God's Word had foretold, and therefore, since Israel knew what the consequences would
be, she was quite inexcusable in what she did.

The assertion is first made that "all Israel" is in
the same condemnation. These words are in the emphatic position in the sentence. Israel has "transgressed" in the sense of having wilfully gone beyond,
'abhar, certain bounds that had been distinctly marked.
Significant is the combination "turn aside," *sôr*, the absolute infinitive replacing the finite verb as in v. 5, and
"so as not to hearken"; first departure from God in the
heart of man, then the outward evidence of the departure in the form of manifest disobedience. The re-

sultant disaster may aptly be described as "pouring out the curse" of God, for such national calamities are not the result of a combination of natural causes but are rather traceable to God's activity. The Hebrew calls the thing poured out "the curse and the oath," which is apparently a hendiadys, "the curse of the oath" = the curse which He swore to bring about. Daniel has in mind passages like Lev. 26:14-39 and Deut. 28:15-68, where God solemnly assured Israel that its persistent iniquities would assuredly be visited upon it. Incidentally, this reference serves to show how completely the whole life of the nation was grounded upon the authoritative basis of the Mosaic law, which Daniel here ascribes to Moses by plainly emphasizing the commission which Moses had as "a servant [not, '*the* servant,' see *K. S.* 304d] of the true God," *ha'elohim*. Here the ultimate cause is again made plain by the straightforward admission: "Because we sinned against Him."

12. The deeper point of view expressed here is that what has happened has served to confirm or "fulfill" God's Word that had been spoken with reference to a case such as that of Israel. That inviolable Word invariably comes to pass, cf. Neh. 9:8; Deut. 9:5. The leaders or rulers are again mentioned (they are called "judges") because theirs is a double responsibility; the common herd always follows the leaders' example. One outstanding feature of the experience of Israel was that it had suffered a great "disaster" (the Hebrew has merely "evil," *ra'ah*) which was utterly without parallel among all the disasters upon which the heavens looked down. The overthrow of Israel, particularly of Judah and Jerusalem, had apparently involved an amount of cruelty and suffering that parallel cases could not claim. Naturally, the greater the measure of divine favor that had been granted, the greater were the responsibility and the resultant guilt.

The *le* before *habhî* indicates the sphere or the resultant direction rather than the purpose; so we translate "by bringing upon us" and not "to bring," etc. (cf., *K. S.* 402a).

13.   The prophet does not weary of tying up all these consequences with the Word of God which they served to fulfill. This attitude is a fine indication of how deeply the thinking of godly men is grounded on the Scriptures. "Exactly as it was written in the Law of Moses," cf., Josh. 8:31; 23:6; I Kings 2:3; II Chron. 23:18; 35:12. Israel has, however, since that disaster further increased the measure of guilt by not seeking to appease its God. "Appease" involves a peculiar but readily understandable figure in the Hebrew. The word is *chalah*, a *Piel*, and means "to stroke the face," cf., Exod. 32:11; I Sam. 13:12. The same use of *le* follows which occurred in the preceding verse. Though we have translated "to turn back," etc., the infinitive is best rendered "by turning back," etc. For nothing could better mollify an angered God than breaking with the sin that displeases Him. Such a departure from sin is the very essence of repentance and so of wise conduct—"to behave wisely in Thy truth." Here lie the roots of true wisdom.

The *'eth* before "all this disaster" introduces this expression with emphasis (see *G. K.* 117m).

Here there appears very clearly one of the chief reasons for Daniel's prayer: about seventy years ago the season for repentance had begun in a very specific way, and as yet Israel had not sincerely repented but apparently only bewailed its sad lot.

14.   God's faithfulness demanded that He punish disobedient Israel. This idea is expressed in the Hebrew by the idiom "God has watched," *shaqadh*, which we have rendered, "God was careful" (cf. Jer. 1:12). A truly penitent man can praise God for His righteousness even under circumstances such as these, even

as Daniel also does (cf., Jer. 12:1). Regarding himself
and his nation he can assert only that they have
been disobedient.

The thoughts of a punishment that was fully deserved and of a righteousness on God's part that was
wholly unimpeachable have thus far predominated in
the confession. These thoughts apparently have so
prominent a place in this confessional prayer because
Israel needed, in a very special sense, to be guided in
the direction of thoroughgoing admission of sin and
guilt without reservations and excuses. This confession
is, of course, at the same time wholly and sincerely
Daniel's own.

Beginning with v. 15 the man Daniel essays to
present his petitions to God for the restitution of the
city and the sanctuary. We cannot know whether
Cyrus' famous edict for the restoration of the Temple
had already been issued (Ezra 1:1ff) and so cannot
determine whether and in how far Daniel had any
connection with this edict.

c. *Daniel's Petition*, v. 15-19

15-17. **"And now, O Lord, our God, who didst
bring Thy people forth from the land of Egypt with
a mighty hand and hast made for Thyself a name
as this day proves, we have sinned, we have done
wickedly. O Lord, according to all Thy righteousness
let Thine anger and Thy hot wrath be turned away
from Thy city Jerusalem, Thy holy mountain, for
because of our sins and the iniquities of our fathers
Jerusalem and Thy people have become a reproach
to all that are round about us. And now, O God,
hearken unto the prayer of Thy servant and to his
petitions for mercy, and for the Lord's sake cause
Thy face to shine upon Thy sanctuary which is
desolate."**

The "and now," *we'attah,* indicates that Daniel is

about to advance to the point of presenting his petition. Before he actually does this, the proper timidity occasioned by a deep sense of guilt induces him to recall how by a mighty deliverance in days of old God established a gracious relationship with His people: He brought them forth from the land of Egypt by displaying great power ("with a mighty hand") and acquired renown by this deliverance. We still say, as the Hebrew does, "make a name" for oneself, cf., Isa. 63:12, 14; Jer. 32:20. This renown remains ("as this day proves," cf., v. 7). The thought implied is: He who did mighty works can still do them. But the deep sense of guilt crowds to the forefront once again and leads Daniel to summarize the entire preceding confession in the words: "We have sinned, we have done wickedly." The broken utterance shows the sincerity of feeling at this juncture.

16. Even now the petition advances no farther than to the point of asking that God's anger be turned aside. How terribly God's saints feel the strength of that anger against sin! This plea is motivated by an appeal to God's "righteousness," which is construed as the quality that will induce God to do the right thing, in this case, to grant pardon as He has promised, to the penitent.

It is further motivated by the observation that Jerusalem is God's city. It is such, however, only by virtue of the fact that God's "holy mountain" is there. Daniel very properly mentions only the *site* of the Temple because at this time the Temple itself was nothing more than a mass of ruins. God's sanctuary was dear to Him because He Himself had ordained it for His people as the place of His habitation among them.

A confession again forges to the forefront of the prayer. To the soul that is familiar with such things it appears very natural that confession should be re-

iterated, for repentance is a deep anguish of heart
over our sins against God, and just because it is so
deep it seeks occasion for repeated utterance. In this
particular instance the confession again combines the
present generation with those that preceded because
the sins of all generations were the same and adds the
tragic result that by such sinning Israel brought shame
or "reproach," *cherpah,* upon itself in the sight of the
heathen, for all the nations round about argued quite
correctly that the miseries that had befallen Israel
were the result of her infidelity to her God.

17. Faith finally becomes emboldened enough to
ask for what was contained in the prophecy of Jeremiah 29:10, "After seventy years are accomplished for
Babylon, I will visit you, and perform My good word
toward you, in causing you to return to this place."
Note that no righteousness that is inherent in himself
or in Israel is pleaded. Daniel asks merely to be heard
in his prayer and "his petitions for mercy," *tachanûnîm,* the latter term directly disavowing all semblance of personal worthiness. To this is added the
plea: "For the Lord's sake," which is more formal than
"for Thy sake." This phrase also disclaims merit. The
doctrine of justification by faith and its corollary, the
utter unworthiness of man, find clearest expression in
these verses.

The nub of the petition is finally reached: "Cause
Thy face to shine upon Thy sanctuary which is desolate." The expression "causing the face to shine," *ha'er
panîm,* means letting the face radiate benevolence and
good-will toward one, the surest token of being
well disposed toward him. Prayer is made first for the
"sanctuary," *miqdash,* "the holy place," because to
have a means of establishing communion with God is
more essential than to have a strong city. It is as
though Daniel would leave it to the Lord whatever He
might be pleased to add of material prosperity as long

as only the sanctuary is restored and free communion with God assured.

18, 19. **"O my God, incline Thine ear and hear; open Thine eyes and look upon our desolations and the city which is called after Thy name; for we do not lay our pleas for mercy before Thee because of our own righteousness but because of Thine abundant mercies. O Lord, do hear; O Lord, do forgive; O Lord, do hearken and act; do not delay—for Thine own sake, O my God, for Thy city and Thy people are called after Thy name."**

The plea around which the whole prayer is built has been uttered in proper humility and is based entirely upon the promise that God's Word had offered for this very situation. The eagerness with which Daniel desires what God holds in prospect finds expression in the manifold pleas to grant this petition as they are uttered in these verses. When men supplicate God earnestly, as is the case here, the matter they pray for lies near their heart. Plea follows closely upon plea with great intensity of feeling.

In addition, this section makes evident in a very particular way how God's saints are grounded in the Scriptures and prefer to pray in the language of the Scriptures. Though this fact is plainly apparent throughout the prayer, it nowhere appears more prominently than it does here. Some prayers of this sort are almost Scripture mosaics, being pieced together out of many Scripture passages, yet not in a dull or mechanical fashion but as fresh creations of the Spirit of inspiration who guides such men to incorporate familiar and inspired utterances into their present pleas. Compare the expression "incline thine ear and hear" with Isa. 37:17; or "behold our desolations" with Ps. 80:14; or "city called by Thy name" with Jer. 7:10-12. "Present our supplication" plainly rests on Jer. 36:7; "defer not" (v. 19) resembles Ps. 44:23; 74:10.

We may also refer to the prominent points of contact with Nehemiah's prayer, in which the circumstances were similar, at least to some extent. See how very directly v. 4 corresponds with Neh. 9:32; v. 9 with Neh. 9:17; v. 15 with Neh. 9:10. The very fact that Daniel lived and prayed almost a century before Nehemiah answers the question as to who was the borrower.

"Incline Thine ear" could be rendered "bend down Thine ear," the thought being that one who is on high stoops down to a lowly one in order to catch his weak requests. "Open Thine eyes" involves a certain boldness by implying that God was like unto a person who had failed to take note or had seemed to be asleep, cf., Ps. 44:23; Isa. 51:9. Yet no disrespect is involved. Faith is merely describing things as they seem to be.

Two matters may be offered as pleas for God to act: the fact that the city is called after God's name (the Hebrew says, "over which Thy name is called"), meaning she belongs to God, cf., II Sam 12:28; and secondly, the fact that this city of God is now a mass of "desolations." These considerations must bear weight with God as they would with man. But far stronger is the next plea: a specific disavowal of all personal worth or merit on Israel's part, i.e., "because of our own righteousness" (*Hebrew:* "righteousnesses," meaning, so and so many righteous deeds) and a pronounced falling back upon God's "abundant mercies." This feature of the prayer shows how clear the understanding of faith on the part of Old Testament saints was. Their conception was soundly evangelical: no natural, human capacity for good; no merit resulting from deeds well done; God's mercy our sole hope. This statement is classical and is on a par with passages such as Tit. 3:5; Eph. 2:8, 9; Rom. 3:28, etc.

We have translated the *Hifil* participle *mappîl* "lay," viz., "our pleas." The verb means "cause to fall." This thought does not seem to be borrowed from the idea of prostrating oneself before God in prayer. To express this idea the *Hithpael* form would have been used. The indicated evangelical character of the prayer is still further emphasized, for the term used to describe prayers is *tachanûnîm,* "pleas for mercy."

19. The prayer becomes more eager at this point. The repeated address to God and the detached petitions give evidence of this. Even here, among the cries for action ("hear, hearken, act, do not delay"), a petition for parden shows how deep and how honest the repentance is—"forgive." Whereas *A. V.* renders "hearken and *do,*" we believe that the *'aseh* is best translated "act." The pleas are expressed by means of the stronger form of the imperative, namely, with the ending *ah, shemaʻah, selachah, haqshibhah,* which is analogous to English forms like, "do hear," "do forgive," etc. As his last plea the prophet advances the thought embodied in the phrase "for Thine own sake, O my God," which surely applies equally to each of the five preceding pleas. This means: "May He do all these things because He has always been wont to do them."

Since critical objections are in some instances advanced with a surprising degree of thoroughness, it behooves us to examine one aspect of the case with greater deliberation. The whole section just treated, vv. 4-19, is rejected as an interpolation, and a very unskillful one at that. *Charles* has advanced seven major arguments against its integrity. We shall examine all of these.

First the evidence of the hand of an interpolator is said to appear in this, that these verses are "unnecessary repetitions of 9:3, 20sq." This being a mere claim, we are not in a position to tell where the repe-

titions lie and therefore cannot refute an argument
that is so vague in character.

It is next claimed that the conclusion of the
chapter "takes no account of the subject of the prayer,
which supplicates for forgiveness and deliverance."
This objection is meant in the sense that enlightenment
is given in the answer that follows the prayer, therefore the prayer should have been a prayer for enlightenment and not a prayer for forgiveness and
deliverance.

A basic error of approach invalidates this interpretation of the critic. He assumes without justification that the whole ninth chapter is practically an
explanation of Jeremiah's prophecy to the effect that
"the seventy years meant seventy weeks of years."
Since the chapter as a whole, here at least to the extent of about fifteen verses (vv. 4-19), does not agree
with what the critic aims to demonstrate, the critic
therefore eliminates the portion that does not fall into
line with his interpretation. However, the obvious and
very good sequence of thought running through the
chapter is this: Daniel sees that God's time of judgment is drawing to a close; he notes that the primary
purpose of God is as yet being achieved very imper-
fectly, in other words, men are not repenting of their
sins, and so he proceeds to lead his nation in the matter
of repentance by an exemplary penitential prayer; in
answer to his prayer he receives, not a mere interpretation of a phrase in Jeremiah's book, but an unfolding
of God's program for the ages, which is in effect this:
Not only am I, the Lord, going to fulfill this promise
but all my promises, and this is the pattern after which
they shall be fulfilled. In other words, what the critic
objects to as being a lack of logic in the chapter is an
astoundingly deep and rich logic.

It is next claimed that the prayer "contains clear
evidence that it was written by one who consciously

expressed himself as a resident of Palestine—and not in Babylon." This claim is supported by a reference to v. 7, where we read of those "that are near and that are far off in all the countries whither Thou hast driven them." In this reference those "that are near" are obviously the Jews in Palestine, it is said. That is not only not obvious, it is unsupported. Daniel could have spoken thus in Babylon with absolute propriety to indicate that he had in mind all Jews as we should say "far and near." Verse 16 is then quoted in further support of this contention, where we read: "Because for our sins and for the iniquities of our fathers Jerusalem and Thy people have become a reproach to all that are *round about us.*" The words italicized are said "to betray the hand of a resident in Judaea." That statement does not demand that the Jews be thought of as being a unit within Palestine. Since they are scattered in all lands, their enemies are naturally round about them everywhere. The critic confuses a possible meaning with the only meaning and has not read impartially.

When we next consider the objection that it is in these verses only (barring 9:2) where the name *Jahweh* is found, and that, therefore, this whole piece must be an interpolation, we reply that such criticism is based on the mechanical conception of the use of the divine name, against which we have protested time and again. Holy writers did not use the divine names in a wooden and a stereotyped manner and perhaps had one only in their vocabulary. Even before Mosaic times the heathen had various names for God, sometimes even the very Biblical names. The assumption that a writer could use or knew only one of these divine names makes these writers men of very limited ability. Daniel had heretofore used *Elohim* and not *Jahweh* because he was not thinking of God in terms of His covenant relation to His people Israel. This latter thought is, however, most prominent in his prayer and is expressly connoted by the name *Yahweh.* The critics fail again and again to see such fine propriety and are influenced by mechanical norms of judgment.

It is then pointed out that the prayer has no Aramaisms whereas they are frequently found in the rest of the book in the portions that are written in Hebrew. The explanation for this lack is very simple. As we have continually pointed out, this prayer is saturated with the prayer language of the Scriptures, especially that of the psalms and the prophets. Since this language is pure Hebrew, the Aramaic is in the very nature of the case not used which, by the way, is an excellent argument for the integrity of the prayer.

In the sixth place the prayer is said to ask "for the immediate advent of the kingdom" in vv. 17-19 whereas according to 8:26 Daniel is said to have known that it could not come for "many days," i.e., "till some distant future." In our interpretation of 8:26 we found that the phrase "many days" indicated that these words about the Old Testament Antichrist applied also to the New Testament Antichrist. But in vv. 17-19, as we saw above, Daniel is certainly not praying for the "immediate advent of the kingdom" but for the very thing that v. 2 had suggested on the basis of the words of Jeremiah, namely, the "accomplishing of the desolations of Jerusalem." Daniel prayed that Jerusalem might be restored after he had led his people in humbling themselves before their Lord in true penitence. The contradiction involved lies in the critic's interpretation and not in the words of the prophet as these are recorded.

It is lastly claimed that a comparison of the passage in question with the obvious parallels in Nehemiah and Baruch shows that these writers did not borrow from one another "but from existing liturgical forms, which each writer adapted more or less fully to his own requirements." Yet it is allowed that a comparison of Daniel with the others just referred to shows also that "the verses in Daniel agree word for word with those passages just mentioned." We fail to see how there can be agreement "word for word" between Daniel and other writers, and that it can yet be demonstrated that these writers have not borrowed one from another but "from existing liturgical forms." The evidence submitted leads to the following conclusions that we have advanced above: Daniel uttered this prayer and committed it to writing; Nehemiah and Ezra, also Baruch, to mention a noncanonical book, were acquainted with the prayer of their predecessor, used it, but used it in the free manner that is common to the Scriptures. This is then another of the arguments that backfires at those who use it to the disparagement of the text of the book as we have it.

d. *Gabriel's Reply*, v. 20-23

20, 21. And while I was yet speaking and praying and confessing my sin and the sin of my people Israel and laying my pleas for mercy before Yahweh, my God, in behalf of the holy hill of my God—I say, while I was yet speaking in prayer, the man Gabriel, whom I, in a state of utter exhaustion, had seen in the vision at the beginning touched me, at the time of the evening sacrifice.

From the manner in which Daniel describes what he was doing it appears that his prayer was not an inarticulate or confused feeling that found a kind of blind utterance. He did what he did with clear purpose and understanding. He was "speaking," for this prayer was too stirring a matter to be restrained within the bounds of unspoken prayer.

He further defines his prayer as being a "confessing." Knowing the potency of the sins that control certain ages or generations, and how practically all are swept along by the prevailing tendency, he confessed his own sin and that of his people all in one breath. He knew, too, that on this basis he had been building "pleas for mercy." These were with definite purpose laid before *Yahweh,* the true and merciful covenant God; and his prime objective was the sanctuary, i.e., "the holy hill" of his God. All this indicates that this sincere prayer, though it may be accompanied by a strong rush of feeling, sees very clearly and knows its objectives.

21. To emphasize the fact that the answer was given before the prayer had terminated, Daniel repeats, "While I was yet speaking in prayer." Though the Hebrew says "in *the* prayer" it here means in the prayer that I was then making. The expression "the man Gabriel," which is used in describing an angel, may seem very out of place until we note that "man," *'ish,* is in the Hebrew also used in the sense of a "retainer or servant." This indicates that the thought involved is that Gabriel is "a man of God," that is to say, His obedient servant. The term "Gabriel" means "man of God," but with this difference: the first root, *gébher,* means "man" as the strong one, and the second root, *'el,* means the "Strong God."

"The vision at the beginning" is the one mentioned in 8:16. That vision marked the beginning of Daniel's experience with Gabriel. Daniel cannot but recall how on that first occasion the seeing of the angel and the listening to his revelation were an exhausting experience as 8:18, 27 indicated. The contact with these supernatural disclosures was so taxing an experience that, when Gabriel appeared, Daniel was wearied to the point of falling into a deep sleep until (8:18) he was touched and strengthened by the angel. After the angel's interpretation had been added to the original vision, the effect produced upon Daniel was that he "fainted and was sick certain days" (8:27). It is not to be wondered at that physical reaction recurred at once, as soon as the angel appeared to Daniel a second time. Memory often suggests certain physical reactions in connection with significant experiences. It is, therefore, most natural to construe the phrase *mu'aph bî'aph*, "in a state of utter exhaustion," literally, "wearied in weariness," as a modier of "I" which is the subject of *ra'îthî*, "saw," even though its position puts its nearer to "he touched," *noghéa'*.

BDB renders the phrase "weary with weariness" and adds the explanation "utterly weary . . . (from winged flight, said of Gabriel)." Surely, such procedure is a case of first misconstruing and then ascribing inferior conceptions to the Biblical writer rather than checking the correctness of one's interpretation. The usual procedure is to make a few textual changes to arrive at the meaning "being sped in swift flight" (*Gordon*). Apart from the precarious business of tampering with a good text, such a view not only gives wings to an angel but supposes that he used them mightily to cover a vast distance from high heaven down to Babylonia, racing against time to arrive before Daniel's prayer was concluded. This confines blessed spirits to the laws of time and space in an unwarranted way. By having this phrase modify *battechillah*, "at the beginning," one would remove the only objection that could be raised against our interpretation. It would then read: "Whom I saw in the vision at the beginning [when I was] in a state of utter exhaustion." Only a desire to find fault with a Biblical book could object to so reasonable a rendering.

Mu'aph is, of course, a *Hofal* participle.

We feel, furthermore, that *noghéa'* should be translated "touched" even as it is in 8:18, though it is there construed with *le*. Yet Num. 4:15 construes the verb with '*el* in the sense of "touch." "The time of the evening sacrifice" was also very commonly the

time for prayer. The memorable incident recorded
here took place at this holy season—a matter that
Daniel feels is deserving of record. Ezra 9:5 and Ps.
141:2 suggest that this hour of the day was used for
prayer by many.

**22, 23. And he instructed me and spoke with
me and said: "Daniel, I am now come forth to grant
thee deep insight. At the beginning of thy pleas for
mercy a word went forth, and I am come to tell
thee; for thou art a man greatly beloved. Now consider the word and understand the vision."**

Whatever rare gifts Daniel may have received
from on high, gifts that were far superior to those of
the learned men of his time, he, nevertheless, knew
himself to be a man who knew nothing unless God enlightened him. So he rightly presents himself as a man
whom the angel "instructs," not, however, by some
enlightenment that is imparted internally as was the
case apparently in 2:19, in chapter 4, and in 5:17ff,
for he says: "And [he] spoke with me and said."
"Come forth" with reference to Gabriel fits the situation excellently, for in the Scriptures God's angels
are regularly represented as standing in His presence
and being delegated to perform their various tasks
(Heb. 1:14; Ps. 103:20; Dan. 7:10). Gabriel describes
the purpose of his coming as "to grant thee deep insight," for which the Hebrew says "to cause thee to
understand insight." Apparently, revelations that
probe deepest are about to be imparted.

23. All this is, however, vitally related to
Daniel's prayer. He was about to receive what he had
asked and could have anticipated. So God, who is more
ready to give than we are to ask, sent this messenger "at the beginning of his pleas for mercy." To
understand this in a manner befitting God and angels
we should do well to suppose that, as soon as he was sent,
the angel was present with Daniel, where he waited

till Daniel had finished his prayer and then "touched" him to secure his attention and, perhaps, to strengthen him. Angels are not hampered by the laws that condition the existence of material beings.

The angel informs Daniel that "a word went forth," *yatsa' dhabhar*, at the beginning of his prayer. This "word" was apparently that remarkable prophecy about to follow (v. 24-27), which is the actual revelation granted by God, and which "word" (again *dabhar*) Daniel is, at the close of the verse, asked to consider. The angel describes his mission thus: "And I am come to tell thee." The evident object of the telling is the "word" that went forth from God (so also *Kliefoth* and *Keil* and others). In order that Daniel may know what prompted God to grant this unusual favor he is informed that this was done for this reason: "For thou art a man greatly beloved," *chamûdhôth*. This form is derived from *chamûdhah*, "preciousness." A higher degree or potency of the idea is expressed by the plural; therefore, *"greatly beloved," (A. V.)*. This seems better than *BDB*, "Thou art a precious treasure." *K. W.* renders quite aptly, *wertgeschaetzte Persoenlichkeit*, "a highly esteemed personality." *Luther*, very appropriately: *lieb und wert*, "beloved and dear." With a double summons to give close heed the preamble to the angel's announcement comes to a conclusion.

e. *The Vision Proper, v. 24-27*

This is one of the grandest prophetic passages; and yet, if there ever was an exegetical crux, this is it. Jerome was already acquainted with nine interpretations. Some interpreters despair completely of arriving at any certainty in their exposition, being overawed by the multiplicity of existing interpretations. Others rather dogmatically align themselves with the one or the other type of interpretation and then proceed to espouse it and to fault those who differ from them. Neither of these two positions is wise. We believe that only at a more recent date—within the last century—has sound, constructive scholarship made substantial advances in interpreting this passage by avoiding the pitfalls of the past and by proceeding on the basis of sound and sober exegetical method. We hope to demonstrate this as we proceed.

It will make our approach much easier if we first summarize the three major constructions advanced by exegetes in expounding this passage.

1. The traditional, conservative approach, in vogue in the days of the Reformation and represented at a later date by such substantial exegetes as *Hengstenberg*, *Pusey*, and *Haevernick*, reckons the seventy weeks from some edict that permitted the restoration of the sanctuary or the holy city—about four edicts can be suggested as a starting point—and then concludes with the time of Christ, where a number of possibilities must again be reckoned with.

2. The critical school of interpreters has a starting point that is analogous to that advocated by the first group and usually prefers the earlier dates and does not continue the vision farther than to the time of the Maccabees and, as a rule, does not consider the passage prophetic but rather as a later account that is put into a form resembling prophecy. Operating basically also with the "year-week" idea, this class of commentators usually has too many years at its disposal, reckoning, as it does, in terms of Antiochus Epiphanes (†164 B. C.) and Onias, the high priest (murdered in 171 B. C.), and so usually advances the claim that the author of Daniel miscalculated. Those in the preceding class usually do not have a sufficient number of years. So it appears that the first-mentioned class regards the passage to be Messianic; the second class, as a rule, finds nothing Messianic in it.

3. The third class is designated by some as the

typical-Messianic, a misleading designation. These commentators, whose best exponents are *Kliefoth* and *Keil*, find distinct references to the Messiah in the passage but refuse to attempt an exact counting of years and state that the passage covers the whole period of time from Daniel *to the consummation of all things*. We hope to show that this position is exegetically sound; that it avoids all the difficulties attendant upon the customary calculations; and that it discerns this passage to be, as it most assuredly is, one of the grandest revelations made in the prophetic Word. Of course, this approach regards the numbers as symbolical, as numbers so often must be regarded in the Scriptures.

This is usually referred to as the passage of the "seventy weeks." This fact immediately suggests some connection with the "seventy years" mentioned in v. 2. Much depends on not confusing issues at the very outset. We must, therefore, examine with great care the various suggestions offered under this head. Surely, the situation is not this, that Jeremiah's seventy years (Jer. 25:11, 12; 29:10) were really offering little hope to the Jews of the exile because the restoration promised for this time was not deserving the name restoration. Therefore, Daniel, it is claimed, substitutes a different "seventy" for Jeremiah's "seventy"—"weeks" for "years"—and attaches to the period that he offers in prospect a truly substantial restoration.

Just as unsatisfactory is the approach which asserts that Daniel's prayer in this chapter was an inquiry about Jeremiah's seventy years, and that the vision unfolds more fully what Jeremiah's seventy years really implied. But it is a faulty assumption that Daniel had been inquiring about the seventy years. The fact of the matter is that Daniel understood clearly enough what Jeremiah meant but in his prayer first offered a very necessary confession in order to teach his people repentance. He then proceeded to pray for the basic essentials promised in Jeremiah's prophecy as we have already seen in examining the former section of this chapter.

Daniel is in reality being granted a favor in this vision of the seventy weeks, a favor he had not asked for, and in the larger favor there is embodied an assurance with reference to the matter that he had asked about in his prayer. It is as though God had said: "Yes, Daniel, as you rightly discern, the seventy years you read about in Jeremiah are at an end. There now begins another seventy within which I shall bring *all* My work to a successful termination; and this is the manner in which events shall follow upon one another in this remaining period. During this time that which you so earnestly desire above all things, the restoration of the sanctuary, shall also be fulfilled most gloriously." God then unfolds for Daniel the divine program for the ages.

It will clarify the issue if we state the case thus: the supposition involved is usually a dilemma which is not true to the facts of the case. It is claimed that there are only *two* possibilities: either a normal week of seven *days* or the unusual week of seven *years*. There are in reality three definite possibilities: *shabû'a* may mean 1) a "week"; it may mean 2) a "heptad" of time; it could perhaps mean 3) a "year-week," although this meaning is not supported by Biblical usage; in other words, *shabû'a* never has the meaning "year-week" in Biblical passages. Postbiblical usage on the part of the Jews may be cited in favor of this meaning, but that usage can serve only as an index of how in the days after Daniel's time the Jews were inclined to use the word on the strength of the traditional but wrong interpretation they put upon this passage. We hold that of the three possibilities just mentioned the second alone is exegetically sound and correct.

But how about these "year-weeks" which are so firmly entrenched in exegetical tradition? We are so sure that they are an erroneous conception that we refuse to continue the use of the term and, therefore, set at the head of this section of this chapter the caption, "the seventy *heptads*." We believe that it will not be a very difficult task to demonstrate that the interpretation "year-week" is untenable.

Let us show, first of all, the weakness of the arguments by which this misleading interpretation is supported. The word involved is *shabhû'a*, which usually means "week." Those commentators who advocate the idea of *year*-weeks do so because they cannot use *ordinary* weeks in their interpretation of this passage. Seventy weeks would be 490 days, a little more than a year. Nothing of moment that involves exactly 490 days is known to have transpired. Since a longer period of time is involved, the only alternative that seems to offer itself is this: if it is not a week of *days*, it must be a week of *years*. In support of this alternative interpreters usually point to 10:2, 3, where the same word for weeks occurs with the appositional word "days," *yamîm*, appended. This is thought to be in contrast to the term "weeks" occurring in the preceding chapter, for if the latter means "a week of days," the former must have meant a "week of years." But it requires no extensive argument to demonstrate that the word needed to give force to the argument (viz., "years") was imported from no valid source and injected into the passage. The logic involved is weak.

Pusey claims that God Himself had supplied the key to the passage in Daniel in Ezek. 4:5, 6 where, in a different connnection, the words appear, "each day for a year." But, surely, in our passage not even the word "day" occurs. Or would any interpreter venture to assert that the Ezekiel passage applies to all cases where the word "day" appears? Or would anyone dare to claim that this use of the word might be resorted to wherever one was minded to use it? That would certainly be an unwarranted license in the field of Scripture interpretation—a matter that is at variance with the usual sobriety of *Pusey*.

The argument advanced most frequently is the one which makes use of the idea of the sabbatical year, found in Lev. 25-26:33ff. *Montgomery* states the case thus: "The term (*shabhû'a*) is not used absolutely of years elsewhere in the Bible, although the seven-year periods culminating in a Sabbath (Lev. 25—26:33ff) would easily suggest such a use." *Farrar* seems to make the case more plausible: "The conception . . . would come to readers quite naturally, since *Shabbath* meant in Hebrew, not only the seventh day of the week, but the seventh year in each week of years." We doubt that the conception would come to readers "easily" or "quite naturally." *Shabbath* does happen to be used with reference to the seventh year, but the word under consideration is *shabû'a,* which is derived from an entirely different root. The logic employed here is weak and farfetched.

It means still less to us when it is pointed out that the so-called Book of Jubilees and the Mishna used the word in question in the sense of "year-weeks." The Bible language is evaluated according to the standard of the Bible and not by Jewish productions that were written five and more centuries later. This late meaning of the term would at the most indicate that the Jews had very likely begun rather early to put this meaning into the word. Though this would suggest a rather long tradition for such usage, tradition must be tested by those means which are the church's ancient safeguards; and only when such tradition can meet every legitimate test can it be accepted. Unfortunately, the tradition involved has no sure foundation.

What, then, is the basic feature of our interpretation? First of all a grammatical factor that must be evaluated carefully. It is the simple fact that *shabhû'a,* "week," regularly has as a plural the *feminine* form *shabhû'ôth,* "weeks." In this chapter (v. 24, 25, 26, 27) Daniel uses a different form, viz., *shabhu'îm, masculine* plural. True, in 10:2, 3 this form recurs, seemingly in reminiscence of our chapter, but with the word "days" appended, *shabhu'îm yamîm.* Now the singular means "a period of seven," "a heptad" (*BDB*) or *"Siebend"* (*K. W.*) or, as some prefer to state it, *"Siebenheit."* Since there is nothing in our chapter that indicates a "heptad of days" as a meaning for *shabhu'îm* or a "heptad of years," the only safe translation, if we do not want to resort to farfetched guesses, of this fundamental expression is seventy "heptads"— seventy "sevens"—seventy *Siebenheiten.* Now, since the week of creation, "seven" has always been the mark of divine work in the symbolism of numbers. "Seventy" contains seven multiplied by ten, which, being a round number, signifies perfection, completion. Therefore, "seventy heptads"—7x7x10—is the period in which the divine work of greatest moment is brought to perfection. There is nothing fantastic or unusual about this to the interpreter who has seen how frequently the symbolism of numbers plays a significant part in the Scriptures.

We are not disturbed by the objection of those who, like *Meinhold,* assert: "To assume [for this word] a measure of time which is entirely indefinite would open the door wide to the most arbitrary interpretations." It would, in fact, do nothing of the kind. It simply refuses to enter upon arithmetical calculations which are forced or unnatural in an attempt to find a figure arrived at beforehand in the historical pattern of dates. As the symbolical figure is indeterminate in the matter of an exact number of years, so must our interpretation be inasmuch as the revelation in terms of years was not what the passage intended.

Meinhold's other objection reasons thus: interpreting the numbers symbolically allows a substantial period to intervene between Christ's first coming and His return for judgment, an "impossible interpretation, because the entire Old Testament knows of only *one* appearance of Christ." He is correct about all the rest of the Old Testament. This passage happens to be an exception just as Rev. 20 stands alone—also a chapter in which the symbolical use of numbers is prominent—in its reference to the thousand years.

The other arguments that can be advanced in favor of our point of view will be presented as we proceed with the interpretation.

24. **"Seventy heptads are determined over thy people and over thy holy city**
> **to restrain the transgression**
>> **and to seal up sin**
>> **and to make reconciliation for iniquity;**
> **to bring in everlasting righteousness**
>> **and to seal up vision and prophecy**
>> **and to anoint the Most Holy."**

According to the interpretation given above, "seventy heptads" is designed to describe all future time from the days of Daniel unto the end of time, the time fixed in God's councils for perfectly achieving His holy work as 7x7x10 suggests symbolically—God's program for all ages. These seventy heptads are "determined," *nechtakh*, from *chatakh*, "to cut off or determine." God has fixed them according to His allwise providence "over" (*'al* also means "concerning or in reference to") the "people" and the "holy city," both of which are assigned to the prophet by the possessive pronoun "thy" because they were a matter of very deep concern to him. These seasons are determined inasmuch as God alone knows how much

time is required for God's people and the holy city, in
which their life and being center, to reach the goal
assigned them in God's purposes. Here, as so often
in prophecy, terms like God's "people" and God's "holy
city" broaden out to the point where they assume a
breadth of meaning like that found in the New
Testament (cf. Gal. 6:16).

The singular passive *nechtakh* either keeps "the
seventy heptads" as a retained object, or "the seventy
heptads" are regarded as a unit—a singular subject.

The six statements that follow cover the sum total
of the purposes of God with man. Besides, when they
are taken as a whole, and when the absolute character
of all of them is noted, they are seen actually to cover
the perfect consummation of the Messiah's work that
will be achieved when the second coming and the
judgment have transpired. We have arranged them
after the pattern indicated in the translation because
they really constitute three triads, the first triad summarizing the things that are to be removed, the second
triad those that are to be attained. The first statement
of each triad is again the summary of the three statements in its group. This arrangement is not original
with us.

In the first or negative group of this series the
initial purpose to be achieved is "to restrain transgression." This verb causes difficulty. It is written
kalle', ending in an *aleph*. The verb *kalla'* means "shut
up, restrain, withhold," but no *Piel* forms are found
elsewhere. But *kalle'* is plainly *Piel*. Consequently most
lexicographers suggest that this must be a *Piel* of
kallah, a verb ending in *h*. But this second verb means
"to make an end of, to finish." It is very true that these
two verbs rather frequently exchange forms as *G. K.*
72nn—rr amply indicates. Yet the safer course is to
let each verb retain its native sense if possible. So we
can retain the consonants and point them *likhlo'*, or

we can retain the vowel points of the Masoretic text and call this the only instance on record of the *Piel* of the verb with the intensive meaning "to restrain completely."

The object of this verb is "the transgression," *pésha'*, from the root meaning "to rebel," and so is a strong term for "sin." However, of the three used in the series, this word (*pesha'*) alone has the article. This seems to convey the idea that this object, being a strong term, is designed to cover all forms of sin. In other words, the vanquishing of sin, which is an objective of divine grace, is to be achieved to such an extent that sin is going to *come under control* and will no longer grow and flourish.

This negative group indicates two types of restraint in the next two terms, restraint first with reference to the sins of the wicked, secondly, with reference to the sins of God's saints. The first of these is "to seal up sin." The verb involved is again in dispute, *chathom*, the form being pointed *chathem*, signifying, as the marginal *Kerî* indicates, that these vowels should be used with *chathem*, *Hifil* infinitive from *thamam* and here signifying "complete" (*BDB*) or better *vollzaeh-lig machen* (*K. W.*)—"to make the number complete." The primary objection to the form found in the text is that in the same verse, in the second member of the second triad, the *same* verb occurs. Since the Hebrew text is so much more dependable than the average critic is willing to concede, we feel justified in retaining the received text except where the text is without a doubt corrupt.

"Sin" may be "sealed up," *chatham*. Two meanings of *chatham* are current. The one is to seal in the sense of affixing a seal for the purpose of attestation. The Greek version (*Theodotion*) construed the word thus. for it offers σφραγίσαι, which, according to New Testament usage, has this meaning (cf. John 3:33; 6:27).

And the Old Testament has the same usage of *chatham*, see I Kings 21:8; Esther 8:8.

A second use of the word is a bit more to the point in the present instance. Sealing may be done for the purpose of fastening so that a thing may be securely kept. This usage appears in Isa. 8:6: "seal up the teaching among My disciples," and also in Deut. 32: 34, where a thing sealed up among *Yahweh's* treasures is thought of as being preserved in the remembrance of *Yahweh*. In our passage this is to be done with the sin of the wicked: it is to be securely kept, locked up, as it were, and not permitted to roam about at random and do its nefarious work. This involves also that sin is on record as the condemnation of the evildoer.

The last negative achievement has reference to the sins of God's saints, for *kapper* is used with reference to sins committed involuntarily. It states: "And to make reconciliation for iniquity." *Kapper* does mean primarily "to cover," but when it is used with reference to sin or the sinner or the sanctuary, it always implies an effective covering that might be called "making atonement" or "making reconciliation." If any man's sins are treated thus they naturally lose all power of condemnation, and the sinner himself is reconciled to God. So in this phrase the godly man's "iniquity," *'awôn*, "guilt," is thought of as being adequately removed by the only effective way that the Scriptures know.

Summing up as far as sin is concerned, the things to be achieved by the time the world has run its allotted course is that sin's free and victorious advance is to be checked, the accumulated sins of the wicked are to be set safely aside as their record of condemnation whereas the guilt of the children of God is to be effectively cancelled.

God's works are never merely negative. A positive good is set up in place of the evil that has been disposed of. Summed up in a comprehensive statement, this good thing is described thus: "to bring in everlasting righteousness." This is without a doubt the imputed righteousness which is not naturally to be found among men, and so God must "bring in," *habhi'*, this much-sought treasure. It is not a thing of a moment only but lasts forever as all God's treasures do, it is "everlasting." Daniel speaks the language of St. Paul at this point. This righteousness, or the Messiah who accomplishes it, was the treasure above all treasures that was most eagerly longed for by the Old Testament saints.

This leads to the next point. Since this righteousness was, in the last analysis, the purpose of all vision and prophecy, after the end has been achieved, the means become outmoded, and so "to seal up vision and prophecy" follows. The same verb "to seal up" is used here that was employed earlier in the verse, *chatham*. The objective is the same: to dispose summarily and finally of a thing that deserves to be relegated to the category of achieved things. Why perpetuate visions if the purpose for which they are given is fully realized, and no higher achievement is possible? For "prophecy" we have the word "prophet," *nabhi'*; though the man is involved, it is primarily his *prophecy* that is under consideration. He, too, needs no longer to function after the things he prophesied are fully attained. The term could be translated, "the vision of the prophet"—hendiadys (*Charles*).

The last positive objective is "to anoint the Most Holy." Anointing—the verb is *mashach*—involves consecration even in the case of inanimate objects, but also implies, in the case of persons, that the gifts of the Spirit, which are symbolized by the oil, are being imparted, though not, of course, sacramentally. But in this instance the difficulty lies in the explanation of the term "the Most Holy," which should, perhaps, because of the absence of the article, be rendered "a Most Holy one." But we retain our rendering because the term may be used as a proper noun.

The original has *qôdesh qodashîm,* "(the) most holy," or "the holy of holies," to be very literal. Recent critics have a ready solution. They are convinced that the outside limit to which this prophecy can extend is the Maccabean Age. According to I Macc. 1:59 it was the altar of burnt offering that had suffered the most flagrant desecration. Its reconsecration is reported in I Macc. 4:44ff. (about the year 165 B. C.). This is what the "anointing of the Most Holy" refers to. But the assumption that "the Most Holy" must refer to this altar because in Exod. 29:37; 30:29; 40:10 it is referred to as a most holy thing, and because Lev. 8:11 reports that it was anointed, is a hasty conclusion. *Qôdesh qodashîm* is used with reference to the most holy place of the sanctuary as well as with reference to the sanctuary as such. More particularly it applies to the altars or to sacred vessels and utensils generally as well as to the priests' portion of sacrifices (Lev. 2:3, 10, etc.) and the like; and it is even used with reference to Aaron (I Chron. 23:13).

In the face of such manifold use to single out one item and to claim that it must be referred to specifically, fails to impress us, all the more so since the account in I Macc. does not mention an anointing at all, only the passage Lev. 8:11, which dates back to Moses' time, refers to this. In his longer account of the purifying of the Temple *Josephus* mentions no anointing. Evidence for this interpretation with reference to the altar is poorly substantiated.

Since this prophecy reaches to the point of New Testament ideals, the mere re-establishment of a visible and material thing which is in some sense designated as "most holy," is almost unworthy of such exalted prophecy, belonging, as it does, to the things that are classified as "beggarly elements" (Gal. 4:9). We

need not be thrown off the track by the rather strong
assertion of some that the expression *qódesh qodashîm*
positively cannot refer to a person, for it is used with
reference to Aaron (I Chron 23:13). But the thing
that was typified by that which was by pre-eminence
designated as "the most holy," viz., the most holy part
of the sanctuary, that, we say, might well be under
consideration. But the most holy with the ark of
the covenant typified the throne of God and so God's
dwelling among His people. That which was prefigured
by the symbol and realized in a measure in the old
covenant, that is here referred to as about to come to
a perfect realization. God will come near to them and
dwell in their midst in truth and verity, being a sun
for them (Rev. 21:23) and a wall of defense round
about them (Zech. 2:5). Revelation 21:3 correctly describes what we mean: "Behold the tabernacle of God
is with men, and He shall dwell with them"—a truth
that is realized to perfection only in the consummation
of all things. To expect too little from prophecy means
to find but little in it. The final goal of God in His
dealings with men is here realized, the thing that also
marks the conclusion of the book of Revelation. Since
the Temple must disappear (Rev. 21:22), "the Most
Holy One" is the Christ among His own.

In these six statements we have the sum of all
the good things that God promised to men perfectly
realized. With this verse we stand at the ultimate goal
of the history of the kingdom of God. What follows
will unfold the successive stages by which this goal is
realized and present the main features to be looked
for and borne in mind by the people of God. We have
just seen the essentials of God's program for all ages.

25.   **"But know thou and understand:**
From the going forth of the command to restore
and build Jerusalem

**Unto an Anointed One, a Prince, there will be
seven heptads.
And for sixty-two heptads she shall again be built
extensively, yet within fixed limits,
And that in distressful times."**

We first of all ask that it be noted that the
familiar versions differ radically from this translation on the matter of counting the groups of "heptads." *A.V.* is representative in that it renders: "Unto
Messiah the Prince shall be seven weeks and threescore
and two weeks." If that were the manner in which the
verse should be rendered, it would represent the
strangest mode of counting to be met with anywhere.
Those that have the conclusion of this period lead up
to the Messiah's first coming must render thus; and,
being under necessity of explaining this strange
method of saying "sixty-nine," viz., seven and sixty-
two, attempt to find an explanation for pointing to the
smaller section seven first and then adding the sixty-
two. Since nothing of moment happened after seven
year-weeks according to their mode of computation,
they offer unconvincing suggestions or else pass the
matter by as though men customarily spoke in such
stilted terms in place of using simple figures. We combine "seven heptads" with one clause to mark the
duration of the first major period and "sixty-two heptads" with the next clause to mark the second
major period.

Our difficulties keep increasing. Some writers add
the very fine caution that, when the difficulties are
manifestly many, there is every reason for believing
that the text has been transmitted with more than
usual care, and that, therefore, attempts at modifying
the text should not be resorted to without very good
reason—a caution that is always in place.

We shall endeavor to avoid going into too many

detailed discussions, but rapid progress is completely out of the question.

The words spoken by Gabriel remind Daniel of the fact that what follows calls for special attention—"know thou and understand." Especial attention must be given to discover the right starting point. Yet this need not cause us as much concern as it does some others because we shall indulge in no arithmetical *computations*. We understand the passage as speaking in terms of general seasons of divine activity—"heptads." The starting point is the momentous event when Cyrus allows captive Israel to return, a new experience in the annals of the nation. Heretofore captive, deported nations had perished by becoming absorbed by their captors or new neighbors. But not so Israel. This decree of Cyrus' is deemed so important that the Spirit of inspiration had it recorded twice verbatim, viz., II Chron. 36:22, 23 and Ezra 1:2, 3, 4. This was a "command"—*dabhar* sometimes has this meaning—and had as its objective "to restore and build Jerusalem."

Now it is true, the above command as reported by Chronicles and Ezra speaks in terms of the restoration of the *Temple*. Our passage speaks of *Jerusalem*. But the divergence is only a seeming one. From his heathen point of view, as a successful conqueror and empire builder, Cyrus prefers to follow a policy of appeasement, especially in the matter of not incurring the displeasure of any of the gods of the conquered nations, for he was a religious man. So he ordains that the Temple at Jerusalem is to be restored. Similar favors were shown to other cities and idols as inscriptions of Cyrus prove.* He could not have implied that the Temple alone should be restored and not the city, for where would the people have lived? All arguments to the effect that Cyrus was averse to the restoration of

---

*Barton, George A., *Archaeology and the Bible* (Philadelphia: 1937), p. 485.

Jerusalem and had not allowed it proceed on an un-warranted assumption. Would some 43,000 exiles have returned merely to build the Temple and have re-frained from building or from hoping to build their homes in Jerusalem? Quite unthinkable. But homes for 43,000 exiles in one place—and they settled mostly in one place—constitute a city.

On the other hand, the words of this vision of Daniel speak only about restoring and building Jeru-salem and say nothing specifically concerning the Temple. But that is readily understood on the basis of two facts. First of all, Daniel had been building his thoughts and his prayers on Jeremiah and his words relative to the "seventy years" (cf. v. 2). Both of the passages that mention the seventy years (Jer. 25:11, 12; 29:10) refer only to the outward aspects of the case: "Whole *land* shall be a desolation, and an aston-ishment"; and, "I will perform My good word toward you, in causing you to return to this place."

In the second place, the Daniel passage, on the whole, emphasizes the eternal and lasting verities (cf. v. 24) and therefore does not say much about a temple that is destined to become outmoded. In other words, the decree of Cyrus mentions the Temple and implies the city; the passage in Daniel mentions the city and implies the eternal temple. That Cyrus' decree and God's permission ran parallel is strongly asserted by Ezra 6:14.

Those who will not accept this decree of Cyrus' of the date 538 B. C. point to the other available decrees. In 517 B. C. Darius reaffirmed the decree of Cyrus with reference to the Temple (Ezra 6:1-12). Arta-xerxes issued the decree that allowed Ezra to lead the second contingent of captives back to Jerusalem (458 B. C.) as Ezra 7:11-26 records, providing, however, again only for the sanctuary. These commentators ac-cept as final that which is referred to in Neh. 2:7, 8, where Artaxerxes (445 B. C.) grants Nehemiah permission to get "timber to make beams for the gates of the castle which appertaineth to the house, and for the wall of the city, and for the house" of Nehemiah. To this end Artaxerxes gave Nehemiah letters. But to find in this episode, which is mentioned briefly in passing, and which almost eludes us at a casual reading, the important decree for the building of Jerusalem, which these commentators assert had not been issued before, quite taxes our credulity.

Hengstenberg is the strongest advocate of this position, but this happens to be one of the weakest causes that he ever espoused. Such unwarranted assertions are resorted to when men make computations on the bases of "year-weeks." In fact, the passage just quoted, Neh. 2:7, 8, does not contain the decree to build the city. It merely involves *permission* to secure the needed materials for "the gates of the castle" which was adjacent to the house, i.e., the Temple, no doubt, as well as for the wall of the city and for Nehemiah's house. To construe this to be a command for the restoration of the city as such disregards the plain meaning of words. Let no one suppose that we here have the correct *terminus a quo*, "starting point," for the "seventy heptads." Though it is the traditional one, this interpretation stands on a most precarious foundation. The decree of Cyrus in 538 B. C. is referred to by the *dabhar* "commandment," yet not so much as marking a year for computations as for marking a great event, a turning point in the fortunes of God's people.

This verse states the first of the details according to which the whole program of God shall unfold itself. There are, first of all, two constructive periods that stand out rather prominently. They are the matter that is discussed in this verse. The first of these two constructive periods is the one that culminates in the coming of an important personage, so important, in fact, that He needs merely to be mentioned by significant names of His, and one at once realizes who is referred to. After He has been brought upon the scene there follows a longer period, one that is quite a bit longer than the one that had to elapse before He could appear on earth as a factor to be reckoned with—even as sixty-two is quite a bit larger a figure than seven. That, by the way, is just about all the importance that is to be attached to the "sixty-two"—its relatively greater extent than that of the first constructive period. All attempts at computation are misleading. This word never intended to encourage calculations. But to get down to the details of this progression in God's program for the ages.

The first seven heptads, as we indicated, come to a culmination in one who is designated as "an Anointed One, a Prince." We hold that the reference to Christ is inescapable. The absence of the article in connection with both the nouns used is readily explained. The emphasis rests merely on the qualities described by the terms as such: this one has an anointing; He is of princely character. But to examine the first term, *Mashi(a)ch*, a bit more closely, we note from the lexicon (*BDB*) that two major uses of the word occur. In the first place it refers to the "king of Israel" in about twenty-eight passages. It then refers to the "high priest of Israel" in five passages. One instance of its use with reference to Cyrus appears, and one with reference to the patriarchs. Besides, there is our passage, which has to be evaluated according to the evidence available. Since the two outstanding uses are primarily under consideration, for a patriarch is not under consideration, and Cyrus cannot be referred to as we shall show in a moment, we must confine ourselves to these two primary uses. The reference to a king is covered by the second term, "a prince," *naghidh*. If, then, one term points definitely to the regal character of the personage expected, the other (*Mashi(a)ch*) would seem to point to his priestly office. This yields an interpretation that is entirely in harmony with another well-established fact, that the Messiah, i.e., of course, *Mashi(a)ch,* is known to have combined these two offices in one person as Ps. 110:4 and Zech. 6:13 show. The New Testament usage of "the Christ," i.e., the Anointed One, is built on this word and plainly refers to Jesus. This is the simplest meaning of the terms involved and lies on the surface but also establishes itself more and more firmly the deeper one probes into the case. Why, for example, should the coming of the Lord's Christ (*Mashi(a)ch*) not be marked in the program of God for the ages? That is one of the most significant junctures of history.

To be exact, the double expression used cannot be translated "the anointed prince" as some have rendered these words. *Haevernick* was the first to draw attention to this fact, and all grammarians support him in his contention. That eliminates the idea that only the princely side of His character and His work is considered, which seems to have been an attempt to cast doubt upon the Messianic character of the statement. The translation can be only "an Anointed One, a Prince," cf. *K. S.* 334θ.

Why should Cyrus be ruled out? Does he not meet all requirements? In Isa. 45:1 Cyrus is without a doubt called *mashi(a)ch*. Besides, no one would dispute the fact that he was a "prince." But two major difficulties arise. The first is the computation of the "seven heptads," the second is the computation of the "sixty-two heptads." Though *Koenig* (*Messianische Weissagungen*) speaks very positively throughout, that fact cannot compensate for the weakness of the argument involved. He claims that the word *dabhar,* which we render "command," should be rendered as plain "word." It then refers to Jer. 25:11-13; 29:10. Neither of these passages nor any of the others that *Meinhold* quotes can be shown to date from 587 B. C. In fact, a different date can be established for them. But only if the date 587 is used as a starting point can 49 years—seven year-weeks—be subtracted and the date of approximately 538, the time of the capture of Babylon by Cyrus, be arrived at.

So the first half of the construction used is open to serious question. When the following sixty-two year-weeks are computed from 538, that is to say, 538 minus 434, the result is 104 B. C., a date that happens to be wrong as far as Antiochus Epiphanes or any other character of the Maccabean age that could be utilized is concerned. This is generally admitted. But the conclusion drawn is unwarranted: Since the figures do not tally with the critic's computations, *Daniel* or the author of the book must be wrong; but not the *commentator* himself in his calculations.

If no more is said about the Messiah at this point, that need not disconcert us because His kingdom and His work are sometimes considered in prophecy, at other times His person, and here the time of His appearing for the inauguration of His work. There are many Messianic prophecies such as Isa. 2:1-4 in which the Messiah's times are described without specific mention of the Messiah. Daniel has other strong references to the Messiah, cf., 2:44, 45; 7:13, 14.

The next constructive era is that of the sixty-two heptads during which the outstanding achievement shall be that "she shall again be built." The subject of these two Hebrew verbs is quite naturally Jerusalem, which is mentioned earlier in the verse, for cities are usually construed as feminines. The two verbs, translated literally, would say: "She shall return, and she shall be built." But in such combinations *shubh* is regularly translated "again," see *BDB*, p. 998, 8. There is no good reason for departing from that common usage here. The "again" then refers to the idea that, whatever rebuilding may have been done after the captivity, it was in reality not a rebuilding that involved a restoration of the actual importance of the holy city. It was little more than an external development that fell far short of Jerusalem's ancient glories. What was the city that Herod had rebuilt in Christ's time? Nothing more than a Jewish town of doubtful spiritual importance. But after the Messiah came, the true Jerusalem was, indeed, going to be built again. In other words, there follows an era of constructive work during which, whether the building goes on rapidly or with some delay, building will go on to an extent that is sufficient to allow men to see that the kingdom—the spiritual Jerusalem—is progressing. The church, the true Zion, will always be making at least some progress in some fields. That can be asserted actually to have been characteristic of all time since Christ.

What about the expression "extensively, yet within fixed limits," usually, but inadequately, translated "with street and moat"? That describes very aptly the type of building that is characteristic of the church during this constructive era. On the one hand there is continual progress, a spreading out, a pioneering. New fields are taken in hand. This work may not always have been carried out with the eagerness that should characterize all the work of the church. Yet there was an extension.

On the other hand, the church did not attempt rash expansion: she was "yet within certain limits." She did not, as a rule, attempt more than she could carry through successfully. She did not venture rashly abroad and begin to cultivate fields that were far beyond her power to care for advantageously. When Paul

was making fine progress in Asia Minor he passed by
Mysia and Bithynia (Acts 16:6, 7) because the Spirit
would not suffer him to enter these, a restraint that
was, no doubt, occasioned by the fact that in God's
providence the time was not propitious to do mis-
sionary work in these countries. When God opens
doors, the church enters and builds. When God keeps
them shut, the church bides her time. Generally
speaking, in spite of all human shortcomings the
church has an ambitious program, yet she builds discreetly, wasting neither men nor resources.

One other important feature of the character of
that period of the church's work is deserving of attention in this connection and necessary for men to
know lest they be unduly surprised when they encounter it: such building is to go on "in distressful
times." The "and that" introducing this phrase is the
"and" explicative, which is frequently used in Hebrew, see *BDB,* p. 252b. The expression says literally
"in distress of times." We should say "in distressful
times." There will hardly be a period worthy of mention when there shall be peace and propitious circumstances and a condition in the affairs of this world that
is conducive to the spread of the gospel. Men shall
suffer; the church shall be a suffering church, *ecclesia
pressa.* That should alarm no one; God has foreseen
and foretold that the church is to expect such a state
of affairs. Building Jerusalem always means toil in
the midst of distressful surroundings. All in all, this is
a rather telling description of what we have always
encountered; and yet there was building.

The *A. V.* renders: "The street shall be built again
and the wall." *A. R. V.* translates: "It shall be built
again with street and moat." This last phrase is the
one that we have rendered "extensively, yet within
fixed limits." How can we fly in the face of so much
tradition, which really goes back to the Septuagint?

This traditional interpretation was but poorly established from the outset. *Rechobh* does sometimes mean
the "broad place" at the city gate but not the "street."
And *charuts,* though it allows various translations, is
conjectural in the translation "moat," for this is the
only passage where that meaning would occur. The
defence that is offered for the translation "street and
moat" goes even so far as to claim that street and
moat are "the characteristic thing for a city" (*Hengstenberg*). Yet, thinking soberly, all men must admit
that the things essential for a city are houses and
walls. Since the traditional rendering is not well established and makes poor sense, the expression must be
re-evaluated. *Rechobh* does come from the root that
means "broad" and *charuts* from the root "to sharpen
or decide." That can well lead to our translation,
and the two terms together constitute an adverbial
accusative.

26. **"And after the sixty-two heptads Messiah
shall be cut off, and there shall be nothing for Him;
and the people of a prince, namely, the one that is
to come, shall destroy the city and the sanctuary;
but his end shall be with a flood; and to the very end
war shall continue—destined desolations."**

After the general pattern for the whole period of
the seventy heptads has been outlined (v. 24) and the
two aspects of the constructive sixty-nine heptads have
been indicated (v. 25), more detailed attention is given
to the last heptad in v. 26, 27, more detailed, we suppose, because it is to be a time of suffering for which
particular guidance is needed.

Modern attempts to simplify problems by altering
the text are unsatisfactory. They have poor substantiation and testify to little more than the original perplexity of men like the translators of the Septuagint,
if they go back to this early version for support.

The startling thing, as far as "the Anointed One"

of the preceding verse is concerned, is that He "shall be cut off." We translated the word "the Anointed One" simply as "Messiah" because we believe that will be most readily understood. The original has no article; yet that does not mean any and all anointed ones but rather everything that goes under this name, that is to say, everything that is involved in His being the Messiah, not merely His life and His person. We can well understand how the interpreters who thought that they had here found a prophecy that pointed to the Christ felt that a most definite reference to the *death* of Christ was involved, for the verb used (*karath*) does frequently refer to a form of violent death. But even so, the parallel statement gives the best clue to what this first sentence means when it says, "And there shall be nothing belonging to Him." This could be translated, "There shall be none belonging to Him," as *A.R.V.* has rendered it. Very literally it reads: "And there shall not be for Him," the subject of the verb being understood. That implies that He shall not have that which normally might be expected to fall to his lot such as followers, influence, and the like. If that is the case, then the preceding statement must have involved his being "cut off" in the sense of losing all influence and prestige that He ever had before men. The season of the successful building of the city and the sanctuary is at an end. As far as the world is concerned, Messiah shall be a dead issue. His cause will seem to have failed. God foresees and foreknows that this shall be one of the developments to be expected at the end of the program that God predicts for the world. The details of what is involved in the Messiah's being cut off are explained in the rest of this and in the next verse.

The active agent that shall bring about this setback for the Messiah is "the people of a prince." There shall be many who shall manifest opposition. They

428   *Exposition of Daniel*

shall be under a rather efficient head. This head is
called "a prince." Since this word *nagidh* is often used
as a synonym of "king" (see *K. W.*), the only feature emphasized is his relatively high position. The
mashi(a)ch nagidh used in the preceding verse cannot
be referred to because the important feature of that
double expression was the first word, "Anointed One."
This "prince" has no anointing, no equipment with the
higher and nobler gifts of the Spirit. But Israel does
not appear to have been utterly in the dark as to who
was to be expected, for a participial modifier follows
with the article *habba'*, "the one that is to come." This
means that, according to the foreknowledge of God,
one is to be destined to appear on the scene for some
last destructive work. Since he is against Christ and
all that Christ stands for, we cannot but describe him
as the Antichrist. The New Testament actually uses
this name; the Old Testament reckons with the idea
as such.

The specific object of the destructive work of the
prince and his people is "the city and the sanctuary,"
ha'ir wehaqqódesh, the very things which the preceding verse said would be built during the sixty-two
heptads. These two terms naturally stress the visible
aspects of the kingdom of God in so far as they represent the visible institution called the church. These
shall be destroyed and with them the influence of the
Christ that we now still know and feel to be abroad
in the earth.

The situation might then be said to be analogous
to that which prevailed in the days of Elijah, when the
Old Testament church, at least in the Northern Kingdom, was brought so extremely low that the prophet
felt impelled to lament: "And I, even I only, am left;
and they seek my life to take it away," I Kings 19:14.
Yet there was more life in the people than even the
enlightened prophet had supposed, for there were still

the seven thousand that had not bowed the knee unto Baal. So whatever there shall be of true life among them that yet fear the Lord will be hid away and count for nothing. As the world regards matters, Messiah will be cut off.

A word by way of explanation may be in place. A parallel is offered in our day, which was not before this time available to throw light on how such a situation might develop. Russia has witnessed such a cutting off of Messiah. Who would have dreamed twenty-five years ago that the then at least numerically large Orthodox Church of Russia could be wiped out, at least as far as its visible forms of worship and its congregations were concerned? But we have since seen forces unleashed that have systematically inaugurated persecution, persecution on a scale which even the early Christian centuries had not heard of, persecution that has seemingly achieved its object. For Antichrist is very ruthless. That one illustration of what can be achieved may throw light upon this passage. Or witness Nazi ruthlessness against the church.

But already here we are at once apprised as to what the outcome with reference to this "prince" shall be: "his end shall be with a flood." The statement contains an allusion to that proverbial opponent of the church of God, Pharaoh. As he was swept away by the waters of the great flood of the Red Sea and perished with his host, so shall this great enemy of the latter days, who shall openly defy the Almighty, also perish. To be entirely accurate our translation should have said "*the* flood," for the article is used before the noun. This fact makes the allusion to the earlier incident all the more definite. The permissible conclusion is then, as God's people once praised His name at the overthrow of the tyrant that sought to work their destruction, so shall His people do in latter days.

Yet the times as such, as long as they last, shall

be grievous indeed: "and to the very end war shall continue—destined desolations." War, which is getting more and more to be the mark of the times, and which is growing increasingly more cruel, shall go on to "the very end." The original has only "the end," *qets,* but since the very last end is meant, the great day of judgment, we have ventured to insert "very." The last appositional statement, "destined desolations," points to the inevitable accompaniment of all wars, which in this last instance, it would appear, will be all the more in evidence. For we have witnessed the fact that, as time went on, the havoc wrought by war is more thoroughgoing than ever. It must be some such fact that this apposition seeks to bring out. Men are, therefore, not to be surprised at finding wars and desolations toward the end. In fact, these are one form of evil that dominates the last great "tribulation," to speak the language of the New Testament in this connection.

For this last expression the original has "the determined desolations," but this is apparently a kind of hendiadys, and the two words should be in the genitive relationship, a thing that is very readily possible in Hebrew, therefore: "the determined," that is, "that which is determined of desolations," which could again simply be rendered "destined desolations."

One interpretation with reference to this twenty-sixth verse should be mentioned. Some refer the *mashi(a)ch* to the High Priest Onias IV, a rather venerable man who was put to death ("cut off") by Andronicus, the governor appointed by Antiochus before his second Egyptian campaign, that is to say, before the pillaging of Jerusalem was taken in hand. The people of the prince are then the soldiers of Antiochus, and the situation that obtained in the days of the Seleucidae seems to be fully met. But this very serious chronological difficulty rules out this interpretation:

the date arrived at (538-434, 62 year-weeks, makes 104) is more than fifty years later than the time of Antiochus. It is again claimed that the author of the book of Daniel miscalculated; he did not know his dates in history. The event referred to is mentioned in II Macc. 4:33f.

Since they have the last week terminate with Christ, another school of interpreters sees in "the people of the prince" none other than the Romans, and the "prince" must be Titus and his hosts who invaded Jerusalem in 70 A. D. But according to that interpretation this verse suddenly jumps ahead of itself to the time of the destruction of Jerusalem and then in v. 27 comes back to the days shortly after Christ's death. The untenableness of this interpretation was shown above at length. The unusual jumping back and forth said to be found in the passage at this point makes this construction unsatisfactory.

27. **"And he shall make a covenant to prevail for the masses for one heptad: and in the midst of the heptad he shall cause the sacrifice and oblation to cease; and upon the wing of abominable idols shall the destroyer come; but only until the destined destruction has poured itself upon the destroyer."**

The preceding verse had told what would occur at the end of the sixty-two heptads only in a general, summary way. All the things mentioned would, therefore, fall within the last heptad, although the point of view is primarily this, that they would bring about the end of the sixty-two heptads. Only the wars and the desolations were described as prevailing unto the end. Now in the last verse the last heptad is taken in hand separately and described.

The person under consideration as making the covenant is naturally still the Antichrist. The verb *highbir* cannot have only the meaning "he shall con-

firm the covenant," for the verb involved is stronger.
We therefore translate: "He shall make a covenant to
prevail." The idea is that, as he seeks to take the place
of the Christ, so he shall imitate Him in some way. As
the Lord made a covenant with His own to give them
strong assurances as to what He would do, so Antichrist will inaugurate a covenant that shall prevail,
that is to say, compel the masses to accept it and to
abide by it. It shall not, therefore, be a gracious covenant of love as are the Lord's covenants, but a covenant
of terror, compulsion, and violence. We should liken it
to the manifestoes of the ungodly, whereby they seek
to gain the upper hand over the masses. Apparently
rabbim, "the masses," aptly describes those that constitute the following of the Antichrist. They are
numerous. That seems to be the most characteristic
thing that can be said about them. They may have
been compelled to submit. They are not the type of devoted followers that are found on the Lord's side.
Antichrist seems, therefore, to dominate the situation
because he has so many following him. But it is only
for the last "one heptad" that this domination prevails. Since it is still designated as a heptad, that
indicates that it is a time in which, after all, God's
influence still prevails, for heptads are seasons in
which a divine work is being carried on.

One particular climax of seeming success will be
granted the Antichrist when he "shall cause sacrifice
and oblation to cease," a thing that is to be expected
in "the midst of the heptad." The double expression,
"sacrifice and oblation," may well be construed to mean
"the totality of the cult" even as the expression occurs
elsewhere, cf., I Sam. 2:29; Ps. 40:7. Sacrifices as well
as other gifts that might be presented at the Temple in
Old Testament days were the very soul of all worship.
When they were made impossible, worship as such had
become impossible.

This presents the other side of the idea touched upon in the preceding verse. There the city and the sanctuary were said to be destined to destruction. Here that which was the chief function of the sanctuary is described as also being destined to be removed. That establishes our contention, made above, that all organized religion and worship as offered by the church of the Lord are to be overthrown when this prince has his day. All this is apparently not accomplished before the midst of the heptad because it shall take the prince a measure of time till he achieves his objective. It seems to be implied that, when it is achieved, this new situation shall prevail for the rest of that heptad. The church will not succeed in re-establishing these things. So we refer "worship and oblation" to those things that man offers to God and not to the sacrifice whose benefits Christ offers to man.

A new name is now used for the "prince": he is designated as the "destroyer," *meshomem,* participle from *shamam.* Since he actually achieves nothing constructive and aims to break down the existing world order, as manifestly certain forms of propaganda do in our day, this appears to be as appropriate a designation as can be found. From one point of view he may be a prince; more correctly he is described as a "destroyer." There must be something that lends impetus and sweep to his onward march and power to allow them to move on victoriously. This something is described by the term "wing" even as we use the phrase "coming on the wing." The strong wing on which the destroyer comes as a mighty bird is "abominable idols." Every movement must have something that is or takes the place of religion. If devotion to the true God is not the impelling motive, it must be devotion to something other than He. But this something that is substituted for Him then becomes an idol. Idols are frequently referred to by the term "abomination," *shiqquts.* We have, therefore, ventured to translate the plural simply as "abominable idols." The idol may be an objective like an earthly paradise achieved by man's unaided powers. It may be material comfort and success. It may be creature comforts made available in equal measure for all. It may be any one of the objectives that certain popular movements in our day proclaim loudly, or it may be new goals that are yet to be enunciated. Whatever good it is, it is apart from God and so furnishes the religious sanction and impetus for the movement. Such objectives and sanctions shall be so strong that on "the wing" of them "the destroyer" shall swoop along on his destructive enterprise.

We must reckon with the traditional rendering: "For the overspreading of abominations he shall make it desolate." So *A. V.* Luther's rendering shows how this translation was used. He follows the course taken by the Septuagint translators and translates *Greuel der Verwuestung,* for which the Greek has βδέλυγμα τῶν ἐρημώσεων. The difficulty becomes acute when the same Greek expression is found in Matt. 24:15, the familiar "the abomination of desolation." That refers definitely to something "standing in the holy place." And so one would seem to be compelled, on the very authority of Christ, so to modify the translation as to make clear a reference to some idol image set up in the Temple, either in the days of Antiochus Epiphanes, as some would have it, or in the days of the Romans, when their standards were set up in the holy place, as others would have it. However, as both *Keil* and *Kliefoth* have amply demonstrated, in Matt. 24:15 and the parallels Christ is not referring to this word of Daniel's but to another, which would be either Dan. 11:3 or 12:11.

We must yet refer to the many peculiar and unwarranted constructions that are put upon the word *kenaph,* i.e., "wing." The commentaries list these peculiar meanings. We refer to certain ones that stand out. Some very unnaturally give the word "wing" the meaning "edge" or "extremity" with the intent of having the word designate the edge of the brazen altar upon which a small image of Zeus was placed by Antiochus. *Meinhold* even claims that the expression "wing of the altar" readily suggests itself for "wing of idol abominations." That is plainly a case where the wish is father to the thought.

Another popular construction regards the term as referring to some extremity of the Temple and translates: "Upon the wing [i.e., of the Temple] shall be an abomination." So *Montgomery.* But the Hebrew does not happen to use the word *kanaph,* as we do the word "wing," with reference to a part of a building. *Koenig* (*Messianische Weissagungen*) finds himself in such difficulties at this point that he, conservative though he usually is about textual emendation, resorts to this favorite critical device and stops short with the first two letters of the word, which he then reads *ken* in the sense of a kind of "frame"—a word which he claims is ironically used for the altar of Zeus. What helpless guesses in order to substantiate a preconceived notion suggested by a misinterpretation!

The last statement brings the whole account to a well-rounded conclusion: "But only until the destined destruction has poured itself out upon the destroyer." So there is a destruction which, in the providence of God, is reserved for this destroyer of the church and so can be regarded as "destined," *wenecheratsah,* literally, "and that cut off" in the sense of "destined" or "determined." The noun *kalah* can, of course, mean "completion" but from that meaning merges over into that of "destruction." The greatest difficulty is that which grows out of regarding the word *'adh* as a preposition and making *kalah* its object. Far easier is the rendering which considers *'adh* as a conjunctive adverb, which together with *we* means "and until" in the sense of "but only until." The figure of a destruction "pouring itself" upon some victim is also a rather common one, and so easily understood.

The "destroyer" is naturally the same personage that was before designated by this title, but the participle is here written without the letter *m* as a prefix, a common enough feature of *Polel* participles. This statement about destruction coming upon the destroyer is in point of fact nothing more than a fuller statement of what was embodied in the words "but his end shall be with a flood" (v. 26). But it is very much in order to have so vital a matter stated twice so that there may be no doubt about the ultimate fate of the destroyer.

The questions may yet be raised: "Does this newer interpretation not display a weakness in that it ends on a negative note? Why did it not let the glorious consummation of Christ provide the marvelous and encouraging climax of all of God's work?" By way of answer we feel that that aspect of the case has been disposed of previously by Daniel when, for example, in 2:35, 44; 7:13, 14 he writes of the glorious victory that shall be Christ's in eternal power and glory. The consummation of Christ's work has, therefore, been set forth in all its glory. Will interpreters not be satisfied unless the same thing is said again and again? Besides, here the emphasis lay more on the overcoming of the forces of the adversary. If that closes our passage with emphasis, as it does, do we not have Christ's victory presented, as it were, in its negative character?

We would again call attention to the inferior close of the whole period which those interpreters arrive at who have the end of the sixty-ninth week marked by the death of Christ. All they have left for the last week and the consummation of the seventy year-weeks is an unimportant date seven years after Christ's death, when something so unimportant happened that the commentators are at a loss as to what they should point to. That interpretation runs out into sand. No one has yet advanced a halfway satisfactory answer as to why such a termination of a glorious work should be selected to close the computation.

On the other hand, we feel that the interpretation which we have offered, and which a number of very sober teachers of our church have freely accepted, by the very inner harmony that pervades it bears its chief recommendation upon its very face. Not the least of its merits is the fact that it refuses to make mathematical computations in matters of years of a type that the Scriptures nowhere encourage in any other passages.

Now that the entire eighth and ninth chapters have passed in review before us, it still remains to show the unusually close connection between the two on one particular score. We intimated in our interpretation of chapter eight that there were two statements that pointed to the fact that the Old Testament Antichrist, Antiochus Epiphanes, was a counterpart of the New Testament Antichrist. These statements were made in 8:17, 26. That was the factor that gave the eighth chapter a far-reaching scope, beyond what appeared on the surface. The ninth chapter gave us a rather comprehensive description of the New Testament Antichrist. The correspondence between the two can now be effectively traced and will be seen to involve a surprisingly large number of separate items. By thus making this comparison at this point the effect will be far stronger than if we had merely injected a remark here and there as we interpreted these two chapters.

To begin with, by making chapter nine the basis for the correspondence this Antichrist of the very last times is described as being "a prince" (9:26). When 8:9 uses the term "horn," the same result is attained, for "horn" typifies strength, and 8:10 indicates that it "waxed great," which again leads to the conclusion that a person who occupies a position of unusual prominence is involved.

When the appositional statement occurring in 9:26 describes this prince as "the one that is to come," we are reminded of the fact that we have statements in the earlier part of the book that lead us to expect this adversary of the church and her Lord. The only premonitions of this sort that are available are those that the eighth chapter offers by this type. Yet from the type the writer deduces that it will suffice to indicate that this oppressor is the one whose coming has been foretold.

Verse 26 asserts that he "shall destroy the city and the sanctuary," but we must admit that reference to Jerusalem as such is not available in chapter 8. But when we are there told (8:10, 13) that the horn shall wax great to the host of heaven and ultimately "trample on the host of heaven," that involves the same thing. One chapter emphasizes the destruction of the city, the other the destruction of its inhabitants. In the matter of the "sanctuary" the correspondence is more striking, in fact, chapter eight is a bit more explicit (v. 11) in that it tells how the "regular daily offerings are to be taken away, and the place of the sanctuary is to be cast down." Here, too, there is an almost literal agreement between these two chapters.

Again, when 9:26 speaks of the catastrophic overthrow that shall be the lot of this cruel tyrant in the words: "His end shall be with a flood," 8:25 says the same thing by the use of an entirely different figure: "He shall be broken without hand." In either case the divine agency is hinted at.

Even the unusual statement used in 9:27 to the

effect that "he shall make a covenant," which we interpreted to mean that he shall ape the Almighty and seek to bind himself and his followers together in their common enterprise by the use of something that resembles the sacred covenants that the Lord made with His own, we find that in 8:11 at least this feature reappears that he apes or tries to climb to the level of the Almighty. For there we read: "He magnified himself even to the Prince of the host." This, as we pointed out above, means that he sought to obtain divine honors.

Then there comes one of the most striking points of comparison. For 9:27 tells how "he shall cause sacrifices and oblations to cease," but 8:11 has it that he "took away the regular daily offerings" (a freer translation).

If the next section of v. 27 is correctly construed it is found to agree with 8:12 ("he shall cast truth to the ground"), for the words "upon the wing of abominable idols shall the destroyer come" meant, as we saw above, that the power that sweeps the destroyer along is the impetus that his ungodly religion gives to his undertakings. What is that other than to "cast truth to the ground" and to operate by means of lies and deceptions? With this agrees the rest of 8:12: "The host was given over together with the regular daily offerings for transgressions." For the transgression that takes the place of the true worship of God is the worst form of "transgression," idolatry.

Lastly there is a pronounced correspondence between the words (9:27) : "Only until the destined destruction has poured itself out upon the destroyer" will the adversary's success continue. That surely means that God has a day in store when the final reckoning shall take place. In the meantime the destroyer can do only what God allows. What is that other than 8:25: "He shall stand up against the Prince of princes, but he shall be broken without hand"?

We need to submit no more evidence to show how the two Antichrists agree in work, method, seeming success, and final overthrow. The correspondence is striking.

HOMILETICAL SUGGESTIONS

Surely, the section vv. 1-19, Daniel's prayer and confession, is a most excellent text for seasons of national confession or for times when God's visitations cause men to feel their sins and to bow in awe before Him. A selection of verses may be chosen for this purpose rather than the whole passage. But one could hardly find a better text to show how confession of sins is to be made and what pleas may be offered by penitent sinners at the throne of God.

As far as the Seventy Heptads proper are concerned, it must be admitted that skillful homiletical procedure is required to treat the text adequately. The chief difficulty will be that the traditional translation is about the most inadequate effort that ever came from the pen of the King James' translators. Even the American Standard Version leaves much to be desired though it gives at least the essential corrections in the margin If a preacher will skillfully present the *results* of careful exegetical procedure rather than the procedure as such he will surely have a remarkable text, which may profit his hearers greatly.

Because of its rich content the section vv. 24-27 could easily be broken up into three separate consecutive texts: v. 24, God's Great Objectives; v. 25, 26a, the Course of the History of the Church from Daniel to the End of Time; 26b, 27, God's Victory over Antichrist.

CHAPTER X

The Preparation For The Last Revelation

a. Daniel's Direct but Unintentional Preparation,
v. 1-3

The last three chapters of the book of Daniel contain the Last Revelation of Things to Come. Chapter ten is introductory; the body of this last revelation is found chiefly in chapter eleven; chapter twelve is a conclusion. Strictly speaking, we shall have to group as follows 10:1—11:1; then 11:2—12:4; lastly 12:5 to the end.

There is hardly anything in the Bible that is just like these chapters, especially like chapter eleven. The word, the vision, and minute prediction are combined in a manner that is found nowhere else in the Scriptures. To correspond with this feature there is an unusually extensive introduction to the chapter. Everything in chapter ten is preparatory to chapter eleven.

Our subheading above implies that Daniel did prepare himself for this last revelation though it was not his intention to make such a preparation.

1. In the third year of Cyrus, king of Persia, a word was revealed to Daniel, whose name is called Belteshazzar—and the word was true and involved great suffering—and he understood the word, and this understanding came to him by means of the vision.

A very specific date is again prefixed to this particular revelation. When God gave a word of truth to His prophets, they well knew the importance of such an experience and must have marked these days as red-letter days in their life. The day and the month of the year are stated in v. 4. This third year of Cyrus was significant. We know that in his first year Cyrus had issued his famous decree permitting the Jews to return to their homeland (Ezra 1:1-4). We know, furthermore, that not many had availed themselves of the privilege of returning. Also that the little band that had returned had encountered many disappointments and difficulties. Also, that the Samaritans had laid not a few obstacles in their way, especially at the Persian court (Ezra 4:4, 5) where they sought to block the way of the Jews by wicked machinations. It is essential to understand this situation in order to understand this entire revelation.

It is objected that the title Cyrus, "king of Persia," is not according to the earlier usage of the monuments and the documents available but savors of later times and the usage of the Greeks. Since the monumental evidence is fragmentary, the documentary, too, we are hardly in a position to make definite assertions about what the usage was in those days. Since Cyrus was king of Persia, it does not seem unreasonable to think that the Spirit of inspiration should have allowed Daniel to use a term which would fit the later usage. Besides, Daniel is not writing for Persians in their idiom but for Jews in theirs.

Those who have examined the available evidence (cf., e.g., Driver) as this is found primarily on contract tablets that have been discovered note that out of 1,560 contracts only one referred to the Persian kings and used the title employed in this chapter. In any case, that will be conceded to indicate the usage in question as being exceptional. Even so, that applies only to usage among the Persians or Babylonians. When the exceptional is found in Babylonian contract tablets, it is not at once attacked as being spurious. Why should the Biblical writer not be permitted to use the exceptional construction, especially when he is writing in a different language and in the peculiar idiom of that language? We fail to see the fairness of this kind of treatment of the writers of sacred Scriptures.

Both *A. V.* and *Luther* prefer to render "a thing" was revealed. This translation of the word *dabhar* is, of course, possible. But to label all of the revelation given in chapter eleven a "thing" is hardly as suitable as to use the broader term "word."

The relative clause, "whose name is called Belteshazzar," is not merely an indication of the somewhat ponderous style of the chapter, as some label it, nor a merely habitual designation, but a reminder, as *Keil* suggests, that, after seventy-two years have elapsed since Daniel came to court as the result of a deportation, it is this same Daniel—surnamed Belteshazzar— who functions in this next revelation.

Since the revelation is so very unusual and the prediction so very exact, they might well tax belief; Daniel therefore adds the assurance: "And the word was true." To this he appends the general tenor of the revelation: it "involved great suffering." This last statement has been so variously translated as almost to pass belief. *A. V.* translates, "The time appointed was long." *A. R. V.* renders, "Even a great warfare." *Luther: und von grossen Sachen.* The Hebrew is *tsabha' ghadhol.* This could mean "great war or warfare." But since war involves suffering, the word gets to mean "suffering," and this is, in the last analysis, the best rendering. The suffering of the people of God is the burden of practically the entire revelation—the things they must suffer at the hands of Antichrist. That is at least far more to the point than the meaning "strain" on the prophet, which is finding quite a bit of favor among modern interpreters.

The next clause is also difficult to interpret. Our rendering is as good as any: "And he understood the word, and this understanding came to him by means of the vision." This at least adds the substantial thought that Daniel was not perplexed beyond measure by what he heard and utterly at a loss to discern what had been told him. 12:8 is not at variance with this interpretation, for this latter passage does not refer to the preceding vision as a whole but to the remark immediately preceding it. Since the verb "to understand" is followed by the noun "understanding," we feel that the connection is readily established in English by translating "this understanding." We take the *beth* in *bammar'eh* to be the *beth instrumentalis*: "by means of the vision," so that the vision that appeared made the word of revelation clear to Daniel—a simple enough statement.

2, 3. In those days I, Daniel, continued in mourning for three full weeks. I ate none of the more attractive foods; meat and wine did not cross my lips; I abstained completely from anointing myself until three full weeks were finished.

Neither the cause nor the purpose of this mourning, coupled with fasting, is mentioned. To assert categorically that Daniel was preparing himself to receive a vision is contrary to what the Scriptures tell us regarding visions. Visions are not brought about by personal preparation. Men could not bring about a state of mind that would be favorable for the Lord to impart a revelation to them. It was not for the prophets to determine whether they would on occasion speak a word or not. They did not attempt to persuade the Lord to give what He would otherwise have been reluctant to give. They do not go about begging for revelations. II Kings 3:15 is not an exception to this rule, for the legitimate ruler of Judah had made a legitimate request of God's prophet, which that prophet, according to God's appointment, was bound to answer. Before he answered, however, he sought to have the bad flavor of the conversation with the unbelieving king of Israel removed from his consciousness and so asked for a minstrel to relieve his mind by soothing music.

Much more plausible is the supposition that on the one hand Daniel grieved over Israel's sufferings and adversities, which were many, in this third year of Cyrus; on the other that he prayed God's mercy upon this His afflicted people. After the analogy of chapter nine we also assume that he grieved over his own sins and shortcomings and saw in them, in part at least, a cause of Israel's adversity. Since a term of three full weeks is spent on his prayers and his mourning, that shows with what faith and persistence he addressed himself to this holy task. Prayer for the church of God was engaged in very assiduously by some of these old saints of God. They believed in the efficacy of prayer and prayed as though everything depended on their prayer. A fine exemplary spirit.

The verb "to be" with the participle is well rendered by *Gordon*, "continued in mourning."

3.   To his prayer and his penitence Daniel added disciplinary ascetic measures that were to be of help in bringing about the requisite spiritual frame of mind. He abstained from at least the more attractive forms of food. *Léchem chamudoth* would be "bread of delight" which means "the more attractive foods" according to the common use of the word "bread." At court, where Daniel still was, he could, no doubt, have found as appetizing a collection of dishes as a man could wish. "Meat and wine" are generally partaken of on days of joy and feasting. To these is added the anointing of the body, cf., Gen. 27:25; Isa. 22:13; Amos 6:6. Daniel made his body feel as his soul felt. This harmony of the external with the internal state was conducive to earnest prayer.

This three weeks' period of mourning included the Passover season (see v. 4). But the unleavened bread of the Feast of Unleavened Bread was called "bread of affliction" (Deut. 16:3). We need not suppose that the expression "the more attractive foods" is in direct contrast with the bread of affliction, for the Passover bread itself was the only item of that festival season that was indicative of self-denial of some sort. Daniel denied himself all forms of food and drink as well as the customary anointing.

The expression used in v. 2 and in v. 3, "three full weeks," requires a bit of examination. For "weeks" we have the word *shabhu'im*, which is otherwise found only in chapter nine. Usually, as we remarked there, the word used for "weeks" has the plural *shabhu'oth*. It appears to us that the recollection of the preceding chapter at this point produced this masculine plural for the word "weeks" by way of exception to indicate that the prophet observed the three heptads of mourning to recall God's heptads of working. The word "days" used in the original, in this connection "three weeks of days," is used in apposition to the word "weeks," yielding the sense "three full weeks." For this use compare *G. K.* 131d; also *K. S.* 333e. The argument that the expression "weeks of days" is in contrast with the "weeks of years" or "year-weeks" used in the preceding chapter is unwarranted. What is there that makes "days" a contrast to "years" without any further indication of what the contrast should be?

b. The Vision of the Glorious Angel, v. 4-9

4-6. And on the twenty-fourth day of the first month, when I was by the side of the great river which is the Tigris, I lifted up my eyes and looked, and, lo, there was a man clothed in fine linen garments; his loins were girded with gold of Uphaz; his body looked like the Tarshish stone; his face flashed like lightning; his eyes were like flaming torches; and his arms and his feet resembled pol-

**ished bronze; and the sound of his words was like
a roaring.**

Most plausible is the assumption that the sequence of the days of the month was as follows: the
first two were festival days, the days of the new moon
(cf., I Sam. 20:18, 19, 34) ; then followed Daniel's
twenty-one days of mourning; then on the twenty-
fourth day of the month came the vision. This first
month is commonly called Nisan. The fourteenth day
was the Passover, then followed seven days of unleavened bread. The nearness of the festival days of
the Passover, which were to commemorate Israel's deliverance, and the fact that under the present circumstances Israel was far from delivered—all this may
have suggested to Daniel to choose this season for his
"mourning."

How Daniel came to be by the side of the great
river, "the Tigris," is more than we are able to determine. To say that this locality enabled him to look
out across the desert to the land of his fathers is hardly
true, for the Euphrates is the river that marks the
eastern boundary of that great intervening desert, not
the Tigris, which is here, as in Gen. 2:14, called the
Hiddekel. To assert that Daniel had gone to this river
to exhort bands of Jews to return to the Holy Land,
now that the decree of Cyrus had paved the way for
them, is as a pure guess. Business may have taken
him to this point in company with others (see v. 7).
He recalls distinctly just where he was when the
vision came.

The textual change that deletes the word "Tigris"
because, it is thought, Daniel should have been at the
Euphrates, is rather arbitrary.

5. There was no preliminary indication of any
sort that a vision was about to appear to Daniel. He
just lifts up his eyes, and lo, there stands "a man."
The *'ech(ch)adh* ("one") after the word "man" is

hardly more than the indefinite article (*K. S.* 291d).
Much has been written about the identity of this
"man." One rather elaborate attempt makes him the
angel Gabriel, partly because in 8:16 it is the angel
Gabriel who helps Daniel to understand the vision, and
in this chapter this "man" leads Daniel to understand
the vision. Another attempt centers on the effort to
identify this man, who is apparently an angel, with
the Angel of the Lord, the Logos, the Messiah. This
conclusion is based on the fact that the description
that is given of the Lord in Rev. 1:13-15 corresponds,
at least as far as the appearance is concerned, almost
to the letter with the description given here. But it
must be remembered that it pleased the Lord as well
as His angels to appear in a form like unto human
beings so as not to frighten the children of men too
greatly. Both these visions of men (viz., in Dan. and
in Rev.) were, indeed, much alike as befits heavenly
beings. Yet when these two passages are compared,
one notes that they have distinct points of difference.
Furthermore, no divine work or quality is ascribed
to the "man" in this chapter. It also seems very strange
that Michael (v. 13) "came to help" him. Though
angels and men may share in God's work, it is never
indicated that they help Him.

All this leads to the conclusion that the personage
involved is one of the mighty angels of God, neither
Gabriel nor the Angel of the Lord but one who is on
a par with other mighty angels like Michael. His marvelous appearance and rare beauty agree with this view.

The fine linen garments (*baddim*) were regularly
worn by priests (Exod. 28:42), and their color was
usually white, symbolizing purity. A girdle of gold was
a cloth heavy with gold embroidery or ornamentation,
and such a garment was a mark of high station (cf.,
I Macc. 14:43). It may be that "gold of Uphaz" is the
same as gold of Ophir, for Uphaz is referred to only in

Jer. 10:9 besides this passage, and Uphaz has not been identified.

6. The description now concentrates on the person of this powerful heavenly messenger. Whatever part of his body is visible has the appearance of the Tarshish stone, for so the name of the stone is transliterated. No one has as yet adequately identified it. *K. W.* quotes with approval a reference from P. Haupt who regards this as a crystal of cinnabar from the quicksilver mines of Almaden, north of Cordova in Spain. Considering the fact that Tarshish is the name of the old town of Tartessus in Spain, this suggestion has, perhaps, as much merit as any though suggestions made by lexicographers include the beryl, turquoise, topaz, and many others. A gem of rare beauty and color is, no doubt, meant.

The face of this angel had the greatest brilliance: it flashed like lightning. And all men know what a startling brilliance lightning has. A great light likewise flamed forth from his eyes, for they were "like flaming torches." That means, of course, burning with the bright light that torches display by night. "His arms and his feet" likewise had a beauty and a glow all their own, being like "polished bronze." The word *margeloth* does mean the region of the feet. But since it is connected to "arms" by "and" it must be that, by metonymy, the feet themselves are meant. For we should the region of the feet glow as the arms do?

Add to this vision of astounding beauty one sound and the picture is complete—"the sound of his words"— for that is like a roaring. *Hamon* may be the roar of a great crowd or the roar of great waters. The latter seems to be the better comparison. There is no denying the fact that this description makes the impression of unusual beauty, brilliance, and heavenly glory and pictures a being that is far above the level of a man though he looked like a man in general appearance.

7. But I, Daniel, alone beheld the vision; but the men who were with me did not see the vision, but great trembling took hold on them, and they fled and hid themselves.

God may reveal Himself ever so clearly, the dullness of the mortal senses, blunted by sin, is such that man may not see what God makes manifest. If the perceptions are sharpened by grace, God's revelations may shine through into man's perception. Daniel was such a man. His companions, with whom he happened to be at the time, had no such finer spiritual sensibility. So he alone beheld the things that were revealed. But the others could sense that an unusual manifestation of some sort was taking place, and that this manifestation came from a higher and better world. This realization caused "great trembling" and led them to flee and to hide themselves. Man may feel the effects of his sinfulness without even being able to discern that the trouble with him is his sin. An analogous case is that of Paul and his companions on the Damascus road (Acts 9:3ff). The companions were able to hear a sound but not to distinguish the words spoken. Daniel's companions, whether they were Israelite or Gentile, seem even duller of spirit.

The Hebrew construction uses a kind of gerundive at this point, saying, "They fled, hiding themselves," "hiding" being an infinitive. That may be translated, "They fled to hide themselves" although the more literal rendering would have been, "They attempted to flee by hiding," the *beth* before the infinitive being a *beth* of sphere (*K. S.* 402s).

8. So I was left alone, and I beheld this great vision, but there was no strength left in me; whatever healthy color I had was utterly destroyed, and I retained no strength at all.

Being left alone, Daniel's first impression is that he is being honored by God to see a "great vision."

Even if Daniel had never heard a word he could well have remembered the exceeding glory of the vision that showed him this heavenly being. But even he was greatly affected by what he saw, for it somehow affects grievously those who are marked by sin when they come into direct contact with that which emanates from the holy God. Many of God's saints of the Old and the New Covenant expected death when such a manifestation came to them. Never did they perceive more truly and correctly than when such feelings took possession of them.

Daniel describes in detail what his reactions to the great vision were. Not only the eighth and the ninth verses make this evident, but throughout the rest of the chapter there are instances of weakness and the removal of this weakness. It must have been in part the directness of the revelation that came to him that affected him so strongly. Dreams and visions veil, as it were, the bright light that comes from on high. The direct word of God is more potent and far harder for the human spirit to endure. Therefore there also had to be successive impartations of strength to carry God's servant through the experience that he was undergoing.

First of all a feeling of utter impotence overpowered Daniel: "there was no strength left in me." On a similar occasion Isaiah felt his *uncleanness* (Isa. 6:5). Daniel felt all strength departing from him. He realized besides that whatever appearance of health and of strength he may have had had left him. The Hebrew uses an almost untranslatable mode of statement which reads thus: "My glory or healthy, glowing color was changed upon me unto destruction." That is much more intense than becoming as pale as a ghost. It would have involved serious impairment of health had not the Almighty neutralized these disastrous effects. Since the feeling of overpowering weakness was so strong upon him, he reiterates in another form the thought expressed a moment before by saying, "I retained no strength at all." It must be due to the fact that there are not many who could endure revelations of this sort and survive that God does not grant them to many. Even a spiritual giant such as Daniel was almost perished under the impact of these divine revelations. Very few have a very deep sense of the damage that sin has actually done to them, and how utterly devastating its effects really are.

The account of Daniel's reaction continues:

9.   Then I heard the sound of His words, and as I heard the sound of his words I swooned completely away upon my face, and my face stayed toward the ground.

Until this moment the prophet had been at least conscious, but he had heard no word. Even as he begins to hear the voice of this heavenly apparition he does not seem to be able at once to distinguish individual words, for he twice uses the expression "sound (*qol*, i.e., 'voice') of his words." The words themselves, it would appear, could not begin to convey meaning as yet. In fact, the immediate effect of them was that "he swooned completely away" upon his face. The verb used is the same as that found in 8:18, and though it originally means to "fall into a deep sleep," yet here the meaning is, no doubt, rather that of utterly losing consciousness. The double use of the expression "upon my face" appears to convey the distinction that he first fell upon his face and then, being as completely overcome as he was, remained utterly prostrate in this position. So complete was the fainting away. We have, therefore, ventured to translate, "And my face *stayed* toward the ground," though the Hebrew says merely, "And my face toward the ground."

Though the events recorded are not of far-reaching moment they yet convey, perhaps better than anything else could, the sense of the frailty of man in the presence of the holiness and the greatness of God, and, it would appear, it was for this very reason that God inspired Daniel to make a record of these less important details.

c. *The Initial Announcement of the Angel's Purpose and the Strengthening of Daniel, v. 10-17*

10, 11. And behold, a hand touched me, rousing me and raising me up on my knees and my hands. And he said unto me: "Daniel, greatly beloved, mark the words that I am telling thee and stand in the place, for I have just been sent to thee." And when he said this to me, I stood there trembling.

God imparts strength to this servant of His in such a way that His personal interest in him is very apparent. Daniel seems capable of detecting the presence of only the hand. The person behind the hand is not discerned. It may well have been the hand of the angel who stood before him. But Daniel, having fallen to the ground, was unable to sense more than the touch of the hand.

The next step, the result of the touch, is stated with a rather pregnant expression: "He shook me upon my knees and my hands." We believe that we have come fairly close to the import of this statement by using the double participle "rousing and raising me." We do not believe that the *A. R. V.m.* gives the correct impression when it renders "set me tottering." The impression that is to be conveyed is that the process of strengthening the man of God was one of consecutive steps, each bringing him a bit nearer to the point of being fully capable of receiving the needed instruction. Even as he collapsed by successive stages, so by successive stages he is restored. Indeed, his weakness must have been very great since it required three contacts to build him up again. Daniel must have presented a rather pitiable spectacle as he crouched on hands and knees, incapable for the present of assuming an upright posture. But Daniel is not trying to make himself the hero in this experience.

Textual changes that are made because of the unsatisfactory translation "set me tottering" are made unnecessary by the better translation.

11.   Daniel is now able to distinguish at least individual words and to catch the sense of these words. The words too, for the present, have the aim of enabling Daniel to discern the major element of the revelation. As a result these words are of an encouraging sort. Daniel is made aware of the fact that he is "dearly beloved." When the Hebrew says "man of delights" it means that God delights greatly in this servant of His; that is the force of the plural. *Luther* seems to have caught the spirit of the phrase with his inimitable *Du lieber Daniel.* There is a part that the prophet can take in the course of this revelation: he can "mark the words," that is to say, use all powers of attention and concentration.

The command to stand in his place apparently imparted the strength needed for such a step, for the word of God is here, too, an efficacious thing. That he may at the same time understand what manner of being he is dealing with he is told: "For I have just been sent to thee." This is a messenger from God on high as Daniel had felt from the outset. That dim feeling now becomes a matter of clear-cut consciousness. The prophet does as he is bidden, but, for the time being, the feeling of weakness and human sinfulness is still so strong upon him that he can do no more than to stand there trembling. Surely, the prophet did not present a very heroic picture. But his concern is rather to state the objective truth, not to magnify himself.

Note that a verb like *bin* is construed with a *beth.*

12. **And he said to me: "Be not afraid, Daniel, for from the very first day when thou didst set thy heart upon understanding and upon humbling thyself before thy God, thy words were heard; and I am now here to answer thy words."**

The penitent man's fears of God have no basis in fact. God is always kindly disposed toward him. Man is by nature so suspicious of God that he will not readily cease mistrusting Him. Proof is given the man Daniel that he need have no fear of God: God had given prompt heed to his prayers and had sent an emissary. Daniel's mourning and fasting—referred to in verses 2 and 3—are now explained in greater detail. They involved the fact that Daniel had set his heart upon understanding and upon humbling himself before his God. All the things that he did not understand sufficiently, as these are related in chapters eight and nine, were still weighing heavily upon his mind, and he did not deem it a curiosity that would be displeasing in the sight of God to pray for an understanding of what was still puzzling him. Note the import of 8:27. But, as we intimated earlier in this chapter, Daniel also humbled himself before his God, for he knew that any man living in a given age shares in the sins of that age and is responsible for the evils that may have been done by him and by the remainder of the people of God.

But the chief feature of the comfort granted to Daniel is this, that from the very moment his prayers were uttered his "words were heard." It is even true, as the Scriptures say, that He hears before we utter our prayer. *Fausset* suggests very properly: "If in our prayers amidst long protracted sorrows we believed God's angel is on his way to us, what consolation it would give us!" The angel implies that, when God heard these words of Daniel, He promptly dispatched His messenger. But the angel says: "I am now here to answer thy prayers." That involves that it has taken him until this time to arrive in Daniel's immediate presence. He then, of necessity, owes Daniel an explanation as to why he came to him no sooner if he was sent forth immediately when the prayer was made. That explanation is given in the next verse.

13.   **"But the prince of the kingdom of Persia took his stand over against me for twenty-one days. But, lo, Michael, one of the princes of the first order, came to help me; and I was left there by the side of the kings of Persia."**

Daniel's prayer had been concerned with the kingdom of Persia. We must refer to the matter discussed in the introduction to this chapter. Daniel's prayer must have made reference to the distressed state of his people and to the wretched plight which had been brought about by the opposition of the Samaritans at the Persian court, where they had slandered the Jews (cf., Ezra 4) and had caused them grievous trouble. The heavenly messenger had apparently been sent to correct this misfortune and to remove the evil influence that was at work against the people of God. But strangely, at court the heavenly helper does not encounter Samaritans or Samaritan intrigues but "the prince of the kingdom of Persia." We are afforded a glimpse behind the scenes of world history. For in the realm of history, too, more is intended than meets the eye. There are powers at work of which some never have a conception. Isa. 24:21 may refer to the same subject.

Who is this "prince of the kingdom of Persia"? Conflicting and confusing answers are given. We may dismiss at once, as hardly worthy of earnest consideration, the idea that this must be some prince of Persian lineage who particularly distinguished himself at that time, for it is hardly logical to suppose that one man will have furnished one angel of God sufficient

opposition to detain this angel for a period of twenty-
one days till the opposition was overcome. If one angel
was able to smite 185,000 Assyrians in the days of
Hezekiah, and that in one night, surely this explanation
involves too many improbabilities.

This approach to the problem leads us to conclude
that an *angel*-"prince" must be meant. Though at
this point many interpreters speak of "guardian
angels" of the nations, there is something very infe-
licitous about the use of that term in this connection.
If this prince opposed the good angel of God he cannot
himself also be good. But if, of necessity, he is an evil
angel he cannot be a guardian angel, for guarding is
a good work. Evil angels cannot do good work. Perhaps this was not meant when the term guardian
angels was referred to but simply one who works in
the interest of a certain kingdom and for the objectives
that this kingdom may happen to represent. Some,
therefore, dilute the terms employed and speak of
angels, not as personal spirits, but as spirits of the
sort that we have in mind when we speak of the spirit
that animates a nation, in other words, a principle.
But that can hardly be the meaning of the term
"prince" in this connection.

Bad angels, called demons in the New Testament,
are, without a doubt, referred to here. In the course of
time these demonic powers gained a very strong influence over certain nations and the government of
these nations. They became the controlling power.
They used whatever resources they could muster to
hamper God's work and to thwart His purposes. It
must have been under the influence of these agents of
the devil that the prevalent forms of idolatry were
built up in the various nations of antiquity. I Cor.
10:20f. may be compared here; also Eph. 6:20.

We get a rare glimpse behind the scenes of world
history. There are spiritual forces at work that are

far in excess of what men who disregard revelation would suppose. They struggle behind the struggles that are written on the pages of history. They explain the Satanic evil that often comes to light under the things that appear on the surface. Since a particular "prince of the kingdom of Persia" is mentioned, it seems to be a valid conclusion that every heathen nation is dominated by some such prince. Whether each evil angel may have but one nation as his domain, or whether there may be broader spheres of activity in which the more powerful among them are active, we shall hardly be able to decide on the basis of Scriptural evidence, for all these issues must be judged on the basis of the canonical Scriptures and not on the basis of pseudepigraphs such as the *Book of Enoch*.

This prince of Persia had been able to withstand God's angel for twenty-one days. Such a conflict, especially such a protracted conflict, seems very strange to us. Our difficulty may arise largely from the fact that in the spiritual world time is not reckoned as it is here on earth where all things are bound by time and space. Since the struggle was difficult, an assistant came to the speaker's aid, "Michael, one of the princes of the first order." This is the first instance in the Scriptures of the mention of an angel by name. We are wont to designate prominent angels as archangels by using a purely Biblical term (cf., I Thess. 4:16). There must be something like rank or orders among God's angels, for this Michael was "of the first order" (the Hebrew has only "the first"). The name Michael is significant. It means: "Who is like God?" It is as though this name recognized the great powers of these pure spirits but protested against forgetting that God's power, being the power of the Creator that made the angels, is much greater.

A helpful thought is suggested here: the good angels of God cooperate harmoniously with one another in the performance of their work in the kingdom

of God. One helps the other where help is needed. That
is one example of how God's will is done in heaven, according to the Third Petition. The perfect unity of the
church is in evidence at least in the kingdom of glory.
And the fact that certain of these angels of God are
great and mighty does not cause any rivalry or opposition among them.

What does the angel mean when he says: "I was
left there by the side of the kings of Persia"? The
verb employed has been variously interpreted and altered when it failed to fit into what the expounder
anticipated it should say. Without making the *Niphal*
(*nothárti*) a *Hiphil,* and without giving it a new object,
namely Michael, it fits so neatly into the situation that
we have just been discussing that it should have caused
little trouble, for the evil angels had held the controlling position at the Persian court. Now that they
had been overcome by the angel who is speaking and
by Michael, the place of influence at the Persian court
was taken over by these good spirits. The others
having been driven out, and Michael having come only
by way of tiding over an emergency, the speaker naturally "was left there by the side of the kings of
Persia." The plural "kings" implies that, after the
present king shall have passed from the scene, the
same position will be held in the case of his successors,
and every good influence will be brought to bear on
these kings successively to cause them to favor God's
chosen people with justice and righteousness. *Luther's*
rendering is more of an interpretation: *behielt den Sieg.*

The sum of the matter is this: There are powerful
forces of evil at work in and through the nations and
their rulers to defeat and to overthrow the people of
God. This may alarm and cause terror when one considers how powerful these demon potentates are. On
the other hand, there are still more powerful agents
of good at work who, by harmonious cooperation, will

prevail over their wicked opponents. So the cause of the kingdom is in good hands, and its success is assured.

This happens to be a truth that is considered too little in our day. Yet it throws light on many a puzzling situation in the course of historical developments and helps God's children to keep a balanced judgment as well as a sure hope.

14. **"And I am come here to help thee to understand what shall happen to thy people after the end of these days. For there is yet vision for these days."**

The specific purpose of the angel's mission, as far as the prophet is concerned, is now to give him that understanding which he so earnestly desired with reference to the revelations that had thus far been made of the times immediately following. It is not for himself that the prophet desires to acquire this understanding. The welfare of his "people" lies near to his heart.

The expression that we have rendered "after the end of these days" is the familiar one of the *A. V.*, "in the latter days." This expression refers to the time immediately after the expiration of a certain time that happens to be under consideration. When the present series of developments comes to an end, then in the "afterperiod," *'acharith,* other developments will follow. In all instances that we know of this term reaches out into the Messianic age. Obvious instances are Gen. 49:1; Num. 24:14; Isa. 2:2. We believe that the same is the case in this instance. Though this aspect of the case will be deferred till we come to the twelfth chapter, this is a very essential portion of the things that the prophet will be granted to understand.

The concluding statement agrees with this: "For there is yet vision for these days." This is an accurate translation of these words. "Vision" is without the article. The article before "days" is the article of relative familiarity, for the "days" were just referred to. So the article practically has the force of the demonstrative. The statement as a whole means that some of the vision given refers to the days after the next series of events, that is, to the Messianic Age. One should, therefore, see the broader scope of the vision and not limit it too closely to impending historical developments.

15. **And as he spake with me after the tenor of these words, I kept my eyes on the ground and remained dumb.**

By this time the prophet is able to follow an explanation. He is not yet in a frame of body and mind that enables him to hear to advantage. He realizes that a revelation is about to be made. But both modesty and weakness keep him from raising his eyes to him that speaks with him, neither has he the ability even to express what still troubles him. For the present he must "remain dumb." His recovery must go through a few more stages till he is able to do justice to what God is about to reveal to him.

16, 17. **And lo, one like a human being touched my lips; and I opened my mouth and spake and said to him that stood over against me: "My lord, as a result of the vision my pains have come back on me, and I have retained no strength. And how can the servant of this my lord speak with this my lord? And as for me, after this no strength remains in me, neither is there any breath left in me."**

It must have been a strange weakness that overcame this prophet so that he was not able even to express the pain and the weakness that still had hold upon him. Though he had been momentarily relieved, the sound of the words of the heavenly messenger brought all his former pain and weakness back to him. He was enabled to utter his complaint only by being again touched by "one like a human being." There is every reason to believe that this one was none other than the angel who was conferring with him. But in Daniel's weakened state such identities were hardly observed by him. In fact, during the speaking of the last words of the angel, Daniel's face had been turned toward the ground. In any case, to have a number of angels present with different functions to perform seems a bit unnatural—one to speak, another to touch and to strengthen. The touching of the "lips" was for the purpose of imparting to the mouth ability to present his petition before the angel in the form of a complaint. The whole episode expresses the New Testament thought that the Spirit presents our unutterable prayers or groanings before God as effectual prayers (Rom. 8:26).

Daniel's answer suggests that he had but one personage to deal with throughout. He first utters his complaint. Having now been made aware of the vision that he is in process of beholding, "the pains," *tsiray*, that he had felt at the outset returned. These must have involved great anguish because this word could also be rendered "pangs," referring to the pangs of childbirth. Coincident with the pains was the great weakness. He feels the need of uttering his thoughts but feels his utter inability to do so. So his complaint amounts to practically this: I know I am to be favored with a vision and revelation, but in my present state I am unable properly to receive it; all I perceive on my part is weakness and inability. In repeated statements and in manifold forms this thought, especially of the weakness felt, finds expression—"no strength; no breath"—so that we cannot but feel that it must have been a most appalling sense of inability that possessed this man. Of course, his free utterance of what grieves him is the equivalent of a prayer to the effect that God might strengthen him through this His representative.

Zeh is used twice after the noun with a suffix, a very unusual construction; at least as unusual as the expression "this my lord." See *K. S.* 334y. *Charles* translates well: "How can so mean a servant of my lord talk with so great a one as my lord?"

d. *The Second Announcement of the Angel's Purpose and Daniel's Final Strengthening, v. 18—11:1*

18, 19. Then again one in appearance like a man touched me and gave me strength. And he said: "Fear not, O greatly beloved; peace be unto thee. Be strong, be strong." And as he spoke with me, I gained strength, and I said: "Let my lord speak with me, for thou hast made me strong."

It is of secondary importance to identify the one who imparted strength by touching Daniel. When Daniel speaks as a result of the touch, we notice that it was again the same angel even though his identification is rather vague, for he is described merely as "one in appearance like a man." The reason for this unusual mode of statement may well be the fact that Daniel records exactly what he experienced. When he was touched, the factor that impressed or perhaps even comforted him was that the one who touched him appeared to be a man like himself. He may for the moment have given little thought to the identity of this individual. But it is at once apparent that he knew who he was because he addresses him as the one who did it. So the unusual mode of statement again has excellent reason for being just what it is.

In addition to the physical touch which imparted strength to the body there was the comforting word that gave strength to heart and mind. A threefold emphasis appears in his words: "fear not"; "peace"; "be strong." This is further reinforced by the repetition of the kindly address used before, "greatly beloved," as well as by a repetition of the word "be strong," a repetition that gives the word an intimate touch.

The effect produced upon Daniel was so immediately apparent that he perceived at once that he had already gained the needed strength and asked that the further revelation might continue at once. With a strong interest in the divine revelation Daniel was as eager to learn as the angel was to impart.

The amount of detail given in connection with the repeated strengthening of the prophet serves the purpose of reminding all readers that the impending revelation must be of a most unusual and important character. The triple strengthening, however, can hardly be said to have any direct connection with the three persons of the Holy Trinity, for nothing, except pure surmise, indicates such a connection. Yet a strange parallel is apparent between the prophet's experience and that of our Lord in Gethsemane. But there again nothing more than the psychological importance of the threefold experience is at stake.

20. **Then he said: "Dost thou know why I have come to thee? At once I must return to wage war with the prince of Persia. And when I come forth from that conflict, lo, the prince of Greece will come forth."**

The text of verses 20 and 21 has been assailed rather strongly as being "confused, weak, and illogical." This criticism is based on the observation that the divine messenger begins by saying, "Knowest thou wherefore I am come?" Yet "in 10:14 he had definitely stated that he had come to make the Seer understand what should befall Israel in the latter days, and that his coming had been due to the Seer's prayers, 10:12." Consequently the above question is labelled as being even a "foolish note of interrogation."

The criticism is again based on preconceived notions and a strange reluctance to enter into the situation as it is given by the text. The purpose of the coming of the heavenly messenger had, of course, been divulged. But Daniel's weak and perturbed state must be considered. He could hardly at once have retained all that he had been told. The angel, therefore, recalls all this to his mind by asking this question. Considered from this point of view, the question appears very proper and logical.

The debate in regard to this statement by the angel centers about the point as to whether this is a new revelation or a summary of what was said above, particularly in v. 12 and 13. It appears to us that neither statement is quite correct. Verse 20 looks neither exclusively forward nor backward; it is *supplementary* to what had already been said. When this purpose of the coming of the angel had been touched upon in v. 12, 13, the chief consideration was the relation of the angel's coming to Daniel's prayer and self-humiliation. Therefore the further purpose of combating the demon princes was introduced only for incidental notice. That matter is, however, of sufficient importance to have further attention given to it. It provides the needed background for the matters mentioned in chapter eleven, which are of a certain historical type. So this supplementary material is inserted before the nature of the revelation changes. The initial question helps the prophet to concentrate still more strongly upon that toward which all the powers of attention are already strongly directed.

The claim that the angel is under necessity of returning "to wage war with the prince of Persia" must be in harmony with the angel's earlier utterance on the subject. If he was victorious in the first instance, the statement cannot now be advanced that the battle is about to be waged. Both claims can be harmonized if this one is taken in the sense that the angel returns to maintain the position which he has won but which will not go unchallenged or unassailed.

The next statement indicates how this conflict will

turn out: the angel will, of course, be victorious. As long as there is a kingdom of Persia, so long will he prevail there and be able to use his influence in such a way that the interests of God's people are properly advanced. When he then "comes forth," *yotse'*, that refers to his departing from a conflict which has ceased. When the Persians pass off the scene as a power to be reckoned with, then he "comes forth." The verb in question is also a military expression that is used with reference to the withdrawal of troops. So the whole Persian period is covered by this remark.

On the use of the term "come forth" cf. II Kings 11:5-7, "of the shift of the guard in the palace" (*Montgomery*).

As soon as the one conflict ends, another takes its place: "lo, the prince of Greece will come forth." Demon influence will endeavor to enlist Greece in the war of destruction of God's people. If the angel who is speaking did not interpose, demon influence might well meet with success. So the prophet is apprized of some of the undercover movements in history but also of the type of checking that God employs to keep them within proper bounds.

The Hebrew construction used here is vigorous; see Driver, *Tenses*, 169.

21. "Howbeit, I shall tell thee that which is recorded in the book of truth. And there is no one that stands by me against these except Michael, your prince."

The adversative *'abhal* is rather strong; it is not a mild "but"; so we have translated it "howbeit." Since the Hebrew seldom employs adversatives but uses the conjunction *waw*, "and," this use of the adversative should be noted. The angel consciously turns away from the subject that he has been discussing as being one of secondary importance to that which is considered in the entire following chapter, as much as to

say, "But revelations concerning the spiritual or
angelic angle of these conflicts are not what I am primarily to offer to you; we, therefore, leave these behind, and I shall take our chief consideration in hand."
But the things that are to be revealed are matters of
which God's book alone bears record, and, as always,
reliable record: "That which is recorded in the book
of truth." The word "book" is not used here. The Hebrew word means merely "writing," *kethabh,* the
thought being that God alone has accurate records of
the things that will happen, or even, that He alone
foreknows. A similar thought is expressed in Deut.
32:34; Rev. 5:1; Ps. 139:16. The entire next chapter
is practically an abstract from God's record, and, of
course, God's record is always "truth." The term
"writing" is not to be taken literally. Heavenly truth
is expressed in earthly terms.

In dropping this subject of the "princes"—good
and bad—that work which is unseen by the eye of man,
the angel has only one supplementary thought to add,
which served to remove a possible misunderstanding.
This is the thought that he has but *one* angel to assist
him, viz., Michael. After hearing about the work and
the power of these princes man might be in danger of
constructing an elaborate theory about countless
angels. Such thoughts might lead to endless, useless
speculations, which are all cut short by the disclosure
that, as far as this protective angelic work for Israel
is concerned, there are only two who share in it: the
speaker and Michael. The strength and the resources
of these two are sufficient. Whether any more are engaged in other parts of God's work in connection with
the nations in their struggle through ages of history,
that we neither know nor can know. It is quite sufficient
to know this bit of truth, for certainly an enticing
field for speculation would be opened up for specu-
lative minds. Of these two again, Michael has a very

special title here, "your prince." That still leaves us in the dark as to the exact title of the speaker. But we do know that Michael has the welfare of God's people assigned to his care in a special way.

11:1.   But in the first year of Darius, the Mede, I for my part stood by to strengthen and defend him.

Nothing could be clearer than that this verse still belongs to what was just considered. Only the fact that it contains a statement of time similar to that of certain other opening verses of chapters (cf. 9:1 and 10:1) led commentators to make an unfortunate chapter division at this point. Surely, the aim of this verse is not to mark the revelation of this chapter as having been received in the first year of Darius, the Mede.

This verse merely looks back and supplies a thought that rounds out the last one that was uttered. The angel had just said, "Michael stands by me." He now adds, "This is quite natural, for we both collaborate; and two years ago I helped him in an emergency." That happened to be the year, as is shown in connection with 9:1, which could also have been designated as the first year of King Cyrus. In that memorable year obstacles were put in the way of the hope of God's people which aimed to prevent their return according to God's promise. Those obstacles at the Persian court had to be overcome, and they were overcome when the angel who was speaking went to Michael's assistance, and they both carried the day.

So it will be seen that the last two verses of chapter ten plus the first verse of chapter eleven are very closely connected and are not a peculiar confusion of sentences that are to be arranged in two parallel columns in an attempt to have some pattern of order or to prove them entirely out of order as most modern commentators do. A simple evaluation and just a bit of confidence in the sound state of the Hebrew text would spare the critics much confusion that arises out of the lack of patience to discover the good order that is inherent in the Word.

HOMILETICAL SUGGESTIONS

This chapter is much in the nature of an interlude or of a mere preface to chapter 11. Yet since it records at some length how Daniel had to be prepared for receiving the revelations that were still impending it cannot be regarded as something trivial or secondary. It surely tells a strange story, which is without parallel elsewhere in the Scriptures, of human frailty in the face of divine disclosures about the future as well as of angelic princes who exert controlling influence on the historic events in the life of great nations.

If a preacher were minded to extract these two subjects separately from the chapter, they are so obviously of a different character as to forbid trying to put them under a common head. One would have to demonstrate in one case how God overcomes the great frailty of man which might seem to make certain revelations impossible. All of this suggests that one reason such scant revelation concerning the future is given to us is that we are not able to bear it.

On the second subject, the hidden angelic forces that help to control the course of history, there is not much material; perhaps just enough to operate with successfully. On this subject, however, the caution is in order, not to indulge in ungrounded speculations.

Many might be of the opinion that the chapter offers no substantial preaching values.

CHAPTER XI

The Immediate Future and the Remote Future

I. The more Immediate Future; Leagues and Conflicts between Egypt and Syria, v. 2-35

This chapter—including the first three verses of chapter 12—must be of unusual importance, for an entire chapter preceded it by way of preparation for it. It at the same time ties back into chapter 9, which, in the Vision of the Seventy Heptads, gave the summary of the course of history in the sequence of all its parts. Our chapter presents the conclusion of the two main sections of all historical developments, the conclusion of the Old Testament period as well as the conclusion of the New Testament period. These concluding sections are to provide the greatest problems for the people of God, and therefore very special preparation must be made for them so that God's people may have the requisite preparation for the evil day.

From all this it is apparent why we had to formulate the double title stated above: "The immediate future and the more remote future." But there is more unity in the title than appears after a superficial examination, for the more immediate future is a type of the more remote future as we have had occasion to note repeatedly.

One can hardly begin to read this chapter before it becomes evident that a very special problem confronts the Bible student. A certain minuteness of prediction in matters of detail is noted after the opening verses of the chapter have been read. It is true that the prophetic Scriptures do not usually seem to go into detail at such great length, except perhaps in matters that are of the utmost importance, such as the minutiae of the life of the Christ. In this chapter covenants, leagues, treacheries, political marriages, intrigues, victories and defeats, as history knows them, follow in swift succession through the reigns of kings of the north and the south. That, to state it mildly, is not the customary pattern and theme of prophecy.

Farrar has voiced this difficulty in terms so strong that one feels that he has left sober reason behind and speaks in words that savor of strong partisanship. He overstates the difficulty thus: "If this chapter were indeed the utterance of a prophet in the Babylonian Exile, nearly four hundred years before the events— events of which many are of small comparative importance in the world's history—which are here so enigmatically and yet so minutely depicted, the revelation would be the most unique and perplexing in the whole Scriptures. It would represent a sudden and total departure from every method of God's providence and of God's manifestation of His will to the mind of the prophets. It would stand absolutely and abnormally alone as an abandonment of the limitations of all else which has ever been foretold." He seems to forget the variety of modes of manifestation of the divine will through the mouth of the prophets. The "divers portions and divers manners" of Heb. 1:1 dare not be lost sight of.

That such a claim is an unwarranted statement becomes apparent when prophecies are inspected with care. *Hengstenberg* furnished an answer to this criticism, an answer which *Farrar* apparently did not read. A few pertinent quotations from *Hengstenberg* follow. He says: "Out of the great multitude of similar prophecies we submit a few examples. The prophecy concerning the conquest of Babylon, Jer. 50 and 51, offers such exact details that history scarcely can present anything more minute—the city is to captured by the Medes and the peoples allied with them—to be exact, by the strategy of laying bare of the bed of the Euphrates River (50:38; 51:32, 36)—during the course of a night where all within the city lie sodden with drink (51:39, 57)—the return of the Israelites to their fatherland shall come as a result of the conquest of the city—the conquest of this city marks the beginning of the utter desolation and the virtual disappearance of it."

Another example deserves to be quoted. He adds: "The prophecy Zech. 9:1-8 may serve as a further example, a chapter in which Alexander's victories are portrayed with remarkable plainness and in strictest conformity with the facts of history—Syria and Phoenicia are to be conquered—Tyre is to be burned after its ramparts have been hurled into the sea— Gaza is to lose its king . . . . Ashdod, after its inhabitants have been driven out, is to be settled by colonists . . . . Jerusalem is to be guarded against all affliction by the protection of the Lord." He then refers to prophecies such as Isa. 21:1-10 and to chapters 13 and 14 of Isaiah, which even *Bertholet* conceded where "of the same sort" as Daniel 11.

Even when we are ready to grant that such specific prophecy is not without analogy and may, for that matter, serve a very constructive purpose, as we also hope to show, our difficulties are thereby not disposed of.

Is that which seems to be such detailed prediction perhaps, after all, not prediction but rather prophecy? In other words, does it have the form of prediction; but is that which seems like prediction really intended to be a general pattern of history, and does it then, perhaps, actually set forth general truth and not specific foretelling of particular events? That is, in general, the attitude of *Keil*. But such a view entails this difficulty that it cannot adequately explain how it comes to pass that the first part of the chapter, being supposedly prophecy, coincides so closely with the actual happenings of history that the sequence of events can be traced through a succession of reigns of Egyptian and Syrian kings with such accuracy as to make the coincidence of the two—prophecy and fulfillment—clear beyond all argument. *Keil* tries to remove this difficulty by pointing to what looks like discrepancies between history and chapter eleven. However, his objections amount only to this, that the statement of the prophet does not agree *in all details* with the historical fulfillment *as we know it*. Yet the two need not be said to disagree if we allow for the fact that the prophet did not in every instance attempt to state the entire case.

If we admit that the section that we are considering, v. 2—35, is prophetic prediction, that does not imply that we admit that the rest of the chapter—v. 36ff.—is also such prediction of historical events. For, as we shall point out in due time, from v. 36 onward a new factor enters into the picture, and especially from v. 40 onward the incidents foretold do not agree with the actual course of events as these are known from history.

To sum up this aspect of the case for the present, this is what we find: the first part of the chapter does offer specific prediction of historical events from about 300 B. C. to about 150 B. C., the second section of the chapter offers pure prophecy, which predicts what events shall occur in the development of the kingdom of God apart from strictly historical developments.

One further difference is to be noted. Some interpreters begin this last portion with v. 36, others with v. 40. We are definitely of the opinion that v. 36 is the proper point of marking the division. The justification for this point of view can best be offered when we present our interpretation of v. 36.

This seems to be the place to explain, at least as far as we are able, why such specific prediction of historical events of seemingly minor importance should find a place in the prophetic word. *Daniel* himself does not answer that question. But it seems quite reasonable to conjecture that the marvels of prophecy may well be expressed in quite a number of ways. Nor is this mode of exact prediction necessarily more marvelous than are other features found in the prophetic oracles. It should be an easy matter for the Spirit of prophecy, who has foretold the marvels of God's grace in Christ Jesus, to foreknow and foretell the course of history in minutest detail. Such prediction could well, in evil days, serve the purpose of reminding the people of God that all things great and small are under the guiding providence of God, for He both knows what will transpire and has all developments in hand as these things transpire. Such prediction offers no problem to the believer; it offers encouragement to faith.

More difficult are the questions: "Why does only a part of the course of history happen to be revealed, that is to say, up to about the year 165 B. C., and why does the prophetic word then go on to the events of the far distant future?" The reason for that distinction apparently lies in the fact that special guidance about the things to befall the Old Testament church was necessary only till the events of the year 165 B. C. had been reached. That date marked a very difficult crisis in the church. When it had passed, ordinary prophetic words were entirely adequate in the wisdom of God. And since the facts recorded were a pattern of the things that were to come to pass at the very end of all time, it seems quite natural that that end of all things should then be presented with particular reference to the persecutions of the last days.

The church took a significant step forward in the interpretation of this chapter in the days of *Jerome* (died 420) as a result of a controversy in which he happened to be engaged with Porphyry, a heathen philosopher who died 304 and who had written extensively attacking the Christian truth. He it was who had discovered the close correspondence between Daniel's prophecy and the actual sequence of historical events in the days of the Ptolemies and the Seleucidæ and had used that correspondence to advance the claim that Daniel's book could not of necessity have been prophecy but must have been written after the events recorded in it had occurred. This attack stirred the able commentator Jerome to take issue with the heathen philosopher, who had died about a century before his time. Jerome became strongly convinced of one thing in the course of his examination of the problem, namely, that this correspondence between secular history and Daniel was indisputable for the most part and had to be reckoned with but was not something whereby prophecy could be discredited as a fraud but a revelation of the marvels of true prophecy. And such is still our conviction.

Let this yet be said about the first part of the chapter: There is another deeper reason why such details as these are worthy of the work of the Spirit of prophecy, and that is that what is foretold here is in reality, with minor variations, the pattern into which all history falls. Is there not an appalling sameness about this business of leagues and pacts between rival nations, of disagreements, of wars, of alliances, of political marriages, of recriminations, of treachery, of temporary ascendancy, of defeat and utter downfall, of recovery through some aggressive leader; and then the same thing all over again with a slightly different sequence of events? From this point of view there is a drab sameness about history which allows

us to say that, in addition to being a prophecy of a particular period of Syrian and Egyptian history, this
may be regarded as a panoramic view of all history in
a picture that is idealized, at least to some extent.

a. *Historical Background*, v. 2-4

2-4. **"And now I shall show thee what shall
surely come to pass: Behold, three more kings over
Persia shall arise, and a fourth one shall accumulate
more riches than they all. But when he has gotten
strong through his riches he shall stir up all his resources against the kingdom of Greece. Then there
shall stand up a hero-king, and he shall rule, holding
mighty sway, and shall do as he pleases. And while
he is still rising, his kingdom shall be broken and
shall fall apart toward the four winds of heaven but
shall not fall into the hands of his posterity; nor
shall it be controlled as he controlled it, for his kingdom shall be uprooted and shall pass into hands
other than these."**

The angel, who had been introduced as speaking
in 10:20, has by this time fully established his identity
and his purpose and considers Daniel sufficiently informed to be able to appreciate the new revelation of
the future which is about to begin. This revelation he
prefaces by a statement that literally reads thus: "And
now I will show thee the truth," as rendered by *A. R.
V.* But we believe that the emphasis of this statement
lies, not on the fact that it is truth and not a lie which
he purposes to offer, but rather on this that the things
he foretells will truly come to pass. Therefore we have
translated as *Luther* also does: "I shall show thee
what shall surely come to pass."

The history of Persia, which is not a major issue
in this instance, is disposed of briefly. Three kings
shall arise in succession, to be followed by a fourth
who shall be enormously rich. Since Cyrus was on the
throne at this time (cf., 10:1), the three next in order

of succession are referred to by the "three more," that is to say, Cambyses who began to reign in 529 B. C.; Pseudo-Smerdis, whose reign began in 522; and Darius Hystaspis, who came to the throne in 521 B. C. The fourth is, without a doubt, Xerxes, of whom history records that he accumulated great riches, especially for his great expedition against Greece. He began to reign in 485 B. C.

There is no reason why the prophet should go any farther into this aspect of history at this point. He never intended to do anything other than to summarize. He cannot be charged with not having had the facts of history correct because he mentions only four out of a possible nine kings. It is obvious to those who try to read sympathetically what the prophet offers that he mentions Xerxes as the one with whom the Persian glory went on the decline so rapidly that hardly one of the remaining kings is worthy of notice. *Fausset* says very correctly: "After his [i.e., Xerxes'] overthrow at Salamis, Persia is viewed as politically dead, though it had *existence*."

The fact that the reference to the fourth king is a reference to Xerxes is apparent from the rest of the verse, where we read: "But when he has gotten strong through his riches he shall stir up his resources against the kingdom of Greece." It is a matter of historical record that Xerxes spent four years gathering his army from all parts of his empire, and that the sum total of his men amounted to more than two and a half million. Daniel's record is silent in regard to the outcome of the expedition. The reason is not hard to find. Nothing is said because the expedition achieved nothing. After the same manner the remaining kings are not mentioned because they achieved nothing. Instead, the momentous occurrences in the Greek Empire under Alexander are taken in hand.

3.   There can be no doubt that the "hero-king"

is Alexander the Great. The Hebrew reads "a king, a hero." That Alexander manifested unusual courage in his military expeditions is beyond the shadow of a doubt. That he showed remarkable ability to rule is equally apparent: "he shall rule, holding mighty sway." The Hebrew reads "he shall rule a mighty rule." That this king was a mighty autocrat appears from the fact that he is correctly described as "doing as he pleased." He rarely felt it incumbent upon himself to consult with counsellors. His decisions were usually much wiser than those of his counsellors.

4.   Alexander is mentioned only by way of transition to a consideration of the situations that are to be examined in greater detail. It is said correctly of this king that his kingdom is broken very prematurely, that is to say, "while he is still rising." Thus we venture to translate the Hebrew *ke'omdho*, which means literally "as he [still] stands." This implies that he had not really become weakened or lost power. His empire was still intact when this monarch died so very young.

But everything at once disintegrated: "his kingdom shall be broken and shall fall apart toward the four winds of heaven." The natural conclusion that after its falling apart it came into the hands of the offspring of the hero-king is shown to be erroneous. Even though Alexander's generals tried to arrange matters in such a way that the young sons of Alexander should be brought up to assume the rule after a time, these plans miscarried. In fact, there was none who was great enough to carry on the kingdom, that is to say: "it shall not be controlled as he controlled it." As a kingdom it was "uprooted" and so practically ceased to be a kingdom. No one, other than some of Alexander's generals, was able to keep his hold on even a portion of what he might have sought to control, and so it did "pass into hands other than these."

Even after the events have taken place, it is hardly possible to give a more accurate description of what actually happened to this greatest of all the empires up to that time. But to the Almighty the future is as clearly present as the past can ever be to the children of men.

By this brief *résumé* the ground is prepared for the things that are now specially to be revealed.

b.   *Ptolemy Lagi, 305-285 B. C.; Ptolemy Phila-*
delphus, 285-247 B. C.; Antiochus
Theos, 261-246 B. C., v. 5, 6

Daniel is not going to attempt to write the history of Egypt and the history of Syria except insofar as they help us to understand the things that bear on the welfare of the people of God. These two verses indicate how these two world powers, between which Israel happened to find herself, were minded toward one another. The first of the Ptolemies is mentioned only in passing. Of the Seleucidae, the rulers of Syria, the second, Antiochus I called Soter (280-262/1 B. C.), is entirely passed by so that a gap of more than fifty years appears in the sequence of the events that Daniel records. That omission does not, however, impair in any way the presentation of the development of things as it is made by Daniel, for he apparently never purposed to write or foretell history as the historians are wont to do by giving a wealth of minute detail which because of its profusion often prevents the reader from seeing the actual issues.

5, 6. "Then the king of the south shall be strong, and one of his princes; and the latter shall be the stronger of the two and shall have dominion. And at the end of a number of years they shall make an alliance; and the daughter of the king of the south shall be married to the king of the north in order to establish harmony. But she shall not retain the strength of her arm, neither shall he prevail nor

his arm; but she shall be given up as well as her escort and he that begat her and he that took her at that time."

Throughout this section, to v. 35, everything turns about the king of the south and the king of the north. These are the king of Egypt and the king of Syria. All attempts to read later or even modern events into this chapter have failed in the face of this fact, which is simply incontrovertible. In v. 8 an exception is made to the usual designation in that Egypt is actually mentioned. The omission of the two names, Syria and Egypt, is motivated by the observation made above that what is here foretold of these two nations applies in a general way to all history, no matter what its setting. Syria is never mentioned because, as *Fausset* very properly suggests, in Daniel's time the kingdom of Syria had not yet been formed and so could not well be referred to by name without causing confusion. This observation also adds weight to the argument that the book is rightly ascribed to Daniel. The *Greek* version very correctly always translates "Egypt" instead of "the south."

The point is that the king did actually become "strong." He was the first of the generals of Alexander to become established in the land that he was to control. With him was Seleucus, later called Nicator, "the Conqueror," who had fled from Antigonus of Babylon and temporarily had to cast his lot with Ptolemy. Since he himself was one of Alexander's generals, it would hardly seem proper to have him designated with reference to Ptolemy as "one of his princes." But *Montgomery* claims that he is correctly described thus "from the Egyptian point of view." That explanation would remove *Keil's* strong objection to classing this man as an Egyptian prince or general.

When it is said of him also that he "shall be the stronger of the two," that means, of course, not as they strive together, for they did not strive, but simply by way of comparative evaluation. Seleucus ultimately built up the stronger of the two kingdoms. To describe this still more effectively it is said that he "shall have dominion." That always involves real capacity for administration, the ability to hold the reins and direct the course of government with success. To confirm the fact that he became the most successful of those who controlled a part of Alexander's old realm, the prediction is made that "his dominion shall be a great dominion." So v. 5 serves the purposes of merely setting the two rival kings on their thrones and indicating that they were prominent kings that history had to reckon with.

6.   A period of history is passed over which some interpreters compute to have been sixty-one years. New kings are on the throne, but they are still the king of the south and the king of the north. The *Hebrew* says only "at the end of years." But that very naturally means an indefinite number of years, and this leads us customarily to insert the word "number" in this expression. The same expression is found in II Chron. 18:2.

The alliance consisted in this that Antiochus II, called Theos, "the divine," was compelled by Ptolemy Philadelphus to take to wife the latter's daughter Berenice and put aside his own wife Laodiceia—"the daughter of the king of the south shall be married to the king of the north." Though the Hebrew uses the expression "come to," we should say "marry." The fact that this was a typical political marriage is indicated by the two statements that express it: "make an alliance" and "establish harmony." The upshot of it all was that, when Ptolemy died two years later, Antiochus abandoned his Egyptian wife and took back Laodiceia. But now the real grief began. In order to gain her revenge, Laodiceia first of all took care to have her husband Antiochus murdered. She then vented her spite on Berenice, who had taken refuge in a temple at Daphne with her son begotten by Antiochus. So everything ended in a welter of blood. There was thus fulfilled in the case of Berenice the prophecy, "she shall not retain the strength of her arm." Also in the case of Ptolemy there was fulfilled the statement: "Neither shall he prevail nor his arm." In addition, the other personages involved, in what may have been a rather colorful parade when Berenice was brought up to Syria, also lost their lives, as well as the king who married her, thus fulfilling the prophecy: "She shall be given up as well as her escort and he that begat her and he that took her [i.e., married her] at that time."

Some object to having her father ("that begat her") listed among those that perished. But the general term is "shall be given up," *tinnathen,* which may apply to violent death or to anything else that comes under the head of being unsuccessful in a given situation. In the latter sense only it applies to the king. But that all the actors in this drama actually fail and fall by the wayside is only too true, and that is all that the account aims to indicate. *Charles* suggests that the father may have died "of shock at Berenice's fate."

Syntax: the *le* before *qets* is the *le* temporal (*K. S.* 331f). The expression *bath* in the phrase "daughter of the king of the south" must be translated as a definite noun, *"the* daughter," though in reality *"a* daughter" is meant. This is merely an outgrowth as in English of an attempt to speak familiarly of notable personages (*K. S.* 304c). For "at that time" the *Hebrew* has *ba'ittim,* "in the times," the article being the article of connection, meaning such times as one would expect under such a connection and therefore to be translated *"that* time" or "those

times." See *K. S.* 299f. The first verb in v. 5 is not the
customary construction of a converted perfect but the
unusual unconverted imperfect which is used to set
off the separate acts of the series more definitely from
one another (*K. S.* 370s).

c. *Ptolemy Euergetes, 246-222 B. C., and Seleucus
Callinicus, 246-226 B. C., v. 7-9*

7. **"Then there shall arise in his place a scion
of her roots, and he shall advance against the army
and shall enter into the stronghold of the king of the
north and shall deal against them and shall prevail."**

All that has been recorded thus far or will be
presented in the section about to be taken in hand has
not yet touched directly upon the people of God. But
by sketching a longer period of the history of these
times the author makes us aware of the inveterate
opposition that grew up between these two powers of
the north and of the south, and how sooner or later
Israel's position, being between the two as she was,
was bound to become dangerous.

After Ptolemy Philadelphus there comes Ptolemy
III, called Euergetes. He is the one spoken of as coming
up in "his [i.e., Ptolemy Philadelphus'] place." This
new king was of the same stock as Berenice and thus
"a scion of her roots." He did in reality make strong
inroads into the Syrian power and laid low all that
the Syrians had built up, so much so that Syria was
brought extremely low, even the "strongholds" of the
king—*ma'oz* may be taken collectively, for we are not
sure whether any particular stronghold of the king of
the north is referred to. By translating "and shall deal
against them" we follow *A. R.* We take these words to
mean that he shall engage in operations of a military
character against him or "them," referring to all that
are associated with the Syrian king; and "shall prevail," that is to say, have success in all these endeavors.

So for the time being the Egyptian power shall be on the ascendant and the Syrian pretty much on the wane.

8. **"And even their gods together with their molten images as well as their precious vessels of silver and of gold he will bring into captivity to Egypt, and he himself shall continue more years than the king of the north."**

The account of the successes of Philadelphus against the Syrians continues. The very temples will be captured and sacked and the idol images carried away by the Egyptians. Whenever that happened, it was regarded as being about as thorough an overthrow as a nation could suffer. For after the gods had been brought low and had been rendered unable to help themselves, the last line of defense of the nation was broken as, for example, Isa. 46:1, 2 indicates with reference to the fall of Babylon. To make the picture of the humiliation as complete as possible there are listed after the "gods" also their images and the "precious vessels of silver and gold." It is also indicated that this was an affliction of more than a passing nature by the fact that the years of the reign of the king of the south shall exceed those of the king of the north, and that he will thus be able to make his conquests of more lasting effect. The vast wealth that Ptolemy brought back to Egypt from his campaigns won for him the name "Euergetes" i.e., the "Benefactor." For as *Jerome* reports (see *Meinhold*) there was a sum of 40,000 talents of silver involved and 2,500 idol statues.

This is the only verse in which "Egypt" occurs for "the south" in the Hebrew text. The Septuagint has it also in vv. 5, 6, 9, 11, 14, 15, 29, 40.

Yet it would be wrong to assume that the Syrian power will be permanently broken. Therefore, one instance of how Syria will strike back is reported (v. 9) before this part of the record is brought to a close.

9. **"But one shall come against the realm of the king of the south but shall return to his own land."**

To translate the verb *ba'* "he shall come" (*A. R. V.*) is ambiguous. To have the king of the south carry on this expedition is a meaningless translation (*A. V.*) Therefore the third person singular should be construed as involving an indefinite subject—"one shall come." This "one" is the Syrian king Seleucus Callinicus who reigned 247-226 B. C., and of whom it is known that he did conduct an expedition against Egypt, though without success. Nevertheless, we see that Syria was not broken, she was merely brought low for the present. The Syrian had to "return to his own land."

d. *Seleucus, 227-224 B. C., and Antiochus III (the Great), 224-187 B. C., vs. Ptolemy Philopator, 222-205 B. C., v. 10-19*

10. **"But his sons shall bestir themselves, and they shall gather a throng consisting of great forces, and the one shall advance right on and sweep along and cross over and shall return and shall make an attack upon his fortress."**

Though Seleucus Callinicus, as we saw above, had attempted to regain what Syria had lost he had succeeded only in making a bold attempt. The rulers who are now mentioned as "his sons" are Seleucus the Third and Antiochus the Third, who jointly carried on what their father had not been able to accomplish. But they did not work together long because the former came to an untimely end. It is for this reason that the gathering of a throng is ascribed to both, and that the verb is then changed to the singular, for it is Antiochus III, called also the Great, who then carries on alone. The Hebrew marginal reading is "his son"— another solution.

The verb plus the infinitive (*ba' bo'*) is the

strengthened form of the verb "go." It is like our "advance right on," for Antiochus did make great and rapid conquests. At that time Egypt was actually in possession of Seleucia on the Orontes as well as of Tyrus and of other lands in northern Syria. All these Antiochus took and did "sweep along and cross over" (cf., Isa. 8:8) and came even so far south as to be able to "make an attack upon his fortress." Between the two expeditions he had been beguiled into making a truce, but when he saw that this had been based on deceptions practiced by the enemy he returned to his campaign, conquered the Egyptians at Sidon, swept on down through Palestine, and was able to penetrate so far south as to attack the Egyptian "fortress" Gaza. Some interpreters claim it must have been Raphia, which is a bit farther south. During all this time the Egyptian, Ptolemy Philopator, had spent his time idly pursuing the vices that were practiced by so many kings of that time, and no substantial resistance had therefore been offered to Antiochus. But the Egyptian monarch now bestirred himself.

11, 12.   **"And the king of the south shall become embittered and shall go forth and shall make war with him, that is, with the king of the north, and shall raise a great army, and the multitude shall be given into his hand. And the multitude shall be disposed of, and his heart shall be exalted, and he shall bring tens of thousands low but shall not prove himself strong."**

The feelings of the Egyptian king are indicated by the expression "he shall become embittered." He is known to have gathered a large force consisting, we are told, of 73,000 men and 73 elephants. The army of Antiochus was even greater: 72,000 foot soldiers, 6,000 horse, and 102 elephants. Antiochus at first gained the advantage in the battle. The tables were later turned because the Syrian king had too soon abandoned caution and had sought to plunder an enemy that was not yet fully conquered. So he lost the battle in the end, and the Egyptian king was victorious as was foretold here: "and the multitude shall be given into his hand." The "multitude" of the opposing army "was disposed of," and "tens of thousands" were "brought low." But since he was so much addicted to luxurious living, it was a matter of little concern to him whether the success was properly utilized to the full or not. He promptly returned to his former indolent mode of life and so proved the truth of the statement that he "shall not prove himself strong."

Though some of the things recorded are of a more or less trivial nature, they are recorded as typical. Just such events as these make up the pages of history.

13, 14. **"Then the king of the north shall return and shall muster a multitude greater than the former; and after a few years he shall come right on with a large force and great equipment. In those times many shall rise up against the king of the south, and such as are given to violence among thy people shall lift themselves up to establish the vision; but they shall fall."**

The serious setback just recorded did not discourage King Antiochus, who is not without reason called "the Great." He raised a greater army and secured better equipment and again attained some of the success that had attended his first efforts. What made it possible for him to "come right on" was the fact that the king of Egypt offered no opposition, and that after his death various uprisings occurred that materially weakened the Egyptian power and broke it by internal dissension: many were "rising up against the king of the south." But that, unfortunately, led some of the Jews ("thy people," says the angel) to attempt an uprising against the Egyptian dominion under which they had fared relatively well. That up-

rising was headed by a certain Tobias. That undertaking was to bring trouble upon them, the trouble that
had been prophesied in the visions of Daniel. The
angel refers to that fact when he says that the Jews
shall do this to "establish the vision." This uprising
on the part of the Jews proved abortive: "but they
shall fall."

We see from this one incident how intimately the
fortunes of the Jews were intertwined with those of
these two warring nations, and how soon the Jews
could become deeply involved in trouble.

15, 16. **"And the king of the north shall come
and shall raise a rampart and shall capture a well-
fortified city, and the forces of the south will not
stand, neither his chosen people, neither shall there
be any power to stand. But he that cometh against
him shall do as he pleases, and there shall be no one
able to stand before him, and he shall stand in the
glorious land, and it shall be entirely in his hand."**

The connecting "and" seems to be used very
loosely. It is practically equivalent to "namely," for
the same matter that was presented in the last two
verses is apparently considered here in greater detail.
There had been an interruption of the victorious advance of Antiochus when his attention was claimed
by difficulties in Pergamum. During his absence the
Egyptian general Scopas had recaptured some of the
territory that Antiochus had just gained. But Antiochus soon ousted him and with great losses drove him
back to the city of Sidon, which seems to be the "well-
fortified city" referred to. The Hebrew has "city of
fortifications," implying many and good fortifications
by the plural of intensity.

When it is said that the king "raised a rampart,"
that refers to his assault upon the city, which, apparently, ultimately succeeded. For though the Egyptians sent three of their best generals to lift the siege

of the city, these were driven back: "and the forces of the south will not stand, neither his chosen people, neither shall there be any power to stand." This triple statement expressing inability is a strong way of stating its intensity.

16. The subject of the first verb is still Antiochus. As we remarked in connection with verses 13 and 14, he encounters practically no opposition and so attains success for a considerable period of time. The uprising of the Jews mentioned in v. 14 led to his going to the "glorious land"—Palestine, of course, cf., 8:9. In this latter passage it had been said that this uprising was instigated by only the "violent among thy people." These apparently constituted a minority, for the bulk of the people had been treated tyrannically by the Egyptian king and as a result had felt impelled to revolt against him and thus to regard the Seleucidae with greater favor. Of Antiochus the Great, Rappopert reports that he "released Jerusalem from all taxes for three years, and afterwards from one-third of the taxes. He also sent a large sum of money for the service of the Temple, and released the elders, priests, scribes, and singing men from all taxes for the future."* Consequently the translation of the last two words of the verse that some offer is unsatisfactory when they understand them to mean, "And destruction shall be in his hand." It is true enough that the words *wekhallah bheyadho* could be rendered thus. But they can also be translated "and [it shall be] entirely in his hand." That certainly squares far better with the facts. It merely emphasizes another angle of the case. When a king remits taxes, one may point to his kindness. Yet the mere fact that he has complete control of the situation is equally apparent and may with equal propriety be stressed and the statement be made that he has things entirely in hand. The latter

S. Rappopert, *History of Egypt* (London, 1904), I, 194.

statement would emphasize how low the nation that was being treated thus had fallen.

17. "And he shall set his face to advance with the full strength of his entire kingdom and with him equitable terms, and he shall perform them; and he shall give to one a girl in marriage to destroy it; but this shall not stand, neither shall it be to his advantage."

This verse speaks of only a purpose on the part of Antiochus. It is claimed that Livy, the Roman historian, also refers to this intention on the part of the king of Syria. But this was a purpose that was never carried out. Nothing more than that is implied in the statement, "He shall set his face." But it may well be asked why mere purposes that do not materialize should be recorded in this series of predictions in which only the bold outline of history is given. The answer, we believe, lies in this, that as the whole chapter has thus far emphasized God's control of the affairs of history by foretelling what will transpire, so God's foreknowledge is here stressed to the point of showing that God knows even the hidden purposes of men which never materialize. The feature that was characteristic of this expedition was apparently that everything attempted was going to be done on "equitable terms" which Antiochus would have faithfully carried out. But that all belongs to the contemplated expedition with a great army that never materialized.

The next item is, however, a matter of history. Since the two main actors on the stage are the king of the north and the king of the south, and since the one under consideration is the king of the north, the "to one" must refer to the king of the south. It is a fact that is verified by history that Antiochus the Great gave his daughter Cleopatra in marriage to Ptolemy Epiphanes, and that it was the purpose of the father to gain an advantage over the king of Egypt by trusting that his daughter would be her father's ally rather than her husband's. That is what is meant by the infinitive of purpose "to destroy it," i.e., the kingdom. The next statement is also verifiable: "This shall not stand, neither shall it be to his advantage." The girl felt it her duty to be faithful to her husband and so refused to be a tool in her father's hands.

18, 19. **"Then he shall turn his face to the coastlands and shall take many of them, and a commander shall make him desist from his presumptuous boasting without repaying him with like boasting. Then he shall turn his face toward the fortresses of his own land and shall stumble and fall and shall be found no more."**

We have translated *'iyyim* "coastlands," which is a more accurate rendering than the more common "isles," for this expression refers to the entire intricate coastline of the Mediterranean plus the islands. Antiochus made this expedition to gain control of Asia Minor and the islands of Ionia, which the Romans sought to control, in addition to assuming a guardianship over the young Egyptian king. This action was, therefore, designed to break the power of Rome. By 196 B. C., he had gotten hold of even a part of Thrace.

Rome resented this particularly because she exercised a kind of mandate over Thrace. The expedition of Antiochus finally called forth the active resistance of Rome, which led to a battle near Magnesia in 190, in which battle Lucius Scipio administered such a sound drubbing to Antiochus that the "presumptuous boastings" of the Syrian were silenced once and for all. Yet Scipio himself was not to make the same mistake that the man whom he had conquered had made. He achieved his victory "without repaying him with like boasting." This implies a nobler and a more restrained conduct on the part of the Roman general. This statement is usually translated:

"Yea, moreover, he shall cause his reproach to turn upon him." The difficulty with this rendering is that *bilti* is a negative, a fact that this translation does not take note of. Our translation was first offered by *K. S.* 388k and seems to be more reasonable.

19.   This statement seems to have a sharp note of sarcasm. He whose face had in warlike conquests been turned against the fortresses of others shall after his humiliating defeat turn to "the fortresses of his own land." Here no trouble or defeat could befall him. So disheartened shall the king become. In fact, his end shall be still more ignominious: he "shall stumble and fall and shall be found no more."

In regard to verses 10 to 19 *Farrar* quotes *Behrmann* with approval that "there is a sort of dance of shadows, only fully intelligible to the initiated." Such criticism is hardly warranted. All that was recorded in this section was intended to be nothing more than a rough, though accurate, outline of the general course of history for a short period that would come to a climax in a season of unusual difficulty for the people of God. Nothing more was to be demonstrated than that God knew what would come to pass. That knowledge again constituted a sure proof that God could also control what He foreknew. It served no purpose to relate a lot of minor detail. To expect that all this could be understood before the events involved transpired is to expect what was never intended.

e.   *Seleucus Philopator, 187-176 B. C.,* v. 20

20.   **"And there shall rise up in his place one that shall cause an exactor to pass through the glory of the kingdom; but after some days he shall be broken, but not in anger nor by war."**

Only that is told about this Syrian king which bears upon the fortunes of the people of God. It is well known that this ruler had an enormous tribute to pay to the Romans annually, even a thousand talents.

This led to heavy exactions from the tributary nations. The manner in which this affected the Jews was that a special tax collector by the name of Heliodorus (see II Macc. 7) was sent to appropriate the rich treasures of the Temple at Jerusalem, report of which had been brought to the king. The "glory of the kingdom" would, therefore, be the Holy Land, which was already previously (v. 16) called by a similar name, "the glorious land." The word which we have translated "exactor," *noghesh*, could mean oppressor of any sort but will here, no doubt, well apply to the Heliodorus just mentioned, remains of two statues of whom, by the way, have been found.

Though our prediction states nothing of the rather unusual overthrow of Heliodorus as this is recorded in II Maccabees, the reason for that may well be the fact that the account in II Maccabees is a piece of pure embellishment written by some writer of a later date. It hardly reads like the sober miracles of which we have accounts in the Scriptures. All that our verse mentions is that after not too long a time, "after some days," the king was broken, apparently by some not unusual overthrow, for it was "not in anger nor in war." These words could hardly refer to Heliodorus, of whom it could at least be said that he was overthrown "in anger" if the account found in the apocryphal book is true.

f. *Antiochus Epiphanes,* v. 21-35

It is at once apparent that a disproportionate amount of attention is given to this king in comparison with all others that have been mentioned. The reason for this is the fact that this was the ruler with whom the Jews were to have unusual difficulties. Previous reference has been made to him in the book of Daniel. In fact, it was he above all others who caused grief to God's people. It was really for the sake of this section that the preceding events of the chapter had been revealed.

21. "Then there shall arise in his place a contemptible person, on whom the royal dignity was not bestowed, and he shall come by stealth and seize the kingdom by intrigues."

This "contemptible person" is the notorious Antiochus Epiphanes, 175-164 B. C. It would seem that the term "contemptible," *nibhzeh,* applies to the rank and station of this newcomer at the time when he appeared on the scene and aspired to become the king of Syria. At the time of his assuming the rule there were three aspirants to this honor: the legitimate heir Demetrius, a hostage at Rome at the time; a younger son, Antiochus, a baby in Syria; and our Antiochus, the late king's brother, who happened to be at Athens at the time. It could later hardly be said of Antiochus Epiphanes that he was primarily a "contemptible person." He actually distinguished himself among the Syrian kings about as much as any of them did though his character is more or less an enigma to historians; yet even they show no inclination to call this man "contemptible."

His manner of coming to the throne is indicated indirectly when it is said, "On whom the royal dignity was not bestowed." That means: it was not given to him; he took it. His manner of taking it was "by stealth" and "by intrigues." In fact, for a while he posed as the guardian of the boy-king Antiochus; and later, when the boy-king was murdered by Andronicus, Antiochus promptly put Andronicus to death. It can hardly be determined whether Antiochus had been privy to this plot. This was apparently some of the "stealth" that Antiochus employed.

22, 23. "And the floods of armies shall be flooded away before him and shall be broken, as well as the prince of the covenant. And after a

league shall be made with him, he shall practice deceit and shall go up and become strong with but a few people by stealth."

For the present the king's method of establishing himself is pictured in general terms. Disregarding for the most part reference to individual historical events, the account describes picturesquely that it shall be a time when armies shall surge back and forth through the land, in fact, "floods of armies." Then to picture the countersurge the verb "flooded away" is used, a detail that is usually not indicated by the translations. Armies shall thus be disposed of before Antiochus as he gains ground in his, at first precarious, position. At that time even a prince of the covenant loses his life. At this point *Keil* protests against the usual interpretation in an attempt to show that this account is not intended to be historical, in fact, as he says, even runs counter to the facts, for the murder of the high priest Onias took place without the previous knowledge of Antiochus; in fact, he actually had the murderer put to death. But does this verse charge Antiochus with the death of this "prince of the covenant" as the high priest may well be called? Strictly speaking, not. If the preceding verb is supplied, then nothing more is indicated than that in these troublous times also the high priest shall lose his life, "shall be broken." Some feel that this is in reality an aposiopesis: "Also the prince of the covenant—." "Covenant" applies only to the holy covenant of God's people, cf., v. 28, 30, 32.

23.   We now see the king at the point where he can begin to deal with other nations as an equal. He forms leagues, the customary device for enhancing one's influence. The *min* before the infinitive is the *min* temporal. On the Aramaic infinitive compare *G. K.* 54k. Whereas he first used force and then formed leagues, his third device, which is only too common in inter-

national politics, was to "practice deceit." If the sequence of the events recorded is to be viewed strictly from the standpoint of time, this might refer to the first Egyptian expedition. This might then be an indication of the mode of operation that was adopted by the king while he was in Egypt when he espoused the cause of Ptolemy Philometor, his one nephew, over against that of Ptolemy Euergetes, his other nephew, all the while pretending that it was only his nephew's interests that he had at heart. Some historians are of of the opinion that he even had himself crowned king of Egypt at Memphis on one of these expeditions of his. The nephews themselves finally saw that their uncle was "practicing deceit," and that he was "becoming strong with but a few people by stealth." But it matters little whether we regard all this as being related in strict historical sequence or as being merely a list of deeds done by him without strict regard for the order in which these deeds occurred.

We have departed from the punctuation of the *Hebrew* by drawing the phrase "by stealth" back into v. 23, where it fits into the picture more easily than in v. 24. "Go up," no doubt, refers to the king's rise to power and not to "going up the Nile" as *Jerome* thought.

24. **"And he shall enter into the fertile spots of the provinces and shall do what neither his fathers nor his father's fathers had done—plunder, spoils, and goods shall he distribute to men, and against fortresses shall he devise devices, but only for a time."**

The other means for strengthening his position is now described. Oriental princes generally plundered their provinces to the fullest extent. This king also does so and concentrates on the "fertile spots of the provinces" or, as *A. V.* translates, "the fattest places." But this ruler did not squander these things on himself in luxurious living but did the unusual thing of distributing lavishly to men "plunder, spoils, and goods." This method certainly helped him to buy men and influence. It was, however, not the traditional thing to do, for neither his "fathers nor father's fathers" had done thus. Among the fortresses against which he "devised devices" might be mentioned Pelusium on the border of Egypt, which fortress he managed to keep garrisoned for himself so as to keep the entrance into Egypt open against any time when he might return. But, as usual, such underhand dealings gave him an advantage "only for a time."

25. **"And he shall stir up his power and his courage against the king of the south with a great army; and the king of the south shall bestir himself to battle with a great and exceedingly powerful army. But he shall not stand, for they shall devise devices against him."**

Since we do not believe, as we have indicated above, that a strict historical sequence is aimed at in this prediction we are not under the necessity of determining whether this refers to the first or to the second expedition of Antiochus. It does point to great preparations on the part of both kings, and this again led to many battles, with defeats being plentiful on both sides. But the outcome is the important thing: "he [the king of the south] shall not stand." But this is only seemingly the final result as we shall see later. It was not the strength or the skill of the king of the south that ultimately saved him. The temporary victory of the king of the north was to be attributed largely to "devices" that he had been able to employ.

26. **"Even they that eat his dainties shall break him, and his army shall be swept away, and many shall fall down slain."**

The subject is still the king of the south. One factor that will work toward his overthrow will be treachery in his very court circles. Men who eat at the very table with the king shall play into the hand of the enemy. So shall "his army be swept away, and many shall fall down slain."

27. **"And as for these two kings, their heart shall be set upon mischief, and they shall speak lies at one table. But it shall not succeed, for yet at the appointed time there shall be an end."**

Neither of the two opponents has honorable motives nor employs honorable methods. In fact, in spite of all claims to the contrary, their only object will be to harm one another. This could refer to Antiochus' dealings with Philometor whom he pretended to help to gain his throne. Whatever special occasion this might refer to when "they shall speak lies at one table," we do not know. From the Oriental point of view the treachery of a host or against a host is particularly odious. So the expression may be figurative to denote the worst kind of treachery.

The last statement, "it shall not succeed," does not seem to indicate an advantage for either of the two contestants. Some think that it points to the ultimate success of Antiochus. But the concluding remark indicates that there is an "appointed time" according to the verdict of the Almighty, when the actual "end" of all that man builds up becomes apparent, and that is the issue that counts.

This harmless statement about "speaking lies at one table" has been given a peculiar interpretation in these times of ours, an interpretation that is silly enough to be called such. Some have found in it a reference to the treaty of Versailles. To the student of Scripture who interprets it sanely there is here only a reference to the things that Antiochus and the Egyptian king did. In a very loose sense, even as all history has something symbolic about it, the words could be applied to all similar occasions where treachery is hatched out at conference tables. But to stamp the statement as a special reference to one event in the twentieth century is a most glaring misinterpretation.

The word that we have rendered "mischief," *mera'*, is the *Hiphil* participle of *ra'a'*.

28. **"Then shall he return to his land with many possessions, and his heart shall be set against the holy covenant, and he shall achieve his purpose and then return to his own land."**

After at least a temporary success and laden with the spoils of war, Antiochus returned to his own land to attend to its affairs. A part of that land was the Holy Land, and he had to pass through it in order to get to Syria proper. But there were difficulties among the Jews that claimed his attention, for a seditious fellow, Jason by name, had staged an insurrection and was causing serious trouble. He had apparently been misinformed as to the security of the position of Antiochus. All these things are reported in II Macc. 5 and in I Macc. 1:20ff. Though the sources that we have seem to indicate that the basis upon which Antiochus dealt with this problem was purely one of policy, namely, to quell the insurrection, our prediction probes deeper into the matter and indicates that there was in the heart of the king an antagonism against the people of God and their destiny—"his heart shall be set against the holy covenant." This attitude is revealed at least in part by the fact that he made the most of the opportunity that presented itself to plunder the Temple. That is not the act of a man whose sole purpose it is to uphold justice. Our verse intimates this when it says: "And he shall achieve his purpose." All this was, of course, done merely in passing through. So we are further informed that his original purpose was realized when he then returned "to his own land." We could reproduce the thought more easily in English if we were to take the first verb with *waw* conversive as being the equivalent of a temporal clause: "And when he shall return" or "and as he returns." Cf. *K. S.* 193b.

29, 30. **"At the time appointed he shall return and come into the land of the south; but on this latter occasion it shall not be as on the former. For ships of Kittim shall come against him, and he shall be intimidated and return and be indignant against the holy covenant and shall achieve his purpose; he shall, in fact, return and take note of those that forsake the holy covenant."**

Depending on how one regards these Egyptian campaigns, this will be called the second or the third Egyptian campaign. Names matter little in this instance. More important is the fact that, when the king believes that the time has come to conduct another campaign, there are forces at work of which he knows but little, for this act of his takes place "at the time appointed," that means, at a time when divine providence sees that this step may further its own purposes. So even the deeds of the wicked must contribute to the achievement of the objectives of the Almighty. In this instance, however, the success that attended his earlier ventures is noticeably absent: "on this latter occasion it shall not be as on the former." What is meant by this is explained in the next verse.

30. In Egypt the two brothers were no longer at odds with one another. Their sister had succeeded in persuading them that their interests lay along the same lines, and that any efforts to allow Antiochus to control the situation for them was pure folly. Besides, these brothers had sought the support of the Romans. This had occurred in 168. These Romans are those who are referred to as the ones that came against him in the "ships of Kittim," for though "Kittim" is without a doubt Cyprus, in instances such as these, cf., Num. 24:24, it refers merely to those regions which, from the standpoint of Palestine, lay directly to the west. Therefore: Cyprus and everything that lay beyond it. The Greek translators understood this so well that they rendered this verse: "And the Romans will come," etc.

What happened is a famous historical episode that has often been retold. C. Popillius Laenas headed the Roman embassy at the time when it encountered Antiochus, who was besieging Alexandria. The Roman apprised him of the demand of the senate that he quit the land. Antiochus hesitated and sought to gain time. With his staff the Roman drew a circle about the king and curtly told him that his decision must be reached before he stepped outside of the circle, or else he would have to meet the Romans in war. Antiochus well knew the strength of the Romans and, above all things, wanted to keep them appeased, and so, though thoroughly disgruntled, he had to give his word that he would withdraw from Egypt immediately. The text refers to this with the statement, "He shall be intimidated and return."

There would seem to be no connection between this vexation and his being "indignant against the holy covenant," except in a very general way, unless the attitude described in the preceding verse actually covered the case, namely, that his heart was set against the holy covenant. The explanation usually given by historians is scarcely plausible, namely, that he sought to vent his spite on the Jews now that the treatment he had received from the Romans had embittered him. Why just the Jews? What the historian has failed to detect, *that* has been revealed by the Scriptures, which search the heart, namely, that this man had a very particular hostility against the people of God. And since this hostility is directed against the very destiny of this holy people it is twice spoken of—here and in v. 28—as being "against the holy covenant," the essence of the relationship between God and His own.

It is at once indicated that his hostile intentions against the Jews were carried out: he "shall achieve his purpose." That is a general statement which covers all the king's efforts and their success, a typical way of writing history in the Hebrew. The details are given in the next five verses. We have, therefore, introduced the expression "in fact" into the next sentence, for when he returned, the first step in line with his hostile policy was to "take note of those that forsake the holy covenant." That was done with the aim of determining how many were really available to be enrolled on the side of the king. This taking note is, therefore, to be viewed as being friendly in character. "Have regard unto them" (*A. R. V.*) is to be understood in this sense. "Have intelligence with them" (*A. V.*) seems less to the point. Now that the king has secured allies among the Jewish people he is ready to carry out the rest of his cruel program as the next verses report.

31, 32. **"And forces going out from him shall arise and profane the Sanctuary—the Refuge, and shall put aside the regular offering and shall set up in its place an abominable idol. And by smooth words he shall cause those who have transgressed against the covenant to apostatize; but those that know their God shall be strong and shall achieve their purpose."**

The word "forces" is really "arms" in the original, namely, the members of the body, not weapons. In this chapter the word repeatedly means "armies." Here it apparently means any group, large or small, for it was not necessary to have a large number of men such as an army to profane the Sanctuary. These shall not do this unholy work merely on their own initiative but prompted by, or with the sanction of, Antiochus. The formal term "shall arise" implies a definite setting forth with an avowed purpose, not merely an incidental act.

The Temple is called by the double name "the Sanctuary—the Refuge," which shows from a twofold point of view what the Temple meant to the true Israelites. *Miqdash* implies that it is "the holy place," and *ma'oz* refers to the spiritual side of it. It is a place where men seek shelter with their God in the evil day. After it had been profaned, the truehearted in Israel realized more keenly than before these spiritual values of which they had been deprived. The translation of the second term as "the fortress," so popular in our day, seems appropriate enough when it is considered that in those days there was actually a citadel at the sanctuary as we read in I Macc. 6:7. But that applies rather to externals. The word is often used with reference to God in the Scriptures.

This profanation consisted of a negative and a positive act: the negative was the discontinuation of the "regular offering," the *tamidh*, "the continual," which means more than the "daily sacrifice" as some translate this term, for all daily Temple rites of the ritual are included. The positive was the setting up of "the abominable idol in its place." We insert the words "in its place" as being implied in the connection. Most interpreters are agreed that this abominable idol, which was so utterly abhorrent to the Jews, was the image of Zeus Olympius, and some add that of Dionysus, the god of wine. Here, as in 9:27, we take the participle *meshomem* to mean "causing horror" or "abominable." Yet we think that *K. W.* is justified in making *profanierend* equal to *verwuestend;* see under *shiqquts.* We must, therefore, also allow for the possibility of the translation "the abomination that maketh desolate" (*A. V.*).

It is to this passage that the Savior refers when he uses the expression "the abomination of desolation"

(Matt. 24:15; Mark 13:14). This strange diversity of translation is the result of the fact that the two meanings "to be desolated" and "to be appalled" are to be ascribed to this root, the latter being the psychological reaction to the former according to *K. W.* Yet, certainly, in this case the two blend into one another: the religious desolation resulting from the desecration on the one hand and the resultant horror on the part of a true Israelite on the other.

In the expression "forces going out from him" we have the equivalent of the genitive construction; it is like "forces of his." The preposition *min* serves as a substitute for the genitive (*K. S.* 278d).

32. The next step in the program of this king to overthrow the religion of God's people is now described. After the sanctuary has been profaned he resorts to words of persuasion, "smooth words." The most suitable material for his purpose are those "who have transgressed against the covenant." They have already incurred the disfavor of the right-thinking majority. By pleas drawn from the thoughts that were current at that time they were to be induced to apostatize.

But another class will be found under these circumstances. They are "those that know their God." Among these we should include all those who consciously and with clear understanding hold the true faith of Israel. They shall face all dangers and persuasions but shall not allow themselves to be unduly impressed or even intimidated; they "shall be strong." In their strength they shall naturally offer opposition to the program of the king, and they "shall achieve their purpose." They shall have a notable measure of success.

33. **"And the teachers of the people shall help many to understand, yet they shall fall by the sword and the flame, by captivity and by spoil for a time."**

Those who were mentioned in the preceding verse as being the ones who knew God are not to be without leadership in those trying times. They shall find men who are capable to "help them to understand" what the issues at stake are. These leaders are called *maskilim* in the original. This word may be rendered either "they that have insight" or even "they that are wise" (*A. R. V.*). Since it is the causative stem of this verb that is used, it can be rendered more appropriately "they that cause to be wise"—and these are usually conceived of as the "teachers" (*A. R. V.m*) as *Luther* also renders this word in 12:3.

Nor will they have a meager measure of success in this godly endeavor of theirs: "they shall help *many*." Yet, on the whole, this period is to be one of persecution for the church, and so, though the "many" come to the point where they "understand," there will yet be many that shall pay the price that times of persecution often demand: "they shall fall by the sword and the flame, by captivity and by spoil." Knowing what it is all about does not give an individual indemnity against the evil that is current. In certain seasons men will be called upon to pay the supreme penalty. But it will usually happen as it is to happen in this instance: they shall suffer these things "for a time." There are ample indications in our historical sources to show that the sufferings predicted came to pass. The following passages from the first book of Maccabees illustrate our point: 1:56; 2:38; 3:41; 5:13; cf. also II Macc. 6:11.

In this verse the word '*am*, "people," is to be rendered "the people" because it came to be regarded as almost a proper noun and therefore needs no article (*K. S.* 292g).

34, 35. "Yet as they fall they shall receive at least a little help, and many shall join them by means of smooth words. And some of the teachers,

too, shall fall in order that there may be a smelting among them and a sifting and a purifying until the time of the end. For yet at the appointed time it shall come."

The whole book of Daniel is primarily a book of comfort. Whatever can be advanced to prepare men for the evil days to come is set forth by preference. So here the fact can be added that, even as good men lose their life in this good cause of the church of the Old Covenant, there shall be evidences that God has not forgotten His own but is giving them "at least a little help." This must be construed as a reference to the deliverance which came through the Maccabees, the sons of old Mattathias, of whom we read in I Macc. 2:1-5, and of whose exploits the two books of the Maccabees are a most interesting and valuable record, the first book making the impression of being very largely a reliable record of things that transpired, the second being an elaborated and less dependable report. But if this remark is a reference to the deliverance wrought by this famous family, it seems strange, indeed, that this should be described as being only a "little help," for it ultimately led to the complete deliverance from the tyranny of the Syrians and was followed by at least a temporary blossoming forth of national glory and independence. This recovery, in fact, continued for the greater part of a century.

There are, however, several considerations that make the statement "a little help" appear as an accurate evaluation of the case. One might use the approach of *Keil* who says that this help is "so named in comparison with the great deliverance which shall come   . . .   in the time of the end by the complete destruction of the oppressor." This explanation has this feature to recommend it that it makes it manifest that the reference is only to the beginning of the entire period of the Maccabees. For, as we shall see presently, at just about this point the account concerning Antiochus Epiphanes breaks off abruptly, and no attempt is made to predict historical developments after this crisis.

We could also adopt this explanation, which does not rule out the explanation of *Keil* just suggested, that this statement is at the same time an evaluation of the whole movement inaugurated by the sons of Mattathias on the basis of their actual importance for the kingdom of God. In other words, God did not rate this deliverance as high as did the Jews, for it had its shortcomings. It was not like the mighty works of the judges or the God-inspired victories of David. It had too much of human, nationalistic feeling and ambition mingled with it. It was overestimated by the men then living. Yet it was not evil or utterly to be despised. This statement gives it as much approval as it deserves.

The critical use made of this expression "a little help" is interesting. Critics argue that this word indicates that, on the one hand, the writer of the book—it could not be Daniel—was not of the party of the Maccabees and therefore not as enthusiastic as a man who was a strong partisan might have been. Besides, they suggest that the Maccabean deliverance was just beginning when this statement was written, and only the first successes were in evidence, and consequently the author could not speak as enthusiastically as could a later writer, who might have had the entire course of achievements before him. So this expression is to help men to determine the time of the writing of the book. But aside from the "pious fraud" involved in having the writer create the impression that this historical account of his was a message from an angel of God, we feel that the double explanation given above is more satisfactory than a theory that involves the rejection of major statements of the book.

This "little help" is, however, only one side of the matter. The other is that "many shall join themselves by means of smooth words" to the party of the deliverers. When it became apparent that leadership and strong influence as well as actual success were on the side of the Maccabees, men who were not really of one mind with the deliverers began to espouse their party. They came with "smooth words," that is, with hypocritical professions of loyalty.

35. It had been said that some of those who would be on the side of the party that had a right understanding of what God had in mind by all these events that transpired would also "fall." We are now apprised of the fact that "some of the teachers, too, shall fall." These teachers must, apparently, be regarded as being more than pedagogues. They were active leaders who taught trust in God and refusal to consent to heathen practices. It hardly seems likely that they were of that political or religious party who were later known as the Asidaeans although it is not impossible that this party may have grown out of this movement. Even though this name—spelled Hasidaeans in I Macc. 2:42—appears in this connnection, this passage does not state that at this time these men formed a party. They were simply a class of men who stood out because of their devotion and allegiance to the law, for the name means only "the Pious." Besides, "teachers" and "the Pious" are not of one and the same connotation.

It is stated in advance what good purpose the falling of the teachers may serve. In such trying days only men of the purest motives are acceptable and usable. Such times do try men's souls, and the incompetent are inadequate as leaders. Facing the issue of death and bringing the supreme sacrifice would serve the purpose of "smelting" and "sifting" and "purifying" the teachers. There is a progression in these terms. All of them are figures of speech. The first is taken from the work of those who prepare metals. It is essential that smelting remove the useless elements in the form of slag. Metals that are not purified thus would prove useless. Teachers who are not purified in the fires of affliction would be unequal to the stress and the responsibility of their holy calling.

The second figure is taken from the treatment of grain. Sifting removes the undesirable chaff and leaves behind the pure grain. This figure does not differ radically from the first.

The last figure refers to the result produced. "Purifying" means "making white," *lalben,* perhaps *Hiphil* infinitive with the *he* elided.

Such painful work of making the teachers become more nearly what they ought to be will not, however, go on endlessly. It shall continue only "till the time of the end." In this case that means the end of all things, for no limitation whatsoever is added to these words. Men may think that this "end" is afar off. They are, however, on that account not to think that the word refers to the remote future. This thought is implied in the last statement: "Yet at the appointed time it [the end] shall come." God has marked out seasons in advance for taking in hand and for terminating the work that the flesh of man feels to be so painful and grievous. Metals are not left in the fire too long. Grain is not sifted endlessly. The unclean are not washed without ceasing.

Near the beginning of this verse we have a construction that bears watching: *litsroph bahem,* "to smelt among them," meaning, of course, "to smelt some among them." The *be* of sphere expresses the partitive genitive, see *K. S.* 84 and 279b.

II. The More Remote Future: the Antichrist and His Overthrow and the Consummation, 11:36—12:3

a. *Antichrist's Policies and Seeming Success,* v. 36-39

This is one of the very difficult passages in the book of Daniel. The problem it offers is this: "Do v. 36-45 still refer to Antiochus Epiphanes?" or: "Are they, perhaps, a description of Antichrist?"

This is certainly a case where first impressions may be wrong. One is liable to resent violently the suggestion that in this passage a person who is different from King Antiochus is referred to. There is nothing that would seem to indicate a transition in thought.

As soon as the attempt is made consistently to apply these verses to the king last spoken of, the difficulties begin to become overwhelming. In the first place, why deal with the king in such detail (from v. 36) and then, after a good portion of his history has been covered, finally present his policies—as these four verses do—and then seemingly resume his history without having indicated why these policies should have been treated at the point where they are inserted?

Then, aside from other strong objections that shall be referred to later, a most obvious objection is this, that if those last verses (36-45) do refer to Antiochus, why does the historical parallel fail so utterly, the parallel with the history of the Seleucid kings that has been traced so facilely till now? Some commentators go so far, especially in connection with v. 40-45, as to claim that there was even a fourth expedition of Antiochus into Egypt, an expedition of which historical sources know nothing.

This problem was felt already as early as the time of Jerome, who parted company with the heathen Porphyry at verse 22 and had the reference to the Antichrist begin there.

The possibilities involved are these: This section

refers to Antiochus Epiphanes, or it is a section which is in a general way typical of the Antichrist, or it is a direct prophecy of the Antichrist. We are committed to the last of these views as offering the fewest difficulties when viewed as a whole.

Our chief reasons for this position are the following. In the first place, over against the contention that there is nothing that would indicate a transition to another subject it must be remembered that there is a factor in v. 35 which is just such a transition though we did not indicate this fact above. This factor is the remark that the smelting, sifting, and purifying were to continue "until the time of the end." That means that the sifting spoken of shall be the mark of all history that follows until the very end. As far as that end may seem to lie in the future, we were assured that "yet at the time appointed it shall come." With that remark the needed transition is complete. By not heeding carefully that it was a transition interpreters have overlooked the fact that a new subject was taken up in v. 36. Enough has been said about this cruel king to fortify the people of God against the ills they shall suffer at his hands. It is remarkable that so much should have been said. We might have expected less. In any case, for the present there is no need of anything more.

One might, however, protest with a show of right that the subject of Antiochus Epiphanes is just dropped, not concluded. Since so much of his life has been related, there ought to be at least a formal conclusion of that life. But we already know about that from 8:25. That may then justly be taken for granted. Besides, there will be occasion to round out the subject in chapter 12, where reference will again be made to it.

Furthermore, the argument advanced by such interpreters as *Kliefoth*, which refers to the article before the word "king," *hammelekh*, at the very be-

ginning of this verse, has greater force than is usually
conceded to it. *Montgomery*, indeed, draws the contrary conclusion from the use of the title with the
article by having it refer to Antiochus when he says:
" 'The king,' [who is] the fascination of the writer,
now stands *alone* upon the stage," that is to say, apart
from the king of the south who has previously appeared on the scene time and again. But one need remember only that Daniel does not regard Antiochus
Epiphanes as a rightful king. In v. 21 he appeared on
the scene as "a contemptible person, to whom they had
not given the honor of the kingdom." Only in v. 27, by
way of accommodation, when he is mentioned together
with the king of the south, does the plural "kings" include him. Consequently *"the* king" would here be un-
apt as a designation of Antiochus.

To this must be added the fact that this section
of the chapter has no correspondence with chapter 8,
where Antiochus had previously been referred to.
Such correspondence could rightly be expected when
the same author comes back to a subject that he has
previously treated.

To this must be added another argument arising
from v. 36, that this verse does not at all apply to
Antiochus. As we shall see, in v. 36 things are predicated concerning the person under consideration that
are not historically true with reference to this king.
He was not the sort of person there described.

All these considerations ought to be deemed
sufficient to establish the correctness of our position.

36.   **"But the king shall do as he wills and shall
exalt himself and shall magnify himself above every
god and shall speak horrible things against the God
of gods; and he shall meet with success until the
indignation is at an end. For that which is determined
shall be done."**

It must be admitted that, if this verse were found in a chapter which happened to be the only chapter of the book of Daniel, it would certainly offer very little evidence that the Antichrist is being referred to. But we have read of the Antichrist before in Daniel, especially in 7:25. Second Thessalonians 2:4 must be a quotation from this verse; this New Testament passage without a doubt speaks of the Antichrist. In like manner he is spoken of in 9:26 although there the title "prince" is used with regard to him; but similar things are predicated concerning him. The more one reflects on the matter, the stronger the conviction becomes that this must refer to someone other than Antiochus Epiphanes. The matter that has confused some interpreters is the fact that King Antiochus is also regarded as a type of the New Testament Antichrist and is, in a sense, the Old Testament Antichrist.

The impatience at being restrained and the stubborn self-will of the Antichrist are first described when it is said of him that he shall do as he wills (*Hebrew*: "according to his own pleasure"). In addition he assumes a high position (he "shall exalt himself") and also attributes greatness to himself (he "shall magnify himself"), even "above every god." That is the highest pinnacle of inflated pride that knows no limit. Such an attitude cannot be attributed to Antiochus Epiphanes. He certainly was an exponent of the cult of Zeus Olympius. Even in Athens he had a temple built in honor of this god. No historian knows even the least of his aspiring to be anything more than a god in the sense in which all Syrian and other monarchs were classed as being divine. He did, indeed, attempt to rob temples, but that was done more because of financial embarrassment than out of disrespect for the gods whose temples he intended to pillage. The correspondence with 7:8 and 11 is striking enough to be pointed out here.

A number of commentators find no difficulty in connection with the statement that this king will "magnify himself above every god," in applying it to Antiochus. *Charles, Bevan,* and *Driver,* for example, point particularly to inscriptions on coins that date from this king's time. First Apollo appears on these, together with the image of Antiochus, later no god, then Zeus Olympius. The conclusion that these men draw appears to us as being an unsupported inference, the conclusion, namely, that Antiochus identified himself completely with Zeus. A strange contradiction would result from their reasoning. As *Charles* especially claims, Zeus Olympius is the god whom the king "identified with the God of the Jews (II Macc. 6:2)." If Antiochus identified himself with Zeus he must have identified himself with the God of the Jews. But our verse indicates that he "shall speak horrible things against the God of gods." We ask: "Against *himself?*" Or, "How could he be so incensed at himself if the above claims are really meant seriously about identifying Zeus with the God of Israel?" We feel that the identification of the king with Zeus Olympius is invented in order to support the interpretation of these commentators. We find no clear statement to this effect in any historical source that we have seen.

More than pride and self-exaltation will be manifested over against the "God of gods." Against Him he shall "speak horrible things." The word for "horrible," *niphla'oth,* is, indeed, "marvelous" (*A. R. V.*); but *Ungeheuerliches* (monstrous) says *K. W.,* and that is certainly meant. Such bitter opposition lies in the very name which the New Testament gives to this personage: *Anti*-christ, i.e., "against" the Christ.

One might think that God would not allow such blasphemies to be spoken. But "he shall meet with success until the indignation is at an end." God shall have just cause for being indignant at the sins of His people and shall allow such horrible things to transpire as part of the suffering which His own have merited, for to hear the name of the Most High blasphemed thus is in itself a most painful experience for the children of God. But, of course, we know, too, that this season of indignation is not to last long; 9:27 had indicated that its duration was to be but one week. This is, as we also know, but a part of the great tribulation of which the New Testament speaks. But not one of these things is happening without the determined counsel and foreknowledge of God, for even the indignation and the blasphemy of the name of God fit so entirely into the careful plans of the Lord that it may well be remarked in this connection: "For that which is determined shall be done."

37. **"And for the gods of his fathers he shall have no regard; nor for the desire of women; nor for any god at all shall he have regard. For he shall exalt himself above everything."**

The unnaturalness of the attitude of this strange ruler is now presented. Three points are under consideration in regard to which men usually agree, loyalties, as it were, that stand out above all others. First of all there is reverence for the ancestral religion, which men, as a rule, do not easily put aside. The "gods of the fathers" commonly get more than usual attention; but not in the case of this unnatural king, for he shall "have no regard" for them.

Another loyalty is that to womankind, which usually takes the form of love for one's wife. The strange, unfeeling nature of this king will, however, lead him to have no regard "for the desire of women." Let us note the plural "women." That would well include all loyalties to womankind, not only to the wife, but also to mother and sister in so far as they have a claim upon a man's regard. This interpretation fits into this connection so much better than does the one that the critical exposition favors that we do well to retain it.

This view certainly allows for the traditional interpretation advocated since the days of the Reformers that the papacy is described here with reference to its forbidding to marry; in fact, such an attitude toward marriage is nothing less than a direct fulfillment of this passage. At the same time the first part of this verse also has a much clearer sidelight thrown on it by this fact, that when the god of his fathers is not regarded, that involves the rejection of the truth concerning the true God, which the early church had held and which the church of the Middle Ages had abrogated by substituting work-righteousness for Christ-righteousness. This feature of *Luther's* interpretation we are ready to retain without hesitation though certain details of his exposition do not strike us as being sufficiently substantiated. As any careful reader may check, these details were advanced by Luther with quite a measure of diffidence.

The commonly accepted interpretation of our day is that "the desire of women" must be a goddess whom women particularly desired and worshiped, that is to say, Astarte, whose worship, as is well known, was accompanied by lascivious practices and common prostitution of womankind. But why mention one whom women desired whereas one that men desired should have been mentioned?

Lastly the sweeping assertion is made that not "for any god at all shall he have regard." Devotion to a god is one of the universal loyalties of human beings. Even if one god, the god of their fathers had been rejected, they would, because of the natural religious inclination of mankind, have accepted at least some other god or gods. Not so this king. And the explanation for this abnormal attitude? Because of that highly inflated ego of his: "for he shall exalt himself above

everything." A more bloated pride could hardly
be imagined.

**38. "Instead of these he shall honor the god
of strongholds. Yea, even a god whom his fathers
knew not he will honor with gold and silver, with
precious stones and all sorts of treasures."**

We can hardly overlook the fact that we were just
informed that this personage shall not have regard
for any god at all. Does v. 38 now make the assertion
that there is after all some one god to whom he offers
allegiance? Hardly. This difficulty is met by the explanation offered by *Keil,* which still covers the case
very adequately. He says, "He will regard no god, but
only war; the taking of fortresses he will make his
god." This attitude of his is in line with the common
observation that, if men will not have the true god,
there must be something to which they will attach the
allegiance of their heart. That which then becomes the
chief object of one's affection is one's god. It is so here.
Warlike conquests, the taking of strongholds—that
he will engage in. To that he will devote great treasures, even "gold and silver, precious stones and all
sorts of treasures." That attitude is not hard to understand because history offers so many illustrations of
it. But what will make it stranger is the fact that this
person will come from a line of ancestors who had
no such ambitions and who were devoted to no such
god. That fact is stated in the words that this is "a god
whom his fathers knew not."

The Hebrew for "god of strongholds" is *'eloah
ma'uzzim,* which *Luther* understood to be the name of
a new god and reproduced in the form *Maussim.* By
doing this he was, however, merely following in the
footsteps of the Greek translator Theodotion, who
rendered in a similar way. In Luther's case this
rendering was motivated by a strange correspondence
which he saw between this form and the Latin name

for the mass, *missa*. Believing this to be a direct reference to the Antichrist, the pope, Luther detected here the central doctrine of the papacy. We cannot follow him in this although the correspondence is a most striking one, for the meaning of the Hebrew word is well established otherwise, and there is nothing to indicate that this is a proper name. But let no man imagine that Luther did not also know of this basic meaning of the word, for his comments show this.

The first word of the verse is construed with a *le* which, after the Aramaic manner, here functions as the exponent of the accusative.

39. **"He shall proceed against the strongest fortresses with the help of the strange god; and he will increase honors to the one that acknowledges him and shall make such to be rulers over many and shall apportion land as a reward."**

The strange god is, of course, his love of warfare and conquest. "The strongest fortresses" will call forth his most enthusiastic endeavors. To take them will be the pride of his heart. Strange, how wars will prevail to the end, and how the Antichrist shall himself be addicted to wars! To bind men to himself he bestows particular honors on those who acknowledge him. He even makes them influential rulers and gives them land grants as favors. As *Kliefoth* rightly remarks, we find here the thoughts that were already expressed concerning the Antichrist in 9:27, especially in the matter of his trying to establish himself firmly with men and give his cause the proper solidity.

The dilemma of the critics is interesting at this point. All this is to be squeezed into a pattern of history concerning Antiochus Epiphanes, a pattern which refuses to fit. It was noted above that the king especially espoused the cause of Jupiter Olympius. In this verse and in the preceding one everything would seem to point rather to Mars when reference is made to the "god of strongholds." But Jupiter must be retained so as not to create a discrepancy. And strenuous efforts are put forth to make Jupiter the patron god of wars or at least fortresses, a procedure which would have amazed the old Greeks, who certainly themselves never knew of any such attainments on the part of their old god.

In this verse, too, we do well to hold to the received text and to reject the marginal reading, which would produce the thought: "The one that he acknowledges, he will honor," by substituting *yakkir* for *hakkir*. We point to this item, not as though it involved any material modification of the sense, but merely to support our general thesis that the Hebrew text as we have it is, for the most part, a most excellent text and does not stand in half as much need of emendation as critics, Jewish or modern Christian, are wont to think. See *K. S.* 129c.

Aside from this, the text of this verse, as we have it, does make good sense and is not in the hopelessly corrupt state which the critics find here.

b. *His Later Fortunes and End,* v. 40-45

The difficulties encountered by those interpreters who still hold the view that Antiochus Epiphanes is the subject of these verses are increased the farther into the chapter they carry this assumption, for the remaining statements of the chapter do not refer to anything that is known about this king and so must be regarded as being only vaguely correct in their prediction that this king would die—a safe prediction in the case of every man. Since the details preceding his death do not fit their view, the assumption is added that this demonstrates that the writer of these words set them down before the events could safely be forecast and so shot wide of the mark.

We have here an account of the last things that shall befall the *Antichrist*: he shall be strongly as-

sailed; he shall defend himself and still further vex
the church; he shall amass wealth; his course shall,
however, be a troubled one, alarms disturbing him the
nearer the end comes; he shall finally prepare for
some great assault, presumably upon the church, and
shall suddenly perish with none to help him.

The terms that are used in this composite picture
are drawn from the conditions of the times when
Daniel wrote although, of course, every word comes
from the angel that reveals these things to Daniel.
These terms, therefore, become symbolical. The king
of the south is no longer Egypt; nor the king of the
north, the Syrian. *Luther's* exposition, though limited
too closely to the pope, nevertheless indicates how
these events may be construed. On the whole we believe that not a specific but a general picture, a composite of the whole, is drawn with a symbolism which,
like that of unfulfilled statements generally in divine
prophecy, is dark and difficult before the fulfillment
has become reality.

40.   **"But at the time of the end the king of the
south shall push at him, and the king of the north
shall come as a whirlwind against him with chariots
and horsemen and many ships, but he shall come
into these lands and shall sweep along and pass
through."**

The time is definitely marked as "the time of the
end." There is nothing in the context that would restrict the force of the word "end," and so the end of
all things must be meant. Attempts to have the expressions "king of the north" and "king of the south"
refer to historical personages are unsatisfactory.
Though earlier in this chapter these expressions had
a particular meaning, the general idea now involved
would seem to be that, as these ancient kings came
against one another from different points of the
compass, so shall new forces that are like unto those

of old in this instance come against the Antichrist simultaneously from the north and the south. *Luther* saw a beginning of this fulfillment in the active opposition that the papacy was meeting in his day after it had for a long time dominated church and state.

The variety of the resources that are to be employed against the Antichrist indicate how great his power must be at the latter end—"chariots, horsemen, and many ships." But the Antichrist will not be slow to repel the attack. He himself shall "come into these lands," that is, the lands of those who have assailed him, and "shall sweep along and pass through." Armies surge back and forth, are alternately victorious, and work the usual devastations that have always been known to attend upon war. But the Antichrist himself will have huge forces of war at his own disposal.

41. **"And he shall enter also into the glorious land, and many shall perish; but these shall escape from his hands—Edom, Moab, and the chief of the children of the Ammonites."**

This is still a symbolical representation. The "glorious land" refers to what the "glorious land" had stood for in the days of Daniel—the church of God. Antichrist's chief aversion to the very end will be God's church. And of that church "many shall perish." There shall be many martyrs to the cause of the Savior. From this point of view it cannot be difficult to determine what "Edom, Moab, and the chief of the children of the Ammonites" represent. These were the proverbial and bitter enemies of the children of God. They must, therefore, stand for that which Antichrist stands for. In his conquests he shall regard common enmity against the church as being equivalent to loyalty to his cause. Why just "the chief of the children of the Ammonites" should be mentioned is more than we are able to detect.

The feminine plural *rabboth,* "many," apparently

has as its antecedent the feminine plural word "lands" in the preceding verse. But it refers to the people of these lands and is therefore construed with a masculine verb. See *K. S.* 249a.

42, 43. **"He shall stretch forth his hand upon the countries, and the land of Egypt shall not escape him. And he shall get control over the treasures of gold and silver and over all the precious things of Egypt; and the Libyans and Ethiopians shall be in his train."**

Having started on a campaign of defence, he shall follow it with a campaign of conquest: "he shall stretch forth his hand upon the countries," which means, of course, any countries that happen to lie in his path. In the course of this campaign he shall engage also the chief world power of his day, for that is what Egypt still symbolized in the days of Daniel, at least at the time of the end of his prophetic activity when Babylon had just fallen and Persia had not as yet been established. Any interpreter would have to concede that Egypt symbolized a major world power.

43. So great will be the power of Antichrist in this last fierce thrust that he makes that he shall get control of the resources of this country which are here described as "the treasures of gold and silver and all the precious things of Egypt." In this connection the Libyans and the Ethiopians can be intended to describe only the empire of Egypt in its broadest extent, for Libya to the northwest and Ethiopia to the extreme south represented the farthest reaches to which greater Egypt attained. If a major world power falls so completely under his control, Antichrist must surely achieve great power before his end.

44, 45. **"But rumors out of the east and the north shall alarm him, and he shall go forth in great fury to destroy and exterminate many. And he shall pitch his tent-palace between the seas and**

toward the glorious holy mountain. But he shall come to his end, and there shall be none to help him."

Due to the symbolic character of the statements involved, we can hardly determine accurately what the "east" and the "north" are to signify in this connection, except that they may, perhaps, be certain distant countries which, like the rumors emanating from them, are vague. In any case, after his great conquests the Antichrist shall have no peace to enjoy them. Rumors of dangers that threaten the security of all that he has built up shall prove very disturbing. His coarser nature is revealed in the fact that these reports shall rouse "fury" in him and the desire "to destroy and to exterminate many." Constructive endeavors do not emanate from him. His path has been marked by destruction and bloodshed; he knows of no other course to follow.

45. One is almost tempted to interpret the terms employed here very specifically, as Luther does, and to regard this as a reference to Rome which lay "between two seas around the glorious holy mountain" (*Luther's* translation). But this type of prophecy is never to be referred specifically to individual items, and so we must regard this as a description of the last desperate assault upon the church, "the glorious holy mountain."

The "tent-palace" refers to the glorious aggregate of tents (plural: *'oholim*) with all manner of luxurious appointments and splendor, practically like a palace, which Oriental monarchs often took along on their warlike expeditions, and which certain Bedouin rulers of the East still carry with them. The Antichrist is thought of as having come in the full strength of his luxury and power.

The rest of the picture is apparently taken from the location of Jerusalem, and so Jerusalem again appears as the prototype of the church of the last days.

This ancient holy city did lie "between the seas," a phrase that is always used without the article because it was evident which two seas are referred to in locating Jerusalem; and he did encamp "toward the glorious holy mountain," which was the object of his assault.

But even as in 7:25, 26 the Antichrist reaches a certain point and then encounters the judgment, so that same event is recorded here in a more dramatic fashion. Just when it seems as if the Holy City must fall before him whom none seemed able to resist, there comes the catastrophic overthrow: "he shall come to his end." And since that end is the judgment of God, there "shall be none to help him." God's judgments cannot be resisted.

So again a chapter has closed with the note of comfort and victory for the church and of a definite and final overthrow of the last great enemy of the church on earth.

Keil remarks rightly at this point: "The placing of the overthrow of this enemy with his host near the temple mountain agrees with the other prophecies of the Old Testament which place the decisive destruction of the hostile world power by the appearance of the Lord for the consummation of His kingdom upon the mountains of Israel (Ezek. 39:4), or in the valley of Jehoshaphat at Jerusalem, or at Jerusalem (Joel 3: 2, 12f.; Zech. 14:2) and confirms the result of our exposition, that the hostile king, the last enemy of the world power, is the Antichrist."

NOTE: *Driver* (*Tenses*), 171 and 175. Obs., draws attention to the fact that a number of jussives occur in this chapter of Daniel, in which this shortened form is used "without any recollection of its distinctive signification." These occur in vv. 4, 10, 17, 18, 19, 25, 28, 30. He regards this use as an indication of the degeneration of the Hebrew language or else of erroneous pointing by the scribes. *Charles* builds up on this observation and lists these forms as "bad Hebrew" (p. 268). As usual, *Koenig's* approach is far more reasonable (*K. S.* 192d) in that he allows for mistakes in affixing vowel points but shows also from these and other instances that the consonants found in a certain form oftentimes have a tendency to crush certain vowels—*i* to *e*, for example. These forms may have the appearance of being jussives but are in reality just modified imperfects. So the charge of "bad Hebrew" is answered.

HOMILETICAL SUGGESTIONS

This chapter might be treated in Bible classes. We do not see how it could be used for a sermon or for sermons.

CHAPTER XII

c. *The Consummation,* v. 1-3

To begin a chapter at this point is a most unfortunate division of the material. These three verses belong to the preceding revelation. Since 11:2 the angel has been speaking of the disclosures that he had promised to make in the tenth chapter. In fact, what we have here is the glorious climax of the work of the Lord. To drop the matter of the future events with the conclusion of the eleventh chapter would yield a conclusion in a negative strain, for it would tell of nothing more than the overthrow of the Antichrist. Certain constructive features of a most glorious sort are added here: Michael's help in the great tribulation; the deliverance of the faithful; the resurrection; the judgment; and eternal glory. This brings the whole vision to a most glorious consummation. In fact, without this conclusion the treatment of the subject matter in chapter eleven would give unseemly emphasis to the importance of the Antichrist.

Those who have referred the conclusion of the preceding chapter to Antiochus Epiphanes are now, at the beginning of chapter twelve, compelled to make as bold a leap into the future as they would have made had they referred 11:36ff to the Last Tribulation and the Antichrist. But that leap is more precarious at this point, for it would be a leap, not from the Old Testament Antichrist to the New Testament Antichrist—a logical progression—but from the Old Testament Antichrist to the Final Consummation of all things.

1. **"And at that time shall Michael, the great prince who stands guard over those who belong to**

thy people, arise; and there shall be a time of distress such as was not since a nation existed even till that same time. And at that time thy people shall be delivered, every one that shall be found written in the book."

There can be no doubt about it that the time referred to in this verse is coincident with that of the events last spoken of. It is the time of the Great Tribulation, the time of the last Antichrist. The quotation that our Lord makes of this verse in Matt. 24:21, 22 with reference to the end of time clinches the matter for us beyond the possibility of a doubt. Compare also "at that time" with 11:40.

In 10:13, 21 we learned of the nature of the activity of Michael. We saw how he was employed by the good Lord for the defense of His people, and how a valiant obligation was laid upon him in the great warfare of the spiritual forces that contend behind the scenes in the conflict of the nations. Though this mighty angelic prince was, no doubt, continually engaged in behalf of God's own, we are here given special assurance that he will not fail to do his part when that last Great Tribulation breaks upon the people of God. That this is his work we are told in the relative clause: "who stands guard over [literally 'stands over'] those who belong to thy people." His getting into action is described by the verb "arise," *'amadh,* a verb that is often used with reference to some warlike activity.

The sequence of the clauses should be noted at this point. The next clause: "And there shall be a time of distress," does not in point of time follow upon the preceding statement. It records merely an attendant circumstance. The "distress" is not the result of Michael's entrance into the conflict. Rather, because the distress is so great, therefore this prince intervenes in behalf of God's people. The distress, of course, afflicts the world. The exceptional nature of this distress is indicated by the fact that the world, which has times without number seen distress of the most acute sort, will never have seen anything like this last distress, even should men for comparative purposes go back to the time "since a nation existed even till that same time." That means, of course, to go back to the time of the existence of the first nation. For the expression compare Exod. 9:18, 24; Joel 2:2; Jer. 30:7. The world is little minded to give heed to the implications of this plain statement, and in the face of it many keep on speaking of the bold and great achievements in culture that men will 'produce as time advances. Yet this great distress will be unavoidable and unparalleled.

The expression "at that time" occurs for the third time to make assurance doubly sure that the point of time has by no means been shifted, but that the entire action moves in the sphere of the very last things. We are now given the assurance as to what results the angel-prince Michael will achieve: "Thy people shall be delivered." When this great prince sets himself to a God-given task he has success.

It would seem as though those to whom deliverance is promised are only the people of the prophet's own nation, a thought that is actually expressed by *Gordon's* translation "your nation." Yet we know that in its New Testament usage the term Israel broadens out to include all who are of the faith of Abraham (Rom. 4:16). This broader implication of the term used here is indicated also by the parallel expression, "every one that shall be found written in the book." This refers specifically to the book of life which we discussed in connection with our interpretation of 7:10. To have one's name inscribed in this book connotes salvation. That a record of heaven with reference to those who are to inherit eternal life should be available is equivalent to saying that God's thoughts for the salvation of His children run back into eternity, and that He loves to busy Himself with their eternal welfare. In the last analysis, the "book of life" is Christ Jesus Himself as our Confessions indicate (*F. C.*, Epit., Art. XI, 6).

Another achievement on the part of the prince Michael seems to be implied in the fact that this verse follows immediately upon the record of the overthrow of the Antichrist which is described in the preceding chapter. It follows almost inevitably that the juxtaposition of these two matters marks Michael as being the agent appointed by God to deliver His people by effecting a tremendous overthrow.

2. **"And many that sleep in the land of dust shall awake, some to everlasting life, and some to everlasting shame and contempt."**

Farrar faults those who make an effort to solve the difficulties of this verse by stating that their efforts "glide with insincere confidence over the difficulties." It is rather unfair to attribute insincerity to an opponent simply because his solution does not coincide with yours. The first difficulty offered by this verse is, "Does this verse teach a partial resurrection of the dead?" We answer, "No," for the following reasons. A partial resurrection would be a precarious comfort for the times under consideration. When our Lord Jesus quotes this verse, as He without a doubt does in John 5:28, 29 (the points of coincidence between Daniel's and the Savior's statements are too many to be an accidental similarity) He substitutes "all" for "many." This substitution is evidently interpretative. Daniel apparently wanted to emphasize the great number that would be arising from the dead. The Savior apparently sought to make the universality of the resurrection more prominent and at the same time to guard against the misinterpretation to which the Daniel passage was exposed. So Scripture interprets Scripture.

There are other considerations that bear upon the case. First of all, the idea of two resurrections grows out of a misinterpretation of Rev. 20:5. A dual resurrection is taught nowhere in the Scriptures. There are also other instances where "many" and "all" are used interchangeably, the one emphasizing the fact that there are numerically *many,* the other the fact that *all* are involved. Who would venture to restrict the "many" used in Matt. 20:28 and 26:28 as excluding the idea of "all," especially in the light of what I John 2:2 says? The same situation prevails in regard to Rom. 5:15, 16 when these verses are contrasted with v. 12 of the same chapter. Two points of view are permissible here, and they are not mutually exclusive.

Now a consideration of the connection between v. 1 and v. 2. The thought implied is that the "distress" referred to will claim the life of many even though the people as such will be delivered through Michael's work. Now what about those who perished? Verse 2 asserts that for them there will be a resurrection. Nor will there be only a small number that shares in this resurrection; there will be "many." The *min* that follows the *rabbim,* "many," is, without a doubt, not partitive but local. In fact, the Hebrew accents suggest that the entire phrase "from the sleeping in the land of dust" should be construed with the verb that follows, i.e., "they shall arise," even as a similar construction is found in the pertinent New Testament passages, cf., Matt. 17:9. That would yield the following sense: "There will be many who will arise from sleeping in the land of dust."

Already in the Old Testament death is called a sleep in such passages as Ps. 13:3; Job 3:13; Jer. 51:39, 57. Yet it must in all fairness be admitted that to "sleep the sleep of death" in no sense as yet involves the comfort that is found in the New Testament expression "asleep in Jesus." The *A. V.* has made the expression "dust of the earth" quite familiar though the translation is not accurate. Better is "land of dust" as *Gordon* quite aptly renders, for the truth of the matter is that "to sleep in the dust of the earth" is very apt to create the impression of one's lying down in some dusty place upon earth and going to sleep. The Hebrew *'adhamah* would seem to mean as much as "region of dust," the genitive being a description of the thing that is characteristic of the region. "Dust" means that fine loam or earth out of which man was originally formed: we go back to what we came from. Isa. 26:19 is a good parallel to this part of the verse. Note *Luther's* good rendering: *Viele, so unter der Erde schlafen.*

In the Old Testament times there was a clear understanding that death did not indiscriminately consign all to the same happiness as a shallow optimism in all ages seems to hold. Some arise unto "everlasting life," *chayyey 'olam*—the only instance of the use of this term in the Old Testament. Others arise to "everlasting shame and contempt." It is true that the adjective "everlasting" is in this instance apparently used only in connection with the last noun. But why should "contempt" be everlasting and not "shame" also when both nouns are so nearly synonymous? It is better to construe the adjective, which follows its nouns, as being written once though it is applicable to both nouns as *Luther* already very properly translated the expression. Isa. 66:24 is again parallel to this half of the verse. *Charaphoth* is a plural of extent to express the idea of *"great* contempt."

To the idea of a saving resurrection the idea of a just and eternal judgment upon the sinners has been added, a thought that very appropriately fits into the situation.

3. **"And they that are wise shall shine like the brightness of the firmament, and they that turn many to righteousness as the stars forever and ever."**

The noun *hammaskilim*, which is rendered "teachers" by *Luther* as well as by *A. R. V.m,* is better rendered "the wise" or "they that are wise," for the parallel expression in the verse shows that a broader classification is implied. The same word was used in 11:33, 35 and will appear again in 12:10. But in no case is it to be limited to the narrower idea of "teachers" though such persons would naturally be included. The word is a *Hiphil* participle and could mean "those that cause to be wise" as well as "those that behave wisely." This verse predicts that glory awaits these persons. But we know that glory is in store for all that behave wisely. Since so many shall be the recipients of glory, why single out the teachers and leave the others without the comfort that this thought imparts?

To the thought of the resurrection expressed in the preceding verse our verse adds the thought of eternal glory, for "they that are wise shall shine like the brightness of the firmament," and that is without a doubt a brilliant glory. When the shining of the firmament is spoken of, the firmament as it appears at bright noonday is meant; and that is a glory that is too brilliant to look into, for it is when the sun displays its full brilliance.

As is readily seen, the verse does not speak of salvation but of glory. Salvation is everywhere in the Scriptures regarded as depending upon faith and not on works. But the glory, which is the reward of God's grace, is in proportion to the works that are done in the power of the Spirit and for Christ's sake. Since the imparting of such glory is a gracious work that

God does, it would be unnatural for man not to regard the prospect of such glory with joy. To charge those that reckon with the prospect of glory as being motivated by a mercenary spirit, and to regard Christ's words as an appeal to low motives is an ungrateful misconstruction of this word.

The parallel statement of the case, which is in a higher strain and has something akin to poetic structure, is this: "They that turn many to righteousness [shall shine] as the stars forever and ever." This suggests that the true wisdom of those just described consists not only in adopting for themselves a wise attitude in the midst of the troubled times that are upon the people of God but also in helping others to adopt the same attitude or to find righteousness, *matzdiqey,* "causing to be righteous." The double description of the glory to be imparted to all such persons indicates that it shall be no mean glory that the God of pure mercy will bestow.

The Lord's quotation of this verse in Matt. 13:43 confirms the broader construction placed upon the first term and by way of comparison uses only "the sun."

Some interpreters find in these verses "the earliest passage where the belief [of the resurrection] is unambiguously set forth" (*Bevan*). If this is to be understood in the sense that the doctrine of immortality was a late development in the faith of Israel, we cannot agree with the statement, for Ps. 16:9-11; Job 19:25-27; Isa. 26:19, rightly interpreted, already teach the resurrection of the body even as many other passages, such as Gen. 25:8, give evidence of the general belief in immortality among the patriarchs at a very early date. We personally doubt that there was ever a time when the faith of God's people did not include the doctrines of immortality and resurrection, though it is hard for us to determine with what measure of clearness they were revealed. These are not truths that the religious genius of Israel began to discern for the first time in the days of Daniel or even as late as the time of the Maccabees.

d.   *The Command to Preserve the Vision,* v. 4

"And thou, Daniel, preserve the vision and seal the book till the time of the end; many shall diligently peruse it, and knowledge shall be increased."

This is the last statement of this last vision. If Daniel had any misgivings as to whether this vision was intended for him personally or was to be offered for the general use of God's people for times to come, he here receives orders from on high to satisfy his mind on this point; and these orders bid him to preserve the book and to make it available for those who in years to come shall need just such a writing as this.

In connection with our interpretation of 8:26 we discussed the correct meaning of the verb *sethom,* which we there and here translate "preserve." The sealing of the book is to serve the same purpose. "The vision" and "the book," of course, refer to the same thing, namely, the vision that began with 11:2. Such a smaller document may in the Hebrew also be called a "book," for *sepher* may mean any document, long or short. When the article is used with "end," that word apparently gets to mean the end of all things. It is then that this part of Daniel's book will come into its own in a special sense. Then "many shall peruse it." The verb *shut* does mean primarily "run to and fro." But with reference to a book that would mean to let the eyes run to and fro, that is, "peruse" it. Since it is an intensive form of the verb (*yeshotetu*), we have sought to give that shade of meaning by rendering "diligently peruse." They will read, reread, and check on what they have read, and so ponder these words diligently in their heart as did Mary on another occasion. And in the process of such earnest searching "knowledge shall be increased." In the light of the developments of the last times the purpose of the book and its meaning will become increasingly clear. Jesus' words point to the same conclusion when He says: "Let him that readeth understand," Matt. 24:15.

e. *The Last Attempt to Determine the Time of the Things Prophesied,* v. 5-13

Aside from being the conclusion, this portion of the book of Daniel may at the same time be regarded as being an instance of that which Peter refers to in I Pet. 1:10, 11, where he indicates that the prophets themselves are known to have sought to determine "what time or what manner of time the Spirit of Christ which was in them did point unto." The fact that an angel takes the initiative in the matter of making inquiries as to the time involved shows that such inquiries may be good and wise. Man can hardly avoid thinking in terms of the time that is being designated. Though an answer is given, it is significant that this answer is for the most part couched in general terms. That is apparently all with reference to the time element that is essential for the knowledge of man though his curiosity might prompt him to desire much information along this line. Aside from that he is bidden to content himself and quietly to go his way and to comfort himself also with the thought of the power of the good Lord to give to all their promised rewards.

5, 6. **Then I, Daniel, looked, and, lo, there were two others standing, the one on this bank of the river and the other on that bank. And one said to the man clothed in linen, who was above the waters of the river, "How long will it be to the end of these wonders?"**

In connection with our consideration of 10:5 we cast our vote in favor of the interpretation which

regards the "man clothed in linen" as being one of the
angels of the very highest order, that is to say, like
unto Michael. When the marvelous vision recorded in
that chapter first revealed him, he was alone in the
presence of the prophet, for the prophet's personal
attendants had fled. As Daniel now glances about
after this angel's communications have been concluded he discerns two others standing near by. These
are without a doubt to be thought of as angelic beings
though they are, perhaps, not of the same order as
the previous speaker. To project what the prophet here
sees back into chapter ten is hardly permissible, for
the possibility must be reckoned with that he did not
see these other two angels any earlier because they,
perhaps, now appeared for the first time.

We confess that there is some difficulty with
regard to these features of the vision. Several questions come to mind: "Why were there two additional
angels when, apparently, only one speaks and the
other does nothing? Does the manner of presentation
imply that both repeated the same question? Why
are they upon the banks of the river? Why does the
one clothed in linen appear above the waters at this
point?" These problems must be at least considered
even though we do not possess sufficient information
to answer them in detail.

We do well to determine, first of all, which stream
is referred to in this verse. The word for river is *ye'or*,
a word which, it is true, is commonly used for the Nile
although, as *K. W.* points out, this may be a cross between an Egyptian and an Assyrian loan word. In
10:4, however, we saw that the river at which the
prophet stood was the Hiddekel or the Tigris. The
word *ye'or* is here used apparently as a reminder of
the experiences of the Israelites in the days when they
were in Egypt by the side of the Nile, which stream
at that time represented the heathen deities and their

antagonism to Israel. As God proved Himself superior to all that the *ye'or* represented at that time, so His representative here stands above the stream to indicate that God still rules over the turbulent forces of opposition.

No interpreter has an adequate answer to the question as to why just *two* additional angels appear. Such passages as Deut. 19:15; 31:28, II Cor. 13:1, where it is demanded that there must be two witnesses in order to make an accusation valid, do not apply to the case in hand inasmuch as this particular demand of the law deals only with criminal charges, not with substantiating all and every sort of statement. We admit freely that we know of no explanation that actually does justice to the case, for it is certainly a forced interpretation, as is, for instance, that of *Kliefoth,* to have the singular verb used in v. 6, *wayyo'mer,* mean, "And *both* said." That rendition does violence to the simple meaning of words in order to devise a solution for a vexatious problem. We may, perhaps, go so far as to say that the presence of two, one of whom speaks what is in the mind of both, is an indication of the fact that these are "things angels desire to look into" (I Pet. 1:12), not only one lone angel. Though that still leaves the question unanswered as to why they stood on the *banks* of the river, this is, perhaps, a mere bit of the framework of the vision, not something essential. They must needs stand somewhere. They are not quite of the same rank as the revealing angel whom Daniel was dealing with till now. So they stand apart from him.

6.   The question as to why the superior angel was clothed with "linen" was discussed in connection with 10:5. The Hebrew construction is a bit different at this point. The participle "clothed" is in the construct state: "clothed of linens," and the latter plural may be explained by the fact that the word "gar-

ments"—a plural—has dropped out; see *K. S.* p. 215, Footnote 1.

The question propounded by one of these two is stated thus: "How long will it be to the end of these wonders?" The word "wonders," *pela'oth,* does not in the Hebrew happen to be used with the demonstrative pronoun which we inserted in our rendering of it. But the word without a doubt refers to the wonderful things that have just been disclosed in chapter eleven and the beginning of chapter twelve. Since these have just been referred to they are in English best indicated by the insertion of a "these" which is covered by the Hebrew article. The point of the question is therefore, "How long will it take for that entire series of wonderful things just foretold completely to unfold itself?" Behind that question lie two alternatives that apparently give rise to the questions: "Will these events that have been foretold follow in quick succession upon one another and so be concluded in a comparatively short time; or will it be a case of a development that is long drawn out and extends over long ages to come?"

To tell the truth of the matter, that would be the first major question that one would ask if he were attempting to learn the general scope of the last revelation as a whole. It is apparently implied that the questioner senses that these revelations extend to the end of time, and so his question really amounts to this: "How long will it be until the end of time?" *Kliefoth,* who is usually one of the most trustworthy of guides, gives a translation of the question which the words as such could yield, but which makes no sense: "How long is the end of these marvelous things going to last?" Just how much would constitute the end of these disclosures? And what does it matter just how long the *end* as such lasts? An answer to this question, if given, would have benefited no man. *Keil* unfortunately has the same rendering. This view is further unacceptable because of the queer constructions that result, for as *Kliefoth* maps out the sequence of thought here followed he comes to the conclusion that vv. 11 and 12 give the answer to the question asked in v. 6 after the question asked in v. 8 and its answer in vv. 9 and 10 had intervened. That would certainly have the prophets set forth their messages in the worst kind of disorder.

7. **Then I heard the man clothed in linen, who was above the waters of the river, and he raised his right hand and his left hand toward the heavens and swore by Him that liveth forever that it should be for a time, times, and a half time; and when an end be made of shattering the power of the holy people, then all these things should be finished.**

The angel "clothed in linen" apparently possesses information beyond that which other angelic beings have. He is, therefore, qualified to interpret even as he is empowered to make revelations. Though the answer corresponds with the question that was asked it is, perhaps, not quite the kind of an answer that Daniel would have been pleased to hear. Men think they would prefer an answer that gives an exact number of years and so precludes all uncertainty. It might be possible that for various reasons such an answer would benefit man least. Perhaps, though God, no doubt, foreknows even what the exact number of years of the future will be, such revelations would prey unduly upon the susceptibilities of man and seem to conflict with man's freedom. Yet for all that the answer given has two very definite points that constitute a full and satisfactory answer to the angel's question.

We know from Gen. 14:22 and Deut. 32:40 that since the very earliest days the raising of the hand was a gesture that accompanied the oath. The raising of both hands would signify the most solemn assurance that the words spoken are reliable. In the oath given as an answer God Himself is most appropriately designated as He "that liveth forever." In this connection that implies that He is the only One who lives beyond the confines of time and so is well able to mark off its limits.

The first answer informs us that the "end of these wonders" shall be "for" or "after" (Hebrew: *le* temporal) "a time, times, and a half time." This expression is the same one that is found in 7:25, and it has the same meaning in both passages. In chapter 7 the expression referred to the duration of times of persecution. It has practically the same force in this verse. Therefore the same interpretation applies in this verse. The opposition shall seem to begin with some measure of success; it shall then seem to wax twice as strong and successful; its power shall then suddenly be much reduced, and with that it shall be at an end. This part of the answer is given in terms of the opposition that the kingdom of God shall experience, and it offers the comfort that this opposition shall collapse after seeming success. That thought should always be borne in mind because we are too apt to be impressed with the threat that emanates from the enemies of the kingdom and their much-vaunted power.

The second half of the answer again centers on a helpful thought rather than on the calculation of times and seasons, to know which would profit man but little. Here, too, the answer to a question such as man would be apt to put is given in terms of bigger values than man reckons with. This part of the answer conveys the solemn news that the holy people must pass through the sad experience of having their power shattered. "Shatter," *nappets*, or "break in in pieces" (*A. R. V.*) involves complete demolition of power.

Hard though this seems, it is merely one of those necessities to which human pride and self-will put the grace of God before God's gracious purposes can be accomplished. Strangely, man is so set on trusting in himself and depending on his own power that, unless that power is reduced to a helpless minimum, he will refuse to put his confidence wholly in the good Lord. Only after we have been rendered weak are we capable of becoming truly strong. Israel of Old Testament days had to be reduced to the impotence of the last times of the old covenant before the Savior could come. So her trust in self will have to be broken again before the Christ can return. It is far more important to know that than to be able to foretell in exact terms of years how long this old world order is still to continue. There is much wisdom behind this double answer.

When we gave the word *yadh,* which originally means "hand," the meaning "power" we were adopting a frequent use of this word, cf., *BDB* p. 390, col. 1, and such passages as Jos. 8:20; Ps. 76:6.

We can see now that both halves of the answer cover the same ground. Both announce what must happen before the end comes, the one relates about the seeming success but ultimate collapse of the opposition to God, the other reminds that God's people shall be seemingly weakened in the process, but for their own good.

8. **And as for me, I heard this without understanding it; and so I said: "My lord, what shall be the final outcome of these things?"**

The Hebrew reads: "I heard and was not understanding," the perfect being followed by an imperfect of attendant circumstance (*K. S.* 154), a construction in which the subordinated imperfect is best rendered as above: "without understanding." By putting the *'ani,* I, first, the writer implies that the angels may well have understood the answer that the superior

angel gave them; but not so he himself. The fact that
Daniel indicates the instances whenever he had trouble
about understanding what was told him shows rather
clearly that ordinarily the prophets did unꞁerstand
and so did not need to inquire further. But when the
revelation was obscure, then those who received it at
once sought to remove the obscurity. In Daniel's case
the problem was, of course, the familiar one that pure
revelation about the future always puzzles the recipient more or less before the fulfillment is realized.
Even though he had not perceived the scope of the
preceding answer he, nevertheless, recorded both the
question and the answer very faithfully in the confidence that in due season the needed understanding
would be arrived at. He did, however, seem to understand fully the question that had been propounded, for
he now asks one that is quite different from the first
though it still bears on the time element. This second
question seems to have been propounded in the hope
that it might clarify what the answer to the preceding
one had not made clear.

Daniel's question is: "What shall be the final outcome of these things?" The address "my lord" is one
merely of respect which in no wise indicates that the
individual addressed is divine. The *'acharith,* the debate about which has been endless, is apparently to be
taken in the sense of "final outcome" as *BDB* suggests
though it uses the term "ultimate issue." *K. W.* allows
for the same rendering. Some would render "closing
stage" (*Driver* cited with approval by *Montgomery*).
Meinhold and *Keil* agree with this. But, if you cannot
understand what things mean, why inquire about what
will be the last things to happen? Though the term
could have this meaning, we believe a question like,
"What will be the final outcome?" is much more in
place under the circumstances. That, too, really in-
quires about the last things, but in the sense: "What

results will be brought about by the last turn of events?" That implies such vital issues as: "Who shall win in this great struggle? What shall the permanent achievements of it all be? How shall all the participants fare?" *A. R. V.* agrees with this interpretation when it renders: "What shall be the issue of these things?" Luther's rendering has the same sense: *Was wird darnach werden?*

9. **And he said: "Go thy way, Daniel, for preserved and sealed are the words until the time of the end."**

The spirit of this answer is: "There is no use trying to get any farther in the understanding of these matters; they simply will not be fully understood until these things come to pass." So Daniel is, in a way, being put off. He is practically being told, "There is no use trying now; let well enough alone." He is not to become wrapped up in meditation and speculation and stand still while engaged in that task. He is rather bidden: "Go thy way." A way of duty is mapped out before him. This way is to be followed.

As for these difficult words, they are "preserved and sealed." These verbs are the same as those used in v. 4, and the latter of the two is found in 8:26. The supposition is that, even as Daniel himself was to take precautions to have these revelations safeguarded for future times, so the providence of God would work in the same direction, and as a result these good disclosures would be made available for the time when they would meet a felt want. Then men will no longer ask in vain what the words mean, for the developing situation itself would apparently throw the needed light on them, and so men should be guided by this light. So the answer means: "You cannot know them now, but men shall know them hereafter." The time, however, when these words will be understood is designated as "the time of the end," meaning, without a doubt, the final end of all things.

10. **"Many shall be purified and made white and refined; but the wicked shall practice wickedness; and none of the wicked shall understand; but they that are wise shall understand."**

The interpreting angel is not getting off his subject. The preceding verse drew one's mind across the whole space of time that intervenes between the present and the final end. That entire time is in a sense, as long as there is an *ecclesia pressa,* a time of tribulation. Those that meet such persecution and tribulation in true faith will have the benefit of being "purified and made white and refined," figurative expressions that are taken respectively from sifting, washing, and smelting (cf., 11:35). Though in a measure tribulation befalls also the wicked, they on their part shall not profit thereby but shall continue to "practice wickedness." This shall again have the result that, when "the time of the end" comes, those who have been rendered wiser by tribulation and trial "shall understand." They will have grown in spiritual capacity, which includes capacity for apprehending the Word. On the other hand, clear as the Word will then be to the wise, "none of the wicked shall understand." In other words, it will not be a clarity of the Word that automatically reveals the Word to all. It will even then still be true that without the enlightenment of God's Holy Spirit none can truly discern what it is that God's Word says. Thus this verse shows that our approach to v. 9 was correct. There is a close sequence of thought also here in the prophetic Word.

The first two verbs are *Hithpaels,* but the trend toward a passive meaning that is manifested increasingly in later Hebrew may be regarded as being found in these forms, and so they may be translated as passives even as is the third verb, cf., *K. S.* 101.

11, 12. **"And from the time that the regular daily offerings are put aside and an abomination that causeth horror is set up there will be a thousand two hundred and ninety days. Blessed is he that awaiteth and cometh to the one thousand three hundred and thirty-five days."**

The situation is hardly as bad as *Vilmar*, for example, would have us believe, who says: "In short, we cannot be sure of anything in the interpretation." To begin with, we must hold fast to the fact that the Word of God does not jump about wildly from one item to another. If that were the case, not even the first canons of literary composition would be observed by Biblical writers—an unthinkable assumption. Verse 8 determines the trend of thought from that point to the end with the question, "What shall be the final outcome?" We are consequently at "the time of the end." Yet without a doubt, for the moment it seems as though we were thrown back into the times of Antiochus Epiphanes by the reference to "the regular daily offerings" and "an abomination that causeth horror," for in 8:11-13 these very words appeared with reference to his times. But there is a solution of this difficult problem in a fact that we have repeatedly been obliged to draw attention to, namely, the fact that the times of Antiochus Epiphanes are typical of the times of the end of all things. He himself, therefore, becomes a type of the Antichrist. It was for this reason that we have again and again referred to him as the Old Testament Antichrist.

This is the plainest instance of how the language that is borrowed from the earlier period is used with reference to the latter period, and so the typical character of this Old Testament persecutor is most

abundantly confirmed. Something will apparently
transpire at the end of time which in the most significant sense will be a putting aside of "the regular
daily offerings." In the place of these something will
then be set up which will just as plainly be "an abomination that causeth horror." History will tragically
repeat itself. Just what form this will take we cannot
know. *Luther's* comment on this verse may be the best
suggestion that has as yet been offered. He says:
"Nevertheless, it may yet come to pass that the world
becomes so entirely Epicurean that throughout the
entire world there may be no pulpit left from which
the gospel is still publicly preached . . . but it will
be preserved only in the home through the father of
the house." But even he does not venture to predict
what the "abomination" might be. Further speculation along these lines would be quite futile. If we
live to see the day we shall, God willing, understand
well enough what is meant.

This double calamity is used here only as marking
the beginning of a reckoning of time. From this point
onward there are to be "a thousand two hundred and
ninety days." This can be computed to be three years,
six months and a half. Heretofore we have found no
indication of *mathematical* computation in the use of
numbers of this sort. It was the *symbolical* use of
numbers that was evident throughout. We dare not
depart from that safe rule here. Even if we were to
reckon the number in terms of some event of the times
of Antiochus we should be quite unable to make it
square accurately with the facts as they are known.
The conclusion should have to be: either *we* are wrong,
or the author of the book is. We prefer to let such a
dilemma drive us to the former of the conclusions.

Nor does anyone know of any future fulfillment
of this number, certainly at least not for the present;
and we on our part believe that the symbolical use of

numbers will then still be seen to have been the safe approach. But three years, six and a half months is just a bit more than the half of seven. If a time of tribulation had been indicated that would have contained seven units, let us say months, it would have been a period of divine affliction. Our number, therefore, seems to refer to a season of affliction that is scarcely more than half a season of divine affliction and, we conclude, therefore quite bearable—not surpassing man's strength to endure. Such an interpretation is in harmony with the symbolical use of figures as it is found in this book.

The last question has been answered. The "final outcome" will be that God's children will be able to bear whatever hard things come to pass. That is an answer of comfort. At the same time a more definite answer, definite enough at least for the present, has also been given for v. 6.

The word *husar* may be either perfect or infinitive; the meaning remains the same in either case.

12. This verse has to build up on the approach that the preceding verse used. "One thousand three hundred and thirty-five days" is to be estimated in comparison with the number that just preceded. If the one was three years, six and a half months, the other is three years and eight months. Or forty-five days more than the first. Again we should not venture to reckon in terms of exact computation. All those who think they have a basis of exact computation in the events that transpired in the time of Antiochus must assume that the first figure might have related to the death of the tyrant. Then happy would be the man who would live a month and a half more, for he would live, perhaps, to *hear* of the death of the tyrant, it being assumed that forty-five days might be consumed till the news of his death in Persia had penetrated back to Judæa. All guesswork!

Much simpler is the construction: Very shortly after the "abomination" has been removed there will come news that is so good as to allow classifying everyone that lives to see that day as "blessed." When the period of affliction, which is but a little longer than half a period such as God might allow, is at an end, then rather shortly thereafter the hand of God in overruling the evil and substituting good for it will be seen to have control of the issues. That statement answers also the latter of the two questions in terms of comforting assurance. It will be a "blessed" thing to be living then.

Some critics have a novel construction of these two numbers. They are said to have been inserted by men in the days of Antiochus. One man expected an overthrow and a deliverance within a certain period. He was wrong. Another man inserted a gloss because he expected deliverance forty-five days later. He was wrong. Though they are wrong the figures still stand as monuments to human fallibility. And this is found within the Holy Scriptures!

13.   **"But as for thee, go thy way until the end comes. And thou shalt rest and rise again for thy lot at the end of days."**

As was the case in v. 9, Daniel is bidden to go on and to do his work by following the course that God had mapped out for him. Taking the two statements of the verse together, we must arrive at the conclusion that, when Daniel does go his way, that will involve the fact that he will ultimately rest in his grave. He will have to wait there "till the end comes." But so sure is the hope of the resurrection of God's saints as is taught in v. 2 and elsewhere, for that matter, that Daniel is to look forward to the prospect that he will "rise again for his lot." We could have translated these words "stand in thy lot" as *A. V.* does, and the thought would have been about the same, for all interpreters practically agree that *'amadh* "to stand," is here used in the sense of *qum*, "to arise." The thing in prospect is to arise for that which God has in store for His own, and that is something worth living and waiting for and rising for by the power of God. As far as Daniel is concerned, the ultimate fulfillment is too far removed for him to live to see it without having passed through death first. But the "end of days" will bring the general resurrection and the rewards and the blessings for the godly as the beginning of the chapter so gloriously taught. Thus the book closes with a ringing note of victory—also a comfort for troublous times.

HOMILETICAL SUGGESTIONS

Verses 1-3 of this chapter are obviously an excellent text on the consummation against the background of the tribulation of the last times, which is referred to in the concluding portion of chapter 11. God's mighty deliverance is described, the glorious resurrection and the eternal glory. These comforting facts about the end of all things should be preached much more frequently than they customarily are in our day. Verse 4 might be added, particularly for the purpose of showing how the last days should drive men faithfully to peruse God's Word and thereby to be well fortified to meet the distressing things that shall come to pass upon the earth.

The section v. 5ff. hardly constitutes a good text. Where strange and disturbing chiliastic interpretations are put upon this passage, and men have become disturbed by the cocksure assertions of errorists, it may become necessary to show how the passage may be construed according to the analogy of Scripture. Even in such a case the comfort note involved would be strongly stressed so as to have as much positive evangelical content in the sermon as possible.